Deciding to Intervene

Deciding to Intervene

The Reagan Doctrine

and American Foreign Policy

James M. Scott

Duke University Press   *Durham and London 1996*

© 1996 Duke University Press
All rights reserved
Printed in the United States of America on acid-free paper ∞
Typeset in Melior by Tseng Information Systems, Inc.
Library of Congress Cataloging-in-Publication Data appear
on the last printed page of this book.

For Lori and Michael,
and their unfailing love and patience.

Contents

Preface

About the time I was participating in my first graduate seminar on foreign policy analysis, the Iran-Contra affair became public news and grabbed my attention. As I began to explore the twists and turns of that dubious episode of the Reagan administration, my fascination with the broader context of foreign policy during President Reagan's terms grew. That interest, coupled with a general emphasis on the theoretical and conceptual study of U.S. foreign policy making, particularly on the subject of legislative-executive relations, served as the foundation for this book. In the end, the two led me to the Reagan Doctrine and a doctoral dissertation on its origins, nature, and the processes by which it was formulated and implemented. After more research and several stages of revision, that dissertation grew into this book.

As in all projects that evolve over many years, the final product is quite distinct from its early components. One of the most important transformations occurred gradually, as I sorted through the secondary literature, many previously unavailable government documents, a wide range of primary material, and the vast public record of the Reagan Doctrine. My initial efforts to comprehend the actions of the United States in Nicaragua, and then Afghanistan, Cambodia, Angola, Mozambique, and Ethiopia, as a function of White House decision making gave way to a more complex, but I think accurate, incorporation of policy makers from Congress and the bureaucracy. This shift eventually resulted in the central argument of this book, which is that the Reagan Doctrine emerged from the interaction of policy makers from the White House, foreign policy bureaucracy, Congress, and the public, who created it through a messy and complex process. This made the policy, its consequences, and the process by which it was shaped and applied complex and sometimes contradictory.

Hence, in this book I have sought to trace the complex process and to account for the many policy makers engaged in it. I have pursued two interwoven paths of analysis. The substantive thread evaluates the origins, nature, and consequences of the Reagan Doctrine, an intriguing initiative developed in the final phase of the cold war. The procedural thread considers the role and influence of various policy makers in the formulation and implementation of the policy and seeks to account for the influence of decision makers throughout the policy-making arena.

When a project of this size bears the name of only one person, there is a tendency to overlook the many contributors that inevitably shape its contents. This book is no exception. While I take full responsibility for any errors of fact or interpretation, I wish to give credit to those whose assistance enabled me to complete the project successfully. Since the idea for this book began during my graduate student days, I gratefully acknowledge the contribution of all my professors in the Department of Political Science at Northern Illinois University for their instruction and advice. Several members of the NIU faculty deserve special thanks, however. The late Thomas C. Wiegele presided over the foreign policy analysis seminar in which the seed for the book first took root. As my professor and first graduate program adviser, he provided important instruction, assistance, and encouragement. In addition, as a professor, department chairperson, and friend, Clark C. Neher provided constant advice, encouragement, and support.

Most important, I should like to give credit to the members of my dissertation committee, each of whom helped me complete my dissertation in such a way that it could provide the basis for this book. Daniel R. Kempton provided valuable suggestions and advice from the conceptual perspective and helped especially with the cases of Angola and Mozambique. Paul Culhane spent much time on the U.S. policy-making side of the project, particularly congressional behavior. Manfred (Kurt) Wenner devoted considerable attention to the Afghanistan case and was particularly helpful in persuading me not to fall too deeply in love with my own words. All spent hours reading draft after draft of a very long manuscript, for which I am thankful. I especially wish to thank my mentor, dissertation director, colleague, and friend, Lawrence S. Finkelstein. The innumerable hours Larry devoted to discussion, advice, editing, suggestions, and, at certain stages, admonition and exhortation provided the intellectual guidance and inspiration that enabled me to complete my dissertation and ultimately this book. His high standards drove me forward and his persistent prodding kept me from settling for easy solutions. I am proud to have studied with him.

Other scholars provided important contributions as well. Alexander George's scholarship on foreign policy and comparative case study methods has influenced me significantly. In addition, the work of James M. Lindsay on Congress and foreign policy has shaped my views on legislative-executive relations. I am especially grateful to have had Professor Lindsay's assistance on the final drafts. The many hours he devoted to critiquing the manuscript were crucial to the development and refinement of the themes in this book, and I appreciate the time he gave to a junior assistant professor that he did not know.

Many scholars and former policy makers provided valuable information and additional sources. Others gave feedback by commenting on various International Studies Association conference papers that contained elements of the larger study; I owe them my thanks, even if I cannot remember all their names. In addition, Peter Schraeder of Loyola University of Chicago provided help on the Africa cases, sharing the results of his own research, commenting on mine, and simply encouraging me to continue. Paul B. Henze of the Rand Corporation generously provided much information, including many of his own publications, to help me sort out the truth of the Ethiopia case. The incisive comments and suggestions of an anonymous reviewer also helped shape a rough draft into a finished book. Finally, my colleagues at Illinois State University provided much advice, support, and encouragement.

My initial research was funded by a dissertation award from the graduate school of Northern Illinois University, for which I am grateful. I was aided substantially by the librarians at Northern Illinois University and the University of Illinois at Urbana, who helped me obtain many of the government documents on which the cases rest. Moreover, the staffs of the Library of Congress, the Congressional Research Service, and the National Archives provided invaluable research assistance. In the process of finishing this book, I received assistance from a number of key people. Valerie Millholland at Duke University Press shepherded the manuscript through the review stages. Pam Morrison and Mindy Conner, my editors at Duke, spent countless hours scrubbing the text to be readable, accurate, and concise. The final book benefited greatly from their thorough attention. Michele Steinbacher-Kemp also contributed countless hours and a practiced eye to copy editing and indexing, and I am very grateful for her careful efforts and her good cheer. I am also grateful for the assistance and friendship of William Capps, with whom I began my graduate studies. He provided a ready sounding board for my ideas and offered many suggestions, critiques, and recommendations throughout my efforts.

Last, but of course not least, I owe my deepest gratitude to my entire family, whose love, patience, and support are directly responsible for this book. My parents, Harold and Marge Scott, my sister and brother-in-law Anne and Brad Brown, and especially my wife Lori never lost faith and always offered me what I needed most to reach my goal. My son Michael, whose birth just days before I defended my doctoral dissertation made that achievement pale in comparison, provided much of the motivation I needed to see the project through. I am indebted to Lori and Michael especially for putting up with the long hours spent in front of the computer, in the library, or at some conference. I do not suppose I will ever be able to repay them for their love and patience.

US policy will seek to . . . weaken and, where possible, undermine the existing links between [Soviet Third World allies] and the Soviet Union. US policy will include active efforts to encourage democratic movements and forces to bring about political change inside these countries. —National Security Decision Directive 75, January 1983, p. 5

1

Introduction

In April 1985, conservative columnist Charles Krauthammer (1985, 54) claimed that "Ronald Reagan is the master of the new idea. . . . [After his political achievements] all that was left for him to turn on its head was accepted thinking on geopolitics. Now he has done that too. He has produced the Reagan Doctrine . . . [which] proclaims overt and unabashed American support for anti-Communist revolutions. The grounds are justice, necessity and democratic tradition." With these words Krauthammer labeled a foreign policy strategy that originated in the worldview of Ronald Reagan and his conservative supporters. The Reagan Doctrine represents one of the most interesting and significant strategic initiatives developed by the Reagan administration. Its authors believed the doctrine would reverse Soviet advances in Africa, Asia, the Middle East, and Central America; rebut the Brezhnev Doctrine; and reassert U.S. power and purpose in the post-Vietnam world by providing aid to anticommunist insurgencies intent on overthrowing Marxist regimes.

This publicly declared policy of intervention was both a product and an innovation of post–World War II foreign policy. It may be seen as a logical extension of other postwar presidential doctrines of foreign policy (Kirkpatrick and Gerson 1989, 24). For example, the Truman Doctrine, the Eisenhower Doctrine, and the Carter Doctrine all shared an overriding concern for preventing "outside powers" from gaining control of certain governments or geographic areas: the Truman Doctrine emphasized Greece and Turkey, though its language was universal; the Eisenhower Doctrine stressed the Middle East; and the Carter Doctrine focused on the Persian Gulf. The Reagan Doctrine was a corollary of the principle behind these earlier credos: while they were concerned with prevention, the Reagan approach emphasized cure. If outside powers happened to gain control of key areas, then a strategy for wresting control from them must exist.

In a more important sense, however, the Reagan Doctrine represented the abandonment of containment. Its advocates held the view that containment was a defeatist strategy that ceded control of important areas to the Soviet Union without offering a remedy. In light of the events of the 1970s, which many interpreted as a period of major advances and victories by the Soviet Union, to continue only to contain the Soviet Union in those places where its influence already existed meant acceding to Soviet inroads into the Third World and acquiescing in the Soviet domination of Eastern Europe. Hence, from this perspective, the containment strategy had failed and a new approach was required. This is precisely what the Reagan Doctrine offered: a guide for U.S. policy when containment failed.

The origin of this strategy had its roots in the highest levels of the Reagan administration and stemmed from the right-wing skepticism of containment dating back to the 1950s. However, the attempt to convert the idea into policy reality (i.e., to implement the initiative in concrete instances) involved a much wider group of policy makers. In fact, the process by which this strategy was formulated and applied was complex, messy, and laden with individual, organizational, and institutional conflict, compromise, and cooperation. Policy emerged from the shifting interactions between the White House, Congress, bureaucratic agencies, and groups and individuals from the private sector. Hence, the formulation and application of the Reagan Doctrine illustrate a characteristic of U.S. foreign policy in general: what goes on inside the American political system is as important for the resulting policy as what goes on in the world without.

This book uses the comparative case study method known as "structured, focused comparison" (see, e.g., George 1979, 1982; George and McKeown 1985) to examine the historical, intellectual, and ideological origins of the Reagan Doctrine and its application to Afghanistan, Angola, Cambodia, Mozambique, and Nicaragua (Chapter 2 treats the "noncase" of Ethiopia).[1] Both the subject and the method are particularly appropriate for several reasons. First, the Reagan Doctrine has been described as the "distinctive" (Tucker 1989, 14) or "signature"

(Lagon 1992, 40) policy of the Reagan administration. Even President Reagan (1989) and certain of his advisers (e.g., Shultz 1993) called attention to it as one of the administration's most significant efforts. It was thus a key strategy in the last phase of the cold war.

Second, as a strategy, the Reagan Doctrine had several distinct applications, or policy implementations. Only six cases were covered by the Reagan Doctrine: Afghanistan, Angola, Cambodia, Ethiopia, Mozambique, and Nicaragua. This means that it is possible to examine the entire universe of Reagan Doctrine cases in one volume. Moreover, the problem the strategy was created to solve required a sustained policy of some duration (the entire two-term Reagan administration at the least), offering a long-term window into policy making.

Third, the cases themselves should reveal general patterns and lessons of American foreign policy making, since they cover a range of issues. For example, while they fall primarily into what Ripley and Franklin (1991, 22–24) and Ripley and Lindsay (1993, 18–22) termed "strategic policy" (long-term, noncrisis policy which identifies the basic goals and tactics of the United States toward other countries and organizations and develops the basic strategies toward achieving those objectives), the cases also exhibit aspects of crisis (short-term reactions to a high-threat situation) and structural policy (which includes procuring and locating personnel and matériel and providing funds for assistance and other programs).

Although this strategy and its application are significant enough to warrant careful analysis, any broad conclusions or inferences about American foreign policy or policy making must be drawn carefully. It is possible that unique or idiosyncratic factors may limit its generalizability, such as the international setting (the end of the cold war), the Reagan administration, President Reagan's management style, or factors stemming from the particular characteristics of the Reagan Doctrine and its application (e.g., that it relied on U.S. financial assistance and thus congressional appropriation). If, in the end, the patterns or themes that emerge from these cases are limited, the background, context, process, and idiosyncratic features of the Reagan Doctrine and the policy makers who formulated and implemented it are an adequate reason for conducting the study.

Two distinct threads in this analysis can be identified: substance and process. The first, focusing on the policy substance, concerns the origins, nature, and consequences of the Reagan Doctrine itself. The second, focusing on the policy process, concerns the actors and their roles in the formulation and implementation of the policy.

The Origins, Nature, and Consequences of the Reagan Doctrine

Six substantive characteristics of the Reagan Doctrine emerge from this study. First, the observers and former administration officials who have argued that no such strategy was developed prior to 1985 or that the Reagan Doctrine was simply a post hoc attempt to justify aid to the contras in Nicaragua are wrong.[2] Although the Reagan Doctrine received its title in 1985, the strategy originated early in the first Reagan term as an intentional, planned initiative devised by high-level members of the executive branch. Just a few months into 1981, the National Security Planning Group (NSPG), a top-level "executive committee" for the National Security Council, proposed to aid rebels in several countries, including Afghanistan, Nicaragua, and Angola. After several drafts, the White House made this strategy official in National Security Decision Directive 75, written in 1982 and signed in January 1983 (see Chapter 2). To be sure, rebels in Afghanistan were already receiving U.S. aid pursuant to a decision made in 1980 by the Carter administration. Nevertheless, it was the Reagan administration's strategy that provided the basis for expanded assistance, linked this ongoing program to several new efforts—which eventually included those in Nicaragua (late 1981), Cambodia (mid-1982), and Angola (early 1986)—and also prompted a debate over the application of the strategy to Mozambique (1985–87).

Second, this strategy stemmed from the long-standing conservative aversion to containment (see Chapter 2 and the other case studies). Hence, the precursor to the Reagan Doctrine was the "rollback" argument of the 1950s, which found supporters in the "true believers" in the Reagan White House and the National Security Council. It was these hard-line advisers who were principally responsible for formulating the strategy, gaining President Reagan's endorsement, and seeking its uniform application as a means to combat Soviet expansionism. Therefore, the hard-liner ideology formed the basic foundation on which the strategy rested.

Third, these zealots failed in their effort to create a universal doctrine. Instead, four different variants of the doctrine emerged, and U.S.

policy developed as a compromise among them. Hard-liners inside and outside the administration saw the Reagan Doctrine as a way to roll back communist expansion, and some, such as William Casey and the foreign policy analysts at the Heritage Foundation, a conservative think tank, desired to use the rationale to *create* anticommunist rebel movements in several countries where none existed. In contrast, some less hard-line policy makers embraced a version that combined Reagan Doctrine aid with diplomacy to win negotiated settlements, some endorsed another that contemplated aid (along with diplomacy) only if foreign combat troops were stationed in the potential target, and still others supported a version that considered aid only if the Soviet Union itself employed combat troops on the target's soil. These diverging views rested on differing assessments of the threat involved and disagreement over the appropriate instruments of foreign policy. The consequence was a case-by-case approach rather than a doctrinaire application of the strategy.

Fourth, the Reagan Doctrine was unevenly applied. American foreign policy makers agreed in only one case—Afghanistan—and applied the strategy consistently only there. Aid to rebels in Cambodia was limited to nonlethal supplies (both covert and, after 1985, overt) and began in earnest only after 1985. Discord among U.S. policy makers, both within and outside the executive branch, contributed to a sometimes contradictory policy toward Angola and southern Africa. Ultimately, while the Reagan Doctrine was applied in Angola, it required five years of internecine struggle to generate enough support to do so. There was even greater disagreement over U.S. aid to the rebels in Nicaragua. The divisions among U.S. policy makers had their greatest impact there, and disputes over the seriousness of the threat and the utility of a U.S.-backed guerrilla war led to an on-again, off-again application of the Reagan Doctrine that was finally suspended as a result of the Iran-contra affair. Finally, in Mozambique, where virulently anticommunist rebels opposed a leftist regime, most U.S. policy makers considered the threat minimal and endorsed the use of diplomacy and inducements to "wean" the regime from its pro-Soviet leanings.

Fifth, the combination of disagreement in the foreign policy community and the uneven application of the strategy that ensued makes the impact of the Reagan Doctrine uncertain. Detailed evaluations follow each case study presented in this book, and an overall evaluation is given in the concluding chapter. In general, these appraisals suggest two broad themes: (1) the Reagan Doctrine had its greatest success in Afghanistan, where the evidence suggests it made a direct contribution to the Soviet Union's decision to withdraw its troops, and had a significant impact on broader changes in Soviet foreign policy. (2) While the rhetoric of the strategy may have persuaded Soviet policy makers that the cost of further adventurism would be too steep, the doctrine's other applications were of limited effectiveness. Some limited benefits can be identified in the strengthening of the noncommunist faction of the Cambodian resistance, and even more limited contributions occurred in the establishment of a stalemate that led to a negotiated settlement in Angola. It is difficult to find a positive contribution in the case of Nicaragua, and the doctrine was not applied in Mozambique—where, it might be noted, U.S. policy succeeded in curbing Soviet influence in the absence of the Reagan Doctrine. Moreover, to the extent that the Reagan Doctrine proved useful, it contributed chiefly to the withdrawal of foreign troops. In no case did this strategy precipitate the overthrow of a regime facing international opposition. In fact, the application of the doctrine to Afghanistan after the Soviet withdrawal, to Angola after the withdrawal of the Cuban troops, and to Cambodia after the withdrawal of the Vietnamese proved costly, problematic, and self-defeating, and may be judged as having failed. In Nicaragua, where no foreign combat troops operated, reconciliation occurred only after Reagan Doctrine aid to the contra rebels was halted.

Sixth, while the purpose of the Reagan Doctrine makes it irrelevant in the post–cold war period, the strategy itself has several substantive implications for future American foreign policy. The foundation of the Reagan Doctrine provides insight into the necessary requirements of any attempt to establish a post–cold war doctrine. This foundation, based on the wedding of strategic and moral justifications, suggests that both a statement of U.S. interests and an articulation of the ethical and moral bases underlying action will be necessary to develop any consensus. Moreover, the underlying features of the Reagan Doctrine suggest a reliance on several deeper themes in American foreign policy that will continue to be relevant in the post–cold war period. Among these are the U.S. penchant for unilateralism and the broad cultural belief in the innocence, benevolence, and exceptionalism of the United States in its world role. In addition, the Reagan Doctrine suggests that, other than serving as rhetorical devices and opportunities for presidents to set a foreign policy agenda, "doctrines" provide little practical guidance for U.S. foreign policy. Even at the end of the cold war, policy proceeded on a case-by-case basis. In the post–cold war environment, with the absence of a clear threat and disagreement over the proper role of the United States in the world, a case-by-case approach is still the most probable course of action.

The Formulation and Implementation of the Reagan Doctrine

This study of the Reagan Doctrine also provides three broad lessons about American foreign policy making. First, the doctrine emerged from the interaction among four circles of actors: the president and his chief advisers, the foreign policy bureaucracy, Congress, and a group of nongovernmental actors. The president and his advisers—the group studied by most analysts—played a key role in every case. In particular, President Reagan and his chief advisers were the initial authors of the strategy, and while they did not take the lead in every case, they made the initial choice on policy toward Nicaragua during 1981 and key decisions regarding Afghanistan in 1985 and 1986. The role of the president and his top aides in the development and application of the Reagan Doctrine depended primarily on the president's position as the chief executive. He and his circle commanded the executive branch and thus had access to its expertise, information, and capabilities for implementing policy. Moreover, the ability of this group to set the agenda, seize the initiative, mobilize opinion, set the bureaucracy in motion, exert pressure on Congress, and force it to react—in addition to such powers as are bestowed on the commander in chief, chief executive, chief diplomat, and chief legislator of the U.S. government— provided opportunities to shape, if not lead, policy making.

The foreign policy bureaucracy circle consists of the State Department, Defense Department, Central Intelligence Agency, NSC staff, and other agencies created by statute to provide advice and executive policy. The bureaucracy's expertise and control of information consistently placed it in a position to shape the formulation of Reagan Doctrine policy. Moreover, the various agencies of the foreign policy bureaucracy shaped the initiative because of their primary role in its implementation. In both roles, disagreements among officials and agencies affected both the nature of the policy and the process by which it was formulated and implemented. The role of this circle was greatest in the Angola and Mozambique cases, in which it exercised policy leadership. In every case, however, it played a role, and therefore general features of the bureaucracy, including its propensity for risk avoidance, routinization, division, disagreement, and "turf wars" among different agencies, are critical for an understanding of U.S. policy.

Congress includes the leadership, committees, and individual members of both houses. Members of Congress played a significant role in all the Reagan Doctrine cases. In the Angola, Mozambique, and Afghanistan cases, members helped to shape the application of the strategy, sometimes racing ahead of the administration. In the Nicaragua and Cambodia cases, Congress actually took the lead. While the case studies reveal many features of Congress that limited its effectiveness—including its size, its decentralized nature, its limited access to information, and its procedures—they also show that the institution and its individual members had access to potentially potent avenues of influence. These included direct paths, such as the ability to pass laws; the constitutional and statutory authority to hold oversight hearings, require reports, and request individual briefings; the advise and consent authority over treaties and appointments; and the "power of the purse." In addition, indirect routes, such as threatening to exercise congressional powers (e.g., legislate), expressing a "mood," issuing requests and warnings directly to executive branch personnel, and passing nonbinding resolutions, constituted tools that sometimes convinced President Reagan and his administration to incorporate congressional preferences into their policies. Members of Congress also enacted procedural legislation that forced policy to be implemented by a specific agency, threatened the legislative veto, and required reporting. Finally, members attempted to influence policy by "framing opinion" and raising awareness, dictating the terms of debate, and shaping public and presidential opinion (Lindsay 1993, 1994a, 1994b).

The broadest circle of nongovernmental actors includes such elements as public opinion—which may act as a constraint, if not a guide, for government policy—and the media, which may also affect policy by acting as a gatekeeper, a source of information, a watchdog, and an agenda setter. Perhaps more significant, interest groups of varying types affect policy as well. Trade, ethnic, ideological, corporate, transnational, and foreign groups (government, business, or otherwise) may lobby, pressure, persuade, publicize, and endorse or oppose candidates for office in order to influence policy in their particular areas of interest. Moreover, a network of think tanks, or research institutions, affect foreign policy through their actions, which include policy studies, endorsements, and providing personnel for government positions. Finally, some nongovernmental individuals affect policy on the strength of their experiences, status, prestige, or relationships. Their views, advice, and ideas may be solicited or heeded by policy makers. For the Reagan Doctrine, and especially with regard to the Angola and Mozambique cases, individuals and groups were an important source of pressure and support for policy makers in the executive and legislative branches who were attempting to apply their version of the strategy.

It is the relationships among these four circles on which this book sheds particular light. The second broad lesson the case studies teach about U.S. foreign policy making is that the importance of each circle can vary. This runs counter to the traditional depiction of American foreign policy, which posits concentric circles, beginning with the president and expanding to include advisers, the bureaucracy, Congress, and the public. This image places the president at the center of foreign policy making and suggests that the influence and relevance of actors decreases with their distance from the center; it may therefore be labeled the "presidential preeminence" image (Figure 1a). The formulation and implementation of the Reagan Doctrine suggest that this image underestimates the independence and influence of presidential advisers, the foreign policy bureaucracy, and members of Congress.

Careful analysis of the Reagan Doctrine indicates that the power of the president over his own advisers and the executive branch fluctuates and that Congress and its individual members matter a great deal. In truth, the policy process for the Reagan Doctrine was complicated and messy, and it exhibited little of the stability and simplicity suggested by the presidential preeminence image. Instead, the relationship among the four circles varied throughout the initiative, producing different patterns of leadership in different applications of the doctrine and in different stages and cycles of the process. Hence, the use of concentric circles to depict policy making should give way to an image that depicts this more complex, shifting set of relations. A "shifting constellations" image may better represent these varied relationships (Figure 1b).

This second lesson rests on several related themes which emerge from a study of the formulation and application of the Reagan Doctrine. The study highlights the distinction between individual policy deci-

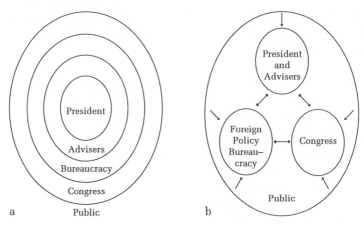

Figure 1. (a) The Presidential Preeminence Image;
(b) The Shifting Constellations Image

sions and policy making itself, and recognizes that the policy-making *process* is significant. While policy decisions involve specific events and an identifiable decision-making group, they are, as a former staffer of the National Security Council noted, "only one aspect of policymaking, a process that began before the decision memorandum reached the president's desk and continues after it has gone into the outbox" (Zelikow 1994, 156). The policy-making process consists of *agenda setting* (in which problems are identified and defined, and priorities are determined), *formulation* (in which options are considered and a choice is made), *legitimation* (in which steps such as simple executive orders or congressional authorization and appropriation are taken to gain approval and provide for implementation), *implementation* (in which specific steps such as the provision and expenditure of funds, the dispatch of personnel, and other actions are taken), and *evaluation* (in which specific actions to implement the policy are reviewed through such actions as executive branch policy reviews, congressional hearings, and budget and funding debates).[3] Moreover, policy may develop from the collective results of discrete actions taken by bureaucrats to deal with day-to-day events. Hence, actions taken at the implementation stage may shape policy as much as specific, formal decisions made at the formulation and legitimation stages.

Several characteristics of the policy-making process shape policy. The process is not linear, with a clear beginning and end; instead,

its stages proceed in cycles, with the implementation and evaluation stages feeding back to the agenda-setting and formulation stages.
Also, the stages allow the involvement of different actors at different
points in the process. Dominance in one iteration or phase does not
necessarily indicate domination of the entire process. Different policy
makers may influence policy at different stages, and each may have
tools that are particularly useful in specific situations (Pastor 1992,
112). These features of the process led to an important pattern in the
Reagan Doctrine. In all cases (on the broad strategy and in each individual application), the initiative began with the White House or the
foreign policy bureaucracies, but subsequently progressed to include
Congress and nongovernmental actors. In fact, in the Afghanistan,
Cambodia, and Nicaragua cases, Congress took over policy leadership in subsequent cycles. Presidential preeminence in policy making
therefore seems to mean initial preeminence only. Moreover, it was the
access to particular stages (e.g., implementation for the foreign policy
bureaucracy, and legitimation and evaluation for Congress) that precipitated involvement and influence by actors other than the White
House. Ultimately, the involvement of many actors in the process made
the strategy evolve as it did.

The four circles of actors varied in their importance and their
impact on the policy-making process. This variation created shifting patterns of policy leadership, or constellations of the circles of
actors. Five different constellations led policy during the Reagan Doctrine cases. No case was dominated by a single constellation; rather,
several applied to each case. Hence, White House leadership (Nicaragua, Afghanistan), foreign policy bureaucracy leadership (Angola,
Mozambique, and Cambodia), interbranch leadership (Nicaragua, Angola, Mozambique, Cambodia, and Afghanistan), subgovernment leadership (Afghanistan, Cambodia), and congressional leadership (Nicaragua, Cambodia) each occurred more than once.

Therefore, the second lesson taught by this analysis of the Reagan
Doctrine also reveals that presidential leadership of foreign policy is a
variable, not a given. In truth, President Reagan's involvement in the
doctrine that bears his name was episodic at best. Most of the time,
President Reagan was a spectator to disputes between advisers, bureaucratic agencies, the executive and legislative branches, and complicated groupings of all three. In fact, President Reagan was active
and assertive only in the cases of Nicaragua and Afghanistan (espe-

cially in 1985–86). This suggests the general conclusion that while the president is *central* to policy making, he is not always the *center* of policy making. Instead, variance in presidential interest, attention, personality, and style creates situations in which the president may exert policy leadership and set the agenda, or presidential advisers and the foreign policy bureaucracy either contest for that role or assume it by default. This characteristic of American foreign policy I label "latent hierarchy" (see Chapter 8).

Moreover, since presidential leadership is not a constant, and since the relationships between the four circles of actors varies, the Reagan Doctrine's "shifting constellation" lesson also indicates that Congress matters in American foreign policy. Individual members and the institution as a whole have various avenues of influence which provide ample opportunity to shape foreign policy. Throughout the cases I discuss here, members used legislation, budgetary powers, treaty and appointment powers, oversight authority, threats to legislate, procedural measures, and attempts to frame opinion in order to play a role in the formulation and application of the strategy. These activities by its members made Congress a full partner in the policy-making process. Significantly, as the Cambodia, Angola, and Afghanistan cases show most clearly, Congress was not limited to a merely reactive role, and its members affected policy even if no specific legislation passed. Furthermore, although many observers argue that members of Congress do not care about foreign policy, these case studies show that member involvement was broad, and that interested individuals in Congress used their access to available avenues to force broader institutional attention. By exercising this leadership, a few members prompted institutional action.

The third broad lesson of this analysis rests on the fact that each of the circles involved in policy making consists of many individuals. As should be expected, the diverse policy makers within each circle have different perspectives and preferences. This characteristic leads to the development of rival alliances that cut across the branches. Rival alliances form when like-minded individuals from different circles unite to force their preferences into policy. Rival alliances thus represent an avenue by which individuals in different circles attempt to pool the resources at their command, thereby increasing their respective influence on the broader policy. Policy, if it emerges, occurs as a result of a vast array of executive, legislative, and public interactions, but it is also quite possible that dissenting alliances will simply block efforts to create and apply policy, creating a stalemate.

Such alliances were common for the Reagan Doctrine and affected policy in every case. Their role in the Angola and Mozambique cases was the most obvious, however. In those cases, a hard-liner faction brought together members of the White House, parts of the foreign policy bureaucracy, members of Congress, and various groups and individuals in the public. A moderate faction brought together a similar group of pragmatists, and a liberal faction consisted of members of Congress and certain public groups. The factions vied with one another: the hard-liners tried to begin sending aid to the rebels in Angola and Mozambique, the pragmatists tried to preserve the diplomatic approach, and the liberals tried to align the United States against South Africa and reject the Reagan Doctrine entirely. The clash shaped the ensuing policy and contributed to contradictions, inconsistencies, setbacks, delays, and stalemates.

In the end, the general patterns exhibited by the Reagan Doctrine have several implications for post–cold war policy making. In short, the process by which the strategy was formulated and implemented—a messy, complicated affair—can be expected to persist. The U.S. foreign policy setting is fragmented, and there is no clear pattern of leadership. If this was true for the Reagan Doctrine, which was formulated in the presence of the Soviet threat and the cold war, it is likely to be even worse in the post–cold war period. In fact, observers might expect Congress and nongovernmental actors to become even more involved for several reasons, including increasing interdependence between foreign and domestic affairs and the absence of consensus over the role of the United States in the world and the nature of threats to U.S. interests.

These lessons on the substance and process of U.S. foreign policy and the Reagan Doctrine are explored in the following pages. Chapter 2 provides an overview of the intellectual, ideological, and institutional origins of the Reagan Doctrine. Chapters 3 through 7 present detailed case studies of the application of the Reagan Doctrine to Afghanistan, Cambodia, Angola, Nicaragua, and Mozambique. These chapters can stand alone as historical examinations, and each contains a concluding section that summarizes the features of that particular case. Finally, Chapter 8 concludes by evaluating the successes and failures of the initiative and drawing out some of the general patterns of foreign policy making suggested by the case studies.

2

The Reagan Doctrine: Challenging the
Soviet Union in the Third World

In January 1981 Ronald Reagan assumed the office of the presidency determined to do something about the apparent tide of Soviet expansionism in the developing world. As one component of his effort, his administration authored a policy initiative to take advantage of the rise of several anti-Soviet insurgencies around the world and provide the rebels with American assistance. This initiative became known as the Reagan Doctrine. The record shows that this strategy was intended by its authors to challenge Soviet advances, rebut the Brezhnev Doctrine, and reassert U.S. power and purpose in the wake of Vietnam. The record also reveals that the strategy provoked a complex struggle among various groups of policy makers, a struggle that resulted in an uneven application of the initiative.

The Origins of the Reagan Doctrine

The Reagan Doctrine originated in the ideological view of the Reagan administration, which provided the lens through which international developments were interpreted. Like most policies, however, it was informed by previous strategies. Its roots can be traced to James Burnham's (1950, 1953) conservative critique of the containment strategy, which he condemned as defeatist. Burnham advocated the pursuit of victory over the Soviet Union rather than its containment to regions already occupied. As part of his agenda, Burnham recommended supporting opposition movements in Soviet-dominated countries to win back certain areas under Soviet domination, especially Eastern Europe.[1]

Burnham's argument languished until the Reagan administration came into power. Although the rhetoric of the Eisenhower administration (which might be labeled the Dulles Doctrine, after its chief proponent, Secretary of State John Foster Dulles) regarding rollback included Republican platform language condemning the "negative, futile, and immoral policy of containment which abandons countless human beings to a despotism and godless terrorism" (Gaddis 1982, 128), that administration limited its efforts to reverse this strategy. As the historian John Lewis Gaddis (1982, 154–55) pointed out, Eisenhower was unwilling to take the steps that the conservative critics desired: the "liberation" strategy adopted in the Republican platform was never seriously considered as anything more than a propaganda effort. A National Security Council document (NSC 162/2) recognized this: "The detachment of any major European satellite from the Soviet bloc does not now appear feasible except by Soviet acquiescence or war." Eisenhower's refusal to respond to the 1956 Hungarian uprising only confirmed this (ibid., 155–57). Still, the covert operations to overthrow governments in Iran (1953), Guatemala (1954), and Cuba (1961) may be viewed as precedents for the Reagan Doctrine (see Prados 1986; Ranelagh 1987).

The transformation of Burnham's argument and the Eisenhower administration's rhetoric into a tangible policy required a series of international and domestic developments. These developments created the opportunity for the Reagan Doctrine, but the interpretation of international events explains the actual rise of the initiative. Domestically, the key factors included the effects of the Vietnam War, the rise of the conservative right, and, most significantly, the election victory of Ronald Reagan in 1980. The international situation consisted of at least three key developments: (1) the Soviet Union appeared to have defeated containment by expanding into all areas of the Third World, and American action seemed necessary to prevent further expansion; (2) the risk of direct confrontation was minimal since the expansion, and thus the arena in which the United States would be challenging the Soviet Union, was the Third World periphery; and (3) the Soviet Union's expansion also increased its vulnerability, and the rise of national liberation movements opposing pro-Soviet regimes created an opportunity to exploit that vulnerability.

As a response to these developments, the Reagan Doctrine had an internal logic that its advocates found compelling. It offered a remedy to the problem of Soviet expansionism; it was, in short, a guide for U.S. policy when containment failed. Moreover, while coping with the "failure" of containment, the Reagan Doctrine also observed the domestic constraints on the use of American forces imposed by the lesson learned in Vietnam: it stated that the United States would only *aid* those trying to liberate their own soil from Soviet-backed regimes. United Nations ambassador Jeane Kirkpatrick (1985a, 14) aptly characterized this point: "It is past time . . . that we should say about all peoples everywhere fighting for their own independence, 'We will do it for you.' What the President and the Reagan Doctrine say instead is 'We will help you do it.'" Hence, as another observer noted, "this version of globalism would require very little treasure and, even more significant, no American blood at all" (Tucker 1989, 15).

In large part, those who advocated the Reagan Doctrine blamed the international developments that called for the strategy on the inaction of the United States. In their view, détente had created a situation in which the Soviets were able to expand their influence without fear of punishment and at the same time derive benefits from U.S.-Soviet relations. In particular, Reagan charged that the Soviets took advantage of the atmosphere of détente to promote and support a series of successful communist revolutions throughout the Third World (Melanson 1991, 139). The policies of President Carter were singled out: Carter, Reagan insisted, had ignored growing Soviet power and influence, abandoned friends, and acquiesced (or assisted) in Marxist revolutions. President Carter was therefore to blame for the new Marxist governments that came to power peacefully or through revolution on three different continents from 1974 to 1980 (in Vietnam, Cambodia, Laos, Afghanistan, Ethiopia, Zimbabwe, Angola, Mozambique, Guineau-Bissau, São Tomé, Cape Verde, Grenada, Suriname, and Nicaragua). Key individuals in the early Reagan administration, including Jeane Kirkpatrick, Secretary of State Alexander Haig, and CIA director William Casey, viewed these developments as a serious threat to U.S. interests (Lagon 1991, 222–45), with Casey reportedly referring to them as "a noose tightening, a rope woven of Communist victories around the globe" (Persico 1990, 217). They believed Soviet influence (and momentum) was increasing and U.S. influence was diminishing, and that the United States needed to halt this trend, to "checkmate them and roll them back" (ibid., 225). Moreover, members of the Reagan campaign and administration, as well as other individuals outside the government, believed in the existence of a worldwide democratic revolution that provided "a unique opportunity to roll back the forces of international communism after decades of Soviet expansion" (Moreno 1990, 110). Hence, the roots of the Reagan Doctrine may be found in conservatives' long-standing dissatisfaction with containment and détente. The rise of the conservative wing of the Republican party in the mid-1970s, which culminated in the campaign and victory of Ronald Reagan in 1980, put into position policy makers who were predisposed to take this view.

The Reagan Doctrine owed its existence to the nearly uniform ideological viewpoint of President Reagan and the top policy makers he brought into his first administration. The essential approach of the Reagan campaign and administration to foreign policy and the world was to divide it into two camps, good and evil. Another administration might not have viewed Soviet influence in backward areas of the developing world with great alarm, and might have considered that the burdens of such relationships were as great as the benefits. Likewise, another administration might have attributed conflict in such areas to local or regional causes instead of blaming the Soviet Union and its allies. A different administration with a different core of beliefs about the cold war and the international system would likely have produced a different doctrine. But President Reagan and his advisers preferred to interpret events in the developing world as a serious threat to the United States, and to blame the Soviet Union for instigating the troubles. In the clearest example of this opinion, Reagan stated in a June 1980 interview, "Let's not delude ourselves, the Soviet Union underlies all the unrest that is going on. If they weren't engaged in this game of dominoes, there wouldn't be any hot spots in the world" (House 1980, 1).

In addition, the president and most of his advisers believed that conflicts in the Third World were part of a "grand design" by the Soviet Union for expansion and world domination. For instance, the president (1981a, 232) stated: "I know of no leader of the Soviet Union . . . that has not more than once repeated, in the various Communist Congresses they hold, their determination that their goal must be the promotion of world revolution and a one-world socialist or Communist state, whichever word you want to use." Other remarks by President Reagan shed further light on his hard-line ideological view of the Soviet Union. In a March 1981 interview with Walter Cronkite, the president (ibid., 232) asserted that the Soviets' "only morality . . . is without God. Their statement about morality is that nothing is immoral if it furthers the cause, which means that they can resort to lying, or stealing, or cheating, or even murder if it furthers their cause, and that is not immoral." Later, in March 1983, the president (1983b, 367) warned that "that while [the Soviets] preach the supremacy of the state, declare its omnipotence over individual man, and predict its eventual domination of all people on the Earth, they are the focus of evil in the modern world," and they follow the "aggressive impulses of an evil empire."

Nor was the president alone in this perspective. Reagan surrounded himself with advisers who shared this conservative or neo-conservative viewpoint (e.g., Richard Allen, Caspar Weinberger, Haig, William Clark, Kirkpatrick, and Edwin Meese). Zealous anticommunists filled the administration's foreign policy positions.[2] Indeed, as Dario Moreno (1990, 83) argued, conformity with this ideological position was emphasized in the selection and appointment of important officials. Other observers have noted that "the striking feature of the Reagan team was its ideological purity. White House political honchos . . . even reached down to ensure purity in positions normally free from politics" (Destler et al. 1984, 109). Many career foreign policy specialists were fired, transferred, or forced into retirement when they failed to meet the administration's ideological standards (ibid., 99–102). Moreover, some officials who deviated from the ideological line were also removed, including Thomas O. Enders, Deane Hinton, Langhorne Motley, L. Craig Johnstone, and John Ferch (Epstein 1989, 16; Moreno 1990, 18).

Guided by these historical and ideological perspectives, the Reagan administration attempted to move beyond containment to develop a policy initiative that would "weaken the links between radical Third World regimes and the Soviet Union, undermine the stability of these Third World governments, and where possible, support or even execute their overthrow" (McFaul 1989, 102). According to Reagan's first secretary of state, Alexander Haig (1984, 96), the Soviets had to be convinced "that their time of unresisted adventuring in the Third World was over." At a minimum, such an initiative would raise the costs to the Soviet Union of maintaining or acquiring clients, discourage them from attempting new acquisitions, and perhaps force them to moderate their foreign policy behavior (Copson and Cronin 1987, 46–47). Interestingly, even Soviet leaders recognized this. According to Moscow, the Reagan Doctrine was intended to "stop the further spread and consolidation of positions of socialism in the world" and "to exhaust the USSR and its allies."[3] To accomplish this, the Reagan Doctrine targeted weak and already unstable Soviet clients facing insurgencies. These weak links in the Soviet sphere appeared to offer the opportunity to succeed at little cost and with little risk of direct confrontation with the Soviet Union.

The Formulation of the Reagan Doctrine

The formulation and development of the Reagan Doctrine began even before Reagan's victory in the 1980 election. At least in its early phases, the strategy was formulated primarily by future members of the administration and its allies in the conservative research institutions. An early contribution may be found in the work of the Committee of Santa Fe from 1979 to 1980. Composed of Latin American specialists led by Lewis Tambs, Roger Fontaine, Lieutenant General Gordon Sumner, Jr., and David C. Jordan (the first three of whom received positions in the Reagan administration), this committee warned of the expansion of Soviet-supported satellites and argued that Central America would be used as a platform from which to threaten the interests of the United States in the region, and ultimately to attack the United States itself. Thus, the report concluded, "containment of the Soviet Union is not enough. Détente is dead. Survival demands a new US foreign policy. America must seize the initiative or perish, for World War III is almost over" (*A New Inter-American Policy for the Eighties* 1980).

As a policy initiative, the Reagan Doctrine was initially shaped by the activities of the National Security Planning Group (NSPG), in particular William J. Casey, director of central intelligence, who "ran his own State Department and his own Defense Department" (Schweizer 1994, xvi) and was responsible for "virtually authoring what would become the Reagan Doctrine" (Persico 1990, 306). By late January 1981, Casey, Secretary of Defense Caspar Weinberger, Haig, National Security Adviser Richard Allen, the president, and Vice President George Bush agreed on the need for a covert strategic offensive against the USSR (Schweizer 1994, 6). In an NSPG meeting in March, Casey proposed a CIA-directed program to provide covert aid to resistance movements in Afghanistan, Angola, Cambodia, Cuba, Grenada, Iran, Laos, Libya, and Nicaragua (Persico 1990, 264; Schweizer 1994, 22–23). According to Peter Schweizer (1994, 23; emphasis added), Casey argued that "we need to be backing these movements with money and political muscle. If we can get the Soviets to expend enough resources, it will create fissures in the system. *We need half a dozen Afghanistans."* This may have been the official "first draft" of the Reagan Doctrine, and President Reagan reportedly responded by asking Casey to develop the idea and identify rebel groups that could be supported. Interestingly, the source for this draft proposal may have been Constantine Menges, the CIA's national intelligence officer for Latin America at the time. According to Menges (1990, 6–7), he presented a similar proposal to the Reagan transition team; his superior at the CIA, William Casey; and administration appointees Haig, Weinberger, and Allen in early 1981. In fact, Menges had called for support of anticommunist "national liberation movements" in 1968. In a report published by the Rand Corporation (Menges 1968), he suggested that democratic insurgencies could topple new communist governments in much the same way that Marxist national liberation movements had toppled other regimes. However, Reagan's undersecretary of defense for policy, Fred Iklé, had made similar recommendations in 1978 with respect to rebellions in Africa and so may deserve some credit as well (Rodman 1994, 262).

By early 1983 the NSPG had furthered the initiative in two national security decision directives (NSDD 32 and NSDD 75). The first of these was coordinated by Thomas C. Reed (a consultant to the National Security Council). The general contents of NSDD 32 were revealed by William Clark (national security adviser) and others. It set out a national strategy (dubbed "Prevailing with Pride" by administration officials) with political, economic, diplomatic, informational, and military components. Among its recommendations the directive suggested providing funds to anticommunist movements as a "forward strategy" to put pressure on the periphery of the "Soviet empire" (Melanson 1991, 142–45; Schweizer 1994, 76–77). It was, however, targeted primarily at Eastern Europe.

The second directive, NSDD 75, was written primarily by NSC staffer Richard Pipes. It committed the administration to seeking out weaknesses on the Soviet Union's periphery and "rolling back" the USSR where possible (Schweizer 1994, 131–32). This directive is especially notable because its language radically altered the fundamental objectives U.S. administrations had pursued since the days of Harry Truman and because it constitutes the "only formal presidential directive during the Reagan Administration on U.S. strategy, goals, and objectives vis-à-vis the Soviet Union" (ibid., 131). According to Robert McFarlane, who was then the deputy national security adviser, its principles included the idea that "the United States does not accept the current Soviet sphere of influence beyond its borders, and the U.S. will seek to roll it back" (ibid., 131).

National Security Decision Directive 75, declassified only in July 1994, contains the strategic rationale of the Reagan Doctrine. According to the directive, the U.S. should try to "contain and over time reverse Soviet expansionism by competing effectively on a sustained basis with the Soviet Union in all international arenas, particularly in the overall military balance and in geographical regions of priority concern to the United States" (NSDD 75, 1). After laying out some areas in which U.S. military and economic pressure would be aimed at Moscow, the directive singled out Afghanistan and the Third World. In Afghanistan, the administration proposed to "keep maximum pressure on Moscow for withdrawal" and "ensure that the Soviets' political, military, and other costs remain high" (NSDD 75, 4). With regard to the Third World, in what was clearly the first official enunciation of the Reagan Doctrine, the directive stated that "US policy will seek to . . . weaken and, where possible, undermine the existing links between [Soviet Third World allies] and the Soviet Union. US policy will include active efforts to encourage democratic movements and forces to bring about political change inside these countries" (NSDD 75, 5). It is quite clear that this document, drafted in 1982 and signed on 17 January 1983, represents the codification of the strategy (already being implemented in Afghanistan, Nicaragua, and Cambodia) that two years later would receive the title "Reagan Doctrine."

In November 1984, the Heritage Foundation, a conservative think tank very influential in both personnel and policy choices during the two Reagan terms, published a report outlining a series of foreign policy initiatives (Butler et al. 1984). A chapter on insurgency and terrorism, written by Richard H. Schultz, Jr. (ibid., 264–70), called for a consistent, integrated strategy for aiding or creating anticommunist insurgents in Iran, Ethiopia, Angola, Afghanistan, Nicaragua, Cambodia, Laos, Libya, and Vietnam. The report urged the Reagan administration to move beyond its "vague and ill-defined" approach to underwrite anticommunist insurgencies by training, arming, advising, and organizing paramilitary assets in Marxist countries threatening U.S. interests. It called for many of the actions that Director of Central Intelligence (DCI) Casey had suggested in 1981, and Richard V. Allen, by then a senior fellow at the Heritage Foundation, predicted that the recommendations contained in the report would "have a significant impact on Administration thinking" (Keller 1984).

These early steps and the simultaneous efforts to provide assistance to rebel groups in Nicaragua, Afghanistan, Cambodia, and Angola led to attempts to develop a public rationale, or declaratory strategy. Initially this was undertaken by key administration personnel, including the president, Secretary of State George Shultz, and DCI William Casey. Although this effort occurred primarily after 1984, some earlier precedents can be found. Among these, several important examples stand out. According to members of the administration, President Reagan's speech to the British Parliament in 1982 set the tone for the Reagan Doctrine. Attorney General Edwin Meese characterized the message as setting the stage for a "crusade for freedom" (Lagon 1991, 321, 370), and Reagan himself (1989, 107–8) described it as the source of the Reagan Doctrine. At a speech at the Heritage Foundation, President Reagan (1983c, 1382–83) remarked: "Throughout the world today the aspirations for freedom and democracy are growing. In the Third World, in Afghanistan, in Central America, in Africa, in Southeast Asia, opposition to totalitarianism is on the rise. It may not grab the headlines, but there is a democratic revolution underway. . . . The goal of the free world must no longer be stated in the negative, that is, resistance to Soviet expansionism. The goal of the free world must instead be stated in the affirmative. We must go on the offensive with a forward strategy for freedom." This call for a "forward strategy" was an explicit appeal for a "Reagan Doctrine."

William Casey was an early, frequent, and outspoken proponent of aiding anticommunist rebels. For instance, in a speech to the Center for the Study of the Presidency in March 1982, Casey stated: "It is much easier and less expensive to support an insurgency than it is for us and our friends to resist one. It takes relatively few people and little support to disrupt the internal peace and economic stability of a small country" (quoted in Woodward 1987, 211).[4] In fact, a speech made by Casey on 9 January 1985 to the Union League Club in New York began the most concerted administration effort to enunciate a clear strategy. Casey explained that "the 1980s have emerged as the decade of freedom fighters resisting communist regimes" and argued that the U.S. should aid them because they "need only modest support and strength of purpose from nations which want to see freedom prevail" (Meyer 1989, 171–72).[5]

Just weeks later, in his State of the Union speech, President Reagan (1985a, 146) declared that the United States "must not break faith with those who are risking their lives—on every continent, from Afghanistan to Nicaragua—to defy Soviet-supported aggression." These remarks were buttressed by George Shultz in a speech in San Francisco and an article in *Foreign Affairs* (Shultz 1985a, 1985b). In the latter, Shultz (1985b, 713) described America's "long and noble tradition of supporting the struggle of other peoples for freedom, democracy, and independence" and warned against acquiescing to the idea that "Communist revolutions are irreversible [thereby] enacting the Brezhnev Doctrine into American law." Shultz's championing of the strategy was followed by a presidential address to the UN General Assembly in October 1985 in which Reagan (1985b, 3) called for a regional peace process for Afghanistan, Cambodia, Ethiopia, Angola, and Nicaragua, while warning that "until such time as these negotiations result in definitive progress, America's support for struggling democratic resistance forces must not and shall not cease."[6]

The following year, in his 1986 State of the Union Address, President Reagan (1986c, 139) made a commitment "to those imprisoned in regimes held captive, to those beaten for daring to fight for freedom and democracy, for the right to worship, to speak, to live, and to prosper in the family of free nations. . . . You are not alone, Freedom Fighters. America will support with moral and material assistance your right not just to fight and die for freedom, but to fight and win freedom—to win freedom in Afghanistan, in Angola, in Cambodia, and in Nicaragua." In a significant policy statement in early 1986 that was the product of NSC staffers Stephen Sestanovich and Donald Fortier— two men who embraced the idea of regional conflict resolution, unlike most of their colleagues (Rodman 1994, 279–80)—the president (1986a, 359) told Congress that "the Soviets and their clients are finding it difficult to consolidate [their gains of the 1970s] . . . mainly because of the courageous forces of indigenous resistance. Growing resistance movements now challenge Communist regimes installed or maintained by the military power of the Soviet Union and its colonial agents in Afghanistan, Angola, Cambodia, Ethiopia, and Nicaragua. We did not create this historical phenomenon, but we must not fail to respond to it."

Though the label "Reagan Doctrine" was not initially used by the administration, columnist Charles Krauthammer (1985) appended it to the 1985 State of the Union reference, and it was soon adopted by administration officials, members of Congress, and others. In 1987, President Reagan (1987a, 966) adopted the appellation, again describing it as a "forward strategy for freedom." Hence, by early 1986 an exposition of the need for, and an outline of, the Reagan Doctrine had emerged from the administration's efforts to fashion a response to the situations in Afghanistan, Nicaragua, Angola, and Cambodia, and from attempts to explain and justify such efforts to the U.S. public.

American Policy Makers and the Reagan Doctrine

Before 1984 the strategy labeled the Reagan Doctrine was primarily the creation of the White House and a generally like-minded group of top-level officials. Two important developments should temper that impression, however. First, even as public efforts to enunciate a declaratory policy were occurring, fissures were revealed within the U.S. policy-making community over the precise nature of the strategy. The disagreements resulted in three broad, identifiable factions in the executive and legislative branches with differing conceptions of and attitudes toward the doctrine. In addition, policy makers from Congress began to get involved in shaping the initiative through case-by-case responses of members of Congress to requests for aid and the attempts by some members to shape the overall initiative. The consequence of both developments was a policy significantly different from that intended by its authors.

Competing Factions in the Foreign Policy Community

Three groups of policy makers with differing views of the Reagan Doctrine can be identified. As Peter Rodman (1994, 248–50) artfully noted, the difference between the three factions centered on their views of the relationship between power (i.e., force) and diplomacy: *advocates* embraced power but rejected diplomacy, *pragmatists* wedded the two approaches, and *opponents* embraced diplomacy but rejected power. Advocates of the initiative had adherents in both the executive and the legislative branches. These individuals considered the initiative to be a broad, comprehensive response to the problem of Soviet expansionism and sought to implement the Reagan Doctrine wherever anticommunist rebels existed—or, for some, could be created. Representatives of this group included Casey, Kirkpatrick, Clark, Fred Iklé, White House Director of Communications Patrick Buchanan, and others in the administration; Toby Roth (R-Wisc.), Dan Burton (R-Ind.), and Jack Kemp (R-N.Y.) in the House of Representatives; and Malcolm Wallop (R-Wyo.), Jesse Helms (R-N.C.), Steven Symms (R-Ida.), and Gordon Humphrey (R-N.H.) in the Senate. Driven by a conservative ideological interpretation of international developments and opportunities, this faction viewed any retreat from this purpose or the use of diplomacy in conjunction with the Reagan Doctrine as a sellout to communism. Former assistant secretary of state for African affairs Chester Crocker (1992, 450) described this group as "viscerally suspicious of any State Department strategy that appeared to rely on the arts of persuasion, seduction, conversion, cooption, and other unnatural acts such as 'weaning Marxists.'" According to George Shultz (1993, 1114), they were "zealous advocates . . . [who] saw little reason to address a comprehensive solution . . . and seemed unwilling to understand the subtle international relationships involved."

The pragmatists, also with members in both branches, viewed the Reagan Doctrine as a more limited instrument of policy. Pragmatists in the State Department, White House, and Congress endorsed the idea of assistance to anticommunist rebels in certain circumstances as a tool to advance regional policy objectives. Representatives of this group included George Shultz, Chester Crocker, Assistant Secretary of State Thomas Enders, Assistant Secretary of Defense Paul Wolfowitz, Undersecretary of State Michael Armacost, Chief of Staff James Baker, Director of Public Relations Michael Deaver, and others in the administration; Dave McCurdy (D-Okla.), Hamilton Fish (R-N.Y.), Steven Solarz (D-N.Y.) in the House of Representatives; and Dennis DeConcini (D-Ariz.), Bill Bradley (D-N.J.), and David Durenburger (R-Minn.) in the Senate. From their perspective, Reagan Doctrine aid to *worthy* rebel groups could be utilized as a part of a broader policy framework that included diplomatic efforts to resolve regional conflicts. But, as Crocker (1992, 292, 297) stated, "aiding anti-Communist rebels was not by itself a strategy. . . . Covert action . . . is not foreign policy." Instead, according to Secretary of State Shultz, the Reagan Doctrine supported diplomacy with force to further American objectives.

The third faction, a group of policy makers in Congress, simply opposed the Reagan Doctrine. These opponents objected to the policy's conception of the world, its purposes, and its methods. Representatives of this group included Michael Barnes (D-Md.), Lee Hamilton (D-Ind.), and David Bonior (D-Mich.) in the House; and Edward Kennedy (D-Mass.), Robert Byrd (D-W.Va.), Alan Cranston (D-Calif.), Christopher Dodd (D-Conn.), and Tom Harkin (D-Iowa) in the Senate. Only in Afghanistan, where the Soviet invasion and direct military operations apparently precluded dissent, did this group quietly acquiesce in the application of the Reagan Doctrine. Otherwise, it maintained a near-perfect record of opposition. Significantly, when the Soviet troops were withdrawn from Afghanistan, members of this group began advocating an end to assistance for the rebels there.

The characteristics and voting records of these factions in the House of Representatives from 1983 to 1989 suggest that the divisions were based on individual beliefs. The most conservative Congress (the Ninety-ninth, 1985–86) was also the most supportive of the Reagan Doctrine, as measured by average scores on the Reagan Doctrine index described in Table 1. The table shows the relationship between ideology and the Reagan Doctrine. Almost all the 124 conservative representatives in the Ninety-eight, Ninety-ninth, and One Hundredth Congresses were advocates of the Reagan Doctrine (115, or 92.7 percent); no conservative was an opponent. Similarly, virtually all of the 130 liberals were opponents of the Reagan Doctrine (127, or 97.7 percent); no liberal was an advocate. Finally, as expected, moderates were split between the categories, with more falling into the pragmatist faction (99, or 35.4 percent) than either the advocate or opponent groups.

Hence, a more moderate administration might not have conceived of the Reagan Doctrine at all, and would certainly not have considered aid to resistance movements a stand-alone strategy. A liberal administration would almost certainly have refrained from enunciating any doctrine at all and, with the exception of aid to the Afghan rebels, would probably have refrained from providing aid to other insurgents. It is also evident (see the case studies) that pragmatists held the key (i.e., the votes) to the Reagan Doctrine: where they supported its application, the doctrine was applied; where they did not, the doctrine was subject to intense debate or was rejected outright.

Table 1. Ideology and Support for the Reagan Doctrine in the House of
Representatives (98th, 99th, and 100th Congresses)

Attitude toward Reagan Doctrine	Ideology		
	Conservatives	Moderates	Liberals
Advocates	92.7% (115)	32.5% (91)	0
Pragmatists	7.3% (9)	35.4% (99)	2.3% (3)
Opponents	0	32.1% (90)	97.7% (127)
Total	124	280	130

Sources: The table was created from Americans for Democratic Action/American Conservative Union (ADA/ACU) ideology scores (0–15 = liberal; 16–85 = moderate; and 86–100 = conservative) and House roll-call votes on Reagan Doctrine assistance. Procedural and undivided votes were eliminated from the selection; the votes, as numbered by *Congressional Quarterly Roll Call Votes*, are as follows: *1983*, 264, 266, 270, 377; *1984*, 162; *1985*, 58, 60, 61, 140, 141, 142, 143, 193, 199; *1986*, 58, 178, 178, 180, 356; *1987*, 30, 168; *1988*, 7, 24, 157.

Note: Reagan Doctrine support was computed by dividing a member's votes for aid by the total number of Reagan Doctrine aid votes for which the member was eligible. An advocate supported the Reagan Doctrine 85 percent of the time or more, a pragmatist 15 to 85 percent of the time, and an opponent less than 15 percent of the time.

Objectives and Objections

The three factions described above disagreed on a series of critical policy issues, which helps to explain why the policy was fully implemented in only one of the cases for which it was designed and considered. The first dispute occurred over objectives. Supporters of the initiative, whether they were advocates or pragmatists, had any of five objectives. The most avid proponents believed that by chipping away at the periphery of the Soviet empire, the United States might succeed in reversing or rolling back the Soviet gains of the 1970s. Supporting insurgencies against small, unstable Soviet clients might result in their overthrow at little cost to the United States. Some thought that a series of defeats on the periphery might cause harm to the Soviet Union itself, perhaps even causing moderation, reform, or failure of the system (e.g., Menges 1988b, 1990). For example, Casey, a strong proponent of this goal, told a CIA officer, "When we win one, the whole house of cards will come tumbling down. It will set off a chain reaction throughout the empire" (quoted in Schweizer 1994, 25). Even among those who generally supported this purpose, however, divisions existed. According to Mark Lagon (1994), some wanted only to destabilize pro-Soviet regimes; some wanted to overthrow those regimes, and perhaps the Soviet Union as well; and some wanted to promote the democratization of the target regimes (and the Soviet Union). The latter group, which included Jeane Kirkpatrick, consisted primarily of neoconservatives.

Some policy makers viewed the Reagan Doctrine as a means to challenge the Soviet Union in the developing world. The policy would respond to Soviet gains in the 1970s and raise the costs of the Soviet effort to consolidate those gains. Moreover, the initiative could discourage new Soviet acquisitions by raising the cost of supporting clients in the developing world. William Casey, for example, emphasized the need for the United States to respond to a Soviet strategy to exert pressure on "strategic chokepoints" in the Caribbean, Cape of Good Hope, Indian Ocean, Persian Gulf, and Red Sea. Casey and others saw a "resource war" in the making and believed that unless the Soviet Union was challenged, it would gain control over vital strategic resources and transit routes (see, e.g., U.S. Congress, House, Committee on Foreign Affairs, Subcommittee on Africa 1981b; Shafer 1982).

Others believed that the Reagan Doctrine would reassert U.S. power and influence in the developing world. In this sense, the policy was an antidote to an America made irresolute and timid by the Vietnam War. By announcing and then pursuing a policy of support for anticommunist insurgencies, the United States could reengage, cope with Vietnam's effect on the U.S. role in the world, and, in the words of Fred Iklé, "demonstrate the United States' capacity as a super power to apply the use of force" when required in the developing world (Lagon 1992, 47).

More cautious supporters of the Reagan Doctrine viewed the policy as a tool with which to achieve regional peace settlements—an objective, it must be noted, that the most fervent advocates of the strategy rejected as appeasement. For pragmatists, the objective was to force the Soviet Union and its clients to negotiate an end to the conflicts, remove Soviet and Cuban troops, and allow elections and participatory governments (i.e., involving the insurgents). This objective was staunchly supported by members of the State Department and some members of Congress (Rodman 1994, 275–79). According to State Department official Peter Rodman, George Shultz was the architect of this "dual track" approach, which attempted to wed the power of the Reagan Doctrine to diplomacy (Rodman 1994). In fact, President Reagan's (1985b) address to the UN General Assembly, which was apparently authored in large part by the State Department, adhered to this approach (Menges 1988b). Michael Armacost (1987, 58) explained: "With respect to conflicts . . . in Afghanistan, Angola, and Cambodia, we are determined to support those resistance forces that are fighting for the independence and freedom. . . . We have outlined a framework for promoting such solutions. The key is a negotiating process between the warring parties to bring an end to violence, national reconciliation, and the withdrawal of foreign troops; we see scope for US-Soviet talks to support such negotiations, ensure a verifiable departure of foreign troops, and stem the flow of outside arms." While many in the U.S. foreign policy community believed that support for anticommunist resistance movements was meant to further regional conflict resolution, serious disagreement over this two-track approach existed because hard-liners opposed negotiations in every instance.

It should also be noted that some proponents of the Reagan Doctrine had a moral objective as well. Copson and Cronin (1987, 2) pointed out that aid to freedom fighters was seen as a moral imperative or obligation to the cause of freedom, democracy, and self-determination. This is evident in President Reagan's speeches and in the speeches and writings of his advisers, including George Shultz and Jeane Kirkpatrick. In this sense, the Reagan Doctrine was equated by some of its advocates with human rights policy—the best way to establish and protect human rights was to rid the world of Marxist governments.

Those opposed to the Reagan Doctrine typically offered one or more of several objections. Some pointed out problems in the ends, means, and consequences of giving aid to guerrilla fighters, concerned that the violence and its victims raised moral problems (e.g., Tucker 1985; R. H. Johnson 1988). Others pointed out the questionable credentials of the freedom fighters themselves (e.g., Carpenter 1986) and suggested that "the movements that the United States supports are not nearly so democratic and the regimes it opposes so totalitarian, so clearly Marxist-Leninist, or so Soviet-dominated as the administration's perspective assumes" (R. H. Johnson 1988, 514).

Others questioned the strategic objectives. Representative Steven Solarz (D-N.Y.) for example, suggested that a doctrine that blindly advocated support for anticommunist insurgencies without examining the nature and level of U.S. interests in the specific country was "manifest absurdity" (Demuth et al. 1987, 7). Others raising this objection argued that doctrines perpetuated the inability to distinguish between vital and peripheral interests (e.g., Tucker 1985; Layne 1988). Even some members of the administration were uncomfortable with the idea of a doctrine, including members of the NSC staff and the State Department (see below).

Some expressed concern that the Reagan Doctrine could be counterproductive. A Congressional Research Service analyst identified a substantial group in Congress that worried about escalation and was concerned that the United States might be creating open-ended commitments that would result in "creeping intervention" (Copson 1987b, 4). Others wondered if the rebels could achieve even the limited U.S. goals, let alone overthrow governments. Critics also worried that the Reagan Doctrine would intensify the conflict and destabilization and exacerbate superpower competition, making settlement of regional conflicts impossible. Some further argued that the Reagan Doctrine would actually entrench Soviet influence as Marxist regimes facing guerrilla war would turn to the Soviet bloc for aid (ibid., 4).

Finally, after General Secretary and then President Mikhail Gorbachev initiated his opening to the West, some worried that his reforms would be scuttled by intensified conflict in the Third World. As time passed, more policy makers questioned the Reagan Doctrine's assumption that the Soviet Union was bent on world conquest and expansionism, which seemed unlikely in view of Gorbachev's internal reform efforts and foreign policy initiatives (e.g., Katz 1991). Ultimately, the unevenness of the application of the strategy can be traced to disagreements over these objectives and disputes over the purposes and appropriateness of the strategy itself.

The Cases and Criteria of the Reagan Doctrine

The complex setting in which policy making took place led to disagreement over the conditions under which the Reagan Doctrine would be applicable. Hard-liners argued that any instance of leftists in power warranted an effort to support or even develop an anticommunist insurgency. This is obvious in the list of countries contained in Casey's 1981 proposal and in the Heritage Foundation recommendation (some were not facing insurgencies). Others saw the doctrine in a more limited sense. For example, Jeane Kirkpatrick and Alan Gerson (1989, 19–25), both members of the UN mission, identified three requirements for Reagan Doctrine assistance to be considered:

1   An indigenous, independent insurgency ("democratic resistance")
2   A government relying on arms, personnel, and advisers from the Soviet bloc to maintain it ("Soviet client")
3   A population denied participation in their own government ("illegitimate government")

Opponents of the doctrine apparently believed that it should be applied only in instances in which the Soviet Union was an invading and occupying force; that is, in Afghanistan (based on voting records in the House of Representatives; see J. Scott 1993, ch. 9).

Even the Kirkpatrick-Gerson guidelines relied on interpretations and judgments (e.g., the definition of a "democratic resistance," a "client," and an "illegitimate government"), and even a loose reading of these requirements suggests that only six countries could be considered as potential Reagan Doctrine cases (i.e., an insurgency was fighting a leftist regime that received Soviet bloc military aid and advice): Afghanistan, Angola, Cambodia, Ethiopia, Mozambique, and Nicaragua. Hard-liners argued for the application of the Reagan Doctrine in each of the six cases, although the Ethiopia case was immediately abandoned. For the rest, some policy discussion ensued. In Mozambique no aid was provided. In Nicaragua and Angola, aid was uneven and inconsistent. In Cambodia, the assistance was nonlethal and limited (less than $10 million annually). Only in Afghanistan was the doctrine implemented consistently and substantially, with roughly $1 billion provided during the Reagan administration, and even there aid was combined with negotiations, to the chagrin of hard-liners. The administration authors of the strategy, intending a comprehensive approach to all the cases, watched the actual policy develop in a more limited manner. Hence, while formal policy statements such as NSDD 75 suggested a grand strategic design, U.S. policy instead emerged from a series of implicit and explicit compromises.

This clearly indicates that the initiative was considered on a case-by-case basis; in no way was it a universal "doctrine." Because of disagreements over objectives, even the administration seemed cautious about its doctrine (R. H. Johnson 1988, 510). Kirkpatrick and Gerson (1989, 21; emphasis added) stressed that "policy under the Reagan Doctrine is established by *prudential determination of the national inter-ests in particular contexts.*" In testimony before a subcommittee of the Senate Appropriations Committee, William Schneider, Jr. (undersecre-tary of state for security assistance, science, and technology) stated that any decision to invoke the Reagan Doctrine toward any specific coun-try or insurgency must be "addressed in [its] particular political and historical context" (U.S. Congress, Senate, Committee on Appropria-tions 1985, 56). Secretary of State Shultz (1985b, 17) maintained that the "nature and extent of US support necessarily varies from case to case." In fact, it was precisely on this point that actors in the foreign policy bureaucracy and Congress shaped the policy, and it is here that the effect of the maneuvering between the three factions can be de-tected. Though hard-liners desired a doctrine that would be observed in all instances, in actuality the Reagan Doctrine outlined "the situa-tion in which the United States [could] intervene with its assistance in the affairs of others." The Reagan Doctrine did not require aid; it per-mitted it (Kirkpatrick and Gerson 1989, 21).

This point provided the basis for another disagreement: What spe-cific criteria would govern the decision to apply the Reagan Doctrine? It may well have been the intention of the authors of the initiative to apply the approach in all the cases, but this did not occur. Thus, the discussion of criteria became a significant debate. Executive branch officials could not agree on a single set of criteria to guide the appli-cation of the Reagan Doctrine, aside from general references to U.S. interests (Lagon 1991, 245). The hard-liners desired universal applica-tion, but other policy makers tried to identify specific circumstances that should trigger the Reagan Doctrine. Roger Kagan, deputy assistant secretary of state for inter-American affairs, suggested that middle-class support of the insurgents and the promise of friendliness to the United States should be considered (Epstein 1989, 21). Richard Armi-tage, assistant secretary of defense for international security affairs, added other considerations (U.S. Congress, Senate, Committee on Ap-propriations 1985, 40–44). Neither these officials nor any others, how-ever, could produce a clearly defined set of guidelines.

The administration's inability or unwillingness to offer such guide-lines prompted several members of Congress to attempt to devise their own set of criteria, and thus to shape the initiative. Again, hard-liners in Congress advocated universal application to all anticommu-nist movements (e.g., Representatives Jack Kemp and Dan Burton, and

Senators Gordon Humphrey, Malcolm Wallop, Steven Symms, and Jesse Helms). Others tried to be more discriminating. Representative Steven Solarz, for example, cautioned:

> Clearly it is one thing to lay out general guidelines for dealing with these matters. It is quite another to apply them in individual circumstances. And I think what we need here is some very clear and systematic analysis. . . . It is incumbent upon us as we consider these various situations to see if we can fashion and formulate a set of criteria which can provide meaningful guidelines for us to determine which insurgencies it is in our interest to support and which insurgencies it is not in our interest to support (U.S. Congress, Senate, Committee on Appropriations 1985, 5).

Consistent with this plea, Representative Robert Torricelli (D-N.J.) argued that U.S. aid should be provided only if the resistance was "genuinely motivated," "democratic," backed by "broad world support," and facing "a genuine foreign intervention, invasion, and not merely a domestic squabble" (U.S. Congress, House, Committee on Foreign Affairs, Subcommittee on Asian and Pacific Affairs 1985a, 657), thus eliminating all cases but Afghanistan (and possibly Cambodia). To these criteria Solarz added that aid should contribute to a negotiated settlement, be consistent with U.S. interests, and be supported by domestic public opinion (U.S. Congress, Senate, Committee on Appropriations 1985, 13; Solarz 1986). While Congress did not succeed in establishing a universally accepted set of criteria either, efforts such as these illustrate attempts by its members to fashion policy.

An Overview of the Strategy

Hence, although some analysts have suggested that the Reagan Doctrine emerged from an elaborate rationale for arming the Nicaraguan contras (e.g., Tucker 1985; Oye 1987; R. H. Johnson 1988), the evidence indicates that the administration developed a strategic initiative in 1982.[7] Key administration officials, including William Casey and Jeane Kirkpatrick, contemplated a broad strategic initiative that would include Nicaragua, Afghanistan, and Angola, at least, and possibly several other areas, and the United States took actions to implement that initiative prior to 1985. The enunciation of the policy in broader terms was intended to provide a firm foundation for ongoing or desired sup-

Table 2. Chronology of the Reagan Doctrine

	Afghanistan	Angola	Nicaragua	Cambodia	Mozambique
Phase 1					
1980	Covert aid, $20–30 million	No aid	No aid	No aid	No aid
1981	Covert aid, $30 million	Aid request rejected	Covert aid program approved	No aid	No aid
1982	Aid increased, $40 million	No aid	Covert aid, $19 million	Covert nonlethal aid, $5 million	No aid
Phase 2					
1983	Aid increased, $80 million	No aid	Aid increased, $25 million	Covert nonlethal aid, $5 million	No aid
1984	Aid increased, $130 million	No aid	Aid halted	Covert nonlethal aid, $5 million	No aid
1985	Aid increased, $450 million	Covert aid program approved	Nonlethal overt aid, $27 million	Covert and overt nonlethal aid, $12–15 million	No aid; conservative pressure
1986	Aid increased, $500 million	Covert aid, $15 million	Overt aid, $100 million	Covert and overt nonlethal aid, $12–15 million	No aid; conservative pressure
Phase 3					
1987	Covert aid, $500 million	Aid increased, $18 million	Overt aid (from 1986), no new aid approved	Covert and overt nonlethal aid, $12–15 million	Aid considered and rejected
1988	Aid decreased,	Aid increased,	Aid ended	Covert and overt	No aid

Table 2. Continued

	Afghanistan	Angola	Nicaragua	Cambodia	Mozambique
Phase 3					
1988 (*cont.*)	$350 million	$40 million		nonlethal aid, $12–15 million	
1989	Covert aid, $350 million	Aid increased, $60 million	No aid	Covert and overt nonlethal aid, $15–20 million	No aid
1990	Aid decreased, $300 million	Aid decreased, $30 million	No aid	Aid ended	No aid
1991	Aid ended	Aid ended	No aid	Aid ended	No aid

port of anticommunist rebels. Although specific cases drove the approach, the principles were much more profound than the individual situations (Krauthammer 1985, 54). At the same time, however, the translation of the original idea into policy resulted in significant alterations to the strategy. The initiative was forced into combination with negotiations to maintain support from enough American policymakers for it to continue; and the strategy was applied fully only to Afghanistan; the other cases received halting, limited, or no support.

Table 2 presents the chronology of the Reagan Doctrine and describes three periods of aid. In the first phase, 1980–82, the administration authored the strategy and took steps to provide anticommunist rebels with American aid, extending assistance to rebels in Afghanistan and Nicaragua in 1981 and Cambodia in 1982. In the second period, from 1983 to 1986, the administration and its supporters moved toward a public rationale, which culminated in 1985–86. Simultaneously, Congress asserted itself in each case as some members took positions on the broad approach, others attempted to define the criteria for the application of the doctrine, and the remainder were involved in votes on individual assistance programs. During this period, aid programs expanded in Afghanistan, Angola, Cambodia, and Nicaragua (briefly). In the third period, 1987–91, the United States continued to apply Reagan

Doctrine in three cases (Afghanistan, Cambodia, and Angola) and rejected in two (Nicaragua and Mozambique). The consensus on Afghanistan, Angola, and Cambodia lasted until Soviet or Soviet bloc troops were withdrawn from each of those countries; aid peaked in 1987 for Afghanistan and 1989 for Cambodia and Angola. Midway through the Bush administration, Soviet reforms and regional developments had effectively ended the need and justification for the Reagan Doctrine.

The Noncase of Ethiopia

Although Ethiopia seemed to meet the basic requirements for Reagan Doctrine assistance, no credible evidence of covert assistance exists, probably because the nature of the resistance movements there prevented any consideration of military aid. The "alphabet soup" of exile, dissident, and resistance groups in Ethiopia was disorganized and factionalized. Moreover, the movements with sufficient organizational and military strength to affect the government—the Eritrean People's Liberation Front (EPLF) and the Tigrean People's Liberation Front (TPLF) —were Marxists themselves until 1989. In fact, prior to 1989, they even described themselves as better Marxists than the government (Henze 1985, 80). Each had received support from the Soviet Union, China, and Cuba prior to the overthrow of the monarchy in Ethiopia in 1974 (Henze 1989, 7). In any case, the groups tended to be so anti-Western that they would not accept U.S. aid. Marina Ottaway (1986, 147) concluded that an "effort to destabilize Ethiopia would [have required] a major commitment to create an anti-Marxist resistance movement where none [existed], and [would have necessitated] direct involvement by the United States, both of which the U.S. proved unwilling to do."

When the Reagan administration took office, the Horn of Africa was a very low priority. As a result, a substantial continuity emerged between the Carter administration's approach and the efforts of the early Reagan administration. Throughout the Reagan administration, the United States supported the territorial integrity of Ethiopia and maintained ties with, and a presence in, Addis Ababa. To counter the radical nature of the regime in Addis Ababa and the presence of Cuban troops and Soviet advisers and weapons, the Reagan administration sought to contain Ethiopia by supporting Somalia, Kenya, Egypt, the

Sudan, Djibouti, and Saudi Arabia. Ironically, the Carter administration had established each of these programs.

In fact, the Reagan administration's policy review for the Horn of Africa did not even commence in earnest until spring 1982, and did not end until July of that year. The results merely codified existing policy (Korn 1986, 56–57). During this review the Reagan Doctrine surfaced briefly, but the idea was quickly rejected (Korn 1986, 57; D. Ottaway 1989, 53). The CIA representative on the interagency review panel appears to have raised the issue along with a request from an exile group that it be given start-up funds (Halliday 1989, 78), but the NSC staff, State Department, and CIA were all opposed to aiding Ethiopian rebels (D. Ottaway 1989, 49). The national security decision directive that emerged from this review (NSDD 57) authorized efforts to improve Somalia's ability to defend itself against Ethiopian attacks. With respect to Ethiopia, the administration decided to join with Europe and regional states (especially Egypt and Saudi Arabia) "to bring pressure on Ethiopia to discourage Ethiopian-Libyan destabilizing activities as well as continuing Ethiopian-Soviet collaboration." In addition, however, NSDD 57 stated the administration's desire to "maintain our presence in Addis Ababa in recognition of . . . our long-term interest in restoring a position of influence in Ethiopia," and explicitly rejected "identification with the Eritrean insurgents" (NSDD 57, 3–4). While rumors persisted that limited covert aid was being supplied to anti-government forces by the CIA (Tinker and Wise 1986), American policy remained centered on containment of the Mengistu regime, primarily through allies and friends in the region.[8]

Officials within the administration appear to have considered applying the Reagan Doctrine in Ethiopia on only one other occasion. In 1985, Undersecretary of Defense for Policy Fred Iklé requested a study of Ethiopia as a potential target for Reagan Doctrine aid. The study, done at the Rand Corporation, detailed the myriad groups and their histories and goals, highlighting their factionalized nature and Marxist ideology, and rejected the claims of some exile groups who asserted that they could start democratic resistance movements with a little U.S. money (Henze 1985). In its conclusions, the report counseled against covert military assistance.

Furthermore, Ethiopia was noticeably absent from President Reagan's State of the Union addresses in 1985 and 1986 (1985a, 1986b), although it was named in several of his other speeches. George Shultz did not include Ethiopia in either of his Reagan Doctrine pronouncements (1985a, 1985b), and at the May 1985 hearings before the Senate Appropriations Committee, no government witness mentioned Ethiopia as a potential recipient. In fact, Undersecretary of State William Schneider, Jr., specifically referred to Ethiopia only to underscore the differences between rebels there and those in Nicaragua, Angola, Cambodia, and Afghanistan, where the administration was advocating assistance (U.S. Congress, Senate, Committee on Appropriations 1985, 47). Assistant Secretary Chester Crocker (1986, 30–32) adamantly maintained that the United States should make no effort to support aggression or offensive forces in the Horn and did not waver in his support of territorial integrity. Crocker referred to the Ethiopian rebel groups as Marxists the Soviets had once supported. In 1988, Crocker testified before the House Foreign Affairs Subcommittee on Africa that "we have never provided equipment or other support to any of the separatist groups active in Ethiopia." He further argued that the only major American involvement was with humanitarian relief efforts, in which the United States worked with the United Nations and private organizations (Crocker 1988, 63).

Outside the administration, voices briefly raised the question of Reagan Doctrine aid to rebel groups in Ethiopia. Private individuals and groups raised the issue occasionally: for example, Jack Wheeler (1985b) included the EPLF and TPLF among "new liberation movements" operating worldwide, and certain Ethiopian exile and dissident organizations in New York and Washington suggested aid programs at times. In the spring of 1986, conservatives in the U.S. Congress, led by Representatives Dan Burton and Toby Roth, suggested that some military support for Ethiopian dissidents should be extended as part of the Reagan Doctrine (Petterson 1986, 627). These efforts had faded by the summer of that year, as these same conservatives argued instead for a strict application of sanctions against the regime. Apparently their anticommunist ideology worked against their desire to support self-proclaimed Marxist rebels in the context of the Horn of Africa (Schraeder 1994, 158–59, personal interview, October 1992).

Hence, American policy makers rejected the application of the Reagan Doctrine to Ethiopia. Opposition existed in the White House, the NSC staff, the State Department, the CIA, and Congress. In the broader policy-making setting, even the natural constituency for the

Reagan Doctrine simply could not ignore the doctrinaire Marxism embraced by the only effective and organized rebel groups. The other factions also found ample reason to reject the strategy.

The Reagan Doctrine was conceived by administration officials eager to devise a means to confront the Soviet Union in the developing world. It was intended to be a reasonably cohesive strategy applied in instances in which an anticommunist insurgency opposed a leftist regime. The process by which this initial idea was translated into a set of U.S. foreign policies involved policy makers outside the White House with different or dissenting views. The consequence of this wider involvement was a gap between the idea and the reality, as three factions struggled to shape the application of the strategy toward Afghanistan, Angola, Cambodia, Nicaragua, and Mozambique. In the end, the implementation of the strategy was inconsistent and depended on the support of enough members of Congress to approve aid requests. In these decisions, members of the pragmatic faction held the key: if they joined with advocates of the doctrine, aid was provided—as in the cases of Afghanistan, Cambodia, Angola after 1985, and Nicaragua in several instances. When they joined opponents of the doctrine, aid was halted or refused, as in the cases of Nicaragua and Mozambique. In order to understand the Reagan Doctrine and its policy applications, it is therefore necessary to look beyond the White House.

3

Afghanistan: Consensus, Cooperation, and the Quest for "Rollback"

Without question, the longest and least controversial application of the Reagan Doctrine occurred in Afghanistan. The Soviet invasion of the country in December 1979 inspired virtually unanimous agreement on U.S. assistance to the Afghan rebels in 1980 during the Carter administration; the Reagan administration continued the policy and codified it as the Reagan Doctrine. The withdrawal of Soviet forces in 1989 prompted disagreement over the wisdom of continued U.S. aid. Until then, the policy debate that did occur concerned the appropriate level, extent, and implementation of the aid—and the relationship of that aid to other tools of policy, including negotiations on Soviet withdrawal— not whether or not the United States should provide assistance.

Background

Historically, the United States has had little interest in Afghanistan. According to Robert A. Peck, a deputy assistant secretary in the State Department, "successive American administrations stretching back to the early Eisenhower years have declined to define a US political or strategic interest in Afghanistan" (U.S. Congress, House Committee on Foreign Affairs, Subcommittee on Asian and Pacific Affairs 1990b, 55). The essential cause of this lack of interest is Afghanistan's location on the southern border of the Soviet Union. Because of simple geography, the United States has long recognized that Soviet interests there exceed its own. In fact, a 1949 U.S. Defense Department study concluded that "Afghanistan is of little or no strategic importance to the United States" because its "geographic location, coupled with the realization by Afghan leaders of Soviet capabilities, presages Soviet control of the country whenever the international situation so dictates" (U.S. Congress, Senate, Committee on Foreign Relations 1984, 5).[1] Hence, until the late 1970s, the United States was content to allow Afghanistan to maintain close relations with the USSR while preserving some degree of nonalignment.

It was the Soviet response to the Afghan revolutions of 1977 and 1978 that triggered a change in the U.S. assessment. After Prince Mohammed Daoud Khan took power in a bloodless coup in 1973, he began to improve relations with conservative Arab states, Pakistan, and Iran, and to pursue a more independent foreign policy. Daoud's attempt to reorient Afghanistan prompted the two factions of the Afghan Communist party, the People's Democratic Party of Afghanistan (PDPA), to unite in 1977 and plan a coup against him. The coup succeeded in April 1978, and the Soviet Union reacted quickly in support of it (Arnold 1983, 59; Hammond 1984, ch. 6; Bradsher 1985, 74–84).

From its inception the PDPA was a Marxist organization.[2] A secret constitution (see Arnold 1983, 137–59) dedicated the party to Marxism-Leninism (article 1) and "democratic centralism" (article 7), and committed it to "expanding and strengthening Afghan-Soviet friendly relations (article 5f). Once in power, the PDPA (with Soviet assistance) began to reorganize the government, party, mass organizations, schools, and economy according to Soviet models (Hammond 1984, 151–53; Arnold 1985, 48–49). Moreover, the regime resorted to high levels of repression to maintain its grip on power. The UN (see, e.g., Ermacora 1985a, 1986, 1987a), Amnesty International (e.g., 1986c), the Helsinki Watch Committee (see, e.g., Laber and Rubin 1984, 1988), and the U.S. State Department (see, e.g., 1981d, 1983c, 1985b, 1988b) all condemned the regime's behavior. Economically the regime became increasingly dependent on the USSR (Noorzoy 1990; Shroder and Assifi 1990). The Soviet interventions of 1979 and 1980 put the regime in power, and as many as 120,000 Soviet troops fought in the civil war to sustain the regime (U.S. Department of State 1981d, 1982d, 1983b, 1983c, 1984b, 1985d, 1986b, 1987c, 1988b).

The consequence of the regime's policies and the Soviet presence was a nearly countrywide revolt. Extensive armed resistance began in early 1978 and soon included much of the Afghan population.[3] Inside Afghanistan, the resistance was led by as many as nine hundred local leaders and guerrilla groups organized by tribal, ethnic, and regional factors. The groups operated independently, although some formed regional "fronts." Local commanders established "parallel governments" that ruled small geographic regions. Outside Afghanistan (in Pakistan), the resistance consisted primarily of seven exile "parties," which were divided into two broad factions. The traditionalist group, which was dedicated to the return of the pre-1973 system of local autonomy and tribalism, separation of Islam and the state, and weak central government, included (1) the National Islamic Front (Mahaz-i-Milli-i-Islami), led by Kabul businessman Sayed Ahmed Gailani; (2) the National Liberation-Salvation Front (Jabha-i-Najat-i-Milli), led by Professor Sibghatullah Mojaddidi, a Kabul cleric; and (3) the Islamic Revolutionary movement (Harakat-i-Inqilab-i-Islami), led by Muhammad Nabi Muhammadi, a religious teacher. A group of Islamist movements composed the other faction committed to a state based on Islamic law and institutions; it included (1) the Islamic Society (Jamiat-i-Islami), led by Professor Burhanuddin Rabbani and composed primarily of Tajiks; (2) the Islamic party (Hizb-i-Islami), led by Gulbuddin Hekmatyar and composed primarily of Pashtuns; (3) the Islamic party (Hizb-i-Islami), led by Yunis Khales and also composed of Pashtuns; and (4) the Islamic Union for the Liberation of Afghanistan (Ittihad-i-Islami Barayi Azadi Afghanistan), led by Professor Abdurrab Rasul Sayaf.

All seven parties received support from the refugee population and, when combined with the local resistance, were broadly representative of Afghanistan, but divisions among the exile resistance groups on political, social, and religious philosophies made it difficult for them to cooperate. Additionally, the exile groups and local leaders were at odds. The local groups, fighting primarily to restore local autonomy and local traditions, often rejected the social and political objectives of the exile groups (U.S. Congress, House, Committee on Foreign Affairs, Subcommittee on Asian and Pacific Affairs 1990b, 127–56; Khalilzad 1991, 2). Moreover, the local groups did the bulk of the fighting; the exile groups served primarily as conduits for supplies to the field commanders. Often the local groups coordinated with the exile parties only to gain access to material and supplies (Roy 1986, 110; B. R. Rubin 1989b, 422).

Hence the Soviet invasion and the rise of the Afghan resistance set the stage for the eventual application of the Reagan Doctrine. These developments prompted the widespread belief among U.S. policy makers that the Soviet intervention threatened U.S. strategic and economic interests in the Middle East and Persian Gulf. President Jimmy Carter noted that the Soviet invasion placed "the Soviet Union within aircraft striking range of the vital oil resources of the Persian Gulf; it [threatened] a strategically located country, Pakistan; [and] it [posed] the prospect of increased Soviet pressure on Iran and on other nations of the Middle East" (*Weekly Compilation of Presidential Documents,* 28 January 1980, 185). Members of the Reagan administration also adhered to this view. According to Joseph E. Persico (1990, 225), William Casey told deputy CIA director John McMahon, "Anyone can see what [the Soviets are] up to. They've pushed their way into Afghanistan, South Yemen, Ethiopia. They're surrounding the oil. They're putting themselves in a position to shut off sixty percent of the world's petroleum sources." President Carter expressed this concern when he warned, in what became known as the "Carter Doctrine," that "an attempt by any outside force to gain control of the Persian Gulf region will be regarded as an assault on the vital interests of the United States of America" (*Weekly Compilation of Presidential Documents,* 28 January 1980, 197).

U.S. Policy and the Reagan Doctrine

The Reagan Doctrine was actually applied in Afghanistan over three presidential administrations, since aid began in the Carter administration and ended in the Bush administration. The Carter administration made the decision to arm the Afghan rebel groups, or mujahidin, which presented the Reagan administration with an existing policy that fit the predisposition of many of its policy makers and enjoyed broad support from Congress and the public. The United States continued to assist the Afghan rebels, pursued a diplomatic settlement, and watched the Soviet Union withdraw in early 1989. In spite of this success, the Reagan Doctrine was extended until 1991 to help the rebels remove the regime that Moscow left in power when it withdrew. That aspect of the policy was unsuccessful and, interestingly, triggered a serious policy debate.

Phase I: The Carter Administration, 1979–1980

The Carter administration responded to the April 1978 coup in Afghanistan with wariness, but not hostility. The administration recognized that the coup leaders were leftist and pro-Soviet, but deferred any action. Theodore Eliot, Jr. (1979, 58), U.S. ambassador to Afghanistan at the time, recalled that the Carter administration decided that severing ties "would only reduce Afghan options and drive the Afghan government deeper into the Soviet embrace." U.S. National Security Adviser Zbigniew Brzezinski, Secretary of State Cyrus Vance, and State Department Soviet specialist Marshall Shulman all concurred, preferring to "wait and see how things turned out" (Brzezinski, quoted in Hammond 1984, 63). According to Vance (1983, 386), the United States was best served "by letting Afghanistan continue its traditional balancing act between East and West."

Widespread rebellion in Afghanistan in early 1979, as well as evidence of Afghanistan's Soviet leanings, radical reforms, repression, and the kidnapping and murder of U.S. ambassador Adolph Dubs finally prompted the United States to respond. Brzezinski began to raise the issue of Soviet involvement in Afghanistan publicly and warned President Carter of the dangers of Soviet domination (Brzezinski 1983, 346). Then, in April 1979, Brzezinski "pushed a decision through the [Special Coordinating Committee of the NSC] to be more sympathetic to those Afghans who were determined to preserve their country's independence" (Brzezinski 1983, 427). According to the chief of the CIA's Near East and South Asian Division of the operations directorate from 1979 to 1984, President Carter signed a presidential finding in July 1979 that started a small program of nonlethal aid—propaganda and medical assistance—for the rebels (Cogan 1993, 74, 76). Finally, over the summer and fall of 1979, the United States issued a series of public and private warnings to the Soviet Union (Hammond 1984, 106–18; Garthoff 1985, 942–44).

The ensuing Soviet invasion prompted the next steps. Alarmed at apparent Soviet expansionism, Carter and most of his top advisers interpreted the Soviet action as a major threat to U.S. interests. American support for the resistance accelerated, accompanied by several public policy actions involving the executive branch and Congress. Responding to what Brzezinski (1983, 429) characterized as "a major watershed . . . in the American-Soviet relationship," the Carter administration and Congress reached a new consensus: the Soviet Union must pay for its deeds (Vance 1983, 389).

Publicly, the revised approach took two forms. First, the administration and Congress stepped up their condemnation of Soviet actions. President Carter described the Soviet move as a "grave threat to peace," an "extremely serious threat to peace," and "the greatest threat to peace since World War II" (quoted in Bradsher 1985, 189). In addition, Carter sent a sharp message to Brezhnev warning that the Soviet invasion "could mark a fundamental and long-lasting turning point in [U.S.-Soviet] relations" (Carter 1982, 472). In late December the United States attempted to secure a UN Security Council condemnation of the Soviet invasion, which the USSR vetoed. However, the UN General Assembly passed a similar condemnation on 14 January 1980 by a vote of 104 to 18 (Garthoff 1985, 950). Finally, on 23 January 1980, President Carter delivered his State of the Union Address (which included the Carter Doctrine), warning of the serious implications of the Soviet invasion and stating that "verbal condemnation is not enough. The Soviet Union must pay a price for their aggression" (*Weekly Compilation of Presidential Documents*, 28 January 1980, 197).

Furthermore, the United States enacted sanctions to punish the Soviet Union, including delaying the SALT II ratification, canceling a large grain sale, boycotting the 1980 Olympic Games, and recalling ("for consultations") the U.S. ambassador to the Soviet Union.[4] In addition, the United States committed to provide Pakistan with more military and other assistance to strengthen its defenses; requested an increase in American defense spending, especially to create a force capable of rapid deployment to the Persian Gulf; and announced its intention to increase security cooperation with China and to expand the sale of military technology. Finally, the U.S. military deployed forces to the area, accelerating the U.S. naval buildup in the Indian Ocean at Diego Garcia and operations that included bomber flights over Soviet vessels (Garthoff 1985, 953–55; Poullada 1990, 60–61).

Most important, the Carter administration expanded its small covert aid program for the resistance. Brzezinski (1983, 449) noted that "plans were made to further enhance [U.S.] cooperation with Saudi Arabia and Egypt regarding Afghanistan." According to the chief of the CIA division responsible for overseeing the program, "just days after the Soviet invasion, Carter signed a new presidential finding on covert action to supply lethal weapons to the Mujaheddin, through the Pakistani authorities, for the purpose of harassing the Soviet occupation forces in Afghanistan. The first arms—mainly .303 Enfield rifles—arrived in Pakistan on January 10, 1980, fourteen days after the Soviet invasion" (Cogan 1993, 76). This finding remained operational until March 1985 and authorized the supply of light weapons primarily to "harass" the Soviet Union; it did not speak of driving the USSR from Afghanistan or defeating it militarily (Coll 1992b). This was a "bleeder" strategy, designed to hurt Moscow and raise the costs of its occupation.

The operation of the program involved several other countries. Just before his assassination in 1981, Egyptian president Anwar Sadat told a journalist that the United States asked, "Please open your stores for us so that we can give the Afghanis the armaments they need to fight." Sadat complied, and "the shipment of armaments to the Afghanis started from Cairo on U.S. planes" (quoted in Bradsher 1985, 223). Sadat supplied weapons from Egypt's armory (gained through Soviet assistance from 1956 to 1972) so the mujahidin could use "battlefield-credible" arms; the United States then replaced Egypt's stores with American weapons. In addition, China, Saudi Arabia, Iran, and other Persian Gulf states provided assistance, mainly financial (although a CIA official estimated that China annually sold $100 million in weapons for this purpose to the CIA in the early 1980s). Pakistan provided the operational control and some additional assistance (Bradsher 1985, 223–24; Coll 1992c; Cogan 1993, 76). Shortly after the policy decision was made and its implementation began, administration officials informed the Senate Select Committee on Intelligence; no objections were raised (Bradsher 1985, 223). Although the specific numbers are still secret, press accounts estimated that, in 1980, the program cost about $30 million (C. Bernstein 1980; Felton 1984b, 1903; *Wall Street Journal,* 9 April 1984).

Phase II: The Reagan Doctrine, 1981–1984

When President Reagan took office in January 1981, he faced no need to formulate a policy and coax Congress into agreement. Debate during Reagan's two terms would address only the level and type of aid provided to the Afghan rebels. The purpose of the program itself was not challenged. In addition, the administration expanded on Carter's diplomatic efforts to create a second track utilizing diplomacy and publicity to try to persuade the Soviet Union to withdraw. The combination of force and negotiations, it was hoped, would convince Moscow to end its occupation of Afghanistan.

Reagan Doctrine aid to the mujahidin. Building on the existing Carter administration program, the second phase of the application of the Reagan Doctrine in Afghanistan was characterized by steadily increasing funding levels, beginning in October 1982. Decisions were made on three occasions to increase the quantity and quality of the weapons provided to the mujahidin. The first was made by the administration but came as a result of congressional prodding. The next two resulted from the efforts of members of Congress; increases in 1983 and 1984 occurred primarily because of the efforts of several congressional leaders, especially Charles Wilson (D-Tex.) and Gordon Humphrey (R-N.H.). On both occasions, Congress added funds to the Afghan program to supplement the administration's request.

The decision to continue the Carter administration program began to take shape even before the Reagan administration assumed office, as members of the intelligence section of the Reagan transition team indicated their desire for continuation, if not actual expansion, of the program. The Carter administration responded by increasing the aid program at the end of its term to provide better equipment to the rebels (Prados 1986, 362). William Casey met with deputy CIA director John McMahon early in 1981 to discuss Afghanistan. Casey remarked that Afghanistan offered a major opportunity for the United States to engage the Soviet Union and said that he believed the administration would expand the program begun by Carter (Woodward 1987, 99–100). Casey insisted that the United States had to do more to "bleed them . . . make them feel the heat" (quoted in Schweizer 1994, 10). In fact, after a review of the CIA program, the administration decided to continue operating under the intelligence finding signed by Carter in December 1979, to maintain the level of funding (approximately $30 million), and to restrict the aid to Soviet-made weapons obtained from Egypt.

The decision to merely continue under the Carter program appears to have been driven by the foreign policy bureaucracy, led by the CIA and the Pentagon, and ratified by the NSPG (Persico 1990, 264; Schweizer 1994, 22). Three factors seem to have been especially important in the decision to maintain the limited nature of the program. First, many U.S. and Pakistani officials feared that greater involvement would provoke the Soviet Union into attacking Pakistan (Cronin 1985, 13, 22; Shultz 1993, 692). Pakistani president Zia Ul-Haq himself expressed this viewpoint, stating his desire to "keep the pot boiling at a certain temperature. We must not allow it to boil over."[5] The chief of the CIA's operation in the Near East and southern Asia recalled that the assistance program "could not be so provocative, or so blatant, as to invite a major Soviet reaction against Pakistan" (Cogan 1993, 80).

Second, U.S. officials did not want to allow U.S. equipment to be used in Afghanistan for fear of a larger Soviet response. Vincent Cannistraro, a CIA operations officer who worked on the NSC staff in the mid-1980s, recalled that "the CIA believed that they had to handle [the Afghan operation] as if they were wearing a condom" (Coll 1992c). Edward Juchniewicz, who became the CIA's assistant deputy director of operations in 1983, emphasized the need for plausible deniability: "We . . . went covert because Afghanistan was different from our other operations. This time, our effort was resulting in the direct death of Soviet boys" (Persico 1990, 310). Others in the administration, especially in the Pentagon, were very cautious about providing American weapons for fear that they would be captured by the Soviets or sold to hostile forces in the Middle East. This was especially worrisome with regard to sophisticated U.S. antiaircraft and antitank weapons (Shultz 1993, 692).[6]

Third, many officials seem to have been certain that the rebels could not win, and this prompted a reluctance to expand the program. Charles G. Cogan (1993, 76) stated that not until 1985 did it appear possible that the Soviet Union could be forced to withdraw. John McMahon reportedly told Casey that it was "unlikely that the Soviet Army would allow itself to be defeated" (Woodward 1987, 100), and remarked to a member of Congress that "US aid cannot be successful" (Harrison 1988, 201). According to Bob Woodward, in 1983 William Casey himself said that "the Soviets will overpower and wear down the rebels" (Woodward 1987, 332). Finally, Senator Malcolm Wallop (R-Wyo.), a staunch supporter of anticommunist rebels around the world, stated in early 1985: "I don't know anyone who believes that we will overthrow the Soviet-supported regime in Afghanistan" (*Washington Post,* 13 January 1985).

On the basis of these considerations, the program proceeded in 1981 and 1982 on a limited basis. Since the program was covert, precise figures are unavailable, but press accounts based on administration and congressional leaks indicate that in both 1981 and 1982 the administration spent approximately $30–40 million. The implementation of the program continued as it had under Carter, and several countries provided facilities, additional assistance, and operational supervision. As described by Coll (1992b), the program basically worked as follows. The United States, through the CIA, provided funds and some weapons, and generally supervised support for the mujahidin, but day-to-day operations were handled by the Pakistani Inter-Services Intelligence agency (ISI). Saudi Arabia agreed to match U.S. financial contributions to the rebels and distributed funds to the ISI. China sold weapons to the CIA and also donated a smaller number directly to Pakistan. Egypt also was involved, both as a source of Soviet-model weapons and as a base for the supply operation (Cogan 1993, 76).

The U.S. part of the program was run entirely by the CIA. The CIA officer in charge of operations in the region stated that "there was no one else involved, except for some of the trainers, who were coopted Special Forces officers" (Cogan 1993, 79). Although the operation grew into the largest CIA operation ever, the number of operatives it used was relatively small: at its height no more than one hundred people, slightly more than half in the field in Pakistan and elsewhere, were involved (ibid., 79). On-site operational control fell to Pakistan, whose officials coordinated their efforts with a working group of representatives from the United States, Saudi Arabia, and China (U.S. Congress, House, Committee on Foreign Affairs, Subcommittee on Asian and Pacific Affairs 1990b, 156). The CIA trained Pakistani instructors, who then trained rebel forces. Pakistan's ISI determined the amount and type of weapons that each rebel party or group would receive and reportedly funneled more and better weapons to the Islamist groups, particularly to Hekmatyar's faction. Pakistani general Mohammed Yousaf estimated that Hekmatyar's party, the most radical Islamist group, received about 20 percent of the assistance, and the four Islamist groups together received about 75 percent (Coll 1992c). Interestingly, on an ABC television report, "The Afghan Connection," aired on *Day One* on 12 July 1993, former ambassador to Pakistan Robert Oakley maintained that the United States knew that Hekmatyar was "a nasty piece of work" but acquiesced in the favoritism because he was "an effective weapon against the Russians."

Operational control of the policy afforded Casey and the CIA the opportunity to act with a substantial degree of independence. As Schweizer (1994, 100–101, 113–19, 149–55, 173–81) suggested, Casey used this freedom to expand U.S. involvement with Saudi Arabia and Pakistan in the areas of intelligence, coordination, and training, and beginning in 1982, he developed a plan for rebel groups to target Soviet officers and conduct raids into Soviet Central Asia, apparently on his own authority.

The first major increase in aid occurred in late 1982. It was primarily an executive branch decision involving presidential advisers and the foreign policy bureaucracy. Two of the main advocates of expanding the program were William Casey and Undersecretary of Defense Fred C. Iklé; in interagency and NSPG meetings these two officials advocated an increase in both the quality and quantity of the weapons. Resistance to the increase came from the CIA bureaucracy, the Pentagon, and parts of the State Department (Codevilla 1988; Harrison 1988, 201; Cannon 1991, 371; Rodman 1994, 336). This opposition produced months of haggling over the potential risks of providing heavier weaponry, prompting one appointee to comment, "I couldn't believe that after all we had said about helping the guerrillas and being tough on the Russians, we weren't really doing much to help. It was outrageous" (Gelb 1983b).

Interestingly, congressional pressure helped to break this impasse. Just before the administration began to consider increasing its assistance to the Afghan rebels, the Senate encouraged the expansion of the program. In September 1982, Senator Paul Tsongas (D-Mass.) introduced a bill (S. Con. Res. 126) "to provide the people of Afghanistan, if they so request, with material assistance, as the U.S. considers appropriate, to help them fight effectively for their freedom" (Felton 1982b, 3056). At its introduction the bill had ninety-nine cosponsors who agreed with its author that it was necessary to persuade the administration to do more. According to Tsongas, current U.S. aid was "not enough to tip the military scale in the Afghans' favor" (ibid., 3056). Charles Mathias (R-Md.) blocked the bill in the Senate Foreign Relations Committee on the grounds that it might instill false expectations of American intervention. It took both committee chairman Charles Percy (R-Ill.) and Tsongas to convince Mathias that the bill was not an aid authorization and that "all of the people we have spoken to in the Afghanistan freedom fighters' groups understand." The resolution then passed the committee by a voice vote (ibid., 3056–57), but it was not brought to the floor for a vote, and thus died when the congressional session ended. Nevertheless, the ongoing debate on the measure indicated Congress's broad support for the program and its belief that the administration was not doing enough.

Ultimately, an agreement was reached and approved by the president in December, and the CIA began to provide bazookas, mortars, grenade launchers, mines, and recoilless rifles of Soviet origin to the mujahidin (Gelb 1983b; *New York Times*, 3 May 1983; Cronin 1985, 23).

The expanded program was incorporated into National Security Decision Directive 75. While addressing broad U.S. strategy vis-à-vis the Soviet Union, this directive also singled out Afghanistan as a primary target and opportunity (see Chapter 2). The directive proposed to "keep maximum pressure on Moscow for withdrawal" and "ensure that the Soviets' political, military, and other costs remain high" (NSDD 75, 4). Administration officials explained that the improved quality and increased number of the weapons was designed to persuade the Soviet Union to agree to a political solution without prompting Soviet retaliation against Pakistan (Harrison 1988, 201). Expanded Soviet efforts on the battlefield also contributed to the decision, as some officials cited the need to increase the rebel supplies simply to maintain a standoff (Gelb 1983b; U.S. Department of State 1983b, 53–55).

The second expansion of the program occurred in late 1983. On this occasion the impetus came entirely from Congress. Bolstered by support from interest groups, including the Federation for American Afghan Action and the Committee for a Free Afghanistan, certain members of Congress began another campaign to expand the application of the Reagan Doctrine. In October 1983, Tsongas reintroduced his amendment (S. Con. Res. 74) with 68 cosponsors. The amendment stated that it would be "indefensible to provide the freedom fighters with only enough aid to fight and die, but not enough to advance their cause of freedom" (Felton 1984b, 1906). A companion resolution in the House (H. Con. Res. 237) was introduced by Representative Don Ritter (R-Pa.) with 169 cosponsors. Neither resolution passed in 1983, largely because of the opposition of the administration. Between December 1982 and the introduction of the new resolution, CIA officials voiced their opposition to the bill based on the argument that public discussion would endanger the secrecy of the program and upset the delicate supply lines. Many policy makers and observers considered a *Time* magazine story describing the tenuous supply links and the rather remarkable efforts of the CIA in Afghanistan to be a CIA-sponsored plant to undermine the criticism from Congress. The story concluded that "the pipeline is probably working at close to its capacity, and the CIA is determined not to upset its delicate system. For that reason, the agency has, in recent months, refused to increase the quality or quantity of U.S. aid to the Afghan rebels" (Iyer 1984, 40). The State Department added its opposition, demanding that the call for direct U.S. aid ("effective material assistance") be eliminated from the bill (Felton 1984b, 1906). Nevertheless, the bill did pressure the administration to expand its Reagan Doctrine aid.

This pressure failed to prompt an immediate change in policy, but the efforts of Representative Charles Wilson in 1983 produced more tangible results.[7] Wilson took advantage of the two-step authorization-appropriation process to adjust the CIA's budget for the Afghan program. Intensely interested in the Afghanistan issue, Wilson visited Pakistan and made unauthorized trips into Afghanistan on three occasions. In the process, he developed relationships with exile leaders and local commanders of the mujahidin and became persuaded that the United States was not sufficiently assisting the rebels. In particular, he maintained that the rebels required an effective antiaircraft gun. When he learned that the CIA's request for the Afghan operation was roughly the same as the previous year's request (around $40 million), Wilson used his position on the House Appropriations Committee to influence the application of the Reagan Doctrine in Afghanistan.

First, Wilson lobbied CIA and Pentagon officials to supply an advanced air defense weapon to counter the devastating Soviet helicopters. When the Intelligence Committee authorization for the Defense Department budget (within which the CIA budget was hidden) came before the House Appropriations Committee, Wilson indicated that he desired only one change: more funding for the Afghan rebels. Arguing that the rebels wanted "some way to knock down Russian helicopters" (U.S. Congress, House, Committee on Appropriations 1984, 242), Wilson maintained that no member of Congress could "be against backing religious freedom-fighters against the atheistic horde from the north . . . you can't make a case" (Felton 1984b, 1903). Wilson offered to vote favorably on matters affecting other members of the committee if they would appropriate an additional $40 million, and the committee agreed.

When the House-Senate conference committee met to reconcile the two versions of the federal budget, Wilson made the same offer and again met with success. Finally, Wilson lobbied the House and Senate Intelligence Committees to obtain their ex post facto authorization of the additional funds. Neither committee was pleased with Wilson's circumvention of their jurisdiction: according to Bob Woodward, Senate Intelligence Committee chairman Barry Goldwater (R-Ariz.) was especially enraged and blocked the authorization request as a matter of ("turf") principle. Goldwater continued his opposition until, in April 1984, Deputy Director of Central Intelligence John McMahon wrote to both committees in favor of having the CIA purchase, test, and (if suitable) provide the guns to the rebels. Goldwater withdrew his objections and the funds were provided. Nine guns were purchased immediately; in 1985 twenty Oerlikon cannons were shipped to the rebels in Afghanistan. In effect, the CIA operating funds for the Afghan program doubled and an advanced antiaircraft weapon was provided to the rebels as a result of the efforts of one member of Congress.

The final increase in aid to the mujahidin occurred in 1984 and again was led by Congress. It was accompanied by renewed congressional pressure to expand the program and the beginning of an attempt by Congress to convert the covert aid program into an overt military and humanitarian assistance plan. The effort was led again by Charles Wilson. Repeating his tactics from the previous fall, Wilson used his position on the House Appropriations Committee to insert an additional $50 million into a supplemental appropriations bill (H.R. 6040), increasing the CIA program to roughly $130 million for 1984. The measure passed the House on 1 August 1984. The amendment was supposed to be secret—the funds were hidden in an air force account ("other procurement") which reportedly is frequently used to hide CIA funds in the budget—but because Wilson's amendment had to be listed as a separate item in the bill, it prompted some curiosity among some journalists, and eventually the information leaked out (Felton 1984b, 1903–4; *New York Times,* 28 July 1984).

Wilson's efforts on behalf of the mujahidin were contagious. In April, a Senate Foreign Relations Committee staff report recommended additional efforts to assist the resistance and suggested that "a Congressional resolution publicly mandating moral and material support for the mujahidin represents a useful, even if far from decisive, antidote to Soviet policy" (U.S. Congress, Senate, Committee on Foreign Relations 1984, 39). Then, on 25 September 1984, the Senate Foreign Relations Committee passed a slightly amended version of the Tsongas resolution, calling on the Reagan administration "to effectively support" the mujahidin (*Congressional Quarterly Weekly Report,* 29 September 1984, 2403). Finally, in October 1984, the Senate passed the resolution by a vote of 97 to 3, and its House counterpart passed by unanimous consent (Cronin 1985, 25).

Other members of Congress attempted to make the application of the Reagan Doctrine in Afghanistan a public policy. The staff study referred to above concluded that "a declaration of direct and overt American aid carries the attraction of conducting a policy and being proud of it" (U.S. Congress, Senate, Committee on Foreign Relations 1984, 40–41). Subsequent pressure from Congress, led by Charles Wilson, Gordon Humphrey, and others, led to a more overt American aid program. Congress persuaded the administration to reprogram $2 million and provide it to the International Red Cross for use in Afghanistan. Another $2 million was reprogrammed from several different accounts into a "Cash for Food" program to alleviate the food shortage inside Afghanistan. Finally, the administration agreed to transfer $4 million in unspent funds originally designated for Syria into the direct American aid program to be dispersed by the U.S. Office of Foreign Disaster Assistance (Cronin 1985, 25; U.S. Department of State 1985d, 15). In short, under pressure from Congress the administration created a humanitarian assistance program for people inside Afghanistan. This new program complemented the considerable refugee relief aid provided by the United States to the UN High Commissioner for Refugees, the World Food Program, and directly to Pakistan. Including the designated aid for 1985, the total U.S. contribution for humanitarian aid to Afghan refugees totaled $430 million between 1979 and 1985 (U.S. Department of State 1985d, 15).

Following the lead of Congress, the administration increased its 1985 funding request to approximately $250 million (Gelb 1984, 1986a, 1986b). Leslie Gelb, a former government official then writing for the *New York Times,* observed that "by all accounts, Congress has been responsible for most of the increases in covert aid [to Afghanistan], sometimes encountering administration resistance" (Gelb 1984). In addition, in late 1984 the administration commenced a policy review to consider a major expansion of Reagan Doctrine aid to Afghanistan, prompted in large part by the pressure by Congress to do more in Afghanistan.

The second track: rhetoric and diplomacy. The United States joined the covert application of the Reagan Doctrine with two additional instruments to try to remove the Soviet Union from Afghanistan. First, the administration and Congress kept up a steady stream of speeches and appearances condemning Soviet actions and extolling the courage of the mujahidin. President Reagan himself repeatedly took up the topic. Many references to the cause of the freedom fighters of Afghanistan appeared in presidential speeches, interviews, press conferences, and impromptu appearances. For example, each year in December (the anniversary of the Soviet invasion) and March (the Afghan New Year, designated as Afghanistan Day by the administration), President Reagan gave a speech or issued a public statement or proclamation on Afghanistan. The speeches typically included words of praise for the mujahidin coupled with attempts to identify the rebels with American ideals.[8] President Reagan always condemned Soviet aggression and brutality and called for continued U.S. action.[9]

Other administration officials joined the effort. For example, in 1984, Secretary of State George Shultz spoke of the mujahidin in glowing terms: "Their sustained countrywide struggle against tyranny and oppression is worthy of our esteem. Their courage and determination is an inspiration to us all" (U.S. Department of State 1984d). In addition, Deputy Secretary of State John C. Whitehead (1986, 1–3) castigated the Soviet Union for its "blatant example of communist colonialism" and its attempt "to destroy everything Afghan—history, tradition, religion, family." After condemning the atrocities committed by the Soviets and praising the courage of the resistance, Whitehead concluded that "we can and must help restore Afghanistan's independence." Finally, Michael Armacost (1988, 19–21), under secretary of state for political affairs, condemned the "brazen act" of aggression by the Soviet Union and praised the rebels for their valor.

The United States also worked to maintain international condemnation of the Soviet Union. The Reagan administration sponsored several UN General Assembly resolutions criticizing Moscow for its actions and continued occupation (building on the 1980 resolution pushed through by the Carter administration).[10] In defense of one resolution, Ambassador Jeane Kirkpatrick (1982, 59) argued that "the struggle of the Afghan nation for survival is consistent with the basic and most cherished purposes of the United Nations. . . . It is only fitting that the United Nations should affirm the basic and most cherished purpose of the Afghan nation, which is to regain its ancient homeland so that it may once again be independent and live in peace." Similarly, in a 1985 address to the General Assembly, Kirkpatrick (1985c, 47) reviewed the pattern of abuse, repression, and devastation; called on the Soviet Union to withdraw; and praised "the Afghan people, who are surely among the most courageous and independent in the world." In other speeches Kirkpatrick and other members of the UN mission called for the Soviet Union to withdraw, again citing its atrocities and aggression while championing the resistance (Kirkpatrick 1983; Walters 1986; Okun 1988). The annual efforts of the administration to report on developments in Afghanistan to Congress and the public formed another thread of this effort (see U.S. Department of State 1981d, 1982d, 1983b, 1984b, 1985d, 1986b, 1987c, 1988b).

The second, and more significant, policy instrument utilized as part of the second track was the American commitment, in conjunction with the UN, to arrive at a political settlement that would require the Soviet Union to withdraw its troops, which was the publicly stated goal of the U.S. policy. Although this track languished, primarily because of the Soviets' disinterest, the broad outlines of a settlement acceptable to the UN and the United States emerged from the efforts of the UN with the support of the U.S. State Department. While the United States did not play a direct role in the negotiations, U.S. representatives were present at the talks and were regularly briefed and consulted by the UN team. For its part, the U.S. State Department's representatives adamantly maintained that the Soviet Union would have to withdraw quickly and that genuine independence that included a role for the resistance in the government should be established.

In February 1981, UN secretary general Kurt Waldheim appointed Javier Perez de Cuellar as his personal representative in the negotiations. Several preliminary meetings between Perez de Cuellar and the Afghan and Pakistani regimes produced a tentative agreement to begin three-sided talks involving the UN. The UN General Assembly formally authorized this approach in a November 1981 resolution. Perez de Cuellar began meetings with the foreign ministers of Pakistan and Afghanistan in New York during that session of the UN (U.S. Department of State 1982b, 25). When Perez de Cuellar replaced Waldheim as secretary general later that year, he designated Diego Cordovez as his replacement; Cordovez began a series of trips between Kabul and Islamabad but made little progress other than settling some procedural issues.

Based on the UN resolution and the initial negotiations, four issues emerged in 1983 as keys to a settlement: withdrawal of foreign troops, noninterference and nonintervention in Afghanistan's affairs, international guarantees of the settlement, and voluntary return of the refugees from Pakistan and Iran (U.S. Department of State 1984b, 79). Although Moscow expressed a commitment to a political solution based on these four components, its insistence on a lengthy withdrawal schedule, initially four years, stymied the talks throughout 1984 (U.S. State

Department 1983b, 79). Cordovez publicly indicated that negotiations were "ninety-five percent complete" but admitted that the unsettled item was Soviet withdrawal—the most significant aspect of the talks. Deputy Secretary of State John C. Whitehead (1986, 3) indicated that "to date, three of the four instruments have been largely completed. The inter-relationships document, in which the withdrawal of Soviet forces from Afghanistan would be addressed, remains to be completed. This is the critical document. The issue of withdrawal lies at the heart of the Afghan problem. . . . The questions addressed in the other instruments . . . are ancillary."

Phase III: Escalating the Reagan Doctrine, 1985-1988

The third phase of U.S. policy saw the acceleration of both tracks of the policy. The administration responded to congressional pressure and greatly expanded the application of the Reagan Doctrine. At the same time, diplomatic efforts intensified as the administration sought to convert the battlefield escalation into a political victory by concluding an agreement on Soviet withdrawal.

Expanding the Reagan Doctrine in Afghanistan. The application of the Reagan Doctrine in Afghanistan was reformulated through two decisions taken in 1985 and early 1986. Both were made almost exclusively in the executive branch, specifically the White House. Congress was involved only secondarily, and the foreign policy bureaucracy functioned as a provider of information and advice. As a result of the decisions, the purposes of the Reagan Doctrine changed and the implementation was adjusted so significantly that it nearly assumed the qualities of a different policy.

The first decision stemmed from the policy review that began in late 1984. William Casey was a frequent traveler to Pakistan, Saudi Arabia, and Egypt, and he used his trips to maintain and expand support for the rebels and improve coordination between the United States and the other contributors (see, e.g., Schweizer 1994, 25–32, 149–55, 173–81). In October 1984, Casey visited Pakistan to confer with U.S. officials involved in the Afghan operation and to discuss the program with Pakistani officials. According to General Mohammed Yousaf of Pakistan, who supervised the operations, Casey's visit produced an agreement to expand the scope and intensity of the war (Coll 1992b). Armed with Pakistan's agreement to support such an escalation, Casey returned to the United States to take part in a high-level policy debate over the Afghan program.

In January 1985, the NSPG review considered expanding the level of covert support. According to intelligence officials, one key aspect of the considerations involved sensitive information gathered in the Soviet Union. From Moscow, the administration learned of Politburo fears that the USSR was "in danger of becoming bogged down" (Coll 1992b). As a result, Mikhail Gorbachev (the new general secretary) and other members of the Politburo had agreed "to make an all-out effort to prevent arms supplies from reaching the anti-Communist mujaheddin" and to conduct "a more vigorous prosecution of the war" (Dobbs 1992b). The intelligence indicated that the Soviet Union's hard-liners had convinced Gorbachev to undertake a final concerted effort to win the war in two years (Coll 1992b). General Mikhail Zaitsev was transferred from command of Soviet forces in Germany to implement the plan, and the Soviet Union increased its troops, conducted more carefully coordinated attacks, and deployed one-third of its special forces, the Spetsnaz. Finally, Moscow sent in sophisticated communications equipment to assist its forces in locating rebel activity by tracking their communications (Coll 1992b; Dobbs 1992b).[11]

This information persuaded senior administration officials that an increased U.S. effort was necessary to match the Soviet escalation. It also revealed that the Soviet Union, and especially Mikhail Gorbachev, was considering the possibility that the costs in Afghanistan might be higher than it was willing to pay. CIA officer Charles G. Cogan (1993, 76) recalled that the idea that the United States might actually be able to force the Soviet Union to withdraw arose at this time. Pentagon officials who examined the intelligence information concluded that the American response should be to provide "secure communications, kill the [helicopter] gunships and fighter cover, [provide] better routes for [rebel] infiltration, and get to work on Soviet targets," and they passed this recommendation up through the channels of the interagency process (quoted in Coll 1992b). President Reagan responded to the information by instructing his advisers to develop an expanded application of the Reagan Doctrine that would "do what's necessary to win" (quoted in Schweizer 1994, 213).

In March 1985, the president and his top advisers met with the NSC to consider policy toward Afghanistan. According to Secretary of State George Shultz (1993, 1087), "with Bill Casey pushing hard and with me in full agreement, the President . . . stepped up sharply our level of assistance to the mujaheddin." Replacing the directive and intelligence finding signed by Jimmy Carter in late 1979, President Reagan signed National Security Decision Directive 166 authorizing increased aid to the rebels. The new directive (which remains classified) called for efforts to force the Soviet Union out of Afghanistan "by all means possible," thus changing the American policy objective from "make Moscow pay a price" to "make Moscow get out" (Gelb 1986b; Cogan 1993, 76). According to Steve Coll (1992b), NSDD 166 "made it clear that the secret Afghan war had a new goal: to defeat Soviet troops in Afghanistan through covert action and encourage a Soviet withdrawal." Specifically, this directive ordered a more effective supply operation; better weapons; expanded intelligence, including satellite photographs; and more international pressure on the Soviet Union. The new objectives were detailed in a long annex to the document committing the United States to victory, not harassment (Schweizer 1994, 213–14). The decision was reported to the congressional intelligence committees soon after Reagan's authorization (Gelb 1986b).

The change in objective and the corresponding increase in aid involved significant adjustments in the role of the United States in the Afghan war. The amount of assistance began to increase markedly. The CIA and other intelligence specialists provided sophisticated satellite photographs and maps to assist the rebels in their operations. The CIA and Pentagon Special Forces personnel provided secure communications gear, along with the training for its effective use. U.S. personnel took a more active role in formulating specific plans utilizing the new weaponry, better battlefield intelligence, and secure communications equipment. General Mohammed Yousaf described "a ceaseless stream" of CIA and Special Forces personnel to Afghanistan beginning in 1985 (Coll 1992b). Finally, the administration requested over $450 million for 1986 and borrowed a page from Representative Charles Wilson's tactics: it reprogrammed more than $200 million from an unspent Defense Department account and then requested authorization from the intelligence committees. The committees eventually approved the request, but not before "heated debate" over the encroachment on the committees' "turf" and the virtual doubling of the Afghan aid program for the second straight year (*Wall Street Journal,* 9 October 1985; *Washington Post,* 10 October 1985).

Thus, the United States redefined its application of the Reagan

Doctrine and took steps to improve the capacity of the rebels to fight the Soviet troops. This escalation of American involvement coincided with the Soviet decision to escalate and nullified any advantages the Soviet Union might have gained with its new tactics. While the underlying pressure by Congress and conservatives cannot be ignored—it was certainly an important factor in the administration's decision to review the application of the Reagan Doctrine and it formed the backdrop for reformulation—the policy review and decision were executive branch products. Congress did not play an active role in the decision itself. Because the CIA had to acquire funding for the program from Congress, however, it is almost certain that the congressional disposition to increase the quantity and quality of that aid weighed in the decision. In particular, the widespread support for the Tsongas resolution calling for U.S. aid to help the Afghans fight and win seems to have indicated to administration personnel that a greater effort to apply the Reagan Doctrine would be supported.

The second significant reformulation of the covert program occurred in early 1986. According to Secretary of State George Shultz (1993, 1087), the administration decided "in April 1986 to provide the Afghan resistance U.S. ground-to-air Stinger missiles." The decision was not an easy one. Although the rebels had wanted Stingers for several years (Persico 1990, 312), a decision to provide the weapon would remove the facade of plausible deniability for the United States and Pakistan, and it would place a highly sophisticated weapon in a position to be captured and copied by the Soviet Union (Cannon 1991, 371; Cogan 1993, 76; Shultz 1993, 692). William Casey, an outspoken proponent, visited Pakistan in March 1983 to persuade President Zia to allow the United States to arm the rebels with this weapon. Zia apparently agreed, provided the first one hundred Stingers went to Pakistan's military (Persico 1990, 312). In 1985, Casey again visited Saudi Arabia and Pakistan and garnered their support for the introduction of the Stinger missiles (Schweizer 1994, 227–32). He was not as successful at convincing the Pentagon or the career officers of the CIA. [12]

George Shultz was another proponent of the decision. In late 1985, after supporting the decision to escalate U.S. aid earlier that year, he determined, on the basis of State Department assessments, that the United States had a window of about one year to turn the tide decisively against the Soviet Union. Morton Abramowitz, director of the State Department's Intelligence and Research Bureau, told Shultz at that time,

"I believe we are not putting significant pressure on the Soviets. We should put in an American weapon: the Stinger" (Shultz 1993, 692). According to Shultz, an interagency conflict arose in early 1986 on this issue: the Pentagon was opposed "for fear [the Stingers] would fall into Soviet hands and thus compromise our technology, or be sold to Third World terrorists for use against American targets" (ibid., 692). Some State Department officials also opposed the idea, fearing that American weapons would antagonize the Soviet Union and ruin other aspects of the U.S.-Soviet relationship (ibid., 692). Shultz disagreed with each of these objections, believing that "unless we hurt the Soviets in Afghanistan, they would have no interest in dealing with us to end the war there" (ibid., 692).

National Security Adviser Robert McFarlane raised the issue in December 1985 with President Reagan, but a bureaucratic dispute created a deadlock that persisted through April 1986 (Schweizer 1994, 253). Favoring aid were Fred Iklé and his assistant, Michael Pillsbury, in the Defense Department, Vincent Cannistraro and Christopher Lehman of the NSC staff, Casey and his top assistants in the CIA, and many members of Congress, including Senator Orrin Hatch (R-Utah) and Representative Charles Wilson. Opposition came from the Joint Chiefs of Staff and the working levels of the CIA, and President Reagan initially deferred to their objections, as he had since 1981 (Cannon 1991, 371; Rodman 1994, 336–39). In March, an interagency group (IG) with representatives from the military, the Office of the Secretary of Defense, the State Department, and the CIA reconsidered the issue (Coll 1992b). Undersecretary of Defense Fred Iklé and William Casey pressured their respective bureaucracies, and Representative Charles Wilson and Senators Gordon Humphrey (R-N.H.) and Orrin Hatch exerted pressure from Congress, but the State Department tipped the scales in favor of the plan. Shultz's decision, pressed by Abramowitz and Michael Armacost, led to vigorous support by the State Department for the introduction of the missile, which broke the deadlock; in March the IG recommended that Stingers be sent to Afghanistan. In the ensuing NSC meeting, Shultz "pushed [the] idea, in the end successfully. Bill Casey was a strong ally in this effort" (Shultz 1993, 692). President Reagan, finally presented with a consensus, approved the recommendation (Gelb 1986b; *Washington Post,* 5 March 1986; Shultz 1993, 1087; Rodman 1994, 339–40).

In June, Pakistani officers were trained in the use of the weapons.

They returned to Pakistan and established a sophisticated training camp for the rebels, assisted by the CIA and U.S. Special Forces (Coll 1992b). According to the CIA officer in charge of operations in southern Asia, the Stingers "became operational in September 1986, and immediately began to take a toll, especially on Soviet helicopters, which were the key element in the Soviets' stepped-up aggressive tactics against the Mujaheddin" (Richelson 1989, 341–42; Cogan 1993, 76). Ultimately, according to General Mohammed Yousaf, the United States provided approximately 250 launchers and more than a thousand missiles (Coll 1992c). Reports of the impact of the Stingers were soon forthcoming. By December, the U.S. government was acknowledging that the rebels were downing as many as one helicopter or plane per day, a dramatic increase from previous months, according to the State Department (see, e.g., Gwertzman 1986d; *New York Times,* 17 December 1986). According to Shultz, "the Stingers . . . made a huge, perhaps even decisive, difference. The Soviets could no longer dominate areas by helicopter or by accurate bombing from low-flying aircraft. High-level bombers were ineffective against the dispersed and mobile forces of the Afghan freedom fighters" (Shultz 1993, 692). American aid increased dramatically again in 1986 and 1987, peaking at between $470 and $650 million (largely the cost of the Stinger missiles).[13] In 1988, Reagan Doctrine aid to the rebels totaled about $350 million (Lardner 1990; Cogan 1993, 76).

Many policy makers regarded this as the turning point of the Afghan conflict, a view that seems to be borne out by recently released Soviet documents on the decision to withdraw from Afghanistan (Dobbs 1992b).[14] According to these documents, the Politburo met on 13 November 1986, two months after the Stingers were introduced. According to the minutes of this meeting, Andrei Gromyko complained that the situation was worse than it had been six months ago and counseled that the Soviet Union "must be more active in searching for a political solution." Marshal Sergei Akhromeyev implicitly acknowledged the effectiveness of the rest of the expanded U.S. aid and support by noting, "We have deployed 50,000 Soviet soldiers to seal the border, but they are unable to close all channels through which arms are being smuggled across the border." The Politburo concluded that the war was no longer winnable unless, as Gorbachev acknowledged, the Soviet Union was willing to fight for another twenty to thirty years.

Gromyko stated that the "strategic goal is to end the war," and Gorbachev asserted that Moscow "must finish this process in the swiftest possible time" (minutes of Politburo meeting, 13 November 1986). Apparently, the increased costs of the war and the Soviets' failure to overcome the Afghan resistance aided Gorbachev in overruling the hard-liners in the Politburo and planning a reversal of Soviet foreign policy in Afghanistan and elsewhere. In the end, the Politburo agreed on a two-year deadline for total Soviet withdrawal, which the Soviet Union ultimately missed by only three months when it completed its withdrawal in February 1989.

The decision to give Stinger missiles to the rebels was primarily an executive branch act, as was the decision to expand the covert program the previous year. Congress was involved in several minor but important ways and exerted consistent background pressure for a stronger policy (Rodman 1994, 330). Pressure to provide greater assistance to the rebels continued from several quarters, most notably through the watchdog efforts of the Joint House-Senate Task Force on Afghanistan, which was cochaired by Senator Gordon J. Humphrey and Representative Robert Lagomarsino (R-Calif.). Charles Wilson continued his advocacy of the Afghan cause as well. Additionally, Senator Orrin Hatch played a key role early in 1986. Hatch, accompanied by Morton Abramowitz, Vincent Cannistraro (NSC staff), Michael Pillsbury (assistant to Undersecretary of Defense Fred C. Iklé), the CIA station chief in Beijing, and the deputy director of the CIA's operations directorate, visited the People's Republic of China and enlisted its support in the covert war. In particular, Hatch helped secure China's promise to support the introduction of the Stingers by interceding with Pakistan. The party then flew to Pakistan and obtained Zia's pledge to accept the missiles (Coll 1992c).

Congress also contributed through its efforts to expand the overt side of the application of the Reagan Doctrine. First, Congress insisted that the United States establish an overt economic and humanitarian assistance program for the people of Afghanistan, building on its efforts in 1984. This program was motivated by the widespread belief that the United States was still responding insufficiently to the Afghan issue. The major villain in this failure, according to hard-liners in Congress, was the State Department. Senator Humphrey, for example, insisted that the department had been "cruelly slow" in providing funds appropriated by Congress, and Benjamin Hart (1986, 5–6), a conservative analyst, argued that only congressional pressure prompted increased aid, which was still being blocked by the State Department.

Under this pressure the administration cooperated with Congress to establish a food, medical, education, and agricultural aid program, administered by the Agency for International Development (AID), that provided $15 million in 1986, $30 million in 1987, and $45 million in 1988 (U.S. Department of State 1987c, 23–24, 1988b, 18). In addition, the U.S. Department of Defense, pursuant to a congressional mandate, provided nonlethal Defense Department property and assisted in the transportation of goods donated by private organizations (U.S. Department of State 1987c, 24). According to the AID budget request, the cumulative effect of these programs would "help the mujahidin to protect and take care of the people who support them" (cited in Harrison 1988, 204).

Some members of Congress, led by Senator Humphrey, tried to persuade the Reagan administration to recognize the rebel umbrella organization, the Islamic Unity of Afghan mujahidin, as the legitimate government of Afghanistan and then provide it with open U.S. military aid. In addition, these members of Congress wanted the administration to close down the U.S. embassy in Kabul. Humphrey again led the charge, publicly complaining that, "on the one hand we are aiding the freedom fighters. On the other hand we still maintain an embassy with an American flag flying daily at the seat of the government against which we are helping the mujaheddin to fight" (U.S. Congress, House, Committee on Foreign Affairs, Subcommittee on Asian and Pacific Affairs 1986, 16). In June 1986, four members of the rebel coalition visited Washington and asked for official recognition (as well as the closing of the U.S. embassy). Humphrey, after meeting with rebel leaders himself, called on the administration to accede to the rebel leaders' requests and to expel representatives of the PDPA regime from the United States as well (Felton 1986, 1390). President Reagan declined, apparently on the advice of the State Department (Felton 1986l, 1390; Gwertzman 1986c). Thus, Congress remained a contributor to the application of the Reagan Doctrine by providing background pressure and by shaping the overt aid program that developed in 1985.

The diplomatic track: State Department leadership and congressional oversight. At the same time the administration was increasing Reagan Doctrine aid, the U.S. government was also cooperating with the UN-led negotiations to reach a political settlement that would remove the Soviet Union from Afghanistan. The U.S. State Department was the principal actor in this effort, but it shared policy-making responsibility with other parts of the administration and with Congress. The negotiations remained stalled through June 1985 over the issue of Soviet withdrawal. The State Department attempted to break the logjam with two offers. According to Robert A. Peck, the deputy assistant secretary of state for Near East and South Asian affairs, in November 1985, after some internal policy discussion, the administration notified the UN "that the United States would be prepared to take on the role of a guarantor . . . if we were fully satisfied with the overall agreement. . . . That was a conditional undertaking and an initiative which was done in order to put pressure on the Soviet Union to discuss the issue of withdrawal" (U.S. Congress, House, Committee on Foreign Affairs, Subcommittee on Asian and Pacific Affairs 1989a, 111). As a part of that guarantee, according to Peck, the United States would be prepared to stop sending military assistance to the Afghan rebels (ibid., 96). George Shultz (1993, 1087) recalled that this position was based on the understanding that "upon Soviet withdrawal from Afghanistan, [U.S.] support for the Mujahiddin, having served its purpose, would cease." According to columnist William Safire (1988), three State Department officials—Peck, Arnold Raphel (U.S. ambassador to Pakistan), and Charles Dunbar—recommended the initiative and extended the offer, after getting approval from Undersecretary Michael Armacost, Secretary of State Shultz, and Donald Fortier of the NSC staff. Safire also indicated that Reagan was consulted, but apparently the president did not understand the implications of, or was misled about, the cessation of U.S. aid. Clearly, however, the offer departed from the administration's previous position, which was that the United States would not guarantee any agreement until its terms had been specified and evaluated.

The mere rumor of the offer prompted immediate criticism. The Heritage Foundation, an influential conservative policy institution, circulated a report in January 1986 that suggested the State Department was retreating from President Reagan's requirements. The report accused the State Department, in its eagerness to conclude an agreement, of abandoning the president's requirements for total withdrawal of the troops, independence and nonalignment, and self-determination in favor of a kind of "sphere-of-influence" agreement that would assign Afghanistan to the Soviet Union (Hart 1986, 6). Members of Congress also reacted suspiciously to the State Department's offer to guarantee an agreement. The "rumor" that the United States would end aid to the rebels on conclusion of an agreement fueled the hostility. Under fire from many quarters, the State Department clouded the record with a series of explanations, qualifications, and denials that left the nature of the commitments unclear, other than the fact that the United States had indeed agreed to be a guarantor (Klass 1988, 930). The flap resulted in a hearing before the House Foreign Affairs Subcommittee on Asian and Pacific Affairs on 1 May 1986.

The principal witnesses at this hearing were Senator Gordon Humphrey and Deputy Assistant Secretary of State Robert A. Peck. Humphrey complained that "the administration has gotten us and the Afghan people into a very tight spot by giving the State Department bureaucracy free reign" (U.S. Congress, House, Committee on Foreign Affairs, Subcommittee on Asian and Pacific Affairs 1986, 5). He then objected to the inordinate secrecy maintained by the State Department and the exclusion of resistance leaders from the talks, denounced the State Department for believing that the Soviet Union was truly interested in withdrawal, and mocked it for assuming that Moscow would abide by an agreement (ibid., 13–15, 65–67, 70–71, 115–19). Finally, Humphrey stated that "with respect to offering to act as a guarantor, as I said in my testimony, a ranking official in the State Department told me that this offer . . . was not cleared by the President" (ibid., 16). Humphrey's accusations prompted panel member Steven Solarz (D-N.Y.) to ask Humphrey whether he thought "the President is some kind of naive dupe who has permitted the bureaucrats in the State Department to pull the wool over his eyes and to conduct an Afghan policy on behalf of the United States of which he does not personally approve" (U.S. Congress, House, Committee on Foreign Affairs, Subcommittee on Asian and Pacific Affairs 1986, 9–10).

In response to Humphrey's charges, Peck maintained that the president supported the negotiating position, which was "an administration position . . . not a State Department position" (ibid., 57). Arguing that U.S. policy focused on the "irrevocable withdrawal of Soviet forces" from Afghanistan "within a fixed and reasonable period," he assured the panel that "the United States has not been engaged in secret negotiations with the Soviets" (ibid., 31). On the issue of aid to the rebels, Peck would say only that the United States would "take into account the undertakings of the other parties" regarding "noninterference and nonintervention" (ibid., 60). He also offered the widely shared opinion that the PDPA regime would collapse almost overnight when the Soviet Union withdrew its forces and argued that the Soviet withdrawal itself, "if accomplished in a reasonably short period of time, would in fact result in Afghan self-determination" (ibid., 70). Therefore, no provisions for a post-Soviet-withdrawal mechanism were required.

Since the negotiations were still incomplete and largely secret at this point, the matter ended. Little was done, however, to assuage the suspicions of members of Congress, especially conservatives, who remained skeptical of the diplomatic option. The initiative appeared to have some effect, though.[15] When the talks reconvened in July and August 1986, the Soviet Union and Afghanistan agreed to discuss a timetable for withdrawal and offered a four-year schedule. The Soviet Union also retreated from its position that halting outside aid to the resistance was a precondition to any deal, agreed that American aid would stop only when the USSR *began* a scheduled withdrawal, and acceded to having a UN monitoring force present to verify withdrawal (U.S. Congress, House, Committee on Foreign Affairs, Subcommittee on Asian and Pacific Affairs 1989a, 12–13). Pakistan's representative to the talks, with American support, rejected the proposal and countered with a four-month timetable (U.S. Department of State 1986b, 18–19).

In March 1987, the Soviet Union offered an eighteen-month withdrawal schedule to replace its initial four-year offering (U.S. Department of State 1987c, 23). Pakistan again rejected the offer and suggested seven months instead. In September, the Soviet-Afghan offer was reduced to sixteen months, and Pakistan countered with a proposal for eight months (ibid., 23). Later, Foreign Minister Eduard Shevardnadze indicated that the Soviet Union was prepared to begin withdrawal on 15 May 1988 if an agreement could be signed by 1 March 1988 (Klass 1988, 932). Responding to this, President Reagan took advantage of the December 1987 summit meeting with Mikhail Gorbachev to urge the Soviet leader to agree to a short timetable and declare a "date certain" for the Soviet withdrawal (U.S. Department of State 1987c, 23).

The final breakthrough came in February 1988. On 8 February, two weeks before the talks were scheduled to resume, Gorbachev announced that the Soviet Union had decided to withdraw from Afghanistan. He publicly recognized that no military solution was feasible, specified the "date certain" that President Reagan had requested

(15 May 1988), and offered a short timetable (ten months) that had most of the troops leaving in the first ninety days. In addition, Gorbachev stated his expectation that all "outside interference" in Afghanistan would cease and announced, in a major concession, that preparations for an interim regime were not of concern to the Soviet Union (hence it would not participate in talks on the subject, U.S. Department of State 1988b, 2–3). In the wake of Gorbachev's proposal, Diego Cordovez asked the United States to observe its 1985 commitment to support the offer (Klass 1988, 932).

Likened by one policy analyst to "a dark tunnel process," in which the negotiations started in public but proceeded in secrecy, only to emerge at the end of the tunnel for public consideration when the agreement was concluded,[16] debate over the diplomatic track began in earnest in 1988 when it became evident that an agreement was imminent and that the United States had agreed to several stipulations regarding the accord and the Reagan Doctrine. When Diego Cordovez called on the United States to fulfill its 1985 commitment, it became known that the United States had indeed agreed to suspend aid to the rebels at the start of the withdrawal (Klass 1988, 932–33; Shipler 1988b). The revelation that Robert A. Peck and his State Department colleagues Arnold Raphel and Charles Dunbar had recommended the offer, apparently with Undersecretary of State Michael Armacost's approval, accompanied reports that Secretary of State Shultz had approved the initiative and that the NSC staff apparently had signed off on it as well.[17] President Reagan denied approving the measure, prompting State Department officials (who declined to be identified) to suggest that either the president had been inattentive or that he had not understood the implication of the measure. These officials insisted that Reagan had approved the 1985 opening (Safire 1988; Shipler 1988b).

Congress reacted immediately. Many members accused the State Department of "selling out" the rebels (Safire 1988). The House Foreign Affairs Subcommittee on Asian and Pacific Affairs called Peck to testify on 25 February 1988. He told the panel:

> We and the Soviet Union would agree to the same basic commitment regarding non-interference and non-intervention. *We would be prepared, if completely satisfied with the overall agreement, to prohibit US military assistance to the Afghan resistance.* We would expect the Soviet Union to show reciprocal restraint under

the Geneva Accords in stopping its military support for the Kabul regime. We will, of course, continue non-military humanitarian assistance and assume the Soviets will do the same. (U.S. Congress, House, Committee on Foreign Affairs, Subcommittee on Asian and Pacific Affairs 1989a, 96; emphasis added)

Although it mentioned an expectation of reciprocity, Peck's statement made it clear that this was not a requirement of the proposed accords. Later in his testimony he offered the State Department's view that the withdrawal of the Soviet troops would cause the PDPA regime to fall almost immediately and stated that "the issue of the continuation of Soviet military supply would not have a material effect on the survivability of the regime" (ibid., 115).

A majority in Congress objected to this policy. Senator Gordon Humphrey and Representative Charles Wilson met with members of the rebel coalition and encouraged them to reject the agreement. Likening the administration's position to Neville Chamberlain's appeasement of the Nazis over the Sudentenland, members of the Senate immediately drew up a resolution (S. Res. 386) urging President Reagan to continue assisting the Afghan resistance until the Soviet withdrawal was irrevocable and the Soviet Union had stopped aiding the Afghan regime. The key provision stated that U.S. aid should continue "until it is absolutely clear that the Soviets have terminated their military occupation, that they are not redeploying their forces to be reinserted again, and that the mujahideen is well enough equipped to maintain its integrity during the delicate period of a transition government leading up to new elections" (Towell 1988, 561). The resolution, energetically supported by Senators Steven Symms (R-Ida.), Claiborne Pell (D-R.I.), John Kerry (D-Mass.), Gordon Humphrey, and Robert C. Byrd (D-W.Va.), passed 77 to 0 (Towell 1988, 561). A similar House resolution was bottled up in the Foreign Affairs Subcommittee on Asian and Pacific Affairs by its chairman, Steven Solarz (*Congressional Quarterly Weekly Report,* 12 March 1988, 686).

The comments of Majority Leader Byrd were indicative of the attitude of the Senate. Responding to the administration's description of the proposed agreement, Byrd stated: "I am not only shocked, I am stunned. . . . This would be a sellout by the United States, if I understand it correctly . . . and it would be a shameful sellout" (*Congressional Record,* 29 February 1988, S1608). Shortly after the February

vote, Senator Humphrey told reporters, "We want to hold the administration's feet to the fire to secure a decent agreement. What they have
been considering is indecent" (N. Lewis 1988). George Shultz (1993,
1092) took a different view, however, suspicious that Humphrey and
other members of the hard-line right "preferred to 'bleed' [the Soviets]
to death through the indefinite continuation of the war" and did not
really want the Soviet Union to withdraw, or an agreement that would
make withdrawal possible.

   This broad opposition—especially in the Senate, where some
members indicated that they might block the recently signed Intermediate Nuclear Force Treaty unless the administration corrected the
problem (P. Lewis 1988)—forced a change in the American position.
Although Shultz (1993, 1087–89) maintained that notice of this change
was provided to the Soviet Union in January, well before the Senate
action, it is clear from his account and press reports at the time that real
efforts to change the accords themselves occurred only after the Senate vote (N. Lewis 1988).[18] Colin Powell, the newly appointed national
security adviser, informed State Department officials who pressed for
Reagan's acceptance of their original proposal that he was not going to
"walk" the President back to where the policy was"; instead, the NSC
staff was going to "walk" the State Department forward to the president's position (Rodman 1994, 346). Hence, during the March 1988
talks between the United States and the Soviet Union, the State Department amended its stance to include a "symmetry" provision: the
United States would retain the right to provide assistance to rebels but
would respond to Soviet suspension of aid to the PDPA regime in kind.
Several days of meetings between Foreign Minister Shevardnadze,
Shultz, Undersecretary Armacost, and National Security Adviser Colin
Powell produced no agreement (Shultz 1993, 1090–91).

   Finally, on 7 April 1988, Gorbachev agreed. Shevardnadze informed Shultz that the Soviet Union recognized that the United States
retained the right under the accords to provide arms to the resistance,
and Shultz replied that the United States intended to assert publicly
this right at the signing (Taubman 1988; U.S. Department of State
1988b, 3; Shultz 1993, 1092). After explaining to Congress that "it is in
our interest to sign onto the Geneva agreements," Shultz added that
the United States had secured Soviet agreement on the principle of
symmetry (Shultz 1993, 1092–93). In Geneva on 14 April 1988, the Afghan regime and Pakistan, with the United States and Soviet Union as

guarantors, signed the Geneva Accords, which provided for full Soviet withdrawal beginning 15 May 1988 and concluding 15 February 1989.[19] Shultz left the room and publicly asserted U.S. rights "to provide military aid to the resistance. We are ready to exercise that right, but we are prepared to meet restraint with restraint" (U.S. Congress, House, Committee on Foreign Affairs, Subcommittee on Asian and Pacific Affairs 1989b, 73).

U.S. Policy after the Geneva Accords. By April 1988, the two-track U.S. strategy combining the Reagan Doctrine with diplomacy had succeeded in achieving a goal that most policy makers and analysts had believed unattainable eight years earlier. As specified by the accords, the Soviet Union began its withdrawal on 15 May 1988. A little over a month later, Michael Armacost informed the Senate that the withdrawal was well under way and that the Soviet Union was adhering to the schedule specified by the agreement (Armacost 1988b, 56). On 16 August 1988, the UN verification team certified that one-half of the Soviet forces had withdrawn (U.S. Department of State 1988b, 4). After a brief suspension in November the withdrawal continued, and by February 1989, all the Soviet troops had left Afghanistan (U.S. Department of State 1989a).

For a number of reasons, however, the triumph of the Reagan Doctrine was marred by subsequent events. First, the American consensus on the Afghan issue that had held together over eight years and two administrations began to unravel almost immediately. Conservatives attacked the administration for its alleged betrayal of the resistance. Gordon Humphrey complained that the agreement constituted "a slow motion sellout, in plain English" (Felton 1988h, 993). He maintained that Moscow would simply return on a new request from the PDPA regime or extend massive amounts of military aid to the regime to sustain it against rebel pressure (ibid., 994). Representative Dan Burton (R-Ind.), a vocal advocate for anticommunist rebels in Africa (see Chapters 5 and 8), believed the United States had betrayed the rebels:

> Had we not signed this agreement in opposition to the leadership of the Mujahedin, they would have kicked [the Soviet Union's] butts all the way to the border, and I think everybody knows it. . . . And so, what we have helped the Mujahedin do is settle for about half a loaf or less when they could have had the whole ball of wax because they were kicking their fanny. . . . And so our State De-

partment with an appeasement policy has embraced [the Soviet Union] and they are helping them get out. . . . I just want to state my, I suppose, disgust that this kind of an agreement would be signed. . . . And our State Department signed an agreement which I believe is full of holes which has led to a semi-sellout of the Mujahedin. (U.S. Congress, House, Committee on Foreign Affairs, Subcommittee on Asian and Pacific Affairs 1989b, 36, 37–38)

Other supporters of the rebels were not so cynical. Representative Charles Wilson, for example, said that the conservatives' fears were unjustified: "Number one, the Russians got their ass kicked. Number two, they're leaving. Number three, the [rebels] will continue to have bullets until [the Soviets] cross the border. . . . The Russians have achieved the most microscopic figleaf in the history of negotiations . . . it's an ignominious withdrawal" (Felton 1988h, 994, 996).

The dissension did not end with the conservatives. Liberal policy makers and analysts began to question whether the United States needed to continue assisting rebels who did not seem to reflect American values or principles. Observers such as Barnett R. Rubin and Selig Harrison, frequent witnesses before Congress on the Afghan issue, began to raise such questions. From a tiny beginning in 1988, this dissension blossomed in Congress in 1989 and 1990 (see, e.g., B. R. Rubin 1989a, 1989b, 1989c; U.S. Congress, House, Committee on Foreign Affairs, Subcommittee on Asian and Pacific Affairs 1990a, 1990b, 1993; U.S. Congress, Senate, Foreign Relations Committee 1990).

Events in Afghanistan in 1988 caused some disappointment as well. The Soviets continued to supply huge amounts of military assistance to the Afghan regime. Apparently the United States had hoped that the Soviet Union would exercise restraint under the symmetry provision of the accords, but it did not. On 13 June 1988, Moscow confirmed that it intended to continue to supply the PDPA regime with military assistance, and departing Soviet troops left behind equipment valued at over $1 billion. According to the U.S. State Department (1988b, 4), "substantial deliveries of military equipment—including tanks, armored personnel carriers, and aircraft—have continued unabated throughout 1988." Such deliveries continued throughout the early Bush administration at roughly twenty-five to forty supply flights per day (B. R. Rubin 1989b, 424).

Another disheartening development was the failure of the rebels to create a viable government. The rebels' condemnation of both the 1988 accords and the Reagan administration added to the sense that the U.S. foreign policy victory was not as decisive as it should have been. Although rebel military successes increased with the Soviet departure, predictions of the regime's immediate collapse did not materialize, in part because of the Soviet aid; however, the rebels' failure to present a unified alternative to the PDPA regime was the chief culprit. Thus, although officials such as Robert A. Peck and Robert Gates of the CIA (Shultz 1993, 1088) were confident of a speedy rebel victory, it did not materialize in 1988 as the Afghan struggle deteriorated into a complex civil war.

In short, while the United States achieved its chief objective, the other goals specified by the Carter and Reagan administrations were not attained. The Soviet Union was gone, but the regime remained, supported by Soviet assistance. In effect, the United States found itself opposing a regime that relied on Soviet aid, rather than a regime defended by Soviet troops. Therefore, Afghanistan had evolved into a situation similar to Nicaragua and, to a lesser extent, Angola and Cambodia after 1988. The application of the Reagan Doctrine changed from a policy to drive out Soviet occupation troops to a policy to depose the regime of a Soviet client. The application of the Reagan Doctrine continued: the United States provided the Afghan rebels with more than $400 million in 1988, and in October 1988 designated $350 million for use in 1989.

Phase IV: The Bush Administration and the
Politics of the Status Quo

In spite of the Soviet withdrawal, U.S. support and assistance in Afghanistan continued well into the Bush administration.[20] American policy in this period exhibited two key characteristics. First, the Bush administration continued the policy pursued in the final months of the Reagan administration: aid to the rebels, funneled through Pakistan and the exile parties in order to replace the PDPA regime. Second, the absence of Soviet occupation troops, who constituted a clear enemy, resulted in the first significant debate over the merits of the Reagan Doctrine since aid was first provided in 1980.

After the Soviet troops withdrew, the situation in Afghanistan developed into a civil war, albeit one with external sponsors. In spite of the changed scenario, however, the Bush administration maintained the Reagan Doctrine for several years. A National Security Council review of the Afghan policy concluded that U.S. assistance should be continued, and Howard B. Schaffer, the new deputy assistant secretary of state for Near East and South Asian affairs, told a House panel in June 1989 that "U.S. goals on Afghanistan remain the same; our policy has not changed" (U.S. Congress, House, Committee on Foreign Affairs, Subcommittee on Asian and Pacific Affairs 1990a, 43).[21] Schaffer cited self-determination, return of refugees, and sovereignty and independence as the goals driving U.S. policy (ibid., 43). The United States continued to provide the Afghan rebels with military assistance to pursue those goals, without specifying how such aid would achieve them (U.S. Congress, House, Committee on Foreign Affairs, Subcommittee on Asian and Pacific Affairs 1990a, 22–23). According to the former director for CIA operations in the region, the United States provided $350 million in 1989 and $300 million in 1990 (Cogan 1993, 76).

The primary focus of the Bush administration's policy was the Afghan interim government (AIG), a government-in-exile created in February 1989,[22] which the administration hoped would present a unified alternative to the PDPA regime. Accordingly, a great deal of attention was given to the AIG, and other alternatives, such as a mutual U.S.-Soviet aid suspension (i.e., "negative symmetry"), were eschewed. According to Deputy Assistant Secretary Schaffer, the AIG was a good start toward an exile government. His optimism soon proved ill-founded (U.S. Congress, House, Committee on Foreign Affairs, Subcommittee on Asian and Pacific Affairs 1990a, 48–53). Internecine fighting among the exile leaders and between the exile leaders and the local commanders prevented effective leadership (Rashid 1990; U.S. Congress, House, Committee on Foreign Affairs, Subcommittee on Asian and Pacific Affairs 1990b, 152). Local commanders were underrepresented or ignored. According to James Rupert (1989, 767–68), local commanders warned the exile parties to include them in the AIG. When that did not happen, many commanders simply sat out the fighting (see also U.S. Congress, Senate, Foreign Relations Committee 1990, 5–6; Khalilzad 1991, 4–16). Moreover, the exile leaders continued to advance their own organizations (B. R. Rubin 1989c, 153–56).

Pressure to continue assistance to Afghanistan came from congressional conservatives. The Congressional Task Force on Afghanistan, led by Senator Gordon Humphrey and Representatives Robert Lagomarsino (R-Calif.) and Don Ritter (R-Pa.), argued that "throwing away ten years of hard-won gains and hard-fought struggle on behalf of self-determination in Afghanistan to negotiate with a criminal regime such as Najibullah's, an Afghan Hitler, would be one of the great sell-outs of this era" (U.S. Congress, House, Committee on Foreign Affairs, Sub-committee on Asian and Pacific Affairs 1990a, 80). Many in Congress continued to regard the problem as an East-West struggle as late as 1990. In a hearing before a House panel, Representative Lagomarsino referred to his belief that "only continued pressure brings the Com-munists to the bargaining table, and only real pressure, not lopsided unilateral efforts like negative symmetry, brings about real conces-sions and real success" (U.S. Congress, House, Committee on Foreign Affairs, Subcommittee on Asian and Pacific Affairs 1990b, 3). In mid-1990 Representative Ritter spoke of the need to continue aid to the rebels because of the "$300 million a month [in] military supplies" that the Soviet Union was pumping into Afghanistan to preserve its client (ibid., 7). At the same time, Representatives Henry Hyde (R-Ill.) and Charles Wilson argued for more aid to achieve what they charac-terized as the "ultimate goal" of the United States: the ouster of the PDPA regime (Hyde and Wilson 1990). The fact that high-level attention was focused on the momentous events taking place in Europe and the Soviet Union contributed to the continuation of existing policy.

As the Bush administration and conservatives in Congress con-tinued to fight the cold war in Afghanistan, other members of Congress began to criticize the policy (e.g., Rodman 1994, 354). Representative Steven Solarz stated that since "some of the fundamental assumptions which had constituted the foundation for our policy are coming into question, we need a comprehensive review of where we are, where we are going, and how best to achieve the desired results" (U.S. Con-gress, House, Committee on Foreign Affairs, Subcommittee on Asian and Pacific Affairs 1990a, 25). Senator Claiborne Pell tried to reori-ent policy by releasing a report on Afghanistan in which he recom-mended "negative symmetry" and a greater effort toward a political solution apart from the AIG. Pell also argued that the United States had no strategic interests in Afghanistan after the Soviet withdrawal, only humanitarian concerns (U.S. Congress, Senate, Committee on Foreign Relations 1990). Dissenting views were heard much more frequently from members of Congress including former aid supporters Steven So-larz and Lee Hamilton (D-Ind.) (see, e.g., U.S. Congress, House, Committee on Foreign Affairs, Subcommittee on Asian and Pacific Affairs 1990b). In October 1990, for the first time since the Afghan program began, Congress reduced the administration's request for the Afghan operation by more than 10 percent, allocating $250 million for 1991 but requiring half of that amount to be subject to an additional congressional vote (Doherty 1990e, 3625–26; Lardner 1990). Amid this bickering and finger pointing, hard-liners were forced to adopt ever more tenuous arguments for continued aid; two representatives even insisted that a change in the Afghan regime had been the principal goal of U.S. policy since 1980, and that the USSR was still committed to cold war goals in Afghanistan (Hyde and Wilson 1990).

Ultimately, three developments combined to force the abandonment of the Reagan Doctrine in Afghanistan. First, the rebels' failure to unite became more and more obvious, and as the various factions began to make war on each other, the Bush administration began new efforts to promote a political solution through the AIG.[23] The United States engaged the Soviet Union in talks on creating a peaceful change of regime (U.S. Congress, House, Committee on Foreign Affairs, Subcommittee on Asian and Pacific Affairs 1990b), but these efforts produced little progress. In June 1991, John Kelly (1991), assistant secretary of state for Near East and South Asian affairs lamented: "If the Kabul regime . . . had been forced to confront a unified opposition, we might have been closer today to a settlement. This has not been the case. Within the resistance, the [AIG] has been plagued by disarray as party leaders continued their rivalries. Most of the [AIG] ministries have suspended operations." As a consequence, Kelly stated, the AIG no longer figured in American policy (U.S. Congress, House, Committee on Foreign Affairs, Subcommittee on Asian and Pacific Affairs 1993, 10–11).

Second, the Gulf War in 1990–91 contributed to a policy change. In addition to diverting attention from, and thus willingness to be involved in, Afghanistan, the Gulf War revealed another problem inherent in U.S. support of the rebels: the group most heavily financed during the Reagan administration and the early Bush administration — Hekmatyar's Islamists — sided with Iraq against the United States. This revealed in a most convincing fashion what some analysts had been arguing for several years: the Islamist groups which received the bulk of U.S. funding were as hostile to the United States as they were to the Soviet Union (U.S. Congress, House, Committee on Foreign Affairs, Subcommittee on Asian and Pacific Affairs 1993).

Third, Soviet cooperation during the Persian Gulf crisis convinced all but the most unregenerate hard-liners that the cold war was over and the Soviet Union was no longer an implacable foe of the United States. In August 1991, after the failed coup attempt by Soviet hard-liners, Boris Yeltsin and George Bush agreed to end assistance to the rebels, thus ending the application of the Reagan Doctrine in Afghanistan after nearly twelve years (Cogan 1993, 77). In April 1992 the Najibullah regime stepped down, but the fighting between various factions continued unabated through 1994. Ironically, as this cold war battlefield degenerated into a civil war, U.S. policy came full circle: in 1994 the Clinton administration began an effort to staunch the flow of weapons into Afghanistan, pressuring former aid partners—Pakistan, Saudi Arabia, and others—to cease their supply to the various former rebel groups (Raphel 1994).

Conclusions: The Reagan Doctrine and Afghanistan

The Reagan Doctrine had its greatest success in Afghanistan. American assistance to the rebels was an important factor in the defeat of the Soviet Union and its subsequent decision to withdraw. Credit for this success goes to virtually the entire U.S. foreign policy community. As the preceding analysis shows, policy makers from the White House, the foreign policy bureaucracy, and Congress agreed on the general purposes of U.S. policy; until the Soviet withdrawal, the only debate was over how best to aid the rebels. With support from public opinion and certain interest groups, U.S. policy makers implemented a surprisingly effective and timely aid program built on a consensus that lasted from the end of the Carter administration to the beginning of the Bush administration.

According to Peter Schweizer (1994), American aid to the rebels in Afghanistan was an integral component of a larger "secret" strategy by high-ranking members of the Reagan administration to win the cold war. This study shows that Congress was a significant policy maker as well, though, and since the policy actually began in the last two years of the Carter administration, some credit for the initiative belongs in that White House. As a former NSC staff officer concluded, however, "you didn't have a major coordinated program" until the Reagan administration, and "you didn't have a coherent [U.S.] response until 1985" (quoted in Schweizer 1994, 214). Within the Reagan administration, William Casey assumed the leadership of policy making prior to 1985, and he and George Shultz drove administration decisions after 1985. Key decisions in 1979, 1980, 1982, 1984, 1985, and 1986 created an increasingly potent American aid program that first sustained the resistance and then provided it with the means to strike back. Beginning slowly, this aid mushroomed from $30 million in 1980 to as much as $600 million in 1986. When combined with U.S. support for Pakistan and the contributions of other countries (especially Egypt and Saudi Arabia), the overall commitment to the mujahidin was quite impressive and simply dwarfs the other cases in which the doctrine was applied.

American policy makers and others who have identified the policy as a major accomplishment include George Shultz, Peter Rodman, Charles Wilson, Robert Oakley, Steven Solarz, Ronald Reagan, John McMahon, and Vincent Cannistraro. According to the Pakistani general in charge of much of the program, the rebels "would have lost" without U.S. aid; "CIA aid was necessary and critical" in the Soviet defeat (quoted in Schweizer 1994, 283). According to Shultz (1993, 1094), "the fact of overwhelming importance was that the Soviets [were] forced to withdraw. The Reagan Doctrine . . . won out over the Brezhnev Doctrine." In fact, the application of the Reagan Doctrine made Afghanistan the Soviet Union's Vietnam and hastened the dramatic reevaluation of Soviet foreign policy led by Mikhail Gorbachev.

Moreover, as William Casey had predicted it would, the Afghan debacle contributed to internal changes within the Soviet Union. There is little doubt that the increasing costs of Afghanistan, caused in no small part by the application of the Reagan Doctrine, contributed mightily to the restructuring of Soviet policy. Politburo documents suggest that the debacle in Afghanistan greatly strengthened both the determination of some within the Soviet leadership including Gorbachev, to reverse course, and the influence of these reformers vis-à-vis the remaining hard-liners. As Schweizer (1994) and Raymond Garthoff (1994) have demonstrated, Afghanistan was a critical factor in the Soviet Union's domestic and international changes.

The success achieved in Afghanistan appears to be the consequence of two factors. The invasion, presence, and operation of Soviet troops in Afghanistan made that situation qualitatively different from any other Reagan Doctrine case. In fact, no Reagan Doctrine was needed for this case, as indicated by the fact that the program began under the Carter administration. Defense against external aggression is a cornerstone of international law, international relations, and the United Nations Charter. Also, American support for the mujahidin affected the Soviet Union more seriously than U.S. support for any other rebel group. Nearly all proponents of the Reagan Doctrine agreed that its general application might raise the price for Soviet adventurism. In Afghanistan, uniquely, that price included the lives of Soviet soldiers. The application of the Reagan Doctrine mired the Soviet Union in a guerrilla war that grew increasingly expensive in money, matériel, and, most important, lives. In particular, U.S. decisions in 1985 and 1986 made it plain to Soviet leaders that victory was not possible without a dramatically greater commitment in time, effort, and price. As the Politburo documents discussed in this chapter show, the U.S. escalation in 1985–86 matched the last Soviet attempt to defeat the insurrection and precipitated the decision to withdraw. It is not clear that the Soviet effort would have failed in the absence of Reagan Doctrine aid. In any event, beginning in 1987, U.S. force (Reagan Doctrine aid) enabled a diplomatic breakthrough: the Soviet Union clearly capitulated in the UN-led negotiations, seeking only international cover for its withdrawal.

Of all the Reagan Doctrine cases, Afghanistan is the single true descendant of the rollback rhetoric of the 1950s: the Reagan Doctrine targeted Soviet forces in Afghanistan just as John Foster Dulles's rhetoric focused on Soviet troops in Eastern Europe. Afghanistan was thus the cornerstone of the Reagan Doctrine and, in conjunction with other pressures on the Soviet Union (economic, political, military, etc.), probably hastened the Soviet demise, as Schweizer (1994) argued. Moreover, as even Soviet leaders recognized, the settlement of the Afghan issue accelerated efforts to settle other regional conflicts (see, e.g., Garthoff 1994, 736, 738). U.S. policy must therefore be viewed as a contribution to those results as well.

Nevertheless, while the results warrant the conclusion that the Reagan Doctrine was a success, several important weaknesses detract from its achievements in Afghanistan. Some involve costs or tradeoffs required by the application of the policy; others concern the ill-advised extension of the doctrine after the Soviet withdrawal. The costs of the program included several virtually inevitable consequences. First, the network of *mujahidin* trained and supplied by the United States turned against its benefactor—the bombing of the Trade Center in New York was apparently perpetrated by volunteers who fought in Afghanistan.

The policy's success at organizing the rebel resistance brought radical, committed fighters who despise the United States as much as they hate the former Soviet Union into contact with each other. Second, as the Defense Department and the CIA feared, sophisticated American anti-aircraft missiles (Stingers) are still unaccounted for, and U.S. officials believe they have been sold by the rebels to Iran and other states, as well as terrorist groups in the Middle East (e.g., Weiner 1993). Some evidence suggests that several were used in fighting in Tajikstan, in the former Soviet Central Asia (Garthoff 1994, 713). Third, the CIA overlooked the involvement of many mujahidin leaders in a growing heroin trade, reportedly the largest in the world (see, e.g., Bonner 1986; P. Scott and Marshall 1991). Finally, the need to retain Pakistan's support and cooperation led the United States to overlook that country's efforts to develop nuclear weapons, which destabilized the region and compromised the U.S. commitment to the Non-proliferation Treaty (Garthoff 1994, 273, 700).

The failure of many policy makers to recognize victory when it was in hand stands out as the most significant weakness revealed by the post-1988 application of the Reagan Doctrine. As both the Carter decision (1979) and the Reagan expansion (NSDD 166) noted, the objective of the policy was Soviet withdrawal from Afghanistan. Yet, when that had been achieved, U.S. policy makers failed to reassess the situation accurately. The insistence by hard-liners that U.S. aid continue until the rebels triumphed over the PDPA regime resulted in the continued application of the Reagan Doctrine to a situation in which its applicability was much less clear. In addition to producing no benefits for the United States, the decision to continue Reagan Doctrine aid—or rather, the absence of a decision to end it when it could have been ended—must be recognized as partly responsible for the continued violence and war in Afghanistan. Of course, the Soviet Union, which continued its military assistance, and the Afghan rebels, who quickly began to fight among themselves, bear heavy responsibility as well. It is mere speculation, but a concerted attempt to pursue a diplomatic settlement aimed at reconciliation and "negative symmetry" beginning in 1988 might have been more appropriate. As more than one observer argued, recognition that the primary goal of U.S. policy was achieved with the Soviet withdrawal should have led to a decision to capitalize on that success and press the local parties, the Soviet Union, and other states to conduct a search for a pragmatic accommodation among the Afghan factions.

Another weakness in the U.S. policy rests in the decision to target the most radical factions of the mujahidin as the primary recipients of the assistance. It is not clear that strengthening these groups, in particular Hekmatyar's Islamist forces, benefited the United States in the long run. While the Pakistani leaders bear the brunt of this responsibility, the United States endorsed or acquiesced and thus is accountable. The groups receiving the lion's share of the U.S. assistance are the ones most responsible for the persistence of the conflict. In particular, Hekmatyar has refused to make peace with other rebel factions, cooperate with an interim government, or observe cease-fire agreements; and as early as 1989 his forces began warring with other rebel groups. After the Soviet Union and the United States suspended their aid in 1991, fighting among the groups increased. In April 1992, the PDPA regime stepped down, but the rebels continued to fight among themselves for power in the new government (Cogan 1993, 78). Attempts in 1993 to form a coalition government failed, and the bloody fighting among rival factions continued; by one account the violence is even more destructive than what occurred during the Soviet invasion and occupation (Darnton 1994).

Ironically, the failure of the exile groups and local factions to make peace prompted the formation in late 1994 of a new force calling itself Taliban (seekers of the truth). In six months this force—which quickly grew to twenty-five thousand fighters, several hundred tanks, and a dozen fighter planes—turned on the various factions and warlords, especially Hekmatyar and Rabbani, with a vengeance. By February 1995 Taliban had captured about 40 percent of Afghanistan, forced Hekmatyar and his forces to flee, and ended the persistent fighting around Kabul. This force, organized around Islamic purists and Afghan patriots, may finally end the civil war, but their policies and the extent to which they are committed to an Islamist society are largely unknown (Burns 1995a, 1995b; Ahmed Rashid 1995).

In the end, the Reagan Doctrine was a successful approach to the regional conflict involving the Soviet Union, Afghanistan, and Pakistan. It was essentially a failure when it was used to address the subsequent civil conflict within Afghanistan. Interestingly, liberals first, and then moderates within the United States recognized this and pressed for a different approach. Only hard-liners, the authors and major proponents of the strategy, failed to grasp this essential fact.

4

Cambodia: Disinterest, Dual Tracks, and
the Search for a Settlement

The application of the Reagan Doctrine to Cambodia was a minor element of a secondary issue. In spite of the fact that the regime in Cambodia had been installed by an invading force of 200,000 Vietnamese troops, the Reagan administration was reluctant to extend itself on behalf of the resistance. In addition to political and humanitarian support, the United States provided limited amounts of nonlethal supplies to elements of the resistance, preferring to follow the lead of Thailand, the Association of Southeast Asian Nations (ASEAN: Thailand, Malaysia, Singapore, Indonesia, the Philippines, and, since 1984, Brunei), and China. The variant of the Reagan Doctrine applied to Cambodia was the two-track version that combined assistance with diplomatic efforts to reach a political settlement which would produce a Vietnamese withdrawal. A basic consensus over American policy lasted until the end of the Reagan administration, when the occupying forces withdrew (in September 1989) and disagreement over policy arose.

Background

Much of Cambodia's history is marked by its position as a pawn in the struggles of external powers.[1] The French established a colonial protectorate over Cambodia in 1863 and maintained a colonial government until 1953. The 1954 Geneva Conference on Indochina created, among other things, an independent Cambodia, and in 1955, Cambodian elections established a regime led by Prince Norodom Sihanouk. As the struggle between North and South Vietnam threatened to engulf Southeast Asia, Sihanouk attempted to maintain Cambodia's neutrality and steer a course between the dangers of alignment with South Vietnam and the United States on the one hand, and North Vietnam, China, and the Soviet Union, on the other. Eventually, his refusal to back South Vietnam caused the United States to consider him procommunist, and to support a coup against him led by the anticommunist Lon Nol. After the 1969 coup, Lon Nol became prime minister and received U.S. backing, but his new Khmer Republic, as Cambodia was renamed, lasted only five years. The combination of American bombing in eastern Cambodia (targeted at the North Vietnamese and the Ho Chi Minh Trail), Cambodian government policies, and North Vietnamese and Chinese assistance spurred the growth of the radical communist Khmer Rouge, which spread its control over Cambodia. Finally, on 17 April 1975, the Communists captured Phnom Penh.

The reign of the Khmer Rouge was a disaster for Cambodia. Given to savagery and brutality, the Khmer Rouge was led by Saloth Sar (Pol Pot), Ieng Sary, and Khieu Samphan, who developed what one analyst labeled a "radical leftist Chinese Communism" (Quinn 1989b, 219). For three years the Khmer Rouge presided over the most brutal period of Cambodian history: an estimated 500,000 to 2 million people were killed by torture, execution, and relocation programs.[2] The Khmer Rouge split with Vietnam and in 1977 began attacks on that country. Vietnam reacted with several "incursions" of its own, and also clashed with China.

In late 1978, events rushed to a climax. On Christmas Day 1978, 200,000 Vietnamese troops drove the Khmer Rouge regime out of Cambodia and replaced it with the Khmer People's Revolutionary Party (KPRP), who christened their new regime the People's Republic of Kampuchea (PRK).[3] The KPRP regime was initially a façade for Vietnamese domination of Cambodia. Vietnamese "advisers" reviewed applications for KPRP membership, and a council from Vietnam's Central Committee "advised" the KPRP on vital issues (Chanda 1986, 372). Vietnamese technicians and bureaucrats staffed the ministries, supervised by another group of Vietnamese officials (Vickery 1984, 221–22; Chandler 1992a, 225). Although this domination diminished over time as Cambodians replaced Vietnamese in positions of authority and the KPRP regime began reforms that greatly enhanced its legitimacy in Cambodia (Brown 1989, 74–77; Chandler 1992a, 227–36), until 1985 most policy makers agreed that the regime was a Vietnamese, and thus Soviet, client.

U.S. interest in Cambodia stemmed from considerations external to Cambodia.[4] Cambodia's position in the larger regional and international context only occasionally garnered attention. When the United States withdrew from Vietnam in 1973, it relegated Southeast Asia to a position of secondary importance, and Cambodia into secondary status in Indochina (Brown 1989, 3, 5–8). Only the Vietnamese invasion in December 1978, which raised the specter of communist expansionism in the region, elevated Cambodia to a position of significance. American security and economic interests, especially with regard to Japan, ASEAN, and China, were served by regional stability and a balance of power, and the principal U.S. concern was that no single country dominate the region (U.S. Congress, Senate, Committee on Foreign Relations, Subcommittee on East Asian and Pacific Affairs 1981, 2; Jordan et al. 1989, 384). One State Department official, for example, described only broad strategic issues when discussing U.S. interests in Cambodia, including the maintenance of a regional balance of power, the promotion and protection of regional stability, and the containment of Soviet influence (U.S. Congress, House, Committee on Foreign Affairs, Subcommittee on Asian and Pacific Affairs 1981c, 164).

Although the Nixon administration viewed Cambodia as a strategically important part of Southeast Asia because of the Vietnam War, after Vietnam, American policy was driven by competing preferences. In the Carter administration, one group, represented by Secretary of State Cyrus Vance and Assistant Secretary of State for East Asia Richard Holbrooke, desired normalization of U.S.-Vietnamese relations. A second group, represented by National Security Adviser Zbigniew Brzezinski, viewed U.S.-Chinese relations as the prize and sought to develop a strategic alliance against the Soviet Union. Brzezinski and his supporters in the NSC staff and elsewhere rejected normalization with Vietnam (a Soviet proxy) in favor of closer ties with China (see, e.g., Brzezinski 1983, 224). American policy thus was tugged in two directions as a result of individual and bureaucratic struggles. Cambodia, which was allied with China, was either completely ignored by the United States or seen through the lens of the broader debate that encompassed Vietnam, China, and the Soviet Union.

Vietnam's invasion of Cambodia in 1978 settled the dispute within the Carter administration and set the stage for the application of the Reagan Doctrine. Brzezinski's faction gained the upper hand, and the United States began to counter what was perceived as Soviet expansionism through its client, Vietnam. The Carter administration backed China, Thailand, and ultimately ASEAN in opposing the Vietnamese invasion (Oksenberg 1982; Garthoff 1985, chs. 20–21; Brown 1989, chs. 3–4). The United States apparently supported (indirectly) initial efforts to organize a noncommunist resistance to the Vietnamese-backed regime, and, according to analyst Elizabeth Becker (1986, 440), Brzezinski acknowledged that the United States supported China's plans to use the Khmer Rouge to make Cambodia "Vietnam's Vietnam." These events established the foundation for the Reagan administration to consider the Reagan Doctrine.

The resistance movement that made the application of the Reagan Doctrine to Cambodia possible consisted of a dubious alliance joining fiercely anticommunist and antiroyalist elements (the Khmer People's National Liberation Front, KPNLF) with royalists (the National United Front for an Independent, Neutral, Peaceful, and Cooperative Cambodia, FUNCINPEC) and radical Communists (the Khmer Rouge).[5] The avidly anticommunist KPNLF was formed on 9 October 1979 uniting thirteen disparate groups (van der Kroef 1990, 202; Corfield 1991, 17). It was dedicated to the liberation of Cambodia and the prevention of the return of either a communist regime under the Khmer Rouge or a monarchy under Prince Sihanouk, the leader of FUNCINPEC (Corfield 1991, 21). By early 1987 the KPNLF comprised about twenty thousand guerrillas, but it was so disorganized and so beset by factional infighting that by mid-1987 it had been reduced to five thousand fighters (van der Kroef 1990, 209; Sutter 1991a, 76).

Most of the defectors turned to the other noncommunist faction, FUNCINPEC, which was led by Sihanouk. Formed in February 1981, FUNCINPEC was an organization dedicated to returning Sihanouk to power. While its political program was ambiguous, consisting primarily of a commitment to independence and neutrality (it was usually described as a "royalist" organization), Sihanouk's long-standing nationalism and dedication to Cambodia's survival undoubtedly made him the most popular political leader in Cambodia (Gordon 1986, 75).

The third faction was the Khmer Rouge, described above. After the Vietnamese invasion, China helped to reorganize the Khmer Rouge and began to provide increasing amounts of assistance. As an insurgency, the Khmer Rouge grew to include about thirty to forty thousand fighters operating from bases in southern and northern Cambodia and out of camps along the Thai-Cambodian border (Sutter 1991a, 72,

1992b, 167). Its leadership remained intact (Chandler 1992b, 185), and its operations and tactics indicated continued repression and brutality (see, e.g., Asia Watch 1989, 1990). More troubling for the resistance coalition, the Khmer Rouge frequently attacked the other factions of the resistance and refused to accept the leadership of any other faction or to compromise on a peace settlement (van der Kroef 1990, 198).

U.S. Policy and the Reagan Doctrine

The application of the Reagan Doctrine to Cambodia was a relatively minor policy initiative that occurred in three phases. The first, from 1981 to 1984, was led by the executive branch, but in the second, from 1985 to 1988, Congress took the lead in developing an overt element of the policy, tying the increased assistance to a negotiating strategy. A diplomatic track was maintained in both phases, as the primary purpose of the Reagan Doctrine aid was to facilitate a negotiated withdrawal of the Vietnamese troops. The third phase, from 1989 to 1991, saw substantial disagreement and an effort by both branches to revise U.S. policy. The withdrawal of Vietnamese troops in 1989 prompted greater attention to establishing a new government and provoked policy debate within the administration and between the administration and Congress. In all phases the issue retained a low profile for American policy makers, although during the Bush administration the issue had slightly greater salience.

One important caveat should be stated regarding this analysis of the Reagan Doctrine in Cambodia. Throughout the Reagan administration, the United States declined to lead on the Cambodia issue. American policy, stated repeatedly, was to follow ASEAN's leadership in bringing political, economic, and military pressure to bear on Vietnam and Cambodia to reach a political solution. The United States supported ASEAN's approach and stayed in the background. Assistant Secretary of State John H. Holdridge explained to Congress in 1982 that "ASEAN is the keystone of American policy toward Kampuchea and Indochina. We fully support ASEAN's strategy and respect ASEAN's leadership role in the region. We share ASEAN's goals . . . and work with ASEAN to realize its objectives" (U.S. Congress, House, Committee on Foreign Affairs, Subcommittee on Asian and Pacific Affairs 1983a, 20–21). Accordingly, the United States did not play a direct role in the military conflict or negotiations, nor did it provide military assistance directly to the rebels.

Phase I: Applying the Reagan Doctrine, 1981–1985

The initial decision to assist the resistance forces in Cambodia was a bureaucratic compromise. Prior to 1982, the United States had condemned the Vietnamese invasion and had shown some sympathy for the resistance, but had provided no material support.[6] In mid-1982 the White House decided to provide about $5 million in covert, nonlethal assistance to the noncommunist factions of the resistance led by Son Sann and Prince Sihanouk. At the same time, the United States maintained its support for a negotiated solution to the conflict, backing ASEAN's efforts to broker an accord.

Providing covert Reagan Doctrine assistance. During its first eighteen months, the Reagan administration moved from a policy of providing only political and humanitarian support for the Cambodian resistance to the covert provision of nonlethal aid that included vehicles, food, uniforms, aid to civilians, and medicine. The American policy toward the situation in Cambodia was to rely on ASEAN to take an active role in the pursuit of a settlement that would include a Vietnamese troop withdrawal. China and ASEAN were the key providers of assistance to forces resisting the Vietnamese-backed regime (e.g., Brown 1989, 44–45, 80). In March 1981, however, CIA director William Casey proposed a plan to aid what he referred to as "universal anti-Soviet resistance movements." As part of this proposal, Casey suggested that the United States provide the noncommunist forces in Cambodia with weapons and aid (Persico 1990, 264; Schweizer 1994, 22–23).

By July, Cambodia was excised from Casey's list of Reagan Doctrine aid recipients. In a hearing before a subcommittee of the Senate Foreign Relations Committee, Assistant Secretary Holdridge explained that the United States was "joining with our ASEAN friends and with others in maintaining the pressure on Vietnam to remove itself from Kampuchea . . . [but] these pressures from our standpoint are going to be political, economic, and psychological" (U.S. Congress, Senate, Committee on Foreign Relations, Subcommittee on East Asian and Pacific Affairs 1981, 3). When Senator S. I. Hayakawa (R-Calif.) asked Holdridge if the United States was considering military assistance to the rebels, Holdridge replied that "the United States intends to maintain pressure on Vietnam. . . . As of now, those pressures quite obviously are political, economic, and military. Now, we have no relationship to the military pressures on Vietnam" (ibid., 7). While acknowledging that ASEAN was providing assistance to the rebels, Holdridge responded unequivocally to Senator John Glenn's (D-Ohio) inquiry about whether the United States was aiding the Non-Communist Resistance (NCR): "We are not, sir. . . . *This is not a policy option which is being contemplated by the United States*" (ibid., 13; emphasis added). Holdridge acknowledged that the NCR factions had requested American assistance, but said that the administration had promised only political, moral, and humanitarian support (U.S. Congress, Senate, Committee on Foreign Relations, Subcommittee on East Asian and Pacific Affairs 1981, 21).

Holdridge's characterization of American policy in mid-1981 was echoed by other administration officials. At a news conference in Manila in June 1981, Secretary of State Alexander Haig (1981a) stated, "I know of no decision, nor do I know of any suggestion of a decision which would lead to the provision of American arms to the United Front resistance movement in Kampuchea." Richard L. Armitage, then deputy assistant secretary of defense, stated that the United States was giving humanitarian assistance to the border refugee camps, "but, other than that, we are not providing matériel" (U.S. Congress, Senate, Committee on Foreign Relations, Subcommittee on East Asian and Pacific Affairs 1981, 39). Moreover, since NCR officials made persistent public requests for U.S. aid throughout 1982, it is evident that assistance had not begun at that point (e.g., U.S. Congress, House, Committee on Foreign Affairs, Subcommittee on Asian and Pacific Affairs 1982, 1983a).

In late 1982, the United States reversed this stand and began to provide covert assistance to the rebels, and the comments of administration officials reflected this change of policy. The key development in this reversal was the formation of the Coalition Government of Democratic Kampuchea (CGDK), which united the three resistance factions into a loose alliance. This elevated the NCR to a role in an internationally recognized exile government at the same time that ASEAN increased its pressure for a larger American role. In this context, the administration conducted a policy review and decided to provide covert assistance. In the process, however, a bureaucratic dispute developed. William Casey and the CIA were the principal advocates for aid. The State Department, which feared that such aid would result in assistance to the Khmer Rouge and would make a negotiated settlement more difficult, opposed assistance (Brown 1989, 82). Eventually, a compromise was worked out between the foreign policy bureaucracies to provide limited nonlethal covert assistance ($5 million), to be funneled through Thailand, and President Reagan signed an intelligence finding to that effect in the fall of 1982 (Babcock and Woodward 1985; Garthoff 1994, 716; Rodman 1994, 452). During the remainder of the Reagan administration the United States provided limited amounts of vehicles, food, uniforms, medicine, and financial aid for construction, training, and other nonlethal purposes, but no lethal (i.e., weapons or ammunition) military aid (Richburg 1991, 116; Thayer 1991, 187–88).

Although this decision was widely reported, it was also closely held, and the documents remain classified. Indeed, administration officials speaking after the decision exhibited a caution and subtlety in their remarks that contrasted with the unequivocal denial of U.S. involvement in 1981 and early 1982. These careful comments appear to confirm the existence of the program reported in the press and in confidential interviews. In September 1982, for example, Assistant Secretary Holdridge explained that "we are considering how we will be of further help. This will not in any event be military assistance. We will not provide assistance of any kind to the Khmer Rouge" (U.S. Congress, House, Committee on Foreign Affairs, Subcommittee on Asian and Pacific Affairs 1983a, 28). Note that Holdridge acknowledged that a review of policy was occurring and seemed to state that the administration was planning to expand its current policy. Finally, Holdridge's distinction between *military* assistance (none was to be provided) and assistance of *any kind* (none was to be provided *to the Khmer Rouge*) suggests that nonmilitary assistance was going to be provided to the noncommunist factions. This telling distinction was also made by Deputy Assistant Secretary of State for East Asian and Pacific Affairs John C. Monjo (U.S. Congress, House, Committee on Foreign Affairs, Subcommittee on Asian and Pacific Affairs 1983b, 5), and by Holdridge's successor, Paul D. Wolfowitz (Wolfowitz 1984, 53).

The United States relied primarily on ASEAN for the implementation of this small program. A Congressional Research Service analyst said that Thailand provided the sanctuaries and supply bases, Singapore contributed arms, Malaysia provided training, and Indonesia supplied clothing (Sutter 1985, 4). According to Frederick Z. Brown (1989, 82), "the Reagan Administration provided financial support to the [NCR], and permitted the Thai and others to carry out the actual organization, sustenance, and strengthening of the resistance forces." An ABC television documentary in 1990 identified a working group of officials from Thailand, Singapore, and Malaysia which supervised

the provision and training of the NCR. Officials from the U.S. State Department and the CIA were also part of this group. In Thailand, where
the supply and training camps were situated, CIA officials cooperated
with Thai officials to try to ensure that no U.S. aid was diverted to the
Khmer Rouge.[7]

Finally, even though the United States provided some assistance,
most of the aid to the NCR came from Thailand, Singapore, Malaysia, and Indonesia, and from China (Chanda 1986, 381–82, 392; Brown
1989, 45, 80). Each of these countries is mentioned as a primary supporter in National Security Decision Directive 158 on U.S. policy in
Southeast Asia, and according to the *Economist* (25 November 1989,
36, 38), assistance from these countries totaled as much as $100 mil-
lion annually (80 percent of which went to the Khmer Rouge). China
provided the most arms, and Singapore and Thailand took the lead in
giving for ASEAN (Richburg 1991, 116). As some analysts have noted,
however, the United States increased its bilateral overt assistance to
Thailand to compensate for Thailand's support for the resistance (e.g.,
Chanda 1984; Quinn-Judge 1984). In 1981, the United States gave Thailand $50 million, and raised that amount to $80 million in 1982, $90
million in 1983, $100 million in 1984, $102 million in 1985, and $104
million in 1986 (U.S. Congress, House, Committee on Appropriations
1983, 184, 1985, 182; U.S. Congress, House, Committee on Foreign Affairs, Subcommittee on Asian and Pacific Affairs 1981a, 38, 1985a, 16,
1988, 15). Even Assistant Secretary of State Wolfowitz acknowledged
that American aid to Thailand related "directly to Thailand's ability to
assist the resistance" (U.S. Congress, House, Committee on Foreign Affairs, Subcommittee on Asian and Pacific Affairs 1985a, 150).

In 1984, the administration conducted an interagency review of its
approach to Cambodia. The CIA representative advocated greater U.S.
assistance, but other participants blocked the idea (Woodward 1987,
425–26). As a result of this review, President Reagan signed NSDD 158
on 9 January 1985. This directive merely codified existing U.S. objectives and reiterated "the main lines of current policies." While recognizing that the United States "should work closely with ASEAN to ensure that the non-Communist resistance elements grow in strength and
influence," the directive also suggested that the United States "should
follow ASEAN's lead rather than getting out in front." Significantly,
especially in light of the debate that erupted after 1987, the directive
also noted that "a return to power by the Khmer Rouge would be un-

acceptable to [ASEAN]," and that U.S. efforts to support the NCR were designed to increase its influence "vis-à-vis the Khmer Rouge as well as the Vietnamese." Finally, the directive conceded that ASEAN "wants us to play a greater role in supporting the non-Communist resistance" (NSDD 158, 1–3).

U.S. support for a diplomatic settlement. The administration tied this minor application of the Reagan Doctrine to a diplomatic track. It is apparent from the actions of the United States, ASEAN, and the NCR leaders that support for the resistance in Cambodia was never intended to produce a military solution to the problem of Vietnamese occupation or domination. Assistant Secretary of State Wolfowitz, for example, explained that the objective was "to somehow get a negotiation with Vietnam that will lead to a political settlement. No one anywhere, that I know of, believes that the Cambodian resistance can ever defeat Vietnam . . . by military means" (U.S. Congress, House, Committee on Foreign Affairs, Subcommittee on Asian and Pacific Affairs 1985a, 151). Instead, the creation and development of the noncommunist factions was embedded in the context of a larger initiative to apply pressure on Vietnam and its client, the PRK, in order to reach a diplomatic solution (*New York Times,* 22 June 1982; U.S. Congress, House, Committee on Foreign Affairs, Subcommittee on Asian and Pacific Affairs 1985a, 151). In addition to the military pressure from the insurgency, this larger context included both political pressures (e.g., withholding from Vietnam the normalization of relations with the United States and withholding from Cambodia international recognition and a seat at the UN) and economic ones (e.g., preventing access to international developmental loans and assistance). As in the paramilitary track, the United States remained a secondary participant, taking "a back seat in defining the shape of a political settlement" (Solarz 1990, 111).

Hence, although the administration supported a diplomatic solution, the task of negotiating was left to ASEAN. Assistant Secretary Wolfowitz described the U.S. purpose to the House Committee on Appropriations in May 1985: "The goal is a political settlement. The incentives for a political settlement on Vietnam's part will in part be the easing of the military pressure. . . . They could gain enormously in economic terms, in diplomatic terms, by a serious settlement of the Cambodian conflict. . . . In that context, I think building up the non-Communist resistance partly contributes to pressure on Vietnam to come to the negotiating table . . . and increases our options when that negotiation takes place" (U.S. Congress, House, Committee on Appropriations 1985, 242). Elsewhere, Wolfowitz (1984, 53) noted that a political settlement providing for Vietnamese withdrawal and free elections would ensure that the Khmer Rouge could not return to power, for the Khmer Rouge could not possibly win in free elections. In support of this effort, the administration maintained pressure on Vietnam (e.g., denying normalization of relations with the United States), supported ASEAN's efforts to negotiate, provided diplomatic and political support to the NCR, helped to prevent recognition of the KPRP regime, and maintained economic and security assistance to ASEAN (ibid., 53). Deputy Assistant Secretary of State for East Asian and Pacific Affairs David Lambertson aptly characterized this approach as the "three no's . . . no trade, no aid, no normal relations except in the context of a political settlement and an end of Vietnam's occupation of Cambodia" (U.S. Congress, House, Committee on Foreign Affairs, Subcommittee on Asian and Pacific Affairs 1989c, 38).

The negotiating position taken by ASEAN was laid out in mid-1981 at the International Conference on Kampuchea, at which a resolution outlining the broad framework of a settlement was drafted and later approved.[8] According to this resolution, a settlement would require (1) a cease-fire and supervised withdrawal of foreign forces, (2) an arrangement to ensure that "armed Kampuchean factions" (i.e., the Khmer Rouge) would not disrupt ensuing elections, (3) measures to administer the country between the withdrawal and the elections, and (4) UN-supervised elections (U.S. Department of State 1981e, 87). These principles were endorsed by the United States and a majority of the U.N. and resolutions incorporating this formula were passed annually by the UN General Assembly.[9]

Even with American support, ASEAN was not able to conclude an agreement; it was, however, able to develop a broad international coalition that denied recognition to the KPRP regime and consistently condemned Vietnam's invasion. It was also successful in overcoming China's opposition to UN-sponsored elections and in persuading China to accept a phased rather than an immediate withdrawal of the Vietnamese troops (Colbert 1984, 147). Moreover, ASEAN succeeded in creating the CGDK to strengthen the position of the noncommunist factions and to convince the Vietnamese that they need not fear a return to power by the Khmer Rouge (Colbert 1984, 143). Nevertheless, by 1985 no progress had been made toward the ultimate objectives: Vietnam simply rejected the proposals (Wolfowitz 1984, 52–53).

Phase II: Expanding the Reagan Doctrine, 1985–1988

In the spring of 1985, Congress expanded the application of the Reagan Doctrine in spite of opposition from the administration. Responding to requests from NCR leaders and ASEAN, and to President Reagan's own State of the Union Address, Representative Steven Solarz (D-N.Y.) devised an overt application of the Reagan Doctrine. Only after Solarz gained broad support for his initiative did the administration endorse the proposal, which it followed for the remainder of President Reagan's second term.

The Solarz initiative. In mid-February 1985, ASEAN released a statement calling on "the international community" to provide more open and substantial support for the NCR in Cambodia (Royal Thai Government 1985, 111). Privately, officials from Thailand and Singapore urged the administration and Congress to begin military aid (Rodman 1994, 452), prompting Representative Solarz to propose expanding the Reagan Doctrine's application in Cambodia. Solarz and Congress grasped the initiative and legislated overt Reagan Doctrine aid, altering the administration's thinking on the overall policy. Congressional leadership on the matter prompted an across-the-board increase in such aid (which climbed from $5 million to about $20 million by the end of the administration) and ultimately generated pressure for increased American diplomatic efforts.

Solarz used the annual foreign aid authorization and appropriation cycle to seize the agenda and reformulate U.S. policy. In hearings on the foreign assistance bill before the House Foreign Affairs Subcommittee on Asian and Pacific Affairs (which he chaired) in early 1985, Solarz began his attempt to invigorate American policy toward Cambodia by addressing the possibility of providing military assistance to the Cambodian resistance. Citing President Reagan's State of the Union Address calling for aid to freedom fighters and the February 1985 ASEAN request, Solarz made four points: (1) a stronger NCR would facilitate a political settlement, (2) resistance leaders believed additional assistance would allow them to expand their operations, (3) ASEAN had requested greater U.S. aid, and (4) the resistance forces comprised the legitimate, recognized government of Cambodia and thus had a greater claim on U.S. assistance than any other resistance movement in the panoply of Reagan Doctrine cases (U.S. Congress, House, Committee on Foreign Affairs, Subcommittee on Asian and Pacific Affairs 1985a, 150–65). Under these circumstances, Solarz suggested, Congress might "put some money in the foreign aid bill up front, overt, not covert . . . limited only to small arms and ammunition" (U.S. Congress, House, Committee on Foreign Affairs, Subcommittee on Asian and Pacific Affairs 1985a, 151, 154). Solarz received early support in his efforts from Representatives Robert Torricelli (D-N.J.) and Toby Roth (R-Wisc.), both of whom agreed that the United States was not doing enough to aid the NCR.

Solarz then arranged a closed session for his subcommittee with representatives from the CIA, the Defense Intelligence Agency (DIA), and the State Department. The subject of this executive session was "the state of the resistance . . . the extent to which they do have the weapons they need . . . the extent to which other countries have or have not been willing to help, and what the implications would be if [the United States] were to provide assistance" (U.S. Congress, House, Committee on Foreign Affairs, Subcommittee on Asian and Pacific Affairs 1985a, 165). The results of this secret hearing led Solarz to add an item to the foreign aid bill to provide $5 million "to be used by Thailand for strengthening the non-communist resistance forces in Cambodia in whatever ways they deem would most effectively strengthen the non-communist resistance" (U.S. Congress, House, Committee on Foreign Affairs, Subcommittee on Asian and Pacific Affairs 1985a, 650). Some members of the subcommittee resisted the proposal: Jim Leach (R-Iowa), for example, referred to it as "interventionism without executive sanction," and he, Sam Gejdenson (D-Conn.), and Michael Barnes (D-Md.) argued that unnecessary American involvement might trap the United States in a quagmire (U.S. Congress, House, Committee on Foreign Affairs, Subcommittee on Asian and Pacific Affairs 1985a, 650–63). Nevertheless, the amendment passed the subcommittee by a vote of 6 to 3. The final language approved by the full Foreign Affairs Committee by a vote of 24 to 9 (*New York Times,* 4 April 1985) stated that Thailand was to provide the funds to the NCR "contingent on an understanding that no assistance will be provided to the Khmer Rouge and that no American personnel will be involved in military activity with the resistance movement" (U.S. Congress, House, Committee on Foreign Affairs, Subcommittee on Asian and Pacific Affairs 1985a, ix).

Having seized the initiative in the House, Solarz then lobbied the Senate for support for his plan. In a hearing held by the Senate Committee on Appropriations on 8 May 1985, Solarz revealed a well-developed rationale for his initiative, arguing that a strong NCR was both essential to convince the Vietnamese to withdraw and necessary to prevent the Khmer Rouge from gaining control and returning to power (U.S. Congress, Senate, Committee on Appropriations 1985, 6–7). Even the relatively minor amount of assistance was carefully considered: "We estimated that the total requirements for the non-Communist resistance forces in the next year to significantly increase the size of their order of battle was in the vicinity of $15 to $20 million, and the $5 million figure would come to between 20 and 30 percent of that amount," acknowledging that "primary responsibility for supporting the . . . resistance lay with the other countries of Southeast Asia" (ibid., 7; based on Solarz's description of the purpose of the executive session with CIA, DIA, and State Department officials, it is apparent that this calculation emerged from information presented in that closed session). In addition to improving the morale of the resistance and encouraging ASEAN to maintain its support and efforts, Solarz argued, an expanded resistance "could substantially increase the cost of the Vietnamese occupation to the point where Vietnam begins to seriously consider a political settlement of the conflict" (ibid., 7). Clearly, Solarz envisioned a strengthened application of the Reagan Doctrine tied to a two-track strategy in which the assistance contributed to a diplomatic solution (see also Solarz 1985, 1986).

The foreign policy bureaucracy opposed the Solarz legislation. At the hearing in which Solarz first broached the subject, Assistant Secretary of State Wolfowitz argued that the resistance could not win and already had all the arms it could handle. Furthermore, he maintained that the danger of inadvertently aiding the Khmer Rouge precluded more American assistance. Denying that ASEAN had requested U.S. aid, he suggested that "the United States ought not gratuitously take up burdens that other people can carry" (U.S. Congress, House, Committee on Foreign Affairs, Subcommittee on Asian and Pacific Affairs 1985a, 159). Insisting that U.S. involvement would complicate the negotiations without providing any appreciable advantage, a State Department spokesman publicly declared that the Reagan administration did not support the bill, and the Defense Department added that the Solarz plan was "needless and ill-considered" (C. Campbell 1985; Crossette 1985c; Felton 1985c, 544). Solarz responded by predicting that the administration would support his idea once it saw a demonstration of support from Congress (Felton 1985c, 544).

Within the administration, the Solarz initiative touched off a debate on the merits of increased U.S. involvement. William Casey again emerged as the principal advocate of greater support for the NCR, and the State Department continued to resist the idea. The emerging support in Congress eventually prompted a compromise similar to the arrangement worked out in 1982; aid, but nonlethal and in limited amounts. The State Department at first said that aid was "not ruled out" but not now needed (Gwertzman 1985a). Finally, after months of debate on 10 April 1985, the Reagan administration announced that it no longer opposed the Solarz initiative and that Secretary of State Shultz was discussing the issue with Sihanouk and Son Sann (*New York Times,* 11 April 1985). The administration continued to maintain that the primary source of aid should be others but applauded the "new mood in Congress in favor of military aid to non-communist insurgents" (Gwertzman 1985a).

When Wolfowitz appeared before the House Committee on Appropriations in May, it was apparent that a major shift had occurred. Wolfowitz presented a letter from the State Department in which he reversed his previous position:

> The administration welcomes the Solarz provision as an important signal to Hanoi regarding congressional and public attitudes toward Vietnam's illegal occupation of Cambodia. . . . As enabling legislation which would allow the U.S. to provide either economic or military assistance to the non-Communist Cambodian resistance, it could be a helpful addition to the other ways we are supporting that resistance. . . . We would . . . prefer that the provision not mandate that the money be channeled through Thailand; the United States Government should retain administrative control of the funds. (U.S. Congress, House, Committee on Appropriations 1985, 236)

The letter added: "It is our understanding that the non-Communist resistance is being provided with all the military equipment it can effectively absorb at this time. We do not believe, therefore, that it is necessary or appropriate for the United States to give weapons to the resistance now. . . . However . . . we would not rule out the possibility of providing military aid at some time in the future" (ibid., 236–37). In answer to questions, Wolfowitz noted that the administration "had begun consideration of a program of overt economic assistance that would concentrate on technical training [and] such things as medical skills, educational skills, and so forth" (ibid., 238), conceding that this might strengthen the NCR and contribute to the pressure on Vietnam to negotiate (ibid., 242, 244).

On 9 July 1985, the House approved a slightly amended version of the Solarz amendment by a vote of 228 to 122. When Representative Leach again tried to substitute a provision for humanitarian assistance, Solarz offered his own substitute, which allowed either economic or military assistance, eliminated the provision that the aid be channeled through Thailand, and prohibited assistance to the Khmer Rouge. In the floor debate, Solarz explicitly identified the assistance as part of a strategy to secure a political settlement that would remove Vietnam from Cambodia and prevent the Khmer Rouge from coming to power (Felton 1985d, 1361; Fuerbringer 1985a). After the full foreign assistance bill passed the House, a conference version reconciling several differences with the Senate bill, which had been approved in May, also passed and was signed into law by President Reagan on 8 August 1985. In effect, Congress, led primarily by Steven Solarz, wrested the agenda from the administration and altered the application of the Reagan Doctrine, then handed the new initiative to the executive branch for implementation.

Because implementation of policy is an executive branch function, however, the administration was able to mold the new initiative to fit the compromise agreement worked out between the CIA and the State Department. Although Solarz anticipated military aid, the administration opted to provide only economic assistance (Christian 1985). Implementation occurred in several stages. First, the State Department conducted a study of the potential needs of the NCR and determined requirements for medical, educational, and political warfare training. When Congress formally appropriated the funds (on 18 December 1985), the State Department established a program to disburse them. Because of budget cuts required by the Gramm-Rudman-Hollings legislation, only $3.35 million was available; this was committed in July

1986 and completely spent in that year (U.S. Congress, House, Committee on Foreign Affairs, Subcommittee on Asian and Pacific Affairs 1988, xxii, 498, 1012). In this outlay all assistance remained nonlethal. The administration continued this policy for the remainder of its second term, requesting $5 million for both 1987 and 1988, and actually spending $3.35 million. Additionally, in the final year of the Reagan administration, a $500,000 program (the McCollum program) allowed excess nonlethal Defense Department supplies to be provided to the NCR (Brown 1989, 80; Lambertson 1989, 38).

The White House also adopted Solarz's rationale in its annual budget requests from 1986 to 1988. For example, in 1987 Assistant Secretary of State Gaston Sigur asserted that the prime goals of the policy were "to respond to ASEAN's February 1985 appeal, . . . to demonstrate tangible U.S. support for the ASEAN strategy on Cambodia, . . . to improve the positioning and strength of the non-Communists vis-à-vis the Khmer Rouge, . . . and to strengthen the actual effectiveness of the resistance forces themselves" (U.S. Congress, House, Committee on Foreign Affairs, Subcommittee on Asian and Pacific Affairs 1988, 21).

Congress (and Solarz) thus set American policy and forced the administration to respond. In the wider context of the U.S. approach to Cambodia, the Solarz initiative had another significant effect. William Casey, who had been pressing for increased covert assistance to the NCR for at least a year, was finally successful. In late 1985, the administration doubled its covert assistance program to about $12 million and maintained it at that level for the following three years (Felton 1988s, 3505; Doherty 1990b, 2724–25, 1990d, 3533). Although Casey was the principal advocate of this increase within the administration (Woodward 1987, 425–26), it clearly came about as a result of congressional support for expanded assistance, which apparently broke a bureaucratic logjam in Casey's favor. This expanded covert program remained strictly nonlethal and was implemented as it had been since 1982.

The diplomatic track: toward a breakthrough. The expansion of Reagan doctrine aid was intended to improve the chances of a political settlement, and numerous efforts were made between 1985 and 1988 to reach an agreement, facilitated in 1987 by the first genuine expressions of interest by Vietnam. Although these efforts stalled until late 1987, chances for a settlement seemed good by the end of the Reagan administration, and it seemed likely that the Bush administration would be able to play a constructive role in the conclusion of an agreement.

At first, the flurry of diplomatic activity resulted in little more than a stalemate. The effort was led by ASEAN, and the United States continued its support, but several proposals produced no progress. In July 1985, a joint communiqué from the ASEAN foreign ministers proposed to mediate indirect or direct talks between the three factions of the CGDK and Vietnam, with the KPRP acting as a member of the Vietnamese delegation (Royal Thai Government 1985, 113–16). This proposal languished when Hanoi insisted that the KPRP would have to be the primary interlocutor and tried to deny the Khmer Rouge representation in the CGDK delegation (Acharya et al. 1991, xxxv). After Vietnam unilaterally announced in August 1985 its plan to withdraw completely from Cambodia by 1990 (Ablin and Hood 1990, 420), the CGDK proposed an eight-point peace plan that included direct negotiations between Vietnam and the CGDK; a phased, UN-supervised withdrawal of Vietnamese troops accompanied by a cease-fire; KPRP-CGDK negotiations to establish a quadripartite interim government under the leadership of Prince Sihanouk; UN-supervised elections; and internationally guaranteed neutrality (Acharya et al. 1991, xxxvi). This proposal also failed to produce any progress, in spite of the fact that it contained a significant concession (direct talks between the CGDK and the KPRP).

In 1987, however, several developments contributed to a series of modest advances. First, and most important, Vietnam retreated from its hard-line position on the talks and also began withdrawing its troops. According to Brown (1989, 52–54), five factors caused the reversal: (1) steady casualties from the CGDK's guerrilla harassment, (2) economic pressure from ASEAN and U.S. blocking of much-needed international financial assistance, (3) continued strong political pressure organized by ASEAN and the United States at the UN, (4) Soviet pressure on Vietnam to withdraw that began with the advent of Mikhail Gorbachev and his "new thinking,"[10] and (5) the PRK's strides in creating an effective government able to withstand the Khmer Rouge. In short, the costs of the occupation—in political, economic, and human terms—simply became excessive, and Vietnam's major source of support, the Soviet Union, began to reduce its political and economic largesse.

Second, Vietnam agreed for the first time to participate in negotiations and its leaders persuaded the KPRP in August 1987 to agree to talks with all the resistance factions. Moreover, under pressure from Vietnam, the KPRP agreed to declare Cambodia neutral, to end the "special relationship" with Vietnam, and to hold elections with foreign

observers. This position was formalized in an October 1987 proposal
by the KPRP regime (G. Porter 1988, especially 820). Sihanouk met with
KPRP leader Hun Sen in December 1987 and January 1988 (Brown 1989,
54–55). Moreover, China ended its insistence that the Khmer Rouge
either be restored to power or be dominant in the new government.
In July 1988, China called for a four-party coalition under Sihanouk
and stated that Cambodian fighters from all factions should "refrain
from getting involved in politics and interfering in the general election" (quoted in Lambertson 1989, 40). In addition, China appeared to
acknowledge that Pol Pot and his top colleagues would not be acceptable members of the new coalition, and to accept the idea of an end to
military assistance after a verified Vietnamese withdrawal. Later, China
accepted a UN peace-keeping force, UN supervision of the interim government and the elections, and limits on the role of the Khmer Rouge
(Ablin and Hood 1990, 422; Zagoria 1991a, 36). But China continued to
support a role for the Khmer Rouge in the interim government and to
ship weapons to the rebel group (Kiernan 1991, 14–15).

Buoyed by these developments, ASEAN revived its proposal for informal talks to be hosted by Indonesia. Dubbed the Jakarta Informal
Meeting, or JIM, the talks occurred in July 1988, just after an announcement by Vietnam that it would withdraw fifty thousand troops by the
end of the year. The four parties met face-to-face for the first time,
but the only breakthrough was an agreement on an interim government consisting of representatives from all four Cambodian factions.
Under ASEAN leadership, a working group was established, however,
and a second round of talks was scheduled for October 1988. The
last diplomatic activity of the Reagan administration in Cambodia occurred when Sihanouk proposed another plan in November 1988 that
called for a specific deadline for Vietnamese withdrawal, an international peace-keeping force, simultaneous dissolution of the CGDK and
the PRK, internationally supervised elections, and the establishment
of a four-party provisional government and a national army (Acharya
et al. 1991, xlii). Vietnam responded on 6 January 1989 by announcing
its intention to withdraw completely by September 1989.

Interestingly, the progress contributed to increasing criticism from
Congress and other observers. In particular, congressional pressure
on the administration to play a more active role increased markedly
through 1987 and 1988. As early as March 1987, amid signs that the

logjam was finally breaking, Solarz expressed disappointment in the administration's lack of a diplomatic strategy:

> I . . . encouraged my colleagues to join me in taking this initiative . . . not because I thought this was a way of driving Vietnam out, but because I thought it was a way of maximizing the prospect for a political settlement. I might add that it was also based on the assumption that we had a viable diplomatic strategy designed to make possible a political settlement. . . . I think if we're going to continue providing support to the non-Communist resistance, it must be accompanied by a diplomatic strategy which has some prospect of being acceptable. (U.S. Congress, House, Committee on Foreign Affairs, Subcommittee on Asian and Pacific Affairs 1988, 532)

As the withdrawal of the Vietnamese (the first and primary policy goal of the Reagan administration) appeared more and more inevitable, congressional pressure began to focus primarily on U.S. efforts to prevent the Khmer Rouge from returning to power (the second policy goal). A number of critics began to note that policy actions in pursuit of the first goal had, perhaps inadvertently, detracted from the prospects of attaining the second. Accusations that the United States had looked the other way or even actively assisted in the strengthening of the Khmer Rouge by China and Thailand had surfaced prior to 1987 (e.g., Shawcross 1984; Becker 1986), and the American decisions to support the seating of the Khmer Rouge at the UN instead of the KPRP after 1978 were frequently criticized (e.g., U.S. Congress, House, Committee on Foreign Affairs, Subcommittee on Asian and Pacific Affairs 1981b; Vance 1983, 126–27; Chanda 1986, ch. 11). The range of choices faced by the United States (i.e., whether to support a government installed by an invading neighbor or a government guilty of horrible crimes) was limited, but the more important question, as noted by a Council on Foreign Relations analyst, was whether the Reagan administration attempted "to do all it could to disassociate itself from the distasteful reality of the Khmer Rouge presence in the CGDK and to examine soberly the longer-term implications" (Brown 1989, 44).

Critics in Congress began to insist that the administration take action to block Khmer Rouge participation in a Cambodian government and prevent the Khmer Rouge from seizing power by force in the aftermath of Vietnam's withdrawal (e.g., U.S. Congress, House, Committee on Foreign Affairs, Subcommittee on Asian and Pacific Affairs 1989c). For example, Solarz asked whether it would be better to have "a political settlement based on the establishment of a quadripartite interim government including . . . the Khmer Rouge . . . or a political settlement which included the two non-Communist factions . . . plus the People's Republic of Kampuchea . . . but excluded the Khmer Rouge" (U.S. Congress, House, Committee on Foreign Affairs, Subcommittee on Asian and Pacific Affairs 1989c, 2). Administration officials appearing before Solarz's subcommittee in June acknowledged the charge that the administration had been too passive, but to the consternation of their listeners proceeded to describe U.S. policy in terms of its support for ASEAN. For example, Deputy Assistant Secretary of State David Lambertson stated, "I think our national interests have been very well served by the posture that we have taken over the last seven or eight years . . . and I think I would say that we ought to continue to . . . coordinate very closely with ASEAN . . . [until] ASEAN themselves . . . come to the conclusion that the United States should be doing some things differently" (U.S. Congress, House, Committee on Foreign Affairs, Subcommittee on Asian and Pacific Affairs 1989c, 63).

While Solarz reacted with a relatively mild warning about the dangers of including the Khmer Rouge in the new government, Representative Chester G. Atkins (D-Mass.) erupted in his desire "to express [his] anger at the policy which [the officials] represent" (ibid., 67). Atkins excoriated the administration for its obsession with a Vietnamese withdrawal—which, he argued, was inevitable—and its lack of concern for the horrible prospect of the return of the Khmer Rouge (ibid., 67–74). To be sure, the administration had endorsed a number of measures specifically designed to minimize, if not entirely exclude, the Khmer Rouge. Secretary of State Shultz, for example, rejected the initial proposals for a quadripartite interim government because of the role it accorded the Khmer Rouge (Chanda 1989a, 38). The perception was that the administration had not been assertive enough, however, and criticisms such as these led Congress to pass a joint resolution calling for withdrawal of the Vietnamese troops; the "protection of the Cambodian people from a return to power by the genocidal Khmer Rouge"; and for the international community to "use all appropriate means available to prevent a return to power of Pol Pot, the top echelon of the Khmer Rouge, and their armed forces, so that the Cambodian people might genuinely be free to pursue self-determination without the specter of the coercion, intimidation, and torture that are known elements of the Khmer Rouge ideology" (H. J. Res. 602). The resolution also encouraged the administration "to seek inclusion, in declarations and resolutions promulgated by the United Nations pertaining to the Cambodia conflict, the principle that those responsible for acts of genocide and massive violations of internationally recognized human rights shall not return to positions of state power in Cambodia upon the withdrawal of the foreign occupation forces" (U.S. Congress, House, Committee on Foreign Affairs, Subcommittee on Asian and Pacific Affairs 1989c, 81–85). This measure passed both houses and was signed by President Reagan in October 1988.

The administration did not immediately insert itself into the negotiations, but these criticisms had several important effects in October and November 1988. First, in the October 1988 UN General Assembly, the United States succeeded in persuading ASEAN to adjust its resolution condemning Vietnam's invasion and calling for its withdrawal to include language stating that the prevention of the return of Pol Pot and his associates was of equal importance. United Nations ambassador Vernon Walters told the delegates that the "newly drafted language . . . is in harmony with my own government's twin goals for Cambodia" (U.S. Department of State 1989e). The resolution, which dedicated the international community to "the nonreturn to the universally condemned practices of the recent past" after it had been sanitized to meet with China's approval, passed 122 to 19, with thirteen abstentions, the largest margin to date (Brown 1989, 57). Second, the administration initiated an interagency national security study to review the developments and reassess U.S. policy, which was completed in October 1988. Third, as a consequence of this review (and congressional prodding), on 14 November 1988 President Reagan signed National Security Decision Directive 319 guiding U.S. policy toward Cambodia.

Although this directive concerned all of Indochina, it made several important adjustments with regard to Cambodia. First, it ordered an increase in U.S. "consultations with ASEAN on the Cambodian conflict" and the establishment of "a more regular framework for collective discussions." In addition, the directive mandated greater efforts to strengthen the NCR and Prince Sihanouk. Also, NSDD 319 stated the administration's willingness to normalize relations with Vietnam in the context of a Cambodian settlement. Finally, the directive repeatedly emphasized the administration's opposition to the return of the Khmer Rouge, noting that "our focus should be to formulate and implement effective measures to prevent their return to power or their attempts to intimidate the Cambodian people" (NSDD 319, 1–3).

Thus, by the end of the Reagan administration, the stage was set for rapid progress. The basic outlines of an agreement had been established and Vietnam had ended its obstructionism. Although the administration had very little to do with the process, it performed three significant tasks: (1) it continued to lend its support to ASEAN, to help to maintain international pressure on Vietnam, and to follow ASEAN's lead; (2) it pressed both the Soviet Union and China to cooperate with the negotiations and to influence their respective clients (Vietnam and the Khmer Rouge) to be more accommodating; and (3) it continued to provide assistance to the NCR. Nevertheless, the Reagan administration had no active diplomatic strategy, and as Reagan left office, a feeling seemed to dominate Washington that the United States would have to act more decisively on a Cambodian settlement in the future.

Phase III: Rethinking the Reagan Doctrine, 1989–1991

The Bush administration assumed office at the very moment that congressional and public concern about Cambodia strengthened in the United States and international efforts to produce a political solution accelerated. Internationally, the second Jakarta Informal Meeting (JIM II) was held, Thailand made an overture to the KPRP regime, and in April 1989 Vietnam announced that it would complete the withdrawal of the fifty to seventy thousand troops remaining in Cambodia by September 1989 with or without a peace agreement (Stern 1990, 136). Moreover, an international conference on Cambodia was scheduled for late July 1989. At the same time, the pressure for more focused U.S. action, especially to prevent the Khmer Rouge from returning to power, heightened.

The Bush administration's policy to deal with this situation had two elements.[11] First, the administration indicated its desire to increase assistance and to provide the first lethal aid to the NCR. In March 1989 the administration requested $7 million for the overt aid component, an increase of 40 percent over the 1988 allocation (Lambertson 1989, 38). Shortly thereafter the administration announced its intention to give military aid to the NCR. Undersecretary of State Robert Kimmit discussed the plan with ASEAN's ambassadors on 2 June 1989, and according to press accounts, an administration official presented the idea to the Senate Select Committee on Intelligence on 13 June 1989 (Chanda 1989b, 22). In a speech before the Heritage Foundation Asian Studies Center on 22 June 1989, Vice President Dan Quayle argued that U.S. military aid would "make it possible for [Sihanouk] to be independent of the Khmer Rouge without becoming a prisoner of the Vietnamese-sponsored puppet government" (quoted in Brown 1989, 81).

Lethal aid had some supporters in Congress. Representative Solarz (1989), for instance, stated that "lethal assistance to the NCR would enhance the prospects for a political solution by sending a signal to Vietnam and the PRK that we are not about to accept the Hun Sen regime as an accomplished fact." Senator Charles Robb (D-Va.) sponsored an amendment in June calling for military aid to the rebels. In spite of opposition from Senators Robert Byrd (D-W. Va.), Claiborne Pell (D-R.I.), and John Kerry (D-Mass.), and with significant assistance from Vice President Dan Quayle, who pressured both the Congress and National Security Adviser Brent Scowcroft and his deputy, Robert Gates, to accept the amendment (Rodman 1994, 461–68), the Senate approved the measure supporting lethal aid to the NCR by a vote of 59 to 39. Undersecretary of State Robert Kimmit's explanation that he had made it clear to the NCR that U.S. aid was contingent on independence from the Khmer Rouge probably turned the tide (Brown 1989, 81; Chanda 1989b, 22; Sutter 1991a, 50).

Second, U.S. officials indicated that the administration was prepared to support a tripartite interim government proposal that excluded the Khmer Rouge (Chanda 1989b, 22). The administration expected Sihanouk, the U.S. "horse in this race" (U.S. Congress, House, Committee on Foreign Affairs, Subcommittee on Asian and Pacific Affairs 1990c, 39), to break from the Khmer Rouge and establish an alliance with Hun Sen at the Paris Conference (Richburg 1991, 122). Although this position was basically passive, predicated on American support for Sihanouk's position rather than an initiative by the United States, it represented a change in the thinking of the administration in recognition of the developing situation.

Both proposals ultimately failed, however. The lethal aid initiative was blocked by Senator Byrd, who chaired the Appropriations Committee. Moreover, the results of the Paris Conference (see below) caused many members who had supported the idea to abandon it, and their criticism convinced the administration, which had never been more than lukewarm to the idea, to abandon the plan (Richburg 1991, 122; Sutter 1991a, 50). The diplomatic initiative died when Sihanouk not only failed to distance himself from the Khmer Rouge at the Paris Peace Conference, but resolutely refused to agree to any plan that did not include the Khmer Rouge in a quadripartite government. Assistant Secretary of State Richard H. Solomon explained that the United States had expected Sihanouk to offer a tripartite arrangement, which the administration would have supported, but when he did not, the United States felt compelled to support his quadripartite proposal (U.S. Congress, House, Committee on Foreign Affairs, Subcommittee on Asian and Pacific Affairs 1990c, 39).[12] American officials were surprised by Sihanouk's actions and went into what one former State Department official labeled "Snooky Shock" (a reference to Sihanouk's nickname; see Rodman 1994, 466–68). The conference closed without any agreement being reached.

After that, the administration lost the initiative to others. On the diplomatic front, Representative Steven Solarz and Australian foreign minister Gareth Evans devised an alternative proposal, eventually dubbed the UN plan. Solarz and Evans suggested that a UN force assume control of Cambodia's government for a transition period, during which elections would be held and a new government formed. This proposal, which was first presented by Foreign Minister Evans at the UN General Assembly in October 1989, represented an attempt to prevent the Khmer Rouge from participating in the interim government (Solarz 1990; Acharya et al. 1991, 498–573). Secretary of State James Baker expressed the administration's support for this initiative at the October UN meeting (Solomon 1991a).

In addition, Congress revolted against the administration's continuation of the Reagan Doctrine. Reports that U.S. aid had benefited the Khmer Rouge prompted an outcry in Congress and the public and motivated the Senate Intelligence Committee to vote on 28 June 1990 to cut off all covert assistance to the NCR. The overt aid program also was challenged but, largely through Solarz's avid backing, passed the House by a vote of 260 to 163 that same month. The administration was thus persuaded to review its entire approach to the Cambodia issue (Doherty 1990a, 2232). In July 1990, seeing aid to the rebels as a dead issue in Congress, the administration announced its conclusions: the United States was withdrawing its support for the resistance coalition and initiating talks with Vietnam and the KPRP regime in Cambodia (Doherty, 1990b, 2724; Rodman 1994, 470–71). An ensuing policy statement reflected the shift in priorities. According to the statement, U.S. objectives were, first, to prevent the Khmer Rouge from returning to power; second, to ensure self-determination for Cambodia; and, third, to verify Vietnam's withdrawal (U.S. Department of State 1991).

Thus the administration began the first active U.S. role in the diplomatic process since the beginning of the Reagan administration. Congress responded to this shift to a more assertive search for an alternative by agreeing in October 1990 to provide $20 million in overt, nonlethal aid to the NCR. This deal, worked out by Senate Majority Leader George Mitchell (D-Maine), prohibited all covert funding and thus actually decreased overall U.S. assistance (Doherty 1990e, 3625–26; Lardner 1990). The aid legislation included strict reporting requirements and the provision that the aid would be suspended if it benefited the Khmer Rouge directly or indirectly. Persistent reports of NCR–Khmer Rouge cooperation caused the funds to be suspended in April 1991 (*Far Eastern Economic Review,* 25 April 1991, 11).

The Bush administration's decision to take a more active role in the diplomatic process occurred amid a series of meetings of the five permanent members of the UN Security Council and resulted in an American decision to endorse the Australian proposal for UN administration of the Cambodian government. The five permanent members of the Security Council agreed on the framework in August 1990, and the four Cambodian factions agreed to the formation of a Supreme National Council (SNC) to serve as the interim authority in Cambodia. In September the Cambodians accepted the UN framework: an SNC composed of six members of the regime and six members of the resistance who would rule until elections could be held (Solomon 1991a; U.S. Congress, House, Committee on Foreign Affairs, Subcommittee on Asian and Pacific Affairs 1991a, 1991b).

The peace accord was finally signed on 23 October 1991, after a year of haggling among the four factions on issues of sovereignty and the role of the SNC. Elections were scheduled for May 1993 (Solomon 1991a, 1991b; U.S. Department of State 1991). The Khmer Rouge refused to take part in the interim organizations or elections—promising to disrupt them—and continued its attacks, even killing UN personnel in several areas of Cambodia. In November 1992, a ten-nation meeting in Beijing failed to resolve the disputes and seemed to presage a return to civil war (Shenon 1992a, 1992b; Wudunn 1992). Although the Khmer Rouge announced in March 1993 that it would not participate, the elections were held in June anyway. In spite of efforts by the Khmer Rouge to disrupt the balloting, the elections took place. Sihanouk won, and Hun Sen finished second. Sihanouk quickly formed a coalition government with Hun Sen, and after waiting two months for the Khmer Rouge to end its insurgency and take up the relatively minor posts Sihanouk offered, the new government launched (on 18 August 1993) an offensive designed to either force the Khmer Rouge to cooperate with the new government or to drive it from Cambodia (*New York Times,* 19 August 1993; Shenon 1993a, 1993b, 1993c, 1993d, 1993e). This, coupled with some instability in the tenuous coalition, prompted another descent into violence as the regime found itself confronted by renewed Khmer Rouge attacks (Prasso 1994).

Conclusions: The Reagan Doctrine and Cambodia

The two key aspects of the application of the Reagan Doctrine to Cambodia were the simultaneous existence of broad agreement on the idea of aid to the NCR and a low level of interest in the issue. The low priority assigned to Cambodia worked against much activism by the White House or the full Congress until the final phase. Nevertheless, both branches were engaged in the application of the Reagan Doctrine. The foreign policy bureaucracy was significant in devising the non-lethal covert element and in implementing the diplomatic approach. It also shaped the implementation of the overt element devised by Congress. The White House played a significant role in the original decision to begin a covert application of the Reagan Doctrine, intervening in a bureaucratic dispute to force a policy decision. President Reagan was, however, largely uninvolved and uninterested. Congress, both in its committees and as a full body, was the principal author of the post-1985 initiatives, creating the overt element, prompting the expanded covert element, and adjusting the diplomatic track. As in the executive branch, certain individual members of Congress were more interested than the entire institution, but they were able to force the institution to act on legislation and resolutions.

Nevertheless, the impact of the Reagan Doctrine on Cambodia is difficult to assess. On the one hand, the results—Vietnamese troop withdrawal and Cambodian elections—indicate a positive contribution. In addition, the Reagan Doctrine's application in Afghanistan probably had a "spillover" effect on the Soviet Union's desire to facilitate a settlement of this conflict in Asia. On the other hand, the passive role of the United States in the negotiations until 1990 and the extremely limited U.S. assistance from 1982 to 1990 suggest that the United States cannot take much credit for the outcome. Part of the difficulty rests in the two somewhat contradictory objectives embraced by the United States. The first, which dominated until 1989, was to force the withdrawal of Vietnamese troops. This objective was interpreted through the lens of broader U.S.-Soviet relations and was affected by Chinese interests in the region. The second, which dominated after 1989, was to prevent a return to power by the Khmer Rouge. This objective, especially after 1989, required the abandonment of the fundamental principle of the Reagan Doctrine: the idea that the KPRP regime, a Vietnamese and Soviet client, had to be removed from power. The logic of the Reagan Doctrine, predicated on the overthrow of Soviet client regimes, worked against the second objective primarily because the only part of the Cambodian resistance with a chance of forcing out the Vietnamese and overthrowing the KPRP regime was the very same Khmer Rouge whose return to power the United States wanted to prevent.

Hence, U.S. reluctance to become deeply involved in the issue, guided in part by the Vietnam experience of the 1960s and 1970s, produced an application of the Reagan Doctrine that was subordinated to other concerns and, wisely, kept limited. The record indicates that U.S. policy makers recognized that the only contribution U.S. aid could make was to strengthen the possibility of a diplomatic solution. Moreover, the efforts of the U.S. government during the Reagan administration suggest that a central, if not major, element of that strategy was to support the creation and strengthening of a noncommunist resistance to replace both the Khmer Rouge and the Vietnamese-installed regime. The administration, Congress, and ASEAN believed that internationally supervised elections would prevent the return of the Khmer Rouge more effectively than a military campaign. Hence, Reagan Doctrine aid as a component of this two-track approach probably served two important purposes. First, the combination of overt and covert assistance may have strengthened the NCR *within the resistance coalition*. It did not, however, improve the military effectiveness of the rebels; their operations remained very limited. A former NSC staff officer wrote in less than glowing terms that "at times [the NCR] have been moderately effective in interdicting lines of communication and attacking Vietnamese outposts, supply depots, and outlying Cambodian towns" (Bach 1986, 80). This more limited contribution helped to sustain the noncommunist factions and improved the NCR's chance to emerge from a diplomatic settlement as the lead faction in a new Cambodian government. Note, however, that this contribution was not consistent with the purposes or logic of the Reagan Doctrine, as it concerned relations between the NCR and the Khmer Rouge, not the KPRP.

Second, the application of the Reagan Doctrine probably strengthened ASEAN's efforts to persuade China to ease its insistence on a return to power of the Khmer Rouge, and to convince the Vietnamese to withdraw and allow elections. In this sense, the doctrine contributed to the UN-sponsored peace accords and to the withdrawal of the Vietnamese forces. As substantiation for the U.S. interest in supporting ASEAN's efforts, it is particularly noteworthy that U.S. policy followed ASEAN's lead and responded to ASEAN's requests; for example, when Congress and the administration devised the overt aid package in 1985. Moreover, the U.S. commitment probably encouraged ASEAN to sustain its much greater support for the NCR and to persevere in its efforts to achieve both of its objectives.

It is, however, important to note what the Reagan Doctrine did not accomplish. Vietnam was not forced out of Cambodia by the rebels; its decision to withdraw was affected much more significantly by decisions in Moscow to reduce assistance to Vietnam and by its own decision (as early as 1985) to cut its costs in Cambodia—costs which were, as Brown (1989, 52–54) noted, chiefly economic and political. The changed stance of the Soviet Union appears to have been more important than anything ASEAN or the United States did. Aside from helping to strengthen the position of the NCR in the resistance coalition, the Reagan Doctrine did not bring about the peace settlement in 1990–91. That occurred primarily because the United States dropped its opposition to the KPRP regime, recognizing its growing legitimacy and support within Cambodia and accepting it as a partner in negotiations (infinitely preferable to the Khmer Rouge). The settlement is also attributable to the plan devised by Representative Solarz and Australian foreign minister Evans for a UN-supervised transition and elections.

U.S. policy, especially after 1985, thus contributed to the positive results without being responsible for them. Moreover, U.S. policy probably did no harm. The elections held in June 1993, although marred by Khmer Rouge violence, resulted in a victory for FUNCINPEC and Prince Norodom Sihanouk, who garnered just over 45 percent of the vote. The KPRP (renamed the Cambodian People's Party) candidate, Hun Sen, received nearly 39 percent; and in the National Assembly, Sihanouk's party won fifty-eight seats to the KPRP's fifty-one (Shenon 1993a, 1993b). Sihanouk and Hun Sen announced the formation of a coalition government with Sihanouk as head of state and he and Hun Sen as co-presidents (Shenon 1993b). Interestingly, as the Khmer Rouge continued its guerrilla warfare, the United States, under the Clinton administration, expanded its effort to aid the coalition government, providing nonlethal assistance and starting the small ($90,000) International Military Education and Training program (Tomsen 1994). In January 1995, Deputy Secretary of State Strobe Talbott revealed that, subject to continued reform of the Cambodian military to reduce its corruption and inefficiency, the United States was considering sending lethal military assistance to help end the Khmer Rouge violence (Shenon 1995a). By early 1995, as a consequence of U.S. aid, the support of other regional actors, and the "carrot" (amnesty for rebels) and "stick" (military operations to destroy rebel units) approach of the Sihanouk–Hun Sen regime, a wave of Khmer Rouge defections occurred that some analysts felt presaged an end to that group's long and violent existence (e.g., Hayes 1995; Shenon 1995b).

5

Angola: Dissensus, Competing Agendas, and the Struggle over Constructive Engagement

During the Reagan administration, Angola emerged as one of the pillars of the Reagan Doctrine. Except for a few instances, however, the president was seldom personally involved in policy making, instead relying on advisers and officials in the foreign policy bureaucracy to lead his administration's efforts. Conflict arose when different elements of the bureaucracy took different approaches to the problem and President Reagan did not act to resolve the disputes. The lack of vigorous White House leadership also prompted Congress to play a vital role. By repealing the 1976 Clark amendment, which banned assistance to Angolan rebels, Congress cleared the way for aid to Jonas Savimbi's National Union for the Total Independence of Angola (UNITA). U.S. policy and the application of the Reagan Doctrine to Angola emerged from a complex interaction of all four circles of policy makers identified in Chapter 1. The State Department generally shaped the overall policy, and other policy makers in the foreign policy bureaucracy, the White House, Congress, and the public attempted to adjust or reformulate the State Department approach, with notable success between 1985 and 1987.

Background

Prior to the Portuguese coup in 1974, the United States exhibited little interest in Angola or its various liberation movements. In fact, Angola—and Africa in general—has been accorded relatively little significance in American foreign policy (Jordan et al. 1989, 433). When attention has been given, it has usually been as a function of the global strategic competition with the USSR (Rothchild and Ravenhill 1987).[1] Consequently, it was only fear that the Soviet Union was engaged in expansionism and was trying to seize Angola in the 1970s that drove the United States to become involved in the Angolan civil war. While Henry Kissinger recognized in 1975 that Angola had no independent strategic significance to the United States, he nevertheless identified U.S. interests as a part of broader East-West geopolitical conflict.[2] William Colby, CIA director at the time, reportedly told Representative Les Aspin (D-Wisc.) in 1975 that the United States backed the National Front for the Liberation of Angola (FNLA) and UNITA only "because the Soviets are backing the MPLA [Popular Movement for the Liberation of Angola]" (quoted in Bender 1988, 188).

Thus, the change in regime prompted by the April 1974 Portuguese officers' coup affected the U.S. calculus. While the new regime in Angola attempted to arrange a peaceful transition to independence, the external sponsors of the movements involved and the rebel groups themselves took actions that undermined the prospects for peace (Davis 1978, 110; Marcum 1978, 245–46; Klinghoffer 1980, 14–15). The United States embraced one of the rebel movements (the FNLA) simply to prevent potential Soviet gains through support of the MPLA (Stockwell, 1978, 43). What followed was a complex cycle of action and reaction, intervention and counterintervention. American support for the FNLA and UNITA, along with even greater assistance from Zaire, China, and South Africa, was paralleled by Soviet and Cuban support for the MPLA. Exactly who moved first is still debated. Ultimately, the Portuguese peace arrangement (the Alvor Agreement) was shattered by Soviet, Chinese, and American support for the competing factions; by Cuban, Zairian, and South African military intervention; and by FNLA, UNITA, and MPLA attacks on each other. The introduction of thousands of Cuban combat troops turned the tide in favor of the MPLA and forced the South African and Zairian troops out of Angola. The MPLA, with Cuban assistance, defeated the FNLA and forced UNITA into a kind of "long march" into sparsely populated southeastern Angola (Stockwell 1978, 240–41; Radu 1990b, 132).

In response to revelations of American involvement, the U.S. Senate voted in December 1975 to prohibit future CIA spending in Angola. That ban was incorporated into the Clark amendment in 1976, which permanently (unless it should be repealed) banned covert action in Angola (Garthoff 1985, 515–16; Bender 1988, 188). The breakdown of the Alvor Agreement thus set parameters for the region that affected American policy from that point forward: the establishment of the MPLA in power, the MPLA's reliance on Soviet military aid and Cuban combat personnel, the destruction of the FNLA and the marginalization of UNITA (forced into the Angolan bush where it turned to South Africa for support), and the presence of South African military units along the border or within the territory of Angola (Marcum 1978, 274; Copson 1986, 13).

Once in power, the MPLA initially strengthened its ties to the Soviet Union and began to create a "vanguard party" after the Soviet model (M. Ottaway 1986, 139).[3] It was rewarded with the Angolan-Soviet Treaty of Friendship and Cooperation in 1976. The organization the MPLA established mirrored the Communist Party of the Soviet Union, with a party congress, central committee, politburo, and general secretary. Consistent with its adoption of this model, the MPLA regime began to emphasize the "structural transformation of the economy," embarking on a program to create state farms, cooperatives, and industries (M. Ottaway 1986, 139). Soviet assistance and Cuban troops, which had helped to install the regime, were increased. Nonetheless, the MPLA was not necessarily ideologically committed to the USSR, as indicated by various disagreements among its leaders and its general commitment to pragmatism (Kempton 1989, 82). Even the regime's military relationship to the Soviet Union and Cuba should be qualified. Neither the arms nor the troops were free. The regime paid $14,000–22,000 per year for each Soviet adviser and Cuban soldier (ibid., 72, 222). Moreover, the Soviet Union was not granted access to bases, which it desired. Many analysts also insist that Cuban troops were present only to defend against South African attacks on Angola (e.g., Bender 1985, 115; Marcum 1989, 161).

After 1975, the MPLA faced resistance from UNITA, which was indisputably an indigenous and nationalist organization, having begun its guerrilla struggle against the Portuguese colonial government in 1966, and against that government's Cuban-supported successor after 1976.[4] It is still a "rebel movement" at the time of this writing, based in the southern and eastern provinces and supported primarily by Savimbi's own Ovimbundo people (Radu 1990b, 143–45). Although it espouses democratic goals, UNITA is organized according to Marxist-Leninist revolutionary principles (Dohning 1984, 8–10).[5] UNITA adopted a socialist program early, reaffirmed that commitment during the liberation struggle, and did not abandon it when it began its guerrilla war against the MPLA regime (Marcum 1978, 160–69). Its official 1984 statement embraced "democratic socialism" and a "comprehensive socialist economic program . . . [within a] socialist-oriented economic superstructure" (Dohning 1984, 25). Though he is viewed by his supporters as an effective, principled, anticommunist, democratic leader, the fact is that Jonas Savimbi exercises complete control over UNITA: its plans, goals, and ideology are indistinguishable from his own. This, coupled with persistent allegations of brutality and atrocities perpetrated by UNITA, undermined the confidence of some U.S. policy makers.

The Carter administration largely ignored the situation in Angola and focused what attention it did give to southern Africa on producing solutions to the Zimbabwe-Rhodesia conflict and the Namibian independence impasse. Although some administration officials expressed a desire to normalize relations with Angola during this period, nothing was done (Bender 1985, 114). Carter turned over to the Reagan administration a situation in Angola basically unchanged from the one he himself had inherited. Carter's major accomplishment in southern Africa was to assist in negotiating a basis for Namibian independence (UN Security Council Resolution 435), but its implementation was blocked by persistent South African objections and preconditions (Crocker 1992, 39). Tentative efforts by the Carter administration to link the withdrawal of Cuban troops from Angola to the independence of Namibia were unsuccessful (Crocker 1992, 42).

U.S. Policy and the Reagan Doctrine

The Reagan administration thus assumed office with an unresolved problem festering in southern Africa. Though UN Resolution 435 provided for Namibian independence, and all the parties had signed it, there had been no movement toward implementation. Moreover, many in the administration and Congress viewed the presence of Cuban combat troops and Soviet bloc advisers in Angola as the real reason for the conflict and instability in the region and preferred to deal directly with that issue. To meet these challenges, many in the administration were determined to alter U.S. policy and apply the Reagan Doctrine. If it was to be applied to Angola, however, the Reagan Doctrine first required a reversal of previous policy, and action by both branches of government. The Clark amendment prohibited covert aid to any faction in

Angola, and Congress had to repeal that measure before the doctrine could be applied, but the development and pursuit of a regional diplomatic strategy minimized the significance of aid to UNITA (and thus the application of the Reagan Doctrine). Consequently, the application of the initiative was delayed until 1985. Four phases in the development of U.S. policy toward Angola can be identified: (1) a regional diplomatic approach from 1981 to July 1985; (2) the initiation of the Reagan Doctrine between 1985 and 1987; (3) a resumption of the diplomatic approach in late 1987 through December 1988, with the Reagan Doctrine as a supplemental policy instrument; and (4) a tenuous maintenance of the status quo from 1989 to early 1991.

Phase I: Constructive Engagement, 1981–1985

A policy review addressing southern Africa, and Angola in particular, was conducted by Chester Crocker, Alexander Haig, Robert McFarlane, Jeane Kirkpatrick, Undersecretary of State Walter Stoessel, Assistant Secretary of State (Europe) Lawrence Eagleburger, State Department Director of the Policy Planning Staff Paul Wolfowitz, Assistant Secretary of State (International Organizations) Elliott Abrams, and others, beginning during the transition to the Reagan administration and lasting until March 1981 (Crocker 1992, 58–63). This review produced a recommendation for a strategy in which the United States would act as a mediator to address both the instability and violence of the region and the Soviet-Cuban presence. As Crocker characterized it, the United States intended "to . . . [build] the confidence necessary for equitable and durable solutions to conflicts and . . . [encourage] the emergence and survival of genuine democratic systems. . . . We will not lend our voice to support those dedicated to seizing and holding power through violence. . . . We . . . will not permit our hand to be forced to align ourselves with one side or another" (Crocker 1981b, 26).

This approach to southern Africa, which acquired the label "constructive engagement," dominated the U.S. policy approach to southern Africa for the entire Reagan administration. It provided a framework for organizing and coordinating various tools of policy—including sanctions, economic aid, military assistance, and assistance to rebels—into a broader policy framework. Its principal architect was former Georgetown University director of African studies Chester Crocker, who was appointed assistant secretary of state for African affairs despite some opposition from members of the right and the left in Congress. Crocker described his approach in a series of articles published in late 1980 (Crocker 1980a, 1980b; Crocker et al. 1981). The strategy promised to eliminate sources of instability and conflict *among* the states of southern Africa (e.g., the Namibia impasse, the South African presence in Angola, and the Cuban threat) in order to create possibilities for peaceful change and development *within* those states (e.g., the dismantling of apartheid and national reconciliation between UNITA and the MPLA). Additionally, as an element of the strategy, the administration decided to request the repeal of the Clark amendment to increase the pressures that could be brought to bear on Angola to secure the withdrawal of Cuban troops (officials within the administration had different reasons for recommending this action, however).

Constructive engagement had four basic features. First, the United States attempted to use its influence with South Africa to encourage positive reform both regionally and domestically (Crocker 1981b, 26; Shultz 1993, 1112). The administration offered better relations with the South African government based on Crocker's belief that "softer language, expanded economic and cultural ties, and diplomatic suasion could nudge South Africa toward regional accommodation" (Marcum 1989, 160). Second, the United States pressed for a Namibian settlement that linked the presence of Cuban troops in Angola to the South African occupation of Namibia; both issues were addressed in tandem, based on the understanding that they were, in fact, connected (Shultz 1993, 1112). As Crocker (1981b, 27) described it, U.S. "diplomacy recognizes openly the intimate relationship between the conflicts in Namibia and Angola. . . . There is a factual relationship on the ground that cannot be denied. We believe that movement on Namibia can reinforce movement toward Cuban withdrawal and vice versa." To reassure other governments and gain acceptance for the U.S. plan, however, the administration insisted that the Angola and Namibia issues were "separate"— "not formally linked" and not part of UN Security Council Resolution 435.[6] Third, the United States worked with southern African states (apart from Angola) to enlist their support for the Namibia-Angola linkage and to generate improved relations with South Africa (Crocker 1981, 26). Finally, the United States pressed for domestic reconciliation between the warring factions within Angola, South Africa, and other states in the region (Shultz 1993, 1112). On this point, as a February 1981 policy memorandum written by Crocker and approved by the review group asserted (leaked to the press and included in P. Baker 1989, 105–12), the United States explicitly affirmed its support for national reconciliation between UNITA and the MPLA. Official policy, however, suggested that this would be secured best through the withdrawal of Cuban troops as a part of the regional settlement (Gelb 1981). Hence, while the consistent position of the United States from 1981 on was that "UNITA is a viable force which must be taken into account in Angola,"[7] Crocker cautioned that sending U.S. aid to UNITA would not necessarily be helpful (Crocker et al. 1981). The four elements of constructive engagement indicate a relatively logical strategy that was to begin by addressing the regional violence and would proceed to the internal disputes only after a more stable framework for peace in the region existed. This approach was authorized by President Reagan in a still-classified national security decision directive from the summer of 1981.

The first and primary focus of constructive engagement was the South Africa–Namibia-Angola triangle. The United States attempted to mediate a settlement to the conflict between South Africa and Angola by insisting on parallel withdrawal of South Africa from Namibia and Cuban troops from Angola. As a part of that effort, the administration opened talks with Angola, other states in the region (e.g., Mozambique, Zimbabwe, Zambia, and Tanzania), and South Africa (Gwertzman 1981d). Additionally, and very controversially, the administration asked Congress to repeal the Clark amendment in March 1981. This request may be understood as the first step toward applying the Reagan Doctrine.

First steps toward the Reagan Doctrine. During the 1980 presidential campaign, a reporter asked Ronald Reagan about Jonas Savimbi and UNITA. He responded by saying: "Well frankly I would provide them with weapons. It doesn't take American manpower. Savimbi, the leader, controls more than half of Angola. I don't see anything wrong with someone who wants to free themselves from the rule of an outside power, which is Cubans and East Germans. I don't see why we shouldn't provide them with weapons to do it" (*Wall Street Journal,* 6 May 1980). In fact, hard-liners in the administration and Congress clamored for immediate repeal of the Clark amendment in order to begin such a program, viewing repeal as the first step toward aiding UNITA (Crocker 1992, ch. 12; Shultz 1993, ch. 50). William Casey was an especially vocal advocate. In March he proposed to the National Security Planning Group (NSPG) that the United States begin a program of assistance to insurgents in several countries, including Angola (Persico 1990, 264; Schweizer 1994, 9–10). Moderates within the administration joined Casey and this faction to request the repeal of the Clark amendment, seeing an opportunity to threaten the Angolan regime with U.S. aid to UNITA as a means to encourage good-faith negotiations. Assistant Secretary Crocker (1992, 137) believed this to be the corollary to the threat of U.S. sanctions on the South African regime and thought the repeal of the amendment would allow the United States to ensure that the MPLA regime would not attempt to defeat UNITA on the battlefield once the Cubans and South Africans had withdrawn.

Neither of these rationales was offered to wary members of Congress to explain the administration's request, however. Instead, several administration officials stated that the request stemmed from a concern for the president's constitutional authority. Alexander Haig told the American Society of Newspaper Editors that the administration considered the Clark amendment one of several "disabling legislative restraints on the conduct of American foreign policy by the President of the United States," and said that the administration "asked for the elimination of these disabling legislation [sic] . . . because we feel that they border on the unconstitutional if they don't cross that line." However, Haig added, the request did "not prejudge that someone has made a decision to pursue actions which would be in violation of the Clark amendment; not at all" (U.S. Department of State 1981c, 9–10). Undersecretary of State James L. Buckley reiterated the "restraint" that the amendment put on the administration in testimony before the Senate Foreign Relations Committee and stated that "there's no implication to be read into this. It's simply a matter of deep principle" (Whittle 1981b, 589). Finally, Acting Assistant Secretary of State Lannon Walker told the House Foreign Affairs Subcommittee on Africa that President Reagan "did not favor [the restrictions imposed by the Clark amendment]," but "any decision as to whether or not we would assist the UNITA forces . . . was a totally separate and different question, which we have not addressed" (U.S. Congress, House, Foreign Affairs Committee, Subcommittee on Africa 1981a, 227, 234–35).

Congress, however, declined to lift the Clark amendment. Members of the House Foreign Affairs Subcommittee on Africa were deeply suspicious of the administration's intentions, and many were not persuaded by the explanations presented to them. Chairman Howard Wolpe (D-Mich.) questioned the administration's rationale: "I frankly am a bit baffled . . . because there are a number of restrictions within the current foreign aid authorization that the administration is not requesting to be lifted" (U.S. Congress, House, Committee on Foreign Affairs, Subcommittee on Africa 1981a, 227). Representative Gerry Studds (D-Mass.) also raised this point, asking whether "the administration will be here fighting to repeal the limitations on Vietnam, Cuba, and Angola" (ibid., 243).

Others suggested that the administration was being disingenuous, maintaining that repeal was the first step toward American intervention in the Angolan conflict. Representative Steven Solarz (D-N.Y.) asked whether "in view of the fact that in the course of the campaign Mr. Reagan publicly indicated he felt we should be helping UNITA, that the Congress should prudently assume that if the Clark amendment is repealed, that there is a very real possibility that the administration might move in that direction" (U.S. Congress, House, Committee on Foreign Affairs, Subcommittee on Africa 1981a, 234). The behavior of some administration officials further increased the level of suspicion: immediately after the inauguration, UN ambassador Jeane Kirkpatrick and other officials met with South African military and intelligence officials (in violation of existing laws prohibiting such contacts), and others met secretly with Savimbi in Morocco (ibid., 229–31). Eventually, although the Senate repealed the Clark amendment by a simple voice vote (Roberts 1981), the House overwhelmingly sustained it. The Africa subcommittee voted 7 to 0 to uphold the ban (U.S. Congress, House, Committee on Foreign Affairs, Subcommittee on Africa 1981a, 442), the Foreign Affairs Committee voted 19 to 5 in its favor (J. Miller 1981b), and the full House included the ban in its foreign assistance bill. In a conference called to reconcile the different versions of the foreign aid bill, the Senate agreed to drop the repeal in order to obtain agreement on other issues, and the Clark amendment was sustained (Tolchin 1981; U.S. Department of State 1982b).

Interestingly, Savimbi, so certain of renewed U.S. aid from the Reagan administration that he planned a visit to the United States to accept the offer, received only an official assurance from the State Department of continued U.S. political support (U.S. Department of State 1982b, 34; Bender 1985, 115). When he departed, Savimbi claimed that the Clark amendment was meaningless because administration officials were encouraging other countries to provide support. Among them, reportedly, was Saudi Arabia. Indeed, some evidence indicates that CIA director William Casey persuaded Saudi Arabia to act as a surrogate for the United States in providing assistance to UNITA, perhaps as a quid pro quo for U.S. arms sales (see Magnuson 1987; Copson and Shepard 1988; Garthoff 1994, 691). On 1 July 1987, the House Foreign Affairs Subcommittee on Africa held a hearing on the allegation, which, though lively, produced no firm corroborating evidence aside from a chronology (1981–87) presenting circumstantial evidence supporting the charge (see U.S. Congress, House, Committee on Foreign Affairs, Subcommittee on Africa 1988b, especially app. 3). It should be noted that reports of U.S. violations of the Clark amendment and Saudi aid to UNITA were common between 1981 and 1987, and, given the role of Saudi Arabia in the Afghanistan and contra operations and the extent of the effort to circumvent congressional restrictions on aid to the contras, the allegations are at least plausible.

The diplomatic initiative. In the absence of congressional permission to apply the Reagan Doctrine to Angola, U.S. policy relied on diplomacy, much of which took place in the background as Crocker attempted to maintain a low profile to escape the criticism of hardliners on both the right and the left. George Shultz (1993, 1114) characterized Crocker's approach as "near-stealth diplomacy." The approach occurred in three stages, which are described in a late 1982 briefing memorandum from Crocker to Shultz.[8] Crocker and his team first approached South Africa to acquire its commitment to their proposed initiative. This effort, which occurred between April and September 1981, involved high-level discussions and a U.S. mission to South Africa headed by William Clark, then Haig's deputy in the State Department. Initially South Africa attempted to engineer a retreat from the UN resolution on Namibian independence by appealing to congressional and administration hard-liners. According to Crocker (1992, 87–92), the South Africans used lobbyists, consultants, and congressional "friends of South Africa," as well as sympathetic administration officials such as William Casey and Jeane Kirkpatrick. In one example of this effort, senior South African military and intelligence officials (including the head of South African military intelligence, General Pieter van der Westhuizen) visited the United States in March 1981 to urge conservatives in Congress, the defense and intelligence agencies, and UN ambassador Kirkpatrick to support their anticommunist efforts in the region.

In addition, the hard-liners attempted to prevent Crocker from being confirmed as assistant secretary of state. After these attempts failed, South Africa endorsed the linkage proposal in September 1981.

An additional year of work was required to sell the proposal to Western allies and to resolve the Namibia issues left over from 1980 (including constitutional guarantees, electoral procedures, and composition of observation teams). During this time the United States also attempted to persuade the so-called front-line states in southern Africa to support the proposed linkage in 1981 and 1982, beginning with an April tour of twelve African countries to assess their reaction and solicit their support (Crocker 1981a, 55). According to Crocker's memorandum to Shultz,[9] these states agreed on the approach in early 1982.

Next, Crocker engaged the Angolans in the summer of 1982; although it took another two years, he eventually engineered an agreement on the linkage concept. Initially, the Angolan regime rejected Crocker's proposal, offering instead to send the Cuban troops home after Namibian independence. Although President José Eduardo Dos Santos of Angola expressed an interest in working with the United States to settle both issues and in normalizing relations between Angola and the United States in December 1981 (Crocker 1992, 138–41), no progress occurred in meetings throughout 1982 (Crocker 1992, ch. 6).[10] The Angolan government and Cuba insisted that the Cuban troops in Angola were their concern alone, completely separate from the South African occupation of Namibia and the UN-mandated withdrawal from that territory.

Faced with the stalled talks, Crocker and the American negotiating team attempted to "create a climate of confidence" and establish the preconditions for a successful settlement of the Namibia-Angola issues (Crocker 1992, 143). In January 1983 the United States proposed a cease-fire between the South African and Angolan armies in Angola, to be followed by a phased withdrawal of South African forces from Angola, monitored by a joint commission.[11] Meetings in January, March, April, and October failed to conclude the accord, however, as the MPLA regime balked at the confidence-building measure. When the South African military increased its presence and activities in Angola in 1983 (culminating in December with Operation Askari, a series of raids deep into Angola involving South African and UNITA troops), and when UNITA's operations also escalated in 1983, the Angolan regime finally indicated its interest in such a deal (Zartman 1989, 217–20).

Moreover, the MPLA received the U.S. decision not to oppose a UN Security Council resolution condemning the South African actions as "an indication of . . . good faith commitment to the negotiating process."[12] With the assistance of President Kenneth Kaunda of Zambia, South Africa and Angola signed on 16 February 1984 in Lusaka, Zambia, that defined an area in which Cuban troops and Namibian guerrillas from the South-West African People's Organization (SWAPO) would not operate, and arranged for a controlled, phased, and verified South African withdrawal from Angola, monitored by a joint South African–Angolan monitoring commission.[13]

The last stage of the diplomatic approach developed because the Lusaka Accord established a momentum that persuaded the MPLA to agree, in principle, to the idea of a Cuban troop withdrawal as a part of a regional peace settlement (Crocker 1992, 175; Gelb 1983a). American diplomacy nearly produced a breakthrough in the regional dispute in 1984 and early 1985. In September 1984 the MPLA presented its first proposal for a parallel agreement, suggesting a three-year schedule for Cuban withdrawal, excluding ten thousand troops around the capital. The South Africans countered with a proposal for a twelve-week schedule for the withdrawal of all Cuban troops (Crocker 1992, 207, 218). The United States responded by working out a "basis for negotiation" that merged the two suggestions into a more reasonable proposal for a two-year withdrawal schedule heavily weighted at the front end (80 percent of the Cuban troops) to occur simultaneously with the South African withdrawal from Namibia (U.S. Congress, House, Committee on Foreign Affairs, Subcommittee on Africa 1985a, 6, 9). While both sides expressed interest in this "split-the-difference" initiative presented to them in March 1985, no final agreement was reached. Ultimately, a combination of factors in South Africa, Angola, and the United States scuttled the promise of an early accord.

The first factor that led to the breakdown of the negotiations was Angola's reaction to South African and UNITA attacks in 1983. South Africa's decision to turn to the battlefield to achieve its security goals prompted the MPLA to sign agreements with the Soviet Union in 1983 and early 1984 for increased arms and advisers (Legum 1988, 320–21; Marcum 1989, 162). By mid-1985, the Angolan military, armed with the new Soviet aid, successfully counterattacked against UNITA (Legum 1988, 345–46, 388–91).

The actions of the South African government within South Africa and in Angola, Namibia, and other regional states also diminished the opportunity for a regional settlement. In late 1984, violence inside South Africa increased as a wave of uprisings and protests was met with increased force by South African security forces (P. Baker 1989, 27). The internal unrest, combined with the heightened international criticism it triggered, caused the South African government to recoil from its internal reforms and its external negotiations (Crocker 1992, 229–30). In addition, South Africa conducted a commando attack on the Cabinda oil fields in northern Angola in May 1985; renewed cross-border raids into Angola and attacks on other states in the region, including Botswana; and increased its direct support for UNITA throughout 1985 (Hanlon 1986, 164; Legum 1988, 341, 352, 390). At the same time, the government of South Africa unilaterally announced that it was about to form an internal government for Namibia and grant it independence. All these acts signaled South Africa's retreat from both the negotiations and its obligations under UN Security Council Resolution 435.

Finally, actions by Congress and the Reagan administration contributed to the breakdown of the diplomatic initiative. Two efforts that began in late 1984 were especially significant. First, the desire of many members of Congress for greater opposition to South Africa's aggression against the front-line states and its repression of the black majority within South Africa led to congressional attempt to apply sanctions to South Africa. This campaign prompted the administration to preempt the legislation by applying some limited measures. This, in turn, angered the Botha regime and probably contributed to its decision to seek a military rather than diplomatic solution.

The attack, involving both Republicans and Democrats, escalated in late 1984. Even some conservatives wanted to threaten sanctions against South Africa: the "Conservative Opportunity Society," a group led by Representatives Newt Gingrich (R-Ga.) and Vin Weber (R-Minn.) and consisting of about thirty-five Republicans in the House of Representatives (P. Baker 1989, 36), broke from the Reagan administration and advocated the use of sanctions to end apartheid. As a part of this effort, the House Foreign Affairs Subcommittee on Africa, chaired by Howard Wolpe, frequently called Chester Crocker before its panel to criticize the American "tilt" toward South Africa and cautioned Crocker against treating the MPLA regime too harshly, or UNITA too favorably. This challenge to administration-led policy persisted throughout

Reagan's first term. The hearings held in March 1981, September 1981, December 1982, February 1983, and February 1985 (U.S. Congress, House, Committee on Foreign Affairs, Subcommittee on Africa 1981a, 1983b, 1983c, 1983a, and 1985, respectively) provide good examples of the broad challenge to administration policy raised by its critics. The struggle over sanctions and South Africa lasted from November 1984 to October 1986 and resulted in limited sanctions imposed by the administration to preempt a tough congressional package in 1985, followed by a congressional sanctions package passed in 1986 over a presidential veto. The rousing battle signified the broad feeling in Congress and the public that South Africa was not cooperating with the U.S. peace initiative and was moving away from rather than toward democratic reforms.[14] In addition, the 1986 action increased South Africa's hostility and intransigence.

Second, beginning in late 1984, other administration officials and members of Congress attempted to force the United States toward more open alignment with South Africa and more active support for UNITA. Many of these conservatives had never been happy with the policy of constructive engagement in the first place, with its emphasis on negotiations and regional peace (Alexiev 1986, 4–6). Crocker (1992, 450) recalled that "conservatives were viscerally suspicious of any State Department strategy that appeared to rely on the arts of persuasion, seduction, conversion, cooption, and other unnatural acts such as 'weaning Marxists.'" Within the administration, William Casey led the effort. With Jeane Kirkpatrick, William Clark, and Caspar Weinberger as allies, Casey persistently undermined the diplomatic initiative by using CIA channels to encourage the South Africans to be "tough" and to maintain U.S. contact with Jonas Savimbi (Crocker 1992, 271, 281; Shultz 1993, 1115–16). Secretary of State George Shultz was extremely troubled by Casey's behavior:

> Bill Casey's pursuit of different foreign policy goals, using the CIA as his platform and his source of influence, was . . . a continuing problem for Crocker and me as we pursued what had been approved as administration policy. . . . Within the administration, Bill Casey viscerally and unswervingly opposed all that Crocker and I were doing; his CIA officers ran channels to the South Africans from CIA headquarters at Langley and used CIA representatives in the field to undermine Crocker with Savimbi and other black

> African leaders. . . . He worked with South African intelligence,
> gave the benefit of the doubt to South Africa, and distrusted any
> negotiation or potential agreement with a Communist government.
> (Shultz 1993, 1113, 1116)

Casey also sent CIA representatives to Congress and private organizations with false or misleading estimates and presentations (Crocker
1992, 284–85; Shultz 1993, 1116). One important consequence of this
campaign was persistent doubt on the part of Savimbi and both South
African and Angolan officials as to whether Crocker really represented
the Reagan administration. Crocker repeatedly had to ask his superiors
to verify his statements as official U.S. policy. For example, he found
it necessary to have Shultz confirm to Savimbi that he spoke for the
president and that Shultz looked to him to carry out U.S. policy.[15]

Casey was aided by like-minded members of the Defense Department, the NSC staff, and the White House, including the Defense Intelligence Agency, Fred Iklé, Constantine Menges, Philip Ringdahl, Oliver
North, Chief of Staff Don Regan, National Security Adviser John Poindexter, and Patrick Buchanan. He was also supported by hard-liners in
Congress, including Jesse Helms (R-N.C.), Steven Symms (R-Ida.), and
Malcolm Wallop (R-Wyo.) in the Senate, and Mark Siljander (R-Mich.),
Robert Dornan (R-Calif.), and Dan Burton (R-Ind.) in the House. These
conservatives were supported by private organizations and lobbyists
who favored U.S. support for South Africa and Savimbi, including
the Heritage Foundation, the American Security Council, the Conservative Caucus, the Cuban-American National Foundation, Citizens for
America, conservative evangelical groups led by Jerry Falwell and Pat
Robertson, and American lobbyists for South Africa Stuart Spencer
and John Sears (Crocker 1992, 268–84; Shultz 1993, 1112, 1116). Shultz
(1993, 1115–16) described the influence of this network on President
Reagan: "Ronald Reagan . . . was . . . disposed to give the benefit of
the doubt to an anti-Communist leader, even if authoritarian and dic-
tatorial" and was thus particularly susceptible to advisers suggesting
alliances with anticommunist entities such as South Africa and UNITA.
Hence, "the South African government's Washington lobbyists, John
Sears and Stuart Spencer, found easy access to White House corridors."
Together this network succeeded in repealing the Clark amendment in
July 1985, prompting Angola to break off the U.S.-sponsored talks immediately.

Phase II: Adding the Reagan Doctrine, 1985–1987

As early as 1983, believing that U.S. policy was ineffective and misguided, the conservative network began a "UNITA project." As a part of
this campaign, individuals and groups maintained that the State Department's policy was ineffective, anti-Western, and hostile to President Reagan's desires.[16] In the summer of 1985, the network and official
U.S. policy collided, resulting in a major reformulation of U.S. policy:
the application of the Reagan Doctrine to Angola. Hard-liners in Congress, the administration, and the public escalated their campaign to
provide aid to UNITA. Their effort, which gained momentum in 1985
after President Reagan's articulation of the Reagan Doctrine in that
year's State of the Union Address, resulted first in the repeal by Congress of the Clark amendment, and then, after a bitter policy review,
the provision of "covert" Reagan Doctrine aid to UNITA in 1986.

Repealing the Clark amendment. The repeal of the Clark amendment in the summer of 1985 was the result of the efforts of conservative members of Congress, especially Senators Symms (who had
visited Savimbi in Angola), James McClure (R-Ida.), and Wallop. Officially, the administration did not seek the action, although some policy
makers worked in the background with the conservative network
identified above (Rodman 1994, 364). A number of important factors
brought about repeal. First, the massive campaign of briefings, opinion
pieces, and lobbying by the hard-line network of intelligence officials,
organizations, and private groups mobilized opinion for Savimbi's
cause. While UNITA representatives, escorted by various conservative
organizations, briefed members of Congress, Stuart Spencer and John
Sears, paid lobbyists for South Africa, further extolled UNITA's virtues
(Crocker 1992, 283–84; Shultz 1993, 1116). Members of the NSC staff
persuaded the Cuban-American National Foundation to pressure members of Congress to oppose the MPLA regime and its Cuban protectors by
aiding UNITA (Rodman 1994, 365). Additionally, although it is not entirely clear when the contract started, UNITA retained the Washington
public relations firm of Black, Manafort, and Stone to "sell" Savimbi to
the American public and Congress. The firm's efforts may have begun
as early as the summer of 1985, although its most important task was
to prepare Washington for Savimbi's February 1986 visit. The firm was
paid $600,000 for a one-year retainer, a fact that became public in 1986
(Felton 1986c, 264–65), and the campaign was managed by Christopher

Lehman, an NSC staffer who resigned his position and took up those responsibilities (see Bridgland 1986, 464; Rodman 1994, 371).[17]

Second, President Reagan's overwhelming victory in the 1984 election generated greater support from members of Congress reluctant to oppose a very popular president. The President's 1985 State of the Union Address articulating the Reagan Doctrine and his identification of UNITA as one of several groups of freedom fighters in the world that deserved U.S. aid further prompted Congress to repeal the Clark amendment and move toward assisting UNITA (P. Baker 1989, 37; McFaul 1989, especially n. 19).

Third, the 1985 Angolan counteroffensive and the large increase in Soviet aid and advisers and Cuban personnel that started in 1984 seemed to indicate that the MPLA was tightly allied with the Soviet Union and was attempting to consolidate its position (see, e.g., Alexiev 1986). This, coupled with the stalemate in the diplomatic effort, persuaded many that constructive engagement had failed. Analysts wrote that "by 1985 it . . . became clear to most observers, except perhaps to Chester Crocker's team, that the Angolan dimension of 'constructive engagement' was a dismal failure" (Alexiev 1986, 6). These developments prompted UNITA proponents to forecast a bleak future for UNITA unless it received American aid (Marcum 1989, 162; McFaul 1989, 106).

The last media gimmick arranged by the conservative network occurred in the first week of June 1985. Armed with a letter of endorsement signed by President Reagan and calling himself "a champion of the Reagan Doctrine," New York gubernatorial candidate Lewis Lehrman convened a "conference of freedom fighters" in Jamba, Angola, Savimbi's headquarters. The meeting was sponsored by Citizens for America (a part of the conservative network that lobbied in three hundred congressional districts) and included representatives from "all the major anti-Soviet guerrilla leaders (except for [the Mozambique National Resistance])."[18] Calling themselves the Democratic International, these organizations called on the United States for expanded assistance and accused the U.S. State Department of undermining White House policy and betraying the president (Cowell 1985a).

Crocker believed that the Casey-Buchanan–South Africa connection arranged the event to put additional pressure on American policy makers. "How exactly," Crocker (1993, 289) asked, "did Lehrman dream up the idea of carrying the Buchanan-Casey battle cry to the remotest reaches of Angola's Cuando Cubango Province? Who do you suppose drafted the letter and lobbied endlessly until it was approved and signed by Reagan or his signature machine? Who coordinated the logistics, communications, press coverage, and security of travelers from around the world into a military camp appearing on no published map in a war zone accessible only to South African military pilots and friendly air service contractors?" In fact, at least one document suggests Crocker was correct. A 21 May 1985 memorandum from NSC staffers Walter Raymond, Jr., and Oliver North makes it very clear that the White House was aware of and was cooperating with the plan, if not actually responsible for it.[19] Referring to "*our* Alliance for Liberation and Democracy" (emphasis added), the memo discussed plans to send a taped speech or a letter from the president and the desire of White House speechwriter Dana Rohrabacher to attend in person. The matter was reviewed by NSC staffers Raymond, North, Raymond Burghardt, Philip Ringdahl, Helen Soos, and Jock Covey; and White House aides Pat Buchanan and Rohrabacher, and was submitted to Robert McFarlane for his decision.

All of these pressures began to produce results just one week after the meeting in Jamba: the U.S. Senate voted 63 to 34 on Symms's bill to repeal the Clark amendment. Following the Senate vote, the battle shifted to the House of Representatives, where the Senate's first attempt at repeal had been defeated in 1981. The debate in the House again took place without official administration lobbying (Rodman 1994, 364). Although conservatives suggested otherwise, the State Department also officially favored repeal in order to strengthen the American hand in the negotiations. However, both Crocker and Shultz decided to "let Congress take the lead" and to offer only "quiet, behind-the-scenes support" (Crocker 1992, 288). Although he feared that it would complicate or scuttle the delicate talks, Crocker (1992, 288, 296) had concluded in July 1985 that repeal "still made sense" and endorsed it. Noting that he "had worked hard for Clark repeal in 1981," Crocker stated that he "cheered the results on C-SPAN in [his] office as sixty Democrats joined in the House's vote for repeal." Of course, his support for repeal did not mean he supported aid to UNITA, a point made clear by Crocker's position in 1981 and by his actions after the July 1985 votes in Congress.

Others in the administration played a more active role in the repeal. In particular, Buchanan and Casey were outspoken proponents, even though they too preferred to remain in the background. According to Constantine Menges (1988b, 235–43), who maintained close links to the director of central intelligence while he served as an NSC staff officer, Casey played a key role in aiding members of Congress and apparently viewed the repeal as a personal victory (Woodward 1987, 490).

The effort in the House of Representatives was led by Jack Kemp (R-N.Y.), Samuel Stratton (D-N.Y.), Trent Lott (R-Miss.), and the Conservative Opportunity Society. They were joined by Claude Pepper (D-Fla.), whose district was 40 percent Cuban American and who was the major target of lobbying by the Cuban-American National Foundation (Rodman 1994, 365). On 10 July 1985 the House voted 236 to 185 in favor of repeal. The bill was attached to the foreign assistance authorization, which passed the House on 11 July 1985 by voice vote. The measure was signed on 8 August 1985 by President Reagan, to become effective in October 1985 (Felton 1985d, 1359–61; Copson and Shepard 1988, 4).

The repeal of the Clark amendment, which required the cooperation of both political branches of the U.S. government, thus provided the essential first step for the application of the Reagan Doctrine to Angola. Conservatives and other supporters of the repeal clearly had this ultimate purpose in mind. Senator Symms celebrated the repeal of the ban and looked forward to providing aid to UNITA. He believed that Angola was "a place where [the United States] can achieve victory, not only an actual victory on the field but a moral victory, psychological victory, which will give strength to free men all over the world" (*Congressional Quarterly Weekly Report,* 15 June 1985, 1143). To Representative Henry Hyde (R-Ill.), repeal was a message "that the United States is no longer paralyzed" (Felton 1985d, 1360), and to Representative Robert Dornan, repeal provided "an opportunity not just to constrain, but to roll back communism" (quoted in McFaul 1989, n. 13).

Some of the members of Congress who voted for repeal did not intend their action to endorse aid to UNITA. Like the State Department, these individuals hoped that repeal would place pressure on the MPLA regime. Representative Lee Hamilton (D-Ind.), who voted for the repeal, stated that the vote for repeal "should not be construed as approval by the Congress" for assistance to UNITA (Felton 1985d, 1360). Instead, Hamilton explained, "I think there is something to the argument that the President needs some flexibility, and the mere fact that the Clark amendment was on the books, I think, limited the President's options to some degree" (U.S. Congress, House, Committee on Foreign Affairs, Subcommittee on Africa 1986c, 22). According to Representative Ted Weiss (D-N.Y.), during the debate, "the administration position set forth very clearly [was] that there was nothing implicit in the repeal as far as aid to Savimbi was concerned. The aid decision was absolutely denied. The President simply wanted in general to have the Clark amendment repealed" (U.S. Congress, House, Committee on Foreign Affairs, Subcommittee on Africa 1986c, 25). The State Department (i.e., Crocker) had maintained that position all along, stating emphatically that the repeal did not imply a decision to provide aid (Gwertzman 1985b). In any event, the repeal of the Clark amendment was necessary for the Reagan Doctrine to be applied to Angola.

The decision to apply the Reagan Doctrine. The removal of the Clark amendment restrictions opened up the option of extending the Reagan Doctrine to Angola. In response, U.S. policy makers began to formulate just such an option. In July 1985, a policy review within the administration commenced, and in August, members of Congress initiated their own attempt, through several amendments, to provide assistance to Savimbi's forces. Divisions existed within each of these channels: within the administration, the essential disagreement rested on differences over how best to aid UNITA and remove the Cuban troops; in Congress, this debate coexisted with disagreement over whether to aid UNITA at all.

The review in the administration's policy channel began after the House voted to repeal the Clark amendment and continued until the end of the year (Crocker 1992, 289, 294). Two positions quickly developed. The State Department, led by Crocker, wanted to fit the *threat* of U.S. assistance to UNITA into the basic diplomatic approach of the previous four and a half years and convince the MPLA to abandon its quest for a military solution. Only if this threat proved ineffective did this group envisage providing aid to UNITA. Crocker (1992, 296) believed that the threat of U.S. aid "would send a signal—a useful one—to Moscow, Havana, and Luanda that we had options if they continued to use our diplomacy as a cover for the pursuit of unilateral military objectives. . . . Now, we could play the assistance card so as to guarantee that UNITA could never become the victim of a Cuban withdrawal settlement; it could give us leverage as the question of Angolan reconciliation ripened." Crocker (1992, 296, 292) expressed frustration with "advocates of immediate aid" who dismissed "all consideration of diplomatic consequences." He argued that "aiding anti-communist rebels was not by itself a strategy" and insisted that without careful integration of the various tools available for American foreign policy, "we could end up with a mortally wounded diplomacy and nothing to replace it. Covert action . . . is not foreign policy" (Crocker 1992, 297). Instead, the African affairs bureau pressed for a phased approach, relying first on the threat of aid to pressure the MPLA, and then moving to "a variety of covert pressures, . . . starting with modest measures and moving toward more coercive ones" as required by the situation.

George Shultz concurred with the thrust of this argument but was much more willing than Crocker to provide aid to UNITA. Shultz (1993, 1118) maintained that "a show of strength would lead to a stronger diplomatic posture" and advocated trying to use the "new leverage to prompt the Dos Santos regime into action at the negotiating table." Moreover, while recognizing that assistance was probably necessary and desirable, Shultz saw that politically it was inevitable, so he advocated covert aid rather than open U.S. assistance as the least damaging and potentially most beneficial addition to American diplomacy. After some disagreement between the two, Shultz ordered Crocker to "develop options for assistance which best supported [the regional diplomatic] strategy, and . . . implement them in a phased manner that supported U.S. diplomacy" (Crocker 1992, 295, 297; Rodman 1994, 367–68).

Opposing this view were the Defense Department, the CIA, and the NSC staff, who insisted that constructive engagement had failed (Crocker 1992, 294) and wanted to confront the Soviet Union and its allies to force their defeat in Angola (New York Times, 29 October 1985). Constantine Menges (1988b, 235–36) reflected their perspective: he believed that the State Department was pursuing a "defective" diplomatic strategy based on the assumption that Marxists could be trusted to keep their agreements, and he advocated the rejection of "this failed State Department policy." These officials were characterized by George Shultz (1993, 1114) as "zealous advocates . . . [who] saw little reason to address a comprehensive solution to the issues of the region and seemed unwilling to understand the subtle international relationships involved." Furthermore, as an official from the intelligence community informed Crocker, "Casey [wanted] to have at least one covert war in each region" (Crocker 1992, 293). Consequently, this group pressed for immediate military aid to UNITA and the suspension of diplomacy.

The review dragged on, frozen by this disagreement. Congress began to press for a decision. As in the administration, significant divisions existed there as well. Leaders of the faction that advocated aid included Representatives Jack Kemp, Bob Michel (R-Ill.), Dan Burton (R-Ind.), Robert Dornan (R-Calif.), Claude Pepper (D-Fla.), and Mark Siljander (R-Mich.); and Senators Steven Symms, Jesse Helms, Malcolm Wallop (R-Wyo.), and Bob Kasten (R-Wisc.). Leaders of the faction opposing aid included Representatives Howard Wolpe, Steven Solarz, Matthew McHugh (D-N.Y.), and Lee Hamilton; and Senators Christopher Dodd (D-Conn.), Joseph Biden (D-Del.), Paul Sarbanes (D-Md.), and Claiborne Pell (D-R.I.). A third faction that preferred covert aid included Representative Dante Fascell (D-Fla.) and Senators Richard Lugar (R-Ind.) and Dennis DeConcini (D-Ariz.).

In August 1985, members from both houses approached Constantine Menges to solicit his assistance in persuading the administration to apply the Reagan Doctrine (Menges 1988b, 236–41). With his help, these individuals submitted letters to Secretary of State Shultz and President Reagan advocating military aid. Then, between September and November, an assortment of resolutions and bills calling for different types of overt assistance were introduced. For example, Representative Siljander introduced a bill for $27 million in direct military aid, including antitank and antiaircraft missiles (TOW and Stinger missiles), and Representatives Pepper and Kemp introduced a bill to provide $27 million in overt humanitarian aid (food, medicine, and clothing) with an attached resolution approving of covert military assistance from the CIA contingency fund. Each bill eventually earned more than one hundred cosponsors (e.g., Felton 1985g, 2505, 1986b, 185; *New York Times,* 29 October 1985; U.S. Congress, House, Committee on Foreign Affairs, Subcommittee on Africa 1986a, 1986b; U.S. Congress, Senate, Committee on Foreign Relations 1986a). Representative Kemp wrote to President Reagan in October denouncing the State Department (*New York Times,* 29 October 1985) and then joined Jeane Kirkpatrick in harsh comments about the State Department's failure to support Savimbi, stating the urgent need for the United States to "prevent the communization of southern Africa" (A. Lewis 1986; also, Kirkpatrick 1985b).

The faction opposed to aiding UNITA also took action. Led by Rep. Howard Wolpe, the Democrats on the House Foreign Affairs Subcommittee on Africa circulated a letter to their colleagues stating their opposition to assistance (*New York Times,* 29 October 1985). One month later Wolpe, Matthew McHugh, and 101 members of the House sent a letter to President Reagan in which they argued that "U.S. involvement in this conflict, whether direct or indirect, covert or overt, would damage relations with governments around Africa and undermine fundamental U.S. policy objectives in southern Africa" (Felton 1985g, 2505–6). The House Foreign Affairs Subcommittee on Africa held two hearings in which the issue was discussed. Administration officials, members of Congress, and a cast of scholars and former government officials testified in support of or in opposition to assistance to UNITA (U.S. Congress, House, Committee on Foreign Affairs, Subcommittee on Africa 1986a, 50–63, 1986b).

While these hearings are too lengthy and detailed to summarize here, a representative example is useful. In one hearing, Representative Siljander declared that "Jonas Savimbi . . . is a true liberation fighter, and he deserves U.S. support, and the Congress has agreed to that by repealing the Clark amendment. . . . As long as we do not have a military option, Angola will remain a Cuban colony. Freedom in Africa will never be a reality" (U.S. Congress, House, Committee on Foreign Affairs, Subcommittee on Africa 1986b, 8). Siljander also argued that "the Russians have never negotiated themselves out of any territory they have ever controlled anywhere in the world," and "there is an alternative to the apparent State Department position of ambivalence toward the Castro domination of Angolan people" (ibid., 7). Wolpe, on the other hand, opposed support for UNITA because "we would be creating greater dependence by the Angolan government on the very Cubans and Soviets that we profess to want to see leave Angola. . . . We permit the Soviet Union to portray the United States as being allied with South Africa. . . . And we would also have American tax dollars flowing directly to an individual that is portraying himself to right-wing circles in the United States as the embodiment of Western capitalistic values and as anti-Communist, but who in fact is an avowed Marxist" (ibid., 1–2). Wolpe also referred to a December 1981 discussion he had had with Savimbi, who had said that he favored socialism on the Chinese model. Siljander responded with a letter from Jeremias Chitunda, the "foreign minister" of UNITA: "This accusation undoubtedly emanates from Dr. Savimbi's preindependent ties to China. . . . Like many other members of the Third World indigenous liberation movements of the 1960s, Dr. Savimbi trained in China. . . . However, Dr. Savimbi has never accepted the principles of Marxism" (ibid., 94–95).

With much of Congress pushing hard for assistance, the administration made several decisions in late October and early November.

The National Security Planning Group (NSPG) principals agreed that U.S. assistance to UNITA, if it were provided, must be covert. Advocates of aid agreed that this was necessary to preserve deniability, protect friendly states in the region whose cooperation was crucial, keep Congress from meddling in the details of the policy, and enhance the role of the CIA and the defense intelligence establishment (Gwertzman 1985c; Crocker 1992, 294–95). In addition, one last attempt at diplomacy was tried. Crocker and Undersecretary of State Michael Armacost engaged in a final bid to convince the Angolans to negotiate. Crocker managed to secure South African support for a proposal for 80 percent of the Cuban troops to be withdrawn in the first year, with the remaining 20 percent removed in the second year, coinciding with the schedule for South African withdrawal from Namibia, elections there, and Namibian independence (Crocker 1992, 298). Unfortunately, when Crocker and Armacost met with MPLA officials, the latter revealed that they had no mandate to negotiate substantively; they only desired to persuade the United States to refrain from assisting UNITA. Crocker broke off the talks and made a detour on his return to the United States, visiting Jonas Savimbi in order to invite him to Washington (Crocker 1992, 299–300; Shultz 1993, 1118).

The failure of this last-ditch effort pushed the stalemate into the lap of the NSPG. At this time, no decision had been taken to provide aid to Savimbi's forces, a fact that State Department press releases emphasized (Gwertzman 1985c; *New York Times,* 29 October 1985), but a preference for covert aid coupled with a renewed diplomatic opening was taking shape (A. Lewis 1985). At this meeting on 12 November 1985, President Reagan and his advisers agreed to begin a covert aid program for UNITA in early 1986 for the purpose of encouraging successful negotiations and national reconciliation (Shultz 1993, 1119). This decision was codified in National Security Decision Directive 212 and confirmed in NSDD 272 and NSDD 274. Directive 212 laid out U.S. objectives (Cuban troop withdrawal, regional peace and stability, and Namibian independence) and stated: "In order to achieve these broad objectives, the US will remain actively involved in Southern Africa, and with respect to Angola, will pursue a two-track strategy of a) continuing to negotiate with the MPLA and South African Cuban troop withdrawal in the context of Namibian independence while b) applying pressure on the MPLA to negotiate seriously and to accept a negotiated solution" (NSDD 212, 1). The directive also noted that the negotiations "have

UNITA's interests in mind. . . . What is required is a national reconciliation based on a political settlement acceptable to all Angolan parties,"
in addition to a number of other measures designed to maintain regional relations, promote the images of the United States and UNITA in
the UN and elsewhere, and increase pressures on the MPLA regime. NSDD
272 added that "UNITA has a valid and critical role to play in Angolan
reconciliation" (NSDD 272, 2); and NSDD 274 ordered increased support
for UNITA and expanded economic pressures on the MPLA regime (NSDD
274, 2).[20] Interestingly, this last directive lists the need for policy to be
"sustainable in Congress" as a reason for the expanded efforts.

Consistent with this White House decision, Secretary Shultz wrote
to House Minority Leader Bob Michel asking him to discourage support for the overt aid legislation. Shultz further stated that Savimbi
agreed that the legislation was unnecessary, and that the MPLA regime
and South Africa had recently expressed renewed interest in the U.S.
"basis for negotiation." Finally, Shultz argued that "the legislation
which Congressmen Pepper and Kemp have proposed is ill-timed and
will not contribute to the settlement we seek. I feel strongly about
Savimbi's courageous stand against Soviet aggression, but there are
better ways to help. A determined effort on our part to pursue negotiation is a good approach" (letter excerpted in U.S. Congress, House,
Committee on Foreign Affairs, Subcommittee on Africa 1986b, 3). This
letter was widely interpreted as evidence of Shultz's hostility to UNITA
and Savimbi (see, e.g., Menges 1988b, 241), and it prompted Jack Kemp
to request Shultz's resignation (Shultz 1993, 1118). As Shultz (1993,
1118) remembered it, "conservatives in Congress, always suspicious of
me and the State Department, went on a virtual rampage." The issue
came to a climax on 8 November 1985 when Jack Kemp met with President Reagan and George Shultz in the White House. Kemp opened with
an attack on Shultz and the State Department regarding the UNITA aid
issue. Shultz responded by trying to explain that overt aid would be
unsuccessful and that covert aid tied to the diplomatic approach was
the best option. According to Shultz (1993, 1118–19), he said, "Why
don't you try thinking, Jack? How are you going to get aid delivered?
Zaire and Zambia cannot openly support insurgencies in another African state. And the aid has to go through there! If this aid isn't delivered,
it's worthless to Savimbi." The meeting ended with Kemp remaining
unconvinced, as indicated by his comments to the New York Times in

which he criticized Shultz and the State Department for opposing aid to UNITA (*New York Times,* 3 December 1985).

Once the administration announced its opposition to the overt aid bills, all the proposals eventually died, many without a vote, as their advocates became satisfied with the covert program (Felton 1986c, 264). In December, the intelligence committees were informed that $15 million for covert aid would be taken from the CIA contingency fund (Gwertzman 1986b; *New York Times,* 31 January 1986; Crocker 1992, 300). The plan prompted Chairman Lee Hamilton and other members of the House Intelligence Committee to write President Reagan and ask him to reconsider (Roberts 1986).

Implementing the Reagan Doctrine. By December 1985 the administration was implementing the decision to apply the Reagan Doctrine to Angola. First, in December, William Casey traveled to Zaire to meet with President Mobuto Sese Seko to arrange to supply the weapons to UNITA through Zaire (Brooke 1987a). Then, an interagency group (IG) led by Crocker and charged with developing aid plans tied to the diplomacy produced a recommendation for nonlethal aid only that was widely criticized by hard-liners in the upper levels of the administration and forced back to the IG for reconsideration (Rodman 1994, 368). Finally, the administration welcomed Jonas Savimbi to Washington in early February, receiving him at the White House and State Department, escorting him to a luncheon at the Heritage Foundation, and accompanying him on visits to Capitol Hill, television networks, major newspapers, the National Press Club, and several think tanks (in a tour arranged by Black, Manafort, and Stone; see Felton 1986c, 265). According to Shultz's 6 February 1986 briefing memorandum,[21] the State Department took the opportunity "to assure Savimbi that we support him, are proceeding on the aid front, and will not abandon him after an agreement on the withdrawal of foreign forces." Shultz also explained to Savimbi why the State Department (and official U.S. policy) opposed making national reconciliation a part of the negotiations.

In February 1986, Crocker explained American policy to members of the Senate Foreign Relations Committee. In comments that closely paralleled the newly approved NSDD 212, Crocker asserted that the United States would provide support to Savimbi "in an effective and appropriate manner," but also emphasized that "the basis and the goals of our policy remain unchanged: we seek a negotiated solution that will bring independence to Namibia and the withdrawal of Cuban forces from Angola. Such a solution opens the way for Angolans to reconcile and achieve peace amongst themselves" (U.S. Congress, Senate, Committee on Foreign Relations 1986a, 5). Crocker added that "diplomacy requires to be effective a degree of pressure that drives the parties toward a compromise. But pressures . . . do not . . . represent solutions. . . . As Secretary Shultz has put it, it takes both power and diplomacy" (ibid., 6). Finally, Crocker stated that Savimbi agreed that no military solution was possible and also desired a political settlement (ibid., 6). Senator Helms challenged Crocker on this point, insisting that only the State Department believed that UNITA was incapable of victory. Crocker responded by maintaining that even Savimbi agreed with the State Department's position (ibid., 13–16).[22] When pushed by Senator Helms to provide assurances of material assistance, Crocker told Helms that "there is such a thing as moral support, there is such a thing as material support. We want to do both, and we want to be effective and relevant to the problem that Dr. Savimbi faces" (ibid., 11).

While Crocker waited for the MPLA to indicate interest in resuming talks, the covert element of the strategy reached full implementation. At a refurbished base in Kamina, Zaire, the CIA and the Defense Department established a supply and training base for UNITA, pursuant to William Casey's preliminary arrangements in December 1985. The base began operation in March 1986; a contract airline called Santa Lucia Airways flew the operations, which grew to four or five flights of C-141 transports per week in 1987, shuttling between the United States, Kinshasa, and the Kamina airbase (Brooke 1987a, 1987b). These flights carried Stinger missiles to assist UNITA against Angolan and Cuban air attacks, a decision made by the NSPG at the same time as the 1986 Afghanistan policy decision (Rodman 1994, 372). In 1987, the administration increased the covert program to $18 million, and in 1988 to $40 million (Shultz 1993, 1124).

The last significant aspect of U.S. policy making in this phase occurred when members of the anti-aid faction in Congress attempted to renew some of the restrictions of the Clark amendment, including those requiring open debate and a congressional vote for aid. Representative Lee Hamilton, angered by the administration's decision to resort to covert aid and then discuss it publicly, offered legislation in March 1986 (H.R. 4276) that some referred to as "Son of Clark" or "Baby Clark" (U.S. Congress, House, Foreign Affairs Committee, Subcommittee on

Africa 1986c, 37, 43). Hamilton's House Intelligence Committee passed the bill on a party-line vote, but Foreign Affairs Committee chairman Dante Fascell and committee member Claude Pepper were adamantly opposed to the bill and killed it without sending it to the House floor (Felton 1986p, 2065–66; U.S. Congress, House, Committee on Foreign Affairs, Subcommittee on Africa 1986c; U.S. Congress, House, Permanent Select Committee on Intelligence 1986). Eventually, Hamilton attached the legislation (now H.R. 4759) to the intelligence authorization bill in July 1986 and forced it through the Intelligence Committee over the objections of all the Republican members. In September, the bill came to the floor and was defeated 229 to 186 (Blakely 1986, 2202–3). This vote marked the last effective challenge to U.S. aid to Savimbi's forces until 1989. By mid-1988, even some former UNITA critics were expressing support for the two-track approach (e.g., Felton 1988m).

Phase III: The Regional Diplomatic Solution Revisited, 1988

Between late 1985 and early 1988, the Angolans and the South Africans both attempted to resolve the conflict in Angola by force; the MPLA used its recently expanded forces to attack UNITA, and South Africa escalated its aid to UNITA and its operations against the MPLA as it had in 1983–84. Neither side was successful, and Crocker and his diplomatic team, who had waited more than a year for an opportunity, quickly seized on the developments. Their efforts produced the Brazzaville Accords, a set of agreements between Angola, South Africa, and Cuba that established a parallel schedule for the withdrawal of South African and Cuban troops from Namibia and Angola, respectively, and for elections and independence for Namibia. A protocol to the accords called for national reconciliation talks between the MPLA and UNITA to convene when the withdrawal process started. In effect, then, the application of the Reagan Doctrine, which many hard-line advocates hoped would replace the pursuit of a regional peace agreement, ultimately helped to produce such an agreement.

From military to diplomatic solutions. The day after the House repealed the Clark amendment, the MPLA regime suspended negotiations with the United States, noting that "the repeal of the Clark amendment will leave the US Administration and international imperialism free to openly and directly intervene in Angola and exercise military and political pressures on the Angolan State" (quoted in Legum 1988,

386). No further substantive talks took place until April 1987, and no progress was made until August 1987 (Crocker 1992, 348–52). During this two-year period a military stalemate developed, and its increasing cost to both sides made it more and more obvious that neither could win military victory (Freeman 1989, 132).

The MPLA offensives in August 1985 and 1987 were matched by increased South African intervention and American military aid to UNITA. Attacks by the MPLA in 1985 were countered by increased South African assistance, and the 1987 MPLA offensive that sent UNITA reeling toward its headquarters was stopped by critical South African support, including air and artillery bombardments and direct use of South African Defense Forces in battle. American aid was important because it increased both the price for MPLA and Cuban pilots and troops, and UNITA's defensive capabilities (Crocker 1992, 462), but it was dwarfed by the South African assistance, which involved vast amounts of supplies, transportation, and six thousand troops in battle (Zartman 1989, 226). A South African–UNITA counterattack sent the MPLA force into a long retreat back to the starting point of their offensive, at which point the U.S. Defense Intelligence Agency began to circulate estimates predicting imminent victory for UNITA (Marcum 1989, 165).[23] Increased Cuban and Soviet assistance blunted the UNITA drive and created another stalemate in central Angola (at the strategically critical town of Cuito Cuanavale). The costs of the new military stalemate reached unacceptable levels for both sides, eventually prompting each to signal its interest in another round of negotiations.

According to I. William Zartman, the most significant act leading up to this new diplomatic opening was a late 1987 Cuban initiative designed to shore up the MPLA, threaten South Africa, and establish the conditions for successful negotiations. Zartman (1989, 225, 227) argued that the Cubans raised the stakes by sending additional troops to Angola, increasing their combat activity at Cuito Cuanavale, and threatening maneuvers near the Namibian border. After indicating a desire to be involved in the negotiations, Castro drastically increased the number of Cuban troops in Angola, and Cuban aircraft dominated the battlefield in spite of the Stinger missiles (Crocker 1992, 353–58). In early 1988, the Cuban forces moved toward the Angola-Namibia border and conducted some limited attacks, threatening South African forces with a significant widening of the conflict (Marcum 1989, 165–66). Interestingly, as Crocker (1992, 384) described these events, both the MPLA and Cuba indicated before commencing the reinforcements and incursions that they intended to negotiate an agreement for the total withdrawal of the Cuban troops; in other words, the maneuvers were simply a bluff to compel negotiations.

In any event, by the spring of 1988 Cuba's gambit had convinced the South Africans that the costs were too high, and South Africa signaled that it too was ready for renewed talks. These developments were further buoyed by the effect of Soviet General Secretary Mikhail Gorbachev's reform efforts. John Marcum (1989, 164) believed that the Soviet Union was no longer willing to pay the political or economic price of having Angola as a client and began to search for ways to secure a peaceful resolution to the conflict (see also McFaul 1989, 115–22; Crocker 1992, 409–11). Crocker aptly characterized the situation as "the right alignment of local, regional, and international events—like planets lining up for some rare astronomical happening" (quoted in Zartman 1989, 234).

To the Brazzaville Accords: the diplomatic endgame. In July and November 1987, Dos Santos and Castro developed a strategy for a successful resolution of the conflict in Angola. Their discussions produced a decision to modify the MPLA's position on Cuban withdrawal to include all forces over a two-year period. Additionally, the MPLA requested that Cuba be granted a seat at the negotiations (Crocker 1992, 353–54). Dos Santos and Castro also decided to deploy Cuban troops to match increased South African and U.S. aid to UNITA and improve the MPLA's bargaining position. A flurry of talks between May and December 1988 produced a tripartite agreement between Angola, South Africa, and Cuba. Crocker's account of this period indicates that the MPLA started the process by agreeing in January 1988 to a two-year schedule for Cuban withdrawal. This was followed by U.S. talks in March with the South Africans, in which Crocker indicated that the MPLA was amenable to agreement on terms favorable to South Africa. The preliminary arrangements for the final diplomatic push were completed when, in January, Shultz approved the inclusion of Cuba in the talks (taking some heat from conservatives) and, in March, the Soviet Union became involved in the talks as a behind-the-scenes facilitator.

These arrangements prompted Representative Dante Fascell and Senator Dennis DeConcini and thirty-seven of his colleagues in the

Senate to protest the exclusion of UNITA from the negotiations (Rodman 1994, 387). However, by this time a change of personnel had occurred within the administration. As Crocker remembered it,

> The bureaucratic and personnel shake-up flowing from Iran-Contra and the departure of Bill Casey created a new foundation for the conduct of US foreign policy. The arrival of Frank Carlucci as NSC Advisor, followed by Howard Baker in place of Donald Regan as White House chief of staff, restored the basic coherence of White House structures. . . . [Carlucci's] selection of Hank Cohen—one of the ranking Africanists in the [Foreign] Service and my eventual successor as assistant secretary in 1989—as NSC Africa director reinforced the change and brought us an ally where we had often faced treachery in the past. (Crocker 1992, 343)

This new NSC staff supported the position developed several years previously by Crocker and Shultz on the question of UNITA. As described in a State Department cable from Crocker to Shultz, UNITA-MPLA reconciliation could not "be a precondition to a Namibia settlement. . . . This is a question for the Angolans themselves to resolve without outside interference—Cuban or South African—and we do not seek to interject ourselves into this problem unless asked by the parties to do so. . . . We believe that the withdrawal of Cuban forces and [Namibian independence] will create conditions for achieving political accommodation in Angola."[24] With the backing of the NSC staff and Shultz, the talks proceeded.

With the Cubans, Angolans, and South Africans all represented, Crocker convened talks in London in May 1988, in Cairo in June, and in New York in July. At the July meeting on Governor's Island, all parties signed the New York Principles, fourteen points that laid out the basic parameters of the negotiated settlement. Further rounds of talks in Cape Verde in late July and in Geneva in early August produced a detailed agreement on ending the war and subsequent procedures for disengagement. Three rounds of talks in Brazzaville in August and September produced progress toward a Cuban withdrawal schedule, but two more rounds in New York in October and early November produced nothing, in part because Savimbi denounced the developing accords. He had been convinced by some of his South African benefactors and several congressional staff members who traveled to Jamba that Crocker was "departing from established U.S. policy" and selling him out (Crocker 1992, 436; Shultz 1993, 1126). Additional efforts to re-assure Savimbi were necessary. After George Bush's election, another round of talks convened in Geneva that resulted in a final schedule for Cuban withdrawal. After two more rounds, on 13 December 1988 all three parties agreed, and the representatives met in New York on 22 December 1988 for final signatures on the document establishing the complex trilateral and bilateral agreements (Crocker 1992, 373–446).

Decried as a "giveaway" by hard-liners (e.g., Menges 1988c, 1990, 131–41), the final schedule (included in the appendix to Crocker 1992) required the initial withdrawal of three thousand Cubans. Then, on 1 April 1989, the seven-month timetable established in UN Security Council Resolution 435 for South Africa's withdrawal from Namibia began; at the same time a twenty-seven-month schedule for total Cuban withdrawal from Angola started. By 1 November 1989 all the Cuban troops had been redeployed to the north, 50 percent had actually left, and Namibian elections were held. By 1 April 1990, two-thirds of the Cubans were out of Angola; by 1 October 1990 76 percent had been withdrawn. Total withdrawal was to be completed by 30 June 1991, but the Cuban troops were all withdrawn five weeks ahead of time (Crocker 1992, 488).

Phase IV: Maintaining the Reagan Doctrine, 1989–1993

The application of Reagan Doctrine to Angola survived into the Bush administration. Bush assured Savimbi after the 1988 elections that U.S. assistance would continue until the Angolan regime agreed to national reconciliation with UNITA (Rodman 1994, 391).[25] American assistance grew from approximately $20 million in 1987 to more than $40 million in 1989 (Weitz 1992, 63). Some reports indicate that aid may have reached as much as $60–90 million in 1990 (Schraeder 1992b, 146; Tvedten 1992, 44). This extension of the strategy to deal with the conflict between UNITA and the MPLA proved problematic. In fact, many of the moderates who had supported aid when the Cuban troops were present were more reluctant after the troops had been withdrawn, and dissent increased between 1989 and 1991, when the aid finally ceased (Rodman 1994, 392–93). In April 1989, for example, the House Foreign Affairs Subcommittee on Africa staged a hearing on the question of continued aid to UNITA, prompted by new reports of atrocities committed by UNITA. Many members of the panel, including some moderates, expressed concern, but hard-liners maintained firm support for Savimbi's forces (see U.S. Congress, House, Committee on Foreign Affairs, Subcommittee on Africa 1989).

Holding to the two-track approach and working with the Soviet Union, the State Department continued to try to hammer out an agreement between Savimbi and the Angolan regime. An early deal brokered by African leaders fell apart in the summer of 1989 over disagreements regarding the role of Savimbi and UNITA in the government, and the MPLA began a new military campaign against UNITA (Gunn 1990, 215–16, 234; Weitz 1992, 64–65). This prompted another hearing, in which Savimbi's commitment to democracy and peace was questioned. Many blamed him for the collapse of the agreement, and the majority of the panel suggested that the United States should abandon its support for UNITA and adopt a more balanced role (U.S. Congress, House, Committee on Foreign Affairs, Subcommittee on Africa 1990).

The Bush administration did not react to the collapse. Instead, the State Department continued its pursuit of a peace settlement while the CIA continued applying the Reagan Doctrine. In the face of the pressing events occurring in Eastern Europe in 1989 and in the Persian Gulf in 1990, the White House had little inclination to focus on Angola. Moreover, several other factors help to explain the adherence to the status quo. First, the continuation of the internal conflict in Angola appeared to be endless, causing some high-level officials to lose interest. Second, throughout 1989 the slow transition between the Reagan administration and the Bush administration left many key mid-level and lower-level foreign policy positions open, which led to the continuation of existing policies. Third, and even more important, hard-liners in Congress and the administration pressed for extension of the aid. Their unity daunted critics, and moderate elements of the administration were unwilling to challenge them (Gunn 1990, 213, 215, 216, 234).

This left the field to Congress, but it too was divided on the issue and diverted by more pressing items. Eventually, however, in the absence of leadership from the White House, Congress began to act. In October 1990, Congress approved $60 million for UNITA but put half of that into a restricted account that required a congressional vote for access. Thus, $30 million was earmarked for 1991, most of which was for lethal assistance (Lardner 1990). Negotiations restarted in 1990 because of two developments: (1) the Soviets agreed to pressure the MPLA regime to make some concessions to UNITA (Weitz 1992, 66–68), and

(2) conservative supporters of Savimbi, reading the handwriting left by the 1990 aid cut, told the UNITA leader that negotiations were the only option left (Rodman 1994, 396).

From mid-1990 on, Portugal chaired a series of talks between UNITA and the regime in an attempt to break the diplomatic deadlock. In December 1990, the United States and the Soviet Union cosponsored a Washington, D.C., meeting between the Angolan factions with Portuguese intermediaries. At these talks, the warring parties agreed to the "Washington Concepts Paper," which laid out a framework for a new round of talks and brought the United States and the Soviet Union into the talks as official observers (H. Cohen 1991). The new framework led to several rounds of negotiations, which culminated in a May 1991 agreement on a cease-fire, disarmament, and free elections in 1992 (Gunn 1990, 234). At this point, American covert military aid, and therefore the application of Reagan Doctrine, ceased, according to a provision in the May 1991 agreement, which also banned Portuguese and Soviet assistance to either party (Holmes 1993b). The Bush administration provided some humanitarian assistance to UNITA and other aid to both sides to assist in the preparations for the elections, but Congress restricted the funds appropriated for the year for use only to transform the guerrilla army into a political party (Finkel 1992, 61).

The problem raised by continued Reagan Doctrine aid to UNITA was revealed after the elections were held as scheduled in October 1992. In a process certified by all observers as free and fair, José Eduardo Dos Santos won, gaining more than 49 percent of the vote to Savimbi's 40 percent. To the dismay of most observers, Savimbi immediately denounced the elections as fraudulent and renewed UNITA's war on the MPLA, actions which suggested that he wanted power, not democracy (Davidow 1992). Efforts by the United States, South Africa, and African leaders to persuade Savimbi to give up the armed struggle and abide by the results failed. When Assistant Secretary of State for African Affairs Herman Cohen contacted Savimbi and encouraged him to accept the results and ask for investigations of the fraud allegations, Savimbi told Cohen to "go to Hell!" (Meldrum 1992, 26).

The MPLA regime drove UNITA back into the bush, and UNITA counterattacked and plunged the country into a general war once again (Finkel 1993, 26–28; Marcum 1993a, 222; Meldrum 1993b, 45–46). In April 1993 the MPLA accepted a Clinton administration peace proposal for a runoff election between Savimbi and Dos Santos, but UNITA rejected the plan. This led the Clinton administration to extend diplomatic recognition to the MPLA-led government, abandoning support for UNITA after seven years of official backing and nearly twenty years of implicit endorsement. On 19 May 1993, the Clinton administration formally recognized the government of Angola led by President Dos Santos, and a short time later officially lifted the ban on selling military matériel to that country (Clinton 1993; Holmes 1993a, 1993b).

The cycle of violence between the MPLA and UNITA increased significantly in 1993–94. One reporter in Luanda described the situation as "probably worse than at any time in the country's history" (Simpson 1993, 594), and another characterized Angola as "the world's worst war" (Shiner 1994, 13). Nearly fifty thousand Angolans died in the renewed fighting, which continued until both sides accepted a cease-fire agreement in November 1994. Preparations for a runoff election between Savimbi and Dos Santos ensued (see *Africa Report*, November–December 1994, 7; Keller 1995).

Conclusions: The Reagan Doctrine and Angola

The application of the Reagan Doctrine to Angola occurred through the complex interaction of three factions that cut across the lines that separate Congress and the executive branch. The three groups —hard-liners, pragmatists, and liberals—took predictable positions. Hard-liners wanted to focus on the communist threat to the region, support South Africa as an anticommunist ally, and provide aid to UNITA to overthrow the MPLA regime and force out the Soviet-Cuban presence. Liberals wanted to force South Africa to abandon its regional aggression and internal repression. Moderates embraced a diplomatic solution that would deal first with cross-border conflict and then address domestic injustice in the region, combining "carrots" and "sticks" for both South Africa and Angola. A surprisingly effective combination of force and diplomacy emerged from the competition between these rival alliances, which resulted in a regional peace settlement in 1988.

Yet, in part because of these divisions and the contradictory actions they prompted, the extent to which U.S. policy, and especially the Reagan Doctrine, contributed to the 1988 and 1991 settlements is difficult to determine. Both Crocker (1992) and Shultz (1993) gave partial credit for the 1988 agreements to U.S. support for UNITA. Some analysts concur with this assessment. Richard Weitz (1992, 68), writing after the 1991 peace agreement between UNITA and the MPLA, argued that "the Reagan Doctrine . . . played a decisive role in moderating the Soviet government's policies toward the conflict." Therefore, "the Reagan Doctrine defeated Moscow in Angola." Ben Martin (1989, 46) agreed in part, noting that the Reagan Doctrine was a component of an effective mix of carrots and sticks. Anthony Pazzanita (1992, 114) was less certain, noting the importance of the U.S. framework for the agreement but concluding that the settlements resulted largely from "events beyond the timing or control" of the United States. Other analysts gave no credit to the Reagan Doctrine at all. Writing before the 1991 settlement between UNITA and the MPLA, Michael McFaul (1989, 100) argued that "the settlement between Angola, Cuba, and South Africa was achieved despite, not because of, the Reagan Doctrine." McFaul attributed the settlement to "the diplomatic efforts of Assistant Secretary of State Chester Crocker, changes in Angolan foreign and domestic policy, and Soviet 'new thinking.' " Inge Tvedten (1992, 32, 52), writing after the 1991 MPLA-UNITA accords, concluded that the application of the Reagan Doctrine, especially after 1988, "significantly delayed finding a lasting political solution to the Angolan problem" and noted "the serious negative consequences . . . of a US policy that was based on ideological misconceptions, as well as a profound misunderstanding of the political and economic realities in Angola." As these contradictory conclusions indicate, the record is mixed. There is some evidence to support both inferences.

Two questions regarding the Reagan Doctrine in Angola require answers. First, did the application of the doctrine help to achieve the regional peace settlement in 1988? The record suggests that, given the events prior to mid-1985, U.S. assistance to UNITA reinforced an internal stalemate, which helped to persuade the MPLA to return to the negotiations in 1987 (see, e.g., Crocker 1992, 463). Nearly all observers agree that both South Africa and the MPLA returned to the bargaining table because of the military stalemate; Reagan Doctrine aid was a limited contributor to that stalemate by helping to improve UNITA's performance, although the estimated $200 million per year provided by South Africa was obviously much more significant. Furthermore, even the highly touted provision of Stinger missiles to UNITA apparently did little good: Angolan and Cuban air power achieved almost total superiority over Angola in 1987–88. Hence, if the situation in mid-1985 is accepted as a given, Reagan Doctrine assistance probably played a positive, though limited, role in the resolution of the regional issue. That the MPLA returned to the bargaining table after failing to achieve a military victory constitutes the primary evidence that Reagan Doctrine aid helped to resolve, not prolong, the conflict.

Several caveats should be noted, however. First, it is by no means clear that the intransigence and obstructionism that stymied the negotiations in 1985 were the fault of the MPLA, as Crocker (1992, 296) candidly admitted. The MPLA military actions that began in 1985 and required U.S. and South African efforts just to reinforce a stalemate were clearly a response to persistent South African and UNITA attacks from 1981 to 1985. Detractors of the Reagan Doctrine's application to Angola are correct in noting that efforts to prevent those attacks prior to 1985 might well have obviated the need for Reagan Doctrine assistance altogether. The MPLA's willingness to negotiate the withdrawal of Cuban troops linked to a simultaneous resolution of the Namibian conflict, which was expressed as late as January 1985, further supports this argument. Second, given the situation as it existed in 1985, increased Cuban and Soviet assistance probably played an important role in convincing South Africa and UNITA that they could not achieve a military victory. Third, Gorbachev's reassessment of Soviet foreign policy was clearly significant in the MPLA's decision to seek a political solution to the conflict (McFaul 1989; Pazzanita 1991). Fourth, it is clear that the U.S. decision to aid Savimbi contributed to a lengthy intermission between substantive talks from 1985 to 1987, as the MPLA sought a military solution. However, given the military situation, the hiatus might well have occurred anyway. Finally, the complex mix of inducements and threats clearly contributed to the settlement. The promise of an end to South African aid to UNITA and South African raids in Angola, the prospects of better ties and increased contacts with the United States (especially economic), and the structured diplomatic framework that addressed the security concerns of each of the parties were at least as important as aid to UNITA.

The second pressing question is whether continued application of the Reagan Doctrine aided in the resolution of the internal Angolan conflict after 1988. Here the answer is clearer, because it is by no means certain that the conflict has been settled. It is, in fact, difficult to find a positive contribution from continued U.S. assistance after the December 1988 accord. Events after 1988 indicate that continued (indeed, increased) American support probably reinforced Savimbi's inclination to reject a power-sharing agreement in mid-1989. Moreover, as Mark Katz (1991) persuasively argued, continued U.S. aid almost certainly prompted the Soviet Union to assist the MPLA in its late-1989 decision to widen military efforts against UNITA. Hence, rather than helping to resolve the conflict, U.S. aid contributed to an additional two years of warfare. However, given the MPLA offensive of 1990, combined with U.S. pressure on Savimbi to negotiate and on Moscow to encourage the MPLA to return to the bargaining table (e.g., Weitz 1992), American aid to UNITA helped to produce the 1991 peace agreement by again reinforcing a stalemate. The fact that U.S. policy helped create the situation in which continued U.S. aid was required cannot be ignored, however.

The costs of continued application of the Reagan Doctrine became even clearer with the 1992 Angolan election fiasco, which revealed the oversimplification on which American policy rested. The logic of the Reagan Doctrine and the Manichaean view of the world that it fostered perpetuated the fiction that the MPLA regime was a Marxist client of the Soviet Union and UNITA was a democratic resistance movement led by "one of the greatest living people in the world today," as Senator Steven Symms once labeled Savimbi (Felton 1986c, 264). In fact, neither image was accurate, and there was little difference between the MPLA and UNITA. The regime was not the totalitarian government that its detractors suggested, and it embarked on a perestroika of its own after 1985. As critics of U.S. policy repeatedly pointed out, the MPLA regime was engaged in significant reforms designed to open Angola to the West (see, e.g., Tvedten 1992; J. Scott 1993, 196–206). Moreover, UNITA was not committed to liberal democracy, either for Angola or within its own organization (see, e.g., J. Scott 1993, 206–17). Savimbi was committed to his own power. Longtime Angola watcher John Marcum (1989, 162) described Savimbi as "a political chameleon of passing persuasion but steady ambition," and one of Savimbi's early supporters, CIA officer John Stockwell, commented that "the only common denominator [in Savimbi's behavior] is his megalomaniacal determination to install himself in power" (Felton 1986c, 265). These realities were driven home with Savimbi's rejection of the election results and his decision to return to war. The carnage that resulted from the next two years of escalating violence must be partly attributed to U.S. policy makers who determined to continue aiding Savimbi.

It seems clear that a much more appropriate decision would have involved an active search for a political settlement and the abandonment of the Reagan Doctrine. As in Afghanistan, the United States lost sight of its primary goal (regional stability and Cuban-Soviet withdrawal). This was, quite clearly, due to the views of hard-liners in the U.S. government, for whom all conflicts were a function of U.S.-Soviet competition. Their determination to see the MPLA overthrown and UNITA installed in power was based on a Manichaean interpretation of the Angolan conflict that barely resembled reality.

Three final comments are in order. First, whatever contribution the Reagan Doctrine made in Angola stems directly from the success of pragmatists in embedding U.S. aid within a broader framework of diplomacy and inducements. The preferred policy of the hard-liners —outright alignment with UNITA and South Africa to overthrow the MPLA regime—did not become U.S. policy. Their adamant position that neither the MPLA nor the Cubans would negotiate in good faith and their view that victory could be achieved only through the direct action of the Defense Department and the CIA proved erroneous. Instead, to the extent that the Reagan Doctrine made a positive contribution, it was to a regional diplomatic settlement that not only required the withdrawal of Cuban troops from Angola but also South African troops from Namibia. In creating the "stick" represented by the Reagan Doctrine, hard-liners contributed, perhaps inadvertently, to the regional accord. That this occurred was due in no small measure to the Shultz-Crocker approach, much maligned by hard-liners in the administration and Congress. It should also be noted, however, that the fears of liberals were misplaced: the application of the Reagan Doctrine did not destroy the regional negotiations or align the United States with South Africa.

Second, it is difficult to identify a connection between U.S. actions in the region and broader U.S.-Soviet relations. The increased costs to the Soviet Union caused by both Afghanistan and Angola may have contributed to Soviet pressure on the MPLA in 1988 to negotiate. It is more difficult, however, to attribute broader Soviet "new-thinking" to the application of the Reagan Doctrine in Angola. Soviet costs were minimal, and the sequence of events suggests that the Soviet reforms began before the Angolan breakthrough. Furthermore, since the Reagan Doctrine did not roll back the MPLA regime, it cannot have had the same effect as U.S. aid to the Afghan rebels.

Finally, although it is purely speculative, the parallel developments in Mozambique (see Chapter 7) give plausibility to another argument: the Angolan "restructuring" was inevitable given economic and political necessities. In this argument, had the policy makers in the United States more accurately assessed the causes of the conflict in southern Africa and anticipated the dynamics of economic and political imperatives within the region, they might have achieved the same results—a regional peace settlement, the withdrawal of Cuban troops, and the realignment of the Angolan regime—through offering "carrots" and opposing South Africa's attempts at destabilization (see, e.g., Bender 1987, 1988; Tvedten 1992). This course, urged by Representatives Howard Wolpe and Steven Solarz, among others, might have produced Mozambique-like results at a lower cost to the United States and, more important, to the Angolan people.

In the end, as in Afghanistan, the Reagan Doctrine probably contributed to the settlement of the regional dispute in southern Africa in 1988, but it is difficult to find a positive contribution from its application to the civil war in Angola after that time. It is perhaps significant that one year after the Clinton administration recognized the MPLA and ceased its support for UNITA, Savimbi was forced to agree to a new cease-fire agreement, in November 1994. As it took effect, observers noted that even among his Ovimbundo people, Savimbi's support in Angola had waned because of his costly decision to return to war.[26]

6

Nicaragua: Polarization, Stalemate, and the Contra War

The most publicized and controversial application of the Reagan Doctrine occurred in Nicaragua. Aid to the insurgency there provoked a six-year struggle between Congress and the administration over the purposes and tactics of U.S. policy. In that struggle, Congress tried to push the administration in a direction that many in the executive branch did not wish to go, and some members of the Reagan administration attempted to evade congressional restrictions and defy the law in order to provide assistance to the anticommunist rebels. The stalemate that occurred after 1983 prevented Reagan administration officials from pursuing the policy they favored. By 1987, the policy that emerged from the clash between members of Congress and the administration reflected congressional rather than presidential priorities.

Background

As a part of the Western Hemisphere, Latin America has long been regarded as the rightful domain of U.S. interests and protection, a kind of backyard that must be kept peaceful and secure.[1] Amos Jordan et al. (1989, 458–65) suggested at least six U.S. interests in Latin America: a peaceful, secure southern flank; the Panama Canal; access to trade, materials, and investment opportunities; stability; support for U.S. foreign and security policies; and democracy and human rights. According to Harold Molineau (1986, 11), the most important objectives of the United States in pursuit of these interests have been the maintenance of friendly states and the prevention of hostile influence in the region. U.S. relations with Nicaragua demonstrate this nicely. Although Nicaragua achieved independence from Spain in 1821 and established its own government in 1838, it has been dominated by the United States for most of its history. In 1893, José Santos Zelaya led an attempt to increase and diversify foreign investment by opening negotiations with Japan and Europe to construct a transisthmian canal. The United States objected and supported an insurrection by landing four hundred U.S. Marines on the Caribbean coast in 1909 (Booth 1985, 24–27; Pastor 1987, 21). U.S. troops continued to occupy Nicaragua for nineteen of the next twenty-three years. In the 1920s, in the face of a guerrilla war led by Augusto Cesar Sandino, the United States created a Nicaraguan National Guard and installed Anastasio Somoza García, who was pro-United States, to lead it (Booth 1985, 41–50).

Over the next few years, Anastasio Somoza García, known as "Tacho," maneuvered his way into supreme political power in Nicaragua.[2] He then had Sandino assassinated and, in 1935, himself elected president. He was succeeded by his sons, Luís and Anastasio Somoza Debayle ("Tachito"). When Tacho was assassinated in 1956, Tachito ensured that power passed to his brother, Luís. Luís and Tachito ruled Nicaragua through the presidency or through puppets until Tachito assumed the office in 1967, where he remained until he was overthrown in 1979. The benefit these autocratic rulers brought to the United States was summarized by Tachito: Nicaragua was "totally aligned with the United States and the Western world" (quoted in Lafeber 1983, 226).

Resistance to the Somoza dynasty began in 1959 but only simmered until the combination of economic stagnation and the Managua earthquake in 1972 prompted new outbreaks (Gilbert 1988, 6). In 1974, the Sandinista National Liberation Front (FSLN) conducted very high profile attacks on the regime (Booth 1985, 141–42). Resistance continued to increase until Pedro Joaquin Chamorro, editor of the opposition newspaper *La Prensa,* was murdered by pro-Somoza forces on 10 January 1978, touching off the final stage of the overthrow of the Somoza regime. The failure of the United States and other Latin American countries to mediate a settlement between Somoza and the opposition in December 1978 prompted the various moderate elements to join with the FSLN (Pastor 1987, 122–23). In May 1979, the resistance began its "final offensive" by invading Nicaragua from Costa Rica and Honduras (Booth 1985, 174–76). The Carter administration scrambled to keep the FSLN from power, attempting to save the National Guard, create a new junta, establish an executive committee to replace Somoza, and create an Organization of American States (OAS) "peacekeeping" force, all in the final four to five weeks of the Somoza regime (Pastor 1987, chs. 8–9). Nevertheless, Tachito fled, the National Guard collapsed, and the FSLN swept into Managua on 20 July 1979.

There is no doubt that the FSLN was guided by Marxist principles and a belief in the destructive nature of U.S. imperialism.[3] Once in power, however, the Sandinistas established a mixed economic and political system incorporating some private ownership and some state-run farms and businesses (Austen et al. 1985, 16; Spalding 1987, 43–60), some political freedom and some repression and intimidation of opposition movements (see, e.g., Gastil 1985, America's Watch 1985a, 1986; Booth 1985, ch. 10; McColm 1991). In addition, the FSLN began a political, economic, and security relationship with the Soviet Union in 1980. The political support began immediately. Economic assistance from the USSR, initially limited, grew with the desperate state of the Nicaraguan economy. Finally, the regime received substantial military assistance; figures published by the U.S. Arms Control and Disarmament Agency showed a steadily increasing flow of Soviet support to Nicaragua. According to the Stockholm International Peace Research Institute (SIPRI), however, weapons sales from Moscow peaked in 1984 and 1986 and fell thereafter.[4] According to the International Institute for Strategic Studies (in the annual *Strategic Survey*), Soviet (100–150) and Cuban advisers (more than 4,000 in 1988) were also present.

Faced with the reality of a Sandinista-led government in Nicaragua, the Carter administration initially tried to forge friendly relations. Carter requested aid for the new regime in 1979 and stated his administration's desire to maintain constructive ties (Lafeber 1983, 240; Christian 1986, 136). When the FSLN began to curtail democratic freedoms, President Carter signed an intelligence finding initiating a covert program of assistance for moderate and democratic elements within Nicaragua, including business and labor groups, political parties, and the press (Christian 1986, 109–10; Pastor 1987, 202–12). When the U.S. Congress blocked the promised economic aid package, the Nicaraguan government turned to the Soviet Union for emergency assistance with oil, agriculture, transportation, and communications (T. Walker 1991a, 119–20).

In June 1980, Congress finally passed the aid bill. The Carter administration considered this aid a critical source of influence on the Nicaraguan government. Assistant Secretary of State for Inter-American

Affairs Viron Vaky argued that the offer of aid and support for debt rescheduling provided the United States with potential levers for inducing moderation from the Nicaraguan regime (Lafeber 1983, 242). However, the aid was not authorized until September 1980, and after evidence that Nicaragua was supporting rebels in El Salvador increased in December, Carter quietly suspended the assistance on 16 January 1981 (de Onis 1981a, 3; Sullivan 1987, 8). This final decision set the stage for the Reagan administration to confront the Sandinista regime.

In the final year of the Carter administration, rebel groups, mainly former Somoza National Guard forces, formed in Honduras, providing the opportunity for the Reagan administration to begin to supply aid. Although a number of groups eventually made up the contras (short for *contra-revolucionarios*), the largest component and recipient of U.S. aid was the Nicaraguan Democratic Force (FDN).[5] The FDN and its military wing were dominated by former members of the National Guard (Pastor 1987, 207; Serafino 1987a, 8); according to the U.S. Congress's Arms Control and Foreign Policy Caucus (1985) forty-six of forty-eight top contra commanders were Somocistas. Although a U.S. State Department analysis maintained that only 30 percent of the 153 top military commanders were from the National Guard (Shultz 1986, 34, 38; U.S. State Department 1986, 1988, 27), both studies are accurate. Thirty percent of 153 is about 46; hence the State Department added low-level officers to dilute the percentage of former national guard present in the FDN to mask their real influence. The political wing, organized by the U.S. State Department, consisted primarily of democratically oriented anti-Somocistas, some of whom had worked with the Sandinistas to overthrow Somoza (Shultz 1986, 34). The rank and file, which increased from a few hundred fighters to fifteen to twenty thousand in 1987, consisted of peasants who joined the resistance because of the failing economy and the policies of the FSLN, the increasingly centralized and polarized political system, the forced conscription, and the repression and forced relocation programs (L. Robinson 1991, 8–16).

The contras had three weaknesses. First, while small groups initially formed on their own, the larger group was hampered by its almost complete dependence on "political, material, and particularly psychological support" from the United States (Radu 1990a, 259). This was especially true of the political wing: according to a 1986 memorandum from Robert Owen, a consultant to the National Security Council Staff, to Oliver North, an NSC staff officer, the political organization was "a creation of the USG [United States government] to garner support from Congress," and it could not control the military wing, which Owen characterized as corrupt, power hungry, and ineffective.[6] Second, there were persistent reports of contra violence and brutality against civilians (e.g., America's Watch 1985b). Third, although optimism survived in certain circles of the administration and Congress, the CIA estimated that "there are no circumstances under which a force of US-backed rebels can achieve a military victory over the leftist Sandinista government" (*Washington Post,* 25 November 1983). By 1984, most observers agreed with deputy CIA director Robert Gates's assessment: "The Contras, even with American support, cannot overthrow the Sandinista regime. . . . Even a well funded Contra movement cannot prevent [the strengthening of the regime and an expansion of influence in Central America]; relying on and supporting the Contras as our only action may actually hasten the ultimate unfortunate outcome."[7]

U.S. Policy and the Reagan Doctrine

The Reagan Doctrine was first applied to Nicaragua in March 1981. The doctrine passed through three phases between then and March 1989, when a bipartisan accord between the new Bush administration and Congress ended the policy. The first phase lasted from March 1981 to December 1982 and amounted to a White House–led policy of aiding the Nicaraguan rebels. The second phase, from December 1982 to August 1987, consisted of an increasingly tendentious interbranch struggle to shape policy toward Nicaragua. The third phase, lasting from August 1987 to March 1989, resulted in the ascendance of congressional priorities over the White House. One caveat must be stated, however: Between June 1984 and October 1986 there was a covert effort to evade congressional restrictions by using the NSC staff and a private network of suppliers to raise funds and provide supplies, training, advice, and intelligence. This effort provided the contras with at least $40 million in aid obtained from private U.S. donors, the governments of Saudi Arabia, Taiwan, and profits from the secret sale of weapons to Iran. Thus, while Congress was asserting itself, the White House was taking steps to limit the effectiveness of such "intrusions." In a broad sense, this evasion is a good example of a potential outcome of White House–Congress clashes.

Phase I: The Application of the Reagan Doctrine, 1981–1982

The White House and the foreign policy bureaucracy dominated the first phase of the Reagan Doctrine as applied to Nicaragua. These groups set the agenda, formulated options, selected a course, and implemented it. Only after the policy was implemented did Congress become involved.

Raising the issue to the agenda. The Reagan Doctrine was raised to the U.S. foreign policy agenda even before Ronald Reagan took office. As a candidate in the 1980 election, Ronald Reagan advocated the elimination of all assistance to the Nicaraguan government (Walsh 1993, 1). He also endorsed the 1980 Republican Platform, which condemned the "Marxist Sandinista takeover of Nicaragua" and supported the "efforts of the Nicaraguan people to establish a free and independent government" (*New York Times,* 3 July 1980). Immediately after Reagan took office, high-ranking policy makers focused on the issue. In January 1981 the Reagan administration threatened to suspend aid unless the Nicaraguan government ceased supporting the El Salvadoran rebels, which the Carter administration discovered was occurring in late 1980 (Pastor 1987, 218–29, 231–33). In February, a State Department report (U.S. Department of State 1981a) assembled the administration's case against Nicaraguan and Cuban interference in El Salvador. Food aid (P.L. 480) was canceled in February (de Onis 1981b, 4), and the remaining $15 million allocated for economic assistance was canceled in April 1981. In its announcement on 1 April, the State Department (1981b, 71) acknowledged that "the Nicaraguan response has been positive. We have no hard evidence of arms movements through Nicaragua during the past few weeks, and propaganda and some other support activities have been curtailed." Despite Nicaragua's compliance with U.S. demands, however, the State Department declared that "some arms traffic may be continuing" and announced that aid would be canceled. U.S. ambassador to Nicaragua Lawrence Pezzullo maintained that the Sandinistas "decommissioned the airplanes . . . released the Costa Rican pilots who were flying . . . and ripped up the whole process" by which aid was provided to the El Salvador guerrillas in response to the U.S. demands. Pezzullo, who had been excluded from the final decision to cancel the aid in April 1981, believed that the decision destroyed an opportunity for peaceful settlement of the issue (Gutman 1988, 36–38).

After the aid cutoff, the administration began to formulate more coercive measures to confront the Sandinista regime. In February 1981, Robert McFarlane, then an assistant to Secretary of State Alexander Haig, submitted a proposal for covert action in Central America calling for a coordinated political, economic, propaganda, military, and covert approach to the crisis.[8] This proposal, the foundation of which CIA director William Casey desired to expand into a global campaign of assistance to insurgents in eight countries (Kornbluh 1987, 23–24; Persico 1990, 264; Schweizer 1994, 22–23), brought the issue to the White House.

Formulating the application of the Reagan Doctrine. The National Security Planning Group (NSPG; William Casey, Alexander Haig, Richard Allen, Jeane Kirkpatrick, and Caspar Weinberger) considered alternative actions in March 1981. This meeting produced a proposal for a $19.5 million covert program to support domestic opposition groups in Nicaragua and to provide some funds to develop the anti-Sandinista forces gathering in Honduras (U.S. Congress, House, Select Committee to Investigate Covert Arms Transactions with Iran, and Senate, Select Committee on Secret Military Assistance to Iran and the Nicaraguan Opposition [ICFR] 1987a, 31). President Reagan signed an intelligence finding authorizing the program after Casey presented his plan at a March meeting of the National Security Council. Casey brought the relatively vague finding to the House and Senate Intelligence Committees, describing political and propaganda activities in Nicaragua and a regional effort to stop the flow of weapons to El Salvador (Pastor 1987, 237).

The covert aid program allocated $19.5 million for clandestine support to business, labor, political parties, and the press, as did the 1980 Carter program (Kornbluh 1987, 23). However, this seemingly innocuous continuation of the Carter program was expanded by Director Casey and Duane Clarridge (chief of the Central American Task Force, CIA, 1981–84) to develop support for the paramilitary forces organizing in Honduras (Moreno 1990, 103). Roy Gutman (1988, 39–57) credited Casey, Clarridge, and Colonel Gustavo Alvarez of Honduras with the early decision to use these forces, most of which were former national guard officers and soldiers. By this time in the spring, some groups were already training with Cuban exiles in camps in Florida and California (Riding 1981e; S. Taylor 1981; Thomas 1981a, 1981b; Lindsey 1982; *New York Times*, 12 January 1982).

At least initially, this limited forerunner to Reagan Doctrine aid was linked to a diplomatic initiative. Assistant Secretary of State for Inter-American Affairs Thomas Enders and Ambassador Lawrence Pezzullo opened negotiations with the Sandinistas to try to convince them to cease their military buildup and their support for the rebels in El Salvador (LeoGrande 1986, 91–94; Gutman 1988, 58–87). Enders and Pezzulo attempted to use the threat of pressure and the promise of U.S. aid as levers to induce the Sandinistas to moderate their foreign policy and reduce their ties to the Soviet Union. In August 1981, Enders offered to enter into a nonaggression treaty with Nicaragua, make an effort to "encourage the Nicaragua exiles [in the United States] to moderate their behavior," and ask Congress to renew economic assistance. In return the United States expected the Sandinistas to "stop training and supplying Salvadoran guerrillas, to give pluralism a chance in their country . . . and to limit their military buildup" (Enders 1982a, 77).

Enders's approach failed for two reasons. First, the Sandinistas rejected the proposal, noting that the United States was promising only to make efforts to satisfy Sandinista concerns regarding paramilitary groups and economic aid (LeoGrande 1986, 92). Second, administration hard-liners Casey, Weinberger, Kirkpatrick, William Clark (consultant to the State Department and friend to Reagan), and others objected to the initiative and blocked it. According to William LeoGrande (1986, 91), this "war party . . . successfully blocked any settlement that would require coexistence with Managua because that would end any hope of getting Nicaragua back from communism." Attempts to follow up on the proposal produced more suspicion, and the diplomatic overture died in October 1981. From that point, within the administration "the covert and overt warriors replaced the diplomats" (Pastor 1987, 235).

The collapse of the diplomatic initiative prompted a second round of policy formulation in 1981, which was heavily influenced by the efforts of Casey and his Latin America division chief, Duane Clarridge, to organize the disparate anti-Sandinista groups in Honduras and Miami into a unified resistance movement. According to Roy Gutman (1988, 57), Clarridge visited Honduras in August 1981 and announced U.S. support for the anti-Sandinista forces "in the name of the president." In fact, according to L. Craig Johnstone, a State Department official in the Bureau for Inter-American Affairs, the approach to the anti-Sandinista forces and Honduras was undertaken on the assumption that Enders's diplomatic approach would fail; if it had succeeded, the paramilitary option being prepared would have been dropped (ibid., 80). Instead, the collapse of the diplomatic initiative—engineered in part by administration officials—prompted a Central American policy review in a restricted interagency group (RIG) consisting of Duane Clarridge, Thomas Enders, General Paul Gorman (representing the Joint Chiefs), Nestor Sanchez (representing the Office of the Secretary of Defense), and either Alfonso Sapia-Bosch or Oliver North (representing the NSC staff). The RIG developed an options paper with a list of alternatives that was presented at a National Security Council meeting on 16 November 1981 (Kornbluh 1987, 24; Arson 1989, 76).[9] According to the options paper, which was leaked to the press, that list included military action against Cuba, an interdiction force in Nicaragua, a paramilitary action to overthrow the Sandinista government, and limited political aid to Nicaraguan opposition groups (*New York Times*, 17 March 1982).

After discussion, the members of the NSC agreed on the paramilitary option, but, according to a memorandum by Robert Gates, there was "no agreement within the administration . . . on our real objectives."[10] Many administration officials felt that the other options were either too costly or too extreme, and "there was no other way to do it" (William Casey, quoted in Rodman 1994, 237). The essential disagreement was between those seeking rollback and those desiring containment (LeoGrande 1986; Cannon 1991, 354–56). In the RIG, for example, Enders supported the paramilitary option as a means to pressure the Sandinistas into accepting the American diplomatic offer, while Clarridge advocated the option to overthrow the Sandinista regime. Casey, the chief proponent of contra aid, argued that aiding the contras would moderate Sandinista behavior and discourage subversion elsewhere. The others at the meeting supported this program for a variety of reasons: Weinberger, James Baker, and Michael Deaver as a way to avoid direct American military involvement; Edwin Meese to prevent inaction; and Haig as a suboptimal substitute for direct action against Cuba (Gutman 1988, 60–81; Cannon 1991, 354–56; Pastor 1992, 68, 198). In a memorandum to Casey, Robert Gates concluded that the compromise produced a "half-hearted policy."[11]

President Reagan signed National Security Decision Directive 17 approving a $20 million program to organize anti-Sandinista rebels against "the Cuban presence and Cuban-Sandinista support structure in Nicaragua and elsewhere in Central America" on 17 November

1981. On 1 December he signed an intelligence finding authorizing the program assigning the responsibility for organizing a five-hundred-member "interdiction force" to the CIA.[12] Classified attachments to NSDD 17 (in National Security Archive 1990) authorized the CIA to take unilateral action against the Nicaraguan government but were not submitted to Congress with the finding. This program, pursuant to Executive Order 12333, which designated the NSC as the "highest Executive Branch entity that provides review of, guidance for, and direction to the conduct of all national foreign intelligence, counterintelligence, and special activities, and attendant policies and programs" (*Weekly Compilation of Presidential Documents,* 7 December 1981, 1336–48), was officially under the control and supervision of the White House. Casey described the program to the House and Senate Intelligence Committees later in December as a "small contained attempt to interdict weapons and to put just enough pressure on the Sandinistas to keep them from delivering their revolution wholly to Communism." He assured the House committee that "nobody was talking about overthrowing anybody" (Persico 1990, 274–75). Thomas Enders (1982a, 80) also emphasized this purpose in his testimony before the Senate Foreign Relations Subcommittee on Western Hemisphere Affairs.

Implementing the Reagan Doctrine. Following the White House decision, the CIA moved quickly to provide aid, support, training, and advice, at first through the Argentine and Honduran armed forces and then directly (Riding 1982d; Pastor 1987, 237–38). Rebel attacks in Nicaragua expanded from largely ineffective raids during 1980–81 to larger coordinated operations. According to the Department of Defense, the rebels conducted at least 106 attacks in Nicaragua between 14 March and 21 June 1982, most of which included sabotage of roads, bridges, and fuel tanks; sniper fire; assassination of government, health, and educational personnel; and destruction and burning of warehouses, buildings, and crops (U.S. Department of Defense, Defense Intelligence Agency 1983, 21–22). After the first major attacks, the Sandinistas declared a state of emergency, closed down the press, and mobilized troops along the Honduran border in March (Riding 1982a).

As the rebel attacks increased, the administration began a verbal assault on Nicaragua, decrying its support for other rebel groups and its internal repression and militarization. The purpose was to generate public and congressional support for the insurgency and to prepare for the possibility that the paramilitary operation, and the U.S.

role in it, might become public. Pursuant to a presidential directive (NSDD 37), and under the overall coordination of an interagency group headed by the NSC staff (Oliver North), the publicity campaign centered on three themes: internal repression, militarization, and international subversion. Administration officials testified to Congress regarding the human rights abuses of the Sandinistas (e.g., Abrams 1982; U.S. Congress, Senate, Committee on Foreign Relations, Subcommittee on Western Hemisphere Affairs 1982) and the Soviet and Cuban military buildup in Nicaragua (e.g., Enders 1982a).[13] Secretary Haig and Assistant Secretary Enders accused Nicaragua of being the primary supplier of arms, soldiers, support, sanctuary, training, and communications for the El Salvadoran rebels (Enders 1982b, 64; Hoge 1982b).

Last, the State Department tried to tie the paramilitary program to a diplomatic initiative, reopening negotiations with Nicaragua on the understanding that the contra program was a bargaining chip to be used to reach a diplomatic settlement (Rodman 1994, 238–39). Early in 1982, with the support of Haig, Enders resumed efforts to negotiate with the Sandinista government. When the Nicaraguan government accepted the U.S. plan and offered counterproposals on several parts of the eight-point agenda, administration hard-liners stonewalled and then rejected the diplomatic effort (Crossette 1982; Gwertzman 1982b; LeoGrande 1986). Increasing pressure from these hard-liners frustrated Enders's attempts to negotiate, especially after William Clark replaced Richard Allen as national security adviser. Clark worked diligently to bring President Reagan's attention to bear on foreign policy and reestablished the coherence, organization, and influence of the NSC staff (Barry Rubin 1985, 224–27). Efforts toward a diplomatic settlement in 1982 assisted by Mexico and Venezuela were halted when Clark, Casey, Kirkpatrick, members of the Defense Department, and the newly strengthened NSC staff argued that negotiations with Communists were futile (LeoGrande 1986, 94–97). These officials advocated negotiations only to keep critics in Congress and the public silent; for example, an NSC paper stated that the administration wanted to "coopt the negotiations issue" because the diplomatic approach "was an obstacle to US policy" (LeoGrande 1986, 96–97). Each time the State Department opened a diplomatic initiative, these hard-liners within the administration cooperated to scuttle it. By 1983 the hard-liners had prevailed, and the administration was committed to the paramilitary option (Gutman 1988; Menges 1988b).

Evaluating the Reagan Doctrine. Although the administration clearly dominated the initial efforts to apply the Reagan Doctrine to Nicaragua, news of the operation piqued the interest of many reporters, and by March 1982 many had begun to write about U.S. support for the Nicaraguan rebel activity (see, e.g., Gelb 1982; *New York Times*, 17 March 1982; Tyler and Woodward 1982). This attention prompted members of Congress to voice their opposition to such activities and begin attempts to restrict U.S. policy (U.S. Congress, House, Committee on Foreign Affairs 1983, 85). For example, in March, Representative Michael Barnes (D-Md.) introduced a bill in the House Foreign Affairs Subcommittee on Western Hemisphere Affairs to stop covert actions in Central America (*New York Times*, 16 March 1982). The first real restriction came in the summer, when the House Intelligence Committee attached classified language to the intelligence authorization act prohibiting the use of CIA funds for the purpose of overthrowing the Nicaraguan government. This restriction passed both houses in September (Serafino 1987b, 2; Sullivan 1987, 14) and served as a "warning shot" for the administration. In December 1982, after a report on "America's Secret War: Nicaragua" in the 8 November issue of *Newsweek*,[14] Representative Tom Harkin (D-Iowa) offered an amendment to the defense appropriations bill to prohibit funds for any operations in or against Nicaragua (*Congressional Record*, 8 December 1982, H9149). Harkin's amendment prompted the House Intelligence Committee chairman, Edward Boland (D-Iowa), to attach the previously classified restriction to the Defense Department appropriations bill for fiscal year 1983 as an alternative to Harkin's measure. Boland I, as the alternative came to be known, passed 411 to 0 and was signed into law by the president on 21 December 1982 (U.S. Congress, House, Committee on Foreign Affairs 1983, 87–88; ICFR 1987a, 33). The president had, however, just confirmed his support for the paramilitary plan in National Security Decision Directive 59, "Cuba and Central America" (5 October 1982, declassified 19 December 1991).

Phase II: The Struggle over the Reagan Doctrine, December 1982–August 1987

In 1983 and 1984, Congress indicated that it would not allow the president to exercise unchallenged control over policy toward Nicaragua. As press reports of contra activity increased throughout early

1983, some members of Congress raised questions about the goals of the program (Felton 1983a, 703–4). Reports from Nicaragua by *Washington Post* reporter Christopher Dickey in March 1983 exposed the inconsistency of administration claims regarding the purposes of the rebel forces: whatever the goals of the United States were, the contras were fighting to overthrow the Sandinistas and liberate Nicaragua (Dickey 1983a, 1983b).[15] Congressional and public criticism increased substantially as a result. Thirty-seven members of the House of Representatives sent a letter to the president warning about the potential illegalities of CIA activities in Central America (in ICFR 1987a, 33). Representative Barnes stated that "Congress intended to prohibit the administration from trying to take paramilitary action against Nicaragua, but they have ignored it. I think they're in pretty obvious violation of the law. . . . I don't care for the Sandinistas, but if one were going to develop a strategy to strengthen the Sandinistas one would do what we have done" (Felton 1983a, 703–4).

President Reagan (1983b) tried to allay congressional suspicions, stating to a joint session of Congress on 27 April 1983, "Let us be clear as to the American attitude toward the Government of Nicaragua. We do not seek its overthrow. Our interest is to ensure that it does not infect its neighbors through the export of subversion and violence. Our purpose, in conformity with American and international law, is to prevent the flow of arms to El Salvador, Honduras, Guatemala, and Costa Rica." The president did not reassure Congress and failed to prevent it from trying to reformulate U.S. policy, especially after William Casey informed the House Intelligence Committee in April that CIA spending was expected to exceed $45 million by the end of the year, and that the contras had increased to seven thousand, far more than the authorized five-hundred-member interdiction force (Copson 1987b, 3; Arnson 1989, 119).

Banning the Reagan Doctrine, 1983–1984. In this first cycle of a series of actions and reactions, Congress seized the initiative, using its legislative powers to set policy. On 12 April 1983 the House Foreign Affairs Western Hemisphere Subcommittee, chaired by Representative Barnes, voted to end all U.S. support for the contras (Arnson 1989, 121). This spurred the House and Senate Intelligence Committees to begin actions to restrict, reshape, or clarify American policy. In the House, the committee also supported an aid ban. The Senate Intelligence Committee, controlled by the Republican majority, voted only to require the administration to submit a new finding that would "articulate, in a clear and coherent fashion, its policy objectives" in Nicaragua (quoted in ICFR 1987a, 33–34).

The administration reacted swiftly to dissuade Congress from interfering with the application of the Reagan Doctrine. A bipartisan commission headed by Henry Kissinger was appointed to study American interests and policy alternatives in Central America and recommend a program of action. The president hoped that the "bipartisan" commission would build "a national consensus on a comprehensive US policy for the region" (Felton 1983d, 1493) and preempt congressional interference. In the end, however, the Kissinger Commission's report was largely ignored, although National Security Decision Directive 124 ("Central America: Promoting Democracy, Economic Improvement, and Peace," 7 February 1984, declassified 19 December 1991) combined some of its recommendations with the results of a National Security Planning Group (NSPG) policy review (Pastor 1992, 72).

The executive branch also conducted a media blitz to generate congressional and public support for Reagan Doctrine aid to the rebels. Administration officials gave speeches and appeared before Congress to characterize Nicaragua as a Marxist-Leninist state tied to Cuba and the Soviet Union (see, e.g., Enders 1983, 76–80; Shultz 1983b). For example, before Congress, Secretary of State Shultz described the Sandinistas as traitors to their own revolution: "Before the Sandinistas came to power . . . they promised free elections, political pluralism, and nonalignment. Today every one of those promises is being betrayed. First the Sandinistas moved to squeeze the democrats out of the governing junta; then to restrict all political opposition, all press freedom, and the independence of the church; then to build what is the largest armed force in the history of Central America; then to align themselves with the Soviet Union and Cuba in subverting their neighbors" (Shultz 1983a, 11). On 27 April 1983, President Reagan (1983e, 4) told a joint session of Congress that "Nicaragua, supported by weapons and military resources provided by the communist bloc, represses its own people, refuses to make peace, and sponsors a guerrilla war against El Salvador." He challenged Congress, saying, "I do not believe that a majority of the Congress or the country is prepared to stand by passively while the people of Central America are delivered to totalitarianism, and we ourselves are left vulnerable to new dangers."

The administration created an office in the State Department to improve "public diplomacy" and win public support for its policies.[16] The Office of Public Diplomacy for Latin America and the Caribbean (State Department abbreviation: s/LPD), coordinated by a working group from the NSC staff, "arranged speaking engagements, published pamphlets, and sent materials to editorial writers. . . . The office used Government employees and outside contractors" (ICFR 1987a, 34). The s/LPD employed tactics that bordered on a deliberate disinformation campaign against Congress and the American public. These efforts, some of which are described in nine-page NSC staff paper written by Daniel Jacobowitz ("Public Diplomacy Action Plan: Support for the White House Educational Campaign," March 12, 1985) and a memorandum from Johnathan Miller to Patrick Buchanan ("White Propaganda Operation," March 13, 1985), were characterized by a congressional panel as "prohibited covert propaganda activities" (ICFR 1987a, 34; see also Parry and Kornbluh 1988).

To mollify its critics in Congress the Reagan administration publicly declared its support for the emerging effort by the foreign ministers of Mexico, Venezuela, Colombia, and Panama to mediate a regional peace settlement. This effort, known as Contadora for the Panamanian island on which the ministers met, began in January 1983 (see Farer 1985; LeoGrande 1986, 98). President Reagan (1983d, 7) declared that "we support negotiations among all the nations of the region to strengthen democracy, to halt subversion, to stop the flow of arms, to respect borders, and to remove all the foreign military advisors. . . . A regional peace initiative is now emerging. We've been in close touch with its sponsors and wish it well." When George Shultz and Thomas Enders tried to work with the Contadora group, however, they found their efforts "relentlessly harassed" by administration hardliners (Rodman 1994, 249).

In fact, apart from the State Department, most administration officials viewed the support of Contadora as a sop for moderates in Congress. Hard-liners, including National Security adviser William Clark, Jeane Kirkpatrick, William Casey, Caspar Weinberger, and President Reagan himself, viewed the negotiations with contempt and suspicion. An NSC staffer referred to Mexico as "closet Sandinistas" (Menges 1988b, 107), and, according to George Shultz (1993, 419), hard-liners tried persistently to block the negotiations, arguing that Communists never honor their agreements. According to an NSC paper from April

1983, for example, serious negotiations were impossible because Marxists could not be trusted, so the administration should co-opt the negotiations to "avoid congressionally mandated negotiations which work against our interests."[17] Undersecretary Fred Iklé (1983, 3–4) announced, "We can no more negotiate an acceptable political solution with these people . . . than the social democrats in revolutionary Russia could have talked Lenin into giving up Totalitarian Bolshevism."

President Reagan also dismissed the Sandinistas as negotiating partners: "I haven't believed anything they've been saying since they got in charge" (*New York Times*, 4 November 1983). Later, in an NSPG meeting, the president stated that "our participation [in the negotiations] is important from that standpoint, to get support from Congress. . . . If we are talking about negotiations with Nicaragua, that is so farfetched to imagine that a Communist government like that would make any reasonable deal with us, but if it is to get Congress to support the anti-Sandinistas, then that can be helpful."[18] The hard-liners "wanted no part of a diplomatic effort to accompany the military effort to defeat the Communists in the region. To them, diplomacy was an avenue to 'accommodation'" (Shultz 1993, 305). Shultz (1993, 305) recounted a striking exchange with Casey in which Casey warned Shultz not to be a "pilgrim," by which he meant "an early settler," or one who gives in to an adversary. Officials who believed in a two-track policy approach faced constant attacks by the hard-liners. A significant portion of Congress suspected this and remained unconvinced that either the president or his administration was interested in negotiations in spite of their public rhetoric (Pastor 1992, 72).

The administration's mobilization of such a wide variety of tools to influence and persuade Congress had mixed results. The House was not persuaded: after a rare four-hour closed session of the full chamber on 19 July 1983 featuring presentations by members of the House Intelligence Committee, the House passed the Boland-Zablocki amendment on 28 July barring funds for "support of military or paramilitary activities in Nicaragua" by a vote of 228 to 195 (the measure also provided $80 million for use by Central American countries to interdict the supply of weapons to rebels) (U.S. Congress, House, Committee on Foreign Affairs 1984, 47, 49–52; ICFR 1987a, 34). The provision was retained in the intelligence authorization bill passed in October 1983 by a 227 to 195 vote (Felton 1983f, 2163). Ironically, on the very day the

House voted to end the application of the Reagan Doctrine, President Reagan signed NSDD 100 reaffirming his commitment to the program and actually expanding U.S. activities in support of the contras.

The administration was more successful in the Republican-controlled Senate, which did not take up Boland-Zablocki. The Senate Intelligence Committee instead settled for a new statement of purpose. An NSPG meeting on 16 September 1983 produced a revised finding that altered the objective of U.S. aid "to induce the Sandinistas and Cubans and their allies to cease their support for insurgencies in the region; to hamper Cuban/Nicaraguan arms trafficking; to divert Nicaragua's resources and energies from support to Central American guerrilla movements; and to bring the Sandinistas into meaningful negotiations and constructive, verifiable agreement with the neighbors on peace in the region."[19] A 19 September 1983 CIA paper entitled "Scope of CIA Activities under the Nicaragua Finding" (in National Security Archive 1990) further explained that contra aid "remained a critical element" of American policy to counter the Sandinista-Cuban-Soviet strategy of "support for insurgent elements whose aim is the overthrow of democratic governments in the region." When the administration sent this finding to the Senate Intelligence Committee, the committee voted to provide funds for the contras (recorded in U.S. Congress, House, Committee on Foreign Affairs 1984, 52–53).

The reconciliation process between the House and the Senate resulted in a cap of $24 million for contra funding and a prohibition on using CIA contingency funds, ensuring that future funds would have to be authorized by Congress (U.S. Congress, House, Committee on Foreign Affairs 1984, 53–54). The new finding committed the administration to a negotiated settlement, a purpose that enjoyed broad support on Capitol Hill. In this way, Congress placed the first real restrictions on the Reagan Doctrine in Nicaragua; the initiative was not reversed (because of disagreements between the House and the Senate), but limits were placed on funding and Congress placed itself "in the loop" for future aid decisions.

Determined to prevent further limits on contra aid, the administration used its control over policy implementation to respond to Congress's actions. Pursuant to a decision made by the RIG and the NSPG between September 1983 and January 1984, the White House authorized the CIA to expand the contras and conduct its own attacks (ICFR 1987a, 36). Between September 1983 and April 1984, the CIA conducted at least twenty-two attacks on Nicaraguan installations (Kornbluh 1987, 29). The most controversial action occurred when the president and the NSPG, on 6 January 1984, agreed to mine Nicaraguan harbors. According to Gutman (1988, 194), the idea originated in the RIG, where Langhorne Motley (new assistant secretary of state for Latin America), Duane Clarridge, Oliver North, and Nestor Sanchez "explored the idea, won the agreement of the RIG, obtained Reagan's approval, organized the operation, and then in their own fashion briefed the congressional oversight committees." Operatives of the CIA placed mines in January and February 1984 at two locations (ICFR 1987a, 36).

This decision was taken without consulting Congress (or even the NSC) and in defiance of congressional restrictions and concerns, and was carried out without a proper briefing of the intelligence committees, prompting Senate Intelligence Committee chairman Barry Goldwater (R-Ariz.) to send an angry letter to Casey stating, "It gets down to one little simple phrase: I am pissed off. . . . Bill, this is no way to run a railroad. . . . This is an act violating international law. It is an act of war. For the life of me, I don't see how we are going to explain it" (Felton 1984a, 833). The few references to mines in briefings to the intelligence committees were specifically designed to obscure CIA involvement and leave the impression that the contras had undertaken the effort themselves. According to a 2 March 1984 memorandum to Robert C. McFarlane from Oliver North and Constantine Menges ("Special Activities in Nicaragua," in National Security Archive 1990), the mines were placed, and, "in accord with prior arrangements, [the contras] took credit for the operation." Edgar Chamorro of the contra directorate was awakened on 6 January 1984 and handed a paper prepared by the CIA. He was instructed to read the announcement on the radio, claiming credit for mining three harbors in Nicaragua (Persico 1990, 371). On 6 April 1984 the *Wall Street Journal* revealed that the CIA had performed the operation and had issued instructions to the contras to claim credit.

Both the House and Senate adopted resolutions condemning the mining (84 to 12 in the Senate, 281 to 111 in the House). More significant, in spite of administration opposition, on 25 May the House voted 241 to 177 to adopt an amendment barring the use of U.S. funds for any military or paramilitary activities against Nicaragua (the amendment was known as "Boland II"). The Senate accepted the ban, attached to a jobs bill, in the summer (recorded in U.S. Congress, House, Committee on Foreign Affairs 1985, 32–34). In October, both houses passed a Continuing Appropriations Resolution (H. J. Res. 648) that included the ban, and the president signed it into law (Sullivan 1987, 21–22). Boland II stated: "During Fiscal Year 1985, no funds available to the Central Intelligence Agency, the Department of Defense, or any other agency or entity involved in intelligence activities may be obligated or expended for the purpose or which would have the effect of supporting, directly or indirectly, military or paramilitary operations in Nicaragua by any nation, group, organization, movement or individual" (*Congressional Record,* 10 October 1984, H11980). According to its author, the amendment ended "US support for the war in Nicaragua" (*Congressional Record,* 10 October 1984, H11974). Later in the fall, reports about the CIA's role in preparing a manual that instructed the rebels on certain tactics, including "neutralizing" Sandinista officials, caused a further row and eliminated any possibility that funding would be restored to the contras (Woodward 1987, 44–49; Arnson 1993, ch. 6).

Thus Congress halted the application of the Reagan Doctrine in Nicaragua by exercising its legislative and budgetary powers to cut off funds. The military aid ban remained in effect until October 1986. However, since the ban was attached to an annual spending bill, it took effect for only one year, and the administration was free to request aid again in 1985. In fact, the intelligence authorization for fiscal year 1985 set aside $14 million to be available after 28 February 1985 if the president requested it and the Congress approved it by joint resolution. This provided the opportunity for the Reagan administration to revisit the issue but also ensured that Congress would be involved in a discussion of the goals and tactics of the Reagan Doctrine.

Modifying the ban, 1985–1986. According to National Security Adviser Robert McFarlane, the president expressed his "strong wish that we not break faith with the Contras" in January 1985 and instructed MacFarlane "to do everything possible to reverse the course of the Congress and get the funding renewed" (ICFR 1987b, 100-2:43). Having lost the initiative to Congress, the administration was forced to attempt to persuade Congress to reverse itself and provide aid. Intense bargaining and often bitter conflict occurred in the process. National Security Council staffer Oliver North began drafting legislative proposals (ICFR 1987a, 46) with the understanding that the strategy was "to bite off a little at a time and start moving back to full support" of the contras (ICFR 1987b, 100-7:268). In the end, the White House achieved authorization for nonlethal aid in 1985, but in the process circumvented congressional restrictions and committed actions that defeated its long-term purposes.

The campaign began on 6 February 1985 with the president's State of the Union Address, in which the Reagan Doctrine was first enunciated. President Reagan (1985a, 146) insisted that the United States "must not break faith with those who are risking their lives on every continent, from Afghanistan to Nicaragua, to defy Soviet-sponsored aggression and secure rights which have been ours since birth. . . . Support for freedom fighters is self-defense . . . [their] struggle . . . is tied to our own security." Since the Reagan Doctrine could not be reapplied without congressional approval of funding for the contras, the Reagan administration employed several tactics to persuade a majority of Congress to reinstate the aid.

First, the administration attempted to renovate the contras' image. The president referred to them as "our brothers," "freedom fighters," and "the moral equal of our founding fathers" (Arnson 1989, 177) in "almost daily presidential speeches and phone calls" (ICFR 1987a, 48). Moreover, Arturo Cruz, Sr., joined Adolfo Calero and Alfonso Robelo to form a new contra civilian directorate known as the Unified Nicaraguan Opposition, marking the second time that a civilian leadership was assembled to generate support for the contra cause.

Second, s/LPD swung into high gear. Administration officials planned a campaign in which the s/LPD prepared themes, talking points, and literature for policy makers and supporters, and generated articles and papers to be published under the names of people not affiliated with the government (e.g., opinion pieces for contra leaders Alfonso Robelo and Adolfo Calero to submit to the *Washington Post* and *New York Times*). A blizzard of activity "projected over seventy publications, conferences, briefings, and meetings with editorial boards to further the Contra cause" in the weeks before the vote in Congress (Arnson 1989, 178).[20]

Finally, President Reagan's request for $14 million in contra aid was coupled with a proposal for a cease-fire, during which negotiations between Managua and the contras would begin. As long as the talks progressed, Reagan promised, the United States would provide only nonlethal aid to the contras (Potter 1987, 8). According to Assistant Secretary of State Langhorne Motley (1985, 80, 82–83), contra aid would pressure the Sandinistas to negotiate in good faith, and the proposal was "an alternative to two extremes the American people want to avoid: a second Cuba . . . and a second Vietnam." Motley's description bracketed the administration's preferred course with unpalatable alternatives (another Cuba or Vietnam), making aid to the contras seem both necessary and desirable. In addition, the president was attempting to convince Congress that the administration sought a political rather than a military solution, a need created in part by his other comments. For instance, in a press conference on 21 February 1985, President Reagan stated that the goal of the United States was to alter the "communist, totalitarian" structure of the Nicaraguan government. He also said that the United States would not seek the overthrow of the FSLN government if they would "say uncle" and accept the contras into a democratic government (*Congressional Quarterly Weekly Report* 2 March 1985, 406–7).

Congress forced the administration to compromise almost immediately. Republican leaders informed the president that a request for military aid was sure to scuttle the initiative, so the White House amended the request to include only nonlethal aid—"food, medicine, clothing, and other assistance [for] survival and well-being and not for arms, ammunition, and weapons of war" (letter from President Reagan, *Congressional Record,* 23 April 1985, S4622–23). The letter was the "crucial element that moved the Senate to pass the administration's request" by a vote of 53 to 46 on 23 April 1985 (Potter 1987, 9). Significantly, the administration's willingness to make such a concession was heavily influenced by Saudi Arabia's secret contribution of $2 million per month to the contras (Walsh 1993, 424).

The House was not similarly persuaded, in part because the president attached to his request a statement that he had currently rejected "direct application" of U.S. military force, but such measures "must realistically be recognized as an eventual option" (Felton and Cohodas 1985, 709). The House rejected the proposal 248 to 180 on 24 April but failed to pass the Democratic alternative (Barnes-Hamilton), which banned contra aid and substituted $10 million in refugee relief and $4 million to assist the peace talks, due largely to a complex procedural strategy adopted by House Republicans (Potter 1987, 8–9; Arnson 1989, 184). Promising "to return to the Congress again and again," the president declared that Congress was "really voting to have a totalitarian Marxist-Leninist government here in the Americas, and there's no way for them to disguise it" (ICFR 1987a, 49). In a unilateral measure, the

White House responded by enacting economic sanctions against Nicaragua on 1 May (U.S. Department of State 1985c, 74–77).

The next day, headlines around the country reported that Nicaragua's president, Daniel Ortega, was to visit Moscow, and the administration's view seemed to be substantiated. Afraid of being cast as "soft on communism," conservative Democrats in the House, led by Dave McCurdy (D-Okla.), presented a $27 million nonlethal aid proposal, which the White House endorsed (Arnson 1989, 186). Still, in a debate laden with red-baiting, a letter from President Reagan to Representative McCurdy was required to turn the tide. The president's letter committed his administration to "political, not military solutions in Central America" and assured McCurdy that "we do not seek the military overthrow of the Sandinista government" (Congressional Record, 11 June 1985, H4093–94). On 12 June, the House passed the bill 248 to 184; after the House-Senate reconciliation process, it was accepted. Since the bill also prohibited CIA or Defense Department involvement, the administration established a State Department Nicaraguan Humanitarian Assistance Office to distribute aid (Reagan 1985b). Later that fall, the intelligence authorization act included a slightly amended version of this provision, which maintained the ban on aid and the use of the CIA's contingency fund but allowed the provision of intelligence and communications equipment and authorized the State Department to solicit funds from third countries (ICFR 1987a, 64; Potter 1987, 18–23).

Thus the White House (and international developments) persuaded Congress to provide nonlethal assistance as a lever to encourage a political settlement, a policy to which the president committed himself and his administration. However, unlike the decision to provide aid, Congress had no control over the diplomatic approach. A December 1985 message from Oliver North to John Poindexter, the new national security adviser, illustrates the problem that ensued. North reported that he had assured U.S. allies during a trip to Central America that the United States intended "to pursue a victory" and would "not be forced to seek a political accommodation with the Sandinistas" (ICFR 1987a, 64). Thus, the Reagan administration proclaimed its support for negotiations to gain congressional support for contra funding while assuring allies in Central America that it had no intention of negotiating.

Restoring Reagan Doctrine aid, 1986–1987. In 1986, the administration again raised the contra aid issue to the agenda. A National Security Council meeting on 10 January resulted in a presidential decision to request full funding for the contras through the CIA (ICFR 1987a, 64). On 25 February 1986, the president attempted the next "bite" and requested $100 million in military and other support. To satisfy Congress's preference for diplomacy, the White House attempted to sell the policy as a necessary component of a wider diplomatic approach. Secretary of State Shultz argued that contra aid would help to counter regional aggression, protect regional democratic advances, promote regional development, and stimulate a regional diplomatic solution (U.S. Congress, Senate, Committee on Foreign Relations 1986). Further, Shultz said, "a vote for military assistance to the democratic resistance will give [the negotiations] a *better* chance to succeed, because it will give the Sandinistas an incentive to negotiate seriously. . . . Absent a credible challenge to their militarized control of Nicaragua, the Sandinistas have no incentive to negotiate a lasting political solution to the conflict in Central America" (Shultz 1986, 39). The administration requested that 25 percent of the aid be made available immediately and suggested that 15 percent should be released every ninety days through September 1987. Thirty million dollars of the $100 million would be nonlethal assistance provided by the Nicaraguan Humanitarian Assistance Office ($3 million to improve the contras' human rights behavior), and, in the event of a diplomatic settlement, whatever money remained would be used for relief, rehabilitation, and reconstruction. An initial element of the administration request, use of CIA contingency funds if necessary, was withdrawn under strong criticism from both houses and both parties (Felton 1986h, 602).

Also, on 7 March, the president announced that he was sending diplomat Phillip C. Habib as a special envoy "to achieve a diplomatic solution" to the regional crisis (Felton 1986g, 535). Ironically, when Habib presented the administration's proposal to the Sandinistas, they accepted it, subject to some revisions. Hard-liners then intervened and prevented the State Department from following up on the talks, creating the embarrassing spectacle of an administration rejecting its own peace proposal (Gutman 1988; Menges 1988b; Shultz 1993).

The White House again resorted to red-baiting to pressure members of Congress. The president stated that it was difficult not to equate opposition to his proposal with support for the Sandinistas (Felton 1986g, 536), and later he accused aid opponents of succumbing to "a great disinformation campaign" that was operating "throughout our country" (Felton 1986h, 601). The partisan rhetoric peaked when White

House Communications Director Patrick Buchanan (1986) wrote: "With the Contra vote, the Democratic Party will reveal whether it stands with Ronald Reagan and the resistance—or Daniel Ortega and the communists." To support its charges, the administration repeated that the Sandinistas were repressive, were engaged in a military buildup, and were attempting to subvert their neighbors (see, e.g., Abrams 1986; Shultz 1986).

The administration succeeded in convincing a majority of Congress, but again the success required substantial lobbying and bargaining, both between the branches and within Congress. The House initially rejected the White House's request. The Appropriations, Foreign Affairs, and Intelligence Committees all concurred that Nicaragua was a problem but thought that military support for the contras would not solve it (U.S. Congress, House, Committee on Foreign Affairs 1986, pt. 2, 4). Although the president tried to reduce opposition by agreeing to suspend the military portion for ninety days while the administration attempted negotiations, this "pause for peace" failed to sway the key swing votes, including Representative Dave McCurdy. After an acrimonious debate, the full chamber voted against the proposal 222 to 210 on 20 March. Many argued that the McCarthyist tactics of the administration led key moderates to vote against the aid (Felton 1986i, 648–50). The president referred to the decision as "a dark day for freedom" and renewed his pledge to "come back again and again until this battle is won" (ibid., 648), which was made possible by Speaker Tip O'Neill's promise to moderates that there would be another vote on alternatives.

Several developments resulted in the House's eventual decision to support the president's proposal. First, the Sandinista army attacked contra camps in Honduras on 22 March 1986. The administration rushed emergency aid to Honduras and blamed the House vote for encouraging the Sandinistas to attack, although it exaggerated the incursion's significance to gain support for the contras (Felton 1986j, 695–96; U.S. Congress, House, Committee on Foreign Affairs, Subcommittee on Western Hemisphere Affairs 1986). Second, the Senate passed Senator Richard Lugar's (R-Ind.) bill containing the administration proposal (S. J. Res. 283) on March 27 by a vote of 53 to 47. Third, in April the proposal by moderate Democrats led by Dave McCurdy was again defeated by a procedural gimmick that frustrated those who wanted contra aid tied to negotiations. The moderates' plan designated $100 million for the contras but restricted the first $30 million to nonlethal aid and tied the release of the other $70 million to progress in the negotiations. Republicans voted for a substitute that included a rule preventing further amendments, and then on final vote abandoned this measure, defeating all attempts to alter the administration's plan (Potter 1987, 36–37). As a consequence, moderates insisted on another vote on the issue in June, to which Speaker O'Neill agreed. Fourth, the White House took the opportunity to lobby furiously for the votes needed to reverse the initial March defeat, using every threat and inducement available. Personal meetings, phone calls, and speeches barraged Congress, especially the few swing votes required to reverse the March results (Felton 1986m, 1986, 1443; Arnson 1989, 197). Finally, the administration toned down its partisan rhetoric and substituted an appeal for bipartisanship (Brenner and LeoGrande 1991, 230).

On 25 June the House passed $100 million in military and non-lethal aid to the contras by a vote of 221 to 209. The McCurdy proposal and the Hamilton amendment were defeated, and after the Senate passed the House bill 53 to 47 in August, both houses passed the continuing appropriations act (H. J. Res. 783) containing the Reagan Doctrine aid for the contras on 17 October 1986 (Felton 1986o, 1876–81; Potter 1987, 41–43). Aid, including weapons, ammunition, training, and guidance provided by the Defense Department and the CIA, resumed on 1 November 1986 (Felton, 1986r). According to President Reagan, the vote signaled "a new era of bipartisan consensus in American foreign policy. . . . We can be proud that we as a people have embraced the struggle of the freedom fighters in Nicaragua. Today, their cause is our cause" (ICFR 1987a, 72).

Hence, over several policy-making cycles, the White House was able to restore funding to the contras. Its domination of the agenda figured prominently in the achievement. As Representative Michael Barnes noted, Reagan's ability and determination to return with new requests again and again simply "wore everybody out" (quoted in Rodman 1994, 418). However, White House euphoria over the success was short-lived. A C-123 cargo plane carrying supplies for the contras was shot down over Nicaragua on 5 October 1986, and U.S. citizen, Eugene Hasenfus, was captured by the Sandinistas. This event began the revelations of secret assistance organized by the White House during the aid ban. The "era of bipartisan consensus" hailed by the president came to an abrupt end.

Iran-contra and the demise of the Reagan Doctrine in Nicaragua.
Although a detailed analysis of the Iran-contra affair far exceeds the
scope of this study,[21] the decision by members of the Reagan administration to evade congressional restrictions on contra aid is important.
In 1984, at the time Congress was moving to bar funding for the contras, the White House began an effort to secure alternative sources of
aid. According to National Security Adviser Robert McFarlane, President Reagan instructed him to "keep the contras together, body and
soul" (ICFR 1987b, 100-2:5, 20–21); and McFarlane's deputy, John Poindexter, testified that "the President wanted to be sure that the Contras
were supported" (ICFR 1987b, 100-8:54). The primary responsibility
for this task was given to Oliver North, NSC staff deputy director for
political-military affairs (ICFR 1987a, 37; Walsh 1993, 105–6). According
to Vincent Cannistraro, a senior CIA official, William Casey informed a
contra leader and the chief of the CIA's Central America Task Force that
President Reagan was committed to the contras and that North was to
be their contact during the Boland aid ban (Walsh 1993, 105–6, 114,
203–4). In fact, as several investigations have made clear, the activities
of North and his colleagues stemmed directly from policy decisions
made in the White House (Walsh 1993, xiv).

The sequence of events that followed the capture of Hasenfus
gradually exposed many of the secrets and deceptions perpetrated by
the White House. Internal investigations revealed connections between
the NSC staff, other parts of the government, and the contras. The Tower
Commission, consisting of former senators John Tower and Edmund
Muskie and former national security adviser Brent Scowcroft, revealed
more details in its February 1987 report (*The Report of the President's
Special Review Board*). This in turn prompted a joint congressional
investigation, which concluded that the administration's policy was
characterized by "secrecy, deception, and disdain for the law" (ICFR
1987a, 11). The independent counsel's investigation by Judge Lawrence
Walsh resulted in the conclusion that members of the administration
"came to accept . . . the mistaken view that Congress couldn't be trusted
and . . . [policy] was better left to a small inside group not elected by
the people . . . a scheme that reflected a total distrust in some constitutional values" (Walsh 1993, 120). Citing the "flawed policy-making
process" (ICFR 1987a, 16), the congressional committees and the Walsh
investigation concluded that "the ultimate responsibility for the events
in the Iran-Contra Affair must rest with the President" (ICFR 1987a, 21;

see Walsh 1993, xv, 445), although all agreed that no direct evidence proved the president had given explicit orders (ICFR 1987a, 149; Walsh 1993, 443).

In fact, all the actions taken by the White House and the NSC staff were consistent with President Reagan's policies and were "not an aberrational scheme carried out by a 'cabal of zealots' on the National Security Council staff" (Walsh 1993, 562). While the president may not have known of the solicitation of money from certain countries prior to June 1984, he was fully engaged in the discussions after that time. The president knew that Saudi Arabia had committed $1 million per month, and he also knew when the Saudis decided to double their contribution in 1985—King Fahd informed him personally (Walsh 1993, 447–48). According to Poindexter, the president wanted to "get what support we could from third countries" (ICFR 1987a, 77). Moreover, the president was aware of private fund-raising efforts. He met and thanked donors, including at least seven major contributors in 1986. Poindexter testified that the president knew of the private efforts and the role of the White House in assisting them (ICFR 1987a, 96). The president himself told a reporter in May 1987 that it was originally his idea (*New York Times,* 16 May 1987). Finally, although no known evidence suggests that the president gave explicit orders to divert funds or establish a private supply network, the attempt was consistent with his general instructions regarding the maintenance of the contras, "body and soul," and some evidence suggests that the president was better informed of his staff's activities than he admitted (Walsh 1993, 8, 132–33, 443, 562).

Perhaps most telling, in the spring of 1986 the president expressed a desire "to take action unilaterally to provide assistance" to the contras if Congress refused to provide aid (ICFR 1987a, 69). According to Poindexter, Reagan was "ready to confront the Congress on the Constitutional question of who controls foreign policy" (ICFR 1987a, 69). These and other statements led Lawrence Walsh (1993, 201) to conclude that there was "abundant evidence that President Reagan was determined that the Contras be sustained." Reagan himself stated that "the consistent policy" of his administration was to sustain the contras, and "administration officials were generally authorized to implement that policy" (ibid., 202). In short, the president's staff responded to his commitment to the contras, his injunction to provide for them, and his willingness to challenge congressional authority in foreign policy.

Significantly, both North and Poindexter defended themselves in their criminal trials with the argument that they were following President Reagan's instructions.

The effort to sustain the contras despite congressional restrictions involved three sources of funds that produced at least $40 million for the contras between June 1984 and October 1986.[22] First, McFarlane and others in the administration solicited funds from other countries pursuant to a January 1984 decision by the NSPG (Walsh 1993, 80). This proceeded despite the fact that at a June NSC meeting (after several countries had already been approached), Secretary of State Shultz stated that James Baker had told him such an effort would be "an impeachable offense."[23] By May 1984 the administration had secured funds from Saudi Arabia and had approached Israel and South Africa for additional assistance. Brunei tried to contribute $8 million, but a typographical error led to the money being deposited in the wrong Swiss bank account. Still another group of countries, including Honduras and Guatemala, received expedited aid and other considerations in return for their support of the contras.[24] Saudi Arabia eventually raised its monthly payment, contributing $32 million in all (ICFR 1987a, 45, 1987b, 100-2:23, 29). McFarlane, North, and other officials also approached Taiwan and South Korea; Taiwan contributed $2 million (ICFR 1987a, 63). Thus, during the ban on lethal aid, $34 million for lethal aid was secured from other countries and administered by Oliver North and former air force general Richard Secord. Moreover, while the White House was making a point of the urgent need for contra funding, North was advising Adolfo Robelo, the recipient of the Saudi aid, "Please do not make *anyone* aware of the deposit. . . . We need to make sure that this new financing does *not* become known. The Congress must believe that there continues to be an urgent need for funding" (ICFR 1987b, 100-2:782 emphasis in original).

Second, a fund-raising network set up by North and run by Carl R. Channell and Richard Miller solicited donations from wealthy U.S. citizens. The operation began in March 1985 and provided nearly $3 million to the contras (while taking in more than $12 million) (Walsh 1993, 187–88). It involved a presentation by North or some other White House official, after which potential donors were sent to see Channell or Miller. At times the president would be asked to express his thanks for the donations (see ICFR 1987a, ch. 4; Walsh 1993, 187–91). At least six group briefings took place at the White House, and at least seven of the top donors had private meetings with the president, who referred to them as "Ollie's people" when discussing alternative sources of funding for the contras (Walsh 1993, 378–79).

Finally, more than $18 million was raised by the secret sale of weapons to Iran at inflated prices. Of that amount, only $3.8 million was given to the contras. The diversion of funds began in late November 1985 and continued until the revelation of the arms sales in November 1986 (ICFR 1987a, ch. 15; Walsh 1993, 159–72).

The administration attempted to conceal its efforts and lied to Congress as well, which Judge Gerhard Gesell ruled was a felony offense (Walsh 1993, 55). On two occasions, press reports about a private financing operation run from the White House by Oliver North triggered congressional attempts to investigate (ICFR 1987a, 121–22). In both instances, White House officials prevented successful oversight activities by lying and withholding documents and other information. In 1985 the House Intelligence Committee chairman, Lee Hamilton, and the Western Hemisphere Affairs Subcommittee chairman, Michael Barnes, wrote letters to Robert McFarlane inquiring about the activities of the NSC staff. Barnes wanted to know about the NSC staff's role in providing "tactical influence on rebel military operations . . . facilitating contacts for prospective financial donors . . . [and] otherwise organizing and coordinating rebel efforts," and Hamilton requested "a full report on the kinds of activities regarding the Contras that the NSC carried out" (ICFR 1987a, 122). In spite of the fact that North had arranged funding, coordinated the purchase of arms, passed on military intelligence, and provided operational and tactical advice to the contras (ICFR 1987a, 122), McFarlane issued a blanket denial: "There has not been, nor will there be, any such activities by the NSC Staff" (ICFR 1987a, 123). In fact, McFarlane's narrowly circumscribed search of the documents revealed six specific memoranda linking North with obvious acts of support for the contras. Both North and McFarlane considered altering them. Yet, McFarlane's denials to Congress were categorical: "None of us has solicited funds or facilitated contacts for prospective donors"; "at no time did we encourage military activities"; North had "not given military advice of any kind to the Contras"; North had not "solicited, accepted, transmitted or in any other way been involved with funds for the Contras" (ICFR 1987a, 123–28; Walsh 1993, 83–88). Later, McFarlane admitted that he had been "too categorical," and North called the denials false, erroneous, misleading, evasive, and wrong (ICFR 1987a, 123).

Hamilton accepted McFarlane's word, asking "how could we take the word of nothing on the one hand against the very specific word of the US national security advisor on the other?" (S. Cohen 1985). Barnes was first stalled and then given one hour to go through a huge stack of documents, printouts, and memoranda in McFarlane's office without staff assistance. He declined and renewed his committee's request that McFarlane turn over the relevant documents. His request was ignored, and the matter was dropped (ICFR 1987a, 129–30).

In 1986 Representative Ron Coleman (D-Tex.) introduced a "Resolution of Inquiry" demanding documents and information on the NSC staff's role in funds and supplies, military activities, and contacts with the private network (H. Res. 485). John Poindexter, the new national security Adviser, responded in a letter that referred to the previous "investigation" by Barnes and Hamilton: "I understand that information on the specific issues raised in H. Res. 485 was provided to your Committee and that this information made it clear that the actions of the National Security Council Staff were in compliance with both the spirit and letter of the law regarding support of the Nicaraguan resistance" (ICFR 1987a, 140). North met with eleven members of the House Intelligence Committee and specifically denied any role in fund-raising, military advice, or supplies (Walsh 1993, 129–30). On these comments he later testified, "I will tell you right now, counsel, and all the Members here gathered, that I misled the Congress" (ICFR 1987a, 141).[25] Remarkably, Intelligence Committee Chairman Lee Hamilton "expressed his appreciation for the good-faith effort that Admiral Poindexter had shown in arranging a meeting and indicated his satisfaction in the responses received."[26] Poindexter congratulated North on his performance with a computer message that said "Well done" (ICFR 1987a, 141), and later testified that "my intention all along was to withhold from the Congress what the NSC Staff was doing in carrying out the President's policy" (ICFR 1987b, 100-8:152).

Phase III: The Abandonment of the Reagan Doctrine,
March 1987–March 1989

The revelations that gradually appeared throughout 1987 provided a justification for members in Congress to reformulate U.S. policy toward Nicaragua. The first indication that the administration was in retreat occurred in February 1987 when the Senate Foreign Relations Committee voted to end all U.S. support for the contras (Pressman 1987a), and the House subsequently voted to cut off the funds remaining from the 1986 authorization. This symbol of increasing congressional opposition was accompanied by an administration effort to regroup. According to NSDD 264 ("Central America"), which was issued that same month, various administration reviews and task forces were assembled to "engage the administration resources in a campaign of public diplomacy regarding the situation in Central America, the threat to US security, and US objectives for the region." Moreover, "a comprehensive action plan to gain sustained congressional support for the Nicaraguan Democratic Resistance will be developed" (NSDD 264, 2).

Nevertheless, in June, the House voted to keep the ban on the use of the CIA's contingency fund, ensuring that any new contra aid would have to be openly debated and voted on in Congress (Towell 1987a). Also, Republican leader Bob Michel (R-Ill.) told reporters that President Reagan's 1987 request for $105 million in additional funds could not pass, and he encouraged more emphasis on negotiations (Pressman 1987c, 460). The threat to deny the remaining funds was largely symbolic, but it served notice that Congress was not agreeable to additional requests for aid.

Two events in August 1987 completed the shift to congressional leadership. First, on 5 August 1987, House Speaker James Wright (D-Tex.) and President Reagan announced a peace proposal. Largely Speaker Wright's initiative, the plan called for a cease-fire in Nicaragua and the simultaneous suspension of U.S. military aid to the contras and Soviet military aid to the Sandinista government over a sixty-day period. If the Sandinistas failed to comply with the cease-fire, the Reagan administration would request new contra aid and Wright would support it (L. Robinson 1991, 31–32; Shultz 1993, 957). According to Cynthia Arnson (1993, 220–22) and Roy Gutman (1988, 345–47), the Wright-Reagan initiative came about as a result of cooperation between Speaker Wright and former congressman Tom Loeffler, who had been appointed special contra aid lobbyist by White House Chief of Staff Howard Baker. Despite resistance from Assistant Secretary Elliott Abrams and the new NSC staff officer for Latin America, José Sorzano, Loeffler and Wright worked out a deal and sold it to Secretary of State George Shultz. Illustrating the administration's ambivalence, the plan was printed on completely blank paper, without any seal or indication that it was official. According to Constantine Menges (1990, 290), Representative Jack Kemp (R-N.Y.) and Defense Secretary Caspar Weinberger advised President Reagan not to agree to Wright's proposal, but the president sided with Shultz (see also Shultz 1993, 963–68; Rodman 1994, 431–32). Though short-lived (see below), the Wright-Reagan plan assured Central American presidents that the United States would not wreck their summit scheduled for two days later.

Even more important than the Wright-Reagan initiative, the Central American peace plan, first proposed by President Oscar Arias of Costa Rica in December 1986, finally provided contra opponents with a viable alternative to the Reagan Doctrine. On 7 August 1987, just two days after the announcement of the Wright-Reagan plan, all five Central American presidents signed the accord at Esquipulas, Guatemala, that became known as Esquipulas I (Pastor 1987, 320–22). This accord was a modified version of the original Arias plan requiring each signatory to negotiate with its opposition, declare amnesty, establish a cease-fire, take steps for democratization and elections, halt militarization, and end support for subversion (L. Robinson 1991, 31). Wright immediately endorsed the accord, and the Reagan administration cautiously embraced it as a starting point (Pressman 1987h, 2178). Then, according to George Shultz (1993, 960–61), proving that "the right wing ideologues did not want a negotiated settlement that would end Contra aid," hard-liners, the new national security adviser, Frank Carlucci, his Latin America staff officer, José Sorzano, and Assistant Secretary of State Elliott Abrams attacked the negotiations, and the president denounced the idea. Nevertheless, when President Arias spoke to members of Congress in the House chamber on 22 September 1987 and urged the United States to "give peace a chance," his remarks won widespread support from both parties.

As a result of these developments, the initiative reverted to Congress. The Arias plan and the Central American negotiations finally offered an opportunity for a diplomatic settlement that did not depend on the administration for implementation, and therefore was not subject to administration obstructionism. Although the administration pledged to stand by the contras and renew requests for aid, it could do little but promise. President Reagan's description of the Esquipulas Accord as "fatally flawed" because of insufficient safeguards for democracy in Nicaragua (Pressman 1987j, 2298), and the State Department's warning against being fooled by "cosmetic gestures of compliance" by Nicaragua (ibid., 2297) failed to shake Congress's commitment. A majority agreed that U.S. policy toward Nicaragua should support the regional initiative and provide only limited nonlethal aid to the contras in Honduras until the peace accord was finalized.

Accordingly, when President Reagan declared his intention to request $270 million in military and nonlethal aid for the contras as a part of the Reagan Doctrine, Speaker Wright stated, "I really don't believe that there's any disposition in Congress to pass military money at the time we're negotiating for peace" (Felton 1987c, 2444). A proposal by Senator Jesse Helms (R-N.C.) to add $310 million for the contras to the defense bill was defeated 61 to 31 (Pressman 1987). Nevertheless, President Reagan appeared before the OAS on 7 October 1987 and warned his listeners to be wary because the Sandinistas did not honor their agreements. Although the Esquipulas Accord was "a step in the right direction," he said, it did not "address US security concerns in the region." He renewed his support for the contras, claiming that they alone had prevented the Sandinistas from attacking their neighbors (Reagan 1987b). Secretary Shultz (1987, 11) then appeared before the House Foreign Affairs Committee to argue that "continued aid to the freedom fighters is, therefore, key to democratization and the full implementation of the Guatemala agreement. . . . The President will request a vote before Thanksgiving on additional aid for the resistance. This assistance . . . is necessary to support the agreement and ensure that it endures."

In view of the attitude in Congress, Reagan's words were toothless and Shultz's pleas were in vain. Opposition to contra aid grew through November, prompting the administration to reduce its request to $30 million, mostly for food, medicine, and clothing. Even this reduction was not enough to satisfy some members, who noted that the Central American peace plan was progressing. Eventually, Congress allocated only $14 million for food and distribution efforts in Honduras, then provided for a further request in February 1988.

In mid-January 1988, following the Sandinistas' agreement to negotiate with the contras and lift restrictions on civil liberties, President Arias requested that Congress reject contra aid. Many members of Congress were swayed by his appeal, but the president tried to rally support for the Reagan Doctrine in Nicaragua on the eve of the February aid vote, going on national television to describe Nicaragua as a "beachhead for aggression against the United States" and the "first step in a strategy to dominate the entire region of Central America and threaten Mexico and the Panama Canal" (Reagan 1988, 32). In his plea, the president also suggested that the Soviet Union was "willing to pay" for the "unprecedented strategic victory" possible in Nicaragua and described Soviet, Cuban, and Nicaraguan plans for the region (Reagan 1988). As critics noted, his statement flew in the face of the INF Treaty; three years of glasnost, perestroika, and *novoye mishlenie* (new thinking); the reforms of Secretary Mikhail Gorbachev; substantial progress in the regional peace process; and Gorbachev's assurance, offered at the INF Treaty signing, that he supported the Arias peace plan (Pastor 1987, 326). The president further insisted that the Sandinistas would never permit free and fair elections without military pressure from the contras (Pastor 1992, 79). Although the administration was again able to force the issue onto the agenda, the $36.25 million request was rejected by the House 219 to 211 on 3 February 1988 (Felton 1988c).

Six weeks later, on 23 March, the contras and the Sandinistas signed a cease-fire agreement at Sapoa, Nicaragua. Though staunch Reagan Doctrine advocates reacted cynically, most observers viewed the development as a step forward in a regional settlement and the death knell for the Reagan Doctrine in Nicaragua. Even contra leader Adolfo Calero described the accord as a realistic step toward peace and "in the interest of Nicaraguans, of national reconciliation, and of stopping war and achieving peace and freedom in our country" (Felton 1988e, 805). Congress quickly passed a $17.7 million humanitarian aid package for the contras on March 30 and 31 (345 to 70 in the House and 87 to 7 in the Senate; Felton 1988g, 839). Then, in its final vote on Reagan Doctrine aid to the contras during the Reagan administration, the House rejected an amendment offered by Representative Henry Hyde (R-Ill.) to allow the CIA's contingency fund to be used for the contras (Felton 1988k).

Each time the peace process stalled during the summer and fall of 1988, the Reagan administration renewed its call for Reagan Doctrine aid. Each appeal was rejected, however, because a majority in the U.S.

government was committed to the peace process. In the final months of the Reagan administration, Nicaragua announced plans for elections, formed an electoral council, and announced its willingness to have international observers monitor the election. In that environment, the Reagan administration simply could not successfully portray the Sandinistas as intransigent, belligerent, totalitarian rulers, and could not persuade Congress of the need for the Reagan Doctrine in Nicaragua.

Two weeks after George Bush won the 1988 election, he contacted Speaker Wright and the two met in Wright's office. There Bush asked Wright to work with the newly designated secretary of state, James Baker, to "search out the ingredients of a common policy" (Pastor 1992, 86). Wright agreed, and on 24 March 1989, Baker and Wright announced a bipartisan agreement that ended the conflict over the contra issue and committed the Bush administration to a policy of support for the planned elections in Nicaragua (Felton 1989; U.S. Department of State 1989c). Thus, the cease-fire at Sapoa eventually led to a March 1989 cease-fire between Congress and the Bush administration, as the two branches agreed to end the application of the Reagan Doctrine. Though President Reagan had warned that the Sandinistas would not follow through with their promises of free elections unless the contras were provided with U.S. military assistance, Congress rejected that argument (Pastor 1992, 79).

The elections were held, and the United Nicaraguan Opposition (UNO) candidate, Violeta Barrios de Chamorro (widow of the assassinated newspaper editor and former member of the first governing junta), defeated President Daniel Ortega. Ortega turned power over to Chamorro and ended the Nicaraguan civil war (Goodfellow and Morrell 1991, 387–92; L. Robinson 1991, 34–56). Yet, as Alex Watson, the Clinton administration's assistant secretary for Latin America, noted in 1993, the years of "dictatorship, war, revolution, and economic mismanagement" exacted a high toll. The fragile anti-Sandinista alliance soon disintegrated in the face of Chamorro's attempts at national reconciliation (instead of revenge). A kind of national paralysis ensued, with the Chamorro government, UNO, and the FSLN as mutually antagonistic competitors. Moreover, in 1993, former contras and Sandinista army members again resorted to violence to gain concessions from the government (Watson 1993).[27]

Conclusions: The Reagan Doctrine and Nicaragua

United States policy toward Nicaragua emerged primarily as the result of a conflict between a relatively unified executive branch, led
by a determined White House, and a Congress characterized by a fundamental division between those opposing and those advocating aid.
One important characteristic of the policy is the involvement of President Reagan. Unlike all the other Reagan Doctrine cases, the president
was actively engaged in policy making for Nicaragua from the outset.
Even so, he was not able to control U.S. policy. After 1983, Congress
was an increasingly significant player, and the most significant arena
for the application of the Reagan Doctrine was Capitol Hill. There were
several consequences of the executive-legislative battle. No group was
able to see its preferences converted into policy: hard-liners were unable to implement an extensive contra program, liberals were unable
to block all aid to the contras, and pragmatists were unable to force
the administration to combine aid with negotiations. This led to a virtual stalemate within the United States. The stalemate, and the president's inability to persuade Congress to adopt his preferences, led to
efforts to circumvent congressional restrictions. Ironically, the president's attempts to assert his authority resulted in Congress taking over
the leadership after mid-1987.

The administration's secret effort to supply the contras demon-
strates both the extent of congressional influence over foreign policy
and the limits to that influence. Congress was so effective in restricting
or eliminating Reagan Doctrine aid to the contras that the White House
found no alternative but to break the law in order to send such aid.
The Reagan administration never convinced a majority of Congress to
support the means or objectives of the Reagan Doctrine in Nicaragua.
However, an administration determined to pursue a specified course
of action regardless of legislated limits may be able to do so. Congress,
after all, is dependent on the executive branch both for information
regarding the conduct of foreign policy and for the actual implementation of policy. If an administration refuses to provide accurate (or even
truthful) information and secretly implements a policy forbidden by
legislation, congressional influence may be limited. Ultimately, after
failing to persuade Congress, and despairing of compromise, the administration instead chose to execute its policy through illegal means.
This was ultimately a result of the constitutional division of power

and responsibility and the fragmented nature of U.S. foreign policy making. In its most constructive form, the shared responsibility may temper policy, stimulate review, and reduce excess and abuse. In this case, however, factions within the separate institutions pursued separate policies; the shared power created the opportunity for stalemate.

In addition to the complex setting, three general problems with U.S. policy exacerbated the dilemma. First, U.S. objectives were never clear (i.e., were the Sandinistas to be restrained, democratized, reconciled with the contras, or removed from power?). This, of course, made it exceedingly difficult to define what a "successful" policy outcome would be. It is clear that different factions of the U.S. government held different views on the policy's goals and the definition of victory. Second, and stemming from the first problem, how the Reagan Doctrine would contribute to U.S. objectives was also unspecified. How, for example, was an insurgency going to prevent the Sandinistas from supporting other rebels? Why was support for a rebel group preferable to other action on a regional security concern? Moreover, even if the objective had been the overthrow of the regime, the contras were a poor choice to achieve that goal. Many policy makers recognized at the time, and most realized later, that the contras had little chance of prompting a countrywide revolt or overthrowing the Sandinistas. Finally, the applicability of the Reagan Doctrine to Nicaragua is more suspect than its applicability to the other three cases in which it was implemented. In Afghanistan and Cambodia, the rebels were freedom fighters in the sense that they were clearly resisting foreign invaders. Hence, aid to those insurgencies could persuade the invader to withdraw by raising the costs of the occupation. In Angola, U.S. aid went to a long-standing, indigenous movement, but such support was embedded in a broad, regional framework that combined inducements with punishment. In Nicaragua, aid was to be provided to a resistance that lacked broad support in the population, was led by members of a despised military, and was seen as a creation of the United States. The target regime was neither put in place by foreign invaders nor a puppet, and Reagan Doctrine aid was not combined with diplomatic efforts. It is difficult to imagine the situation in which U.S. aid to such a rebel group could possibly have attained the kind of goals for which it was considered, even given the range of objectives.

Recognizing the fits and starts of the Reagan Doctrine's application caused by this setting, what can be said about the contribution of the Reagan Doctrine to the peace accords of 1988–90? As in the case of Angola, there is disagreement on the impact of the doctrine. In general, supporters of contra aid argue that the existence and threat of the contras was the most important factor that persuaded the Sandinistas to make peace and hold elections. Opponents of contra aid make the opposite point, noting that it was only after U.S. assistance ended that the Sandinistas agreed to a regional peace settlement. These individuals argue that increased U.S. assistance along the lines of President Reagan's intended request in late 1987 would have accelerated the militarization of the conflict and prevented a peace accord.

Weighing these claims is difficult because both are based on counterfactuals (i.e., "if the contras had not existed," and "if U.S. aid had continued"). The principal claim for an impact asserts that it was the threat of renewed assistance to the contras that made the Arias peace plan successful. Peter Rodman (1994, 434, 437), for example, claimed that the possibility of resumed aid placed "the burden of proof for political good conduct" on the Sandinistas, and that the 1989 bipartisan accord contained a threat to resume aid if the Sandinistas did not honor their obligations. Conversely, as Bruce Jentleson (1991, 67) noted, "by the time of the election, US military aid to the Contras had already been cut off for two years and . . . US domestic political realities made it highly unlikely that military aid would be resumed." Interestingly, in spite of his previous argument, Rodman (1994, 437) also acknowledged that "the military pressure of the Contras was being dropped as an instrument of US policy," and that this instrument "was, in fact, long dead in the Congress." On balance, if the Reagan Doctrine did contribute, it was in a very indirect way.

There is little use in arguing that U.S. aid countered the hostile intentions of the Soviet Union in Central America. The evidence indicates otherwise. For one, the Soviet position from 1980 onward was political support for Nicaragua, limited economic aid, and military assistance as required to prevent the forceful overthrow of the regime (e.g., Korolyov 1987). As John Booth (1985) indicated, there is a congruity between increased U.S. aid and increased Soviet aid, but the former preceded the latter.[28] Both U.S. and Stockholm International Peace Research Institute figures show limited Soviet economic and military commitment to Nicaragua prior to 1984. In fact, the application of the Reagan Doctrine had a self-defeating quality. Its underlying purpose was to prevent Soviet influence and expansionism, but the pattern of contra aid and Sandinista response suggests that U.S. assistance actually "justified the militarism of the Sandinistas and deepened their dependence on the Soviet Union and Cuba" (Pastor 1992, 236). Moreover, the Soviet Union consistently expressed support for a negotiated settlement and regularly encouraged the Sandinistas to negotiate, especially after 1983 (see, e.g., Duncan and Ekedahl 1990; Valenta and Cibulka 1990).

In addition, there is no way around the fact that it was only after Reagan Doctrine assistance ended that the Central American states managed to settle the conflict themselves and the Sandinistas and contras reached a cease-fire agreement. Moreover, this occurred in spite of the Reagan administration's efforts to undermine the process. In the absence of U.S. intervention, the Sandinistas, contras, and other Central American states peacefully resolved the dispute. It is likely that continued U.S. assistance to the contras would have confounded those efforts, as Costa Rican president Oscar Arias argued in 1987 and 1988. In fact, a Nicaraguan defector in 1988 revealed Sandinista plans to cope with an expanded contra insurgency by engaging in an even greater military buildup. The Reagan administration used this defector, Major Roger Miranda, to argue that support for the contras was required because of these plans. A better reading of the material he provided, in light of Soviet support for the settlement and subsequent actions, is that continued support for the contras would indeed have ruined the Arias plan, since the Sandinistas would have increased their efforts to resist the contras. Interestingly, Miranda was later reported to have received $800,000 for unspecified consulting services to the United States (*New York Times,* 14 December 1987, 5 February 1988).

In fact, the commitment of the White House to the Reagan Doctrine appears to have *delayed* resolution of the conflict. The evidence indicates that the administration refused to conduct anything resembling genuine diplomacy because of the a priori assumption held by its hard-line faction that Communists would not conduct good-faith negotiations. Hence, by defining the Sandinista regime as a "communist, totalitarian" regime, itself a dubious proposition given the Nicaraguan government's policies, the administration dismissed negotiations out of hand. By definition, that regime could not be trusted (e.g., Menges 1988b). Those who dissented from this view were harassed or excluded, and some therefore decided simply to go along despite their reservations. McFarlane, for example, refrained from criticizing policy for fear that "Bill Casey, Jeane Kirkpatrick, and Cap Weinberger would have said I was some kind of Commie" (quoted in Pastor 1987, 284).

This reluctance to use diplomacy translated into at least three missed opportunities to negotiate an acceptable settlement that addressed legitimate U.S. security concerns. As Roy Gutman (1988), Frank McNeil (1988), Robert Pastor (1987, 1992), and others have shown, an agreement was probably attainable early in 1981, in 1982, and again in 1983, after the U.S. invasion of Grenada shocked the Sandinistas into the conclusion that a similar U.S. invasion of Nicaragua was imminent. Perhaps as important, the administration's determination to send aid to the Contras weakened the internal opposition to Sandinista rule. As a function of this, the administration's success in pressuring the internal opposition movement to boycott the 1984 election stands as a monumental mistake. In elections that gave advantages to the Sandinistas but were judged by most observers to be reasonably fair, the FSLN received only 63 percent of the vote, and the opposition won thirty-five seats in the ninety-six-member national assembly (Pastor 1987, 247–50).

Far from being the result of the Reagan administration's efforts to apply the Reagan Doctrine, credit for the resolution of the conflict should be given to three other participants. President Arias of Costa Rica designed the plan that provided the framework for the regional settlement and the ensuing Nicaraguan elections and was directly responsible for ending the conflict (Jentleson 1991, 67). Secretary Gorbachev, who repeatedly pressed the Sandinistas to engage in the regional negotiations and adhere to the Arias plan, also performed an important role. It is perhaps in this area that the Reagan Doctrine had an impact. To the extent that Afghanistan hastened the "Gorbachev revolution," it encouraged Moscow to support regional conflict resolution elsewhere. This is, however, a tenuous thread. Finally, some credit must be assigned to the majority in the U.S. Congress. It was, after all, the members of this institution who repeatedly emphasized the negotiating track and steadfastly supported the Arias plan, in spite of the administration's attempts to wreck it. If, in the end, the application of the Reagan Doctrine to Nicaragua was important as a source of pressure on the Sandinistas to negotiate, it was the version of that strategy that the administration rejected, not the version it embraced and tried to implement. As late as 1988, for example, President Reagan was describing the grand strategy of the Soviet Union for the region and arguing that the Sandinistas would never adhere to the peace accord, much less hold elections, without continued military aid to the contras. Of course, President Reagan was wrong.

Several other consequences of the application of the Reagan Doctrine cannot be ignored. First, the means used to apply the strategy led almost inexorably to violations of the law. That the covert approach utilized by the administration enabled it to defy congressional restrictions, circumvent the law, and provoke a constitutional crisis must be weighed. Second, the decision to support the contras had international ramifications as well. Whereas most countries supported U.S. policy on Afghanistan and Cambodia and U.S. diplomacy in Angola, on the question of Nicaragua even U.S. allies dissented. Moreover, the decision to mine the Nicaraguan harbors eventually resulted in a World Court decision that found the United States in violation of international law—a decision the United States promptly condemned and ignored. Hence, the U.S. commitment to the principles of international law also was compromised by the administration's determination to aid the contras. Finally, the cost of the Reagan Doctrine to the Nicaraguan people was heavy. Even at their most potent, the contras did not so much engage the Sandinista army as attack Nicaraguan infrastructure and society to make it ungovernable. The toll, measured in thousands of lives, is attributable to the decision to apply so-called low-intensity force, the strategy on which the Reagan Doctrine rested.

In the end, it is exceedingly doubtful that the Reagan Doctrine produced the results of 1988–90. Moreover, any contribution it made emerged from the efforts by Congress to press for a two-track solution, which ended when the administration rejected the U.S. diplomatic track and President Arias offered his own. Finally, given the minimal cost to the Soviet Union that Nicaragua posed, it cannot be said that this case affected the Soviet Union. Rather, the reverse seems to be true: changes in the Soviet Union affected the situation in Nicaragua. In fact, the Soviet Union made it clear from 1979 on that it had no intention of adopting another client, so the argument that the Reagan Doctrine dissuaded Moscow from greater commitment is dubious.

7

Mozambique: Factions, Fights, and the Rejection of the Reagan Doctrine

At first glance, Mozambique would seem a likely candidate for Reagan Doctrine aid.[1] It appeared to meet the Kirkpatrick-Gerson (1989, 19–25) requirements of a leftist regime with ties to the Soviet bloc facing an anticommunist insurgency. It was also targeted by some of the key authors and supporters of the Reagan Doctrine. To the dismay of some hard-liners, however, the United States did not grant any aid to the Mozambique National Resistance (RENAMO, from the Portuguese). Moreover, the Reagan administration refused any official contact with RENAMO. Instead, the United States pursued a policy of improving ties to the government of Mozambique, providing food and developmental assistance, and soliciting its aid in the broader context of southern African regional problems and policy. In 1984 an identifiable group of hard-line dissenters tried to apply the Reagan Doctrine in Mozambique and force a policy decision that would extend assistance to RENAMO. This "RENAMO lobby" was a network composed of conservative senators and representatives, a handful of administration officials in several agencies, and a group of private citizens and interest groups. Pressure by this network on the rest of the administration and Congress was especially intense in 1986 and 1987, but by the end of 1987 their efforts had failed, and U.S. policy continued on its established course.

Background

Until 25 June 1975, Mozambique was a Portuguese colony that served as a source of raw materials and hired labor for Portugal, South Africa, and Rhodesia (now Zimbabwe) (Isaacman and Isaacman 1983, 18; Hanlon 1984, 16). While these countries benefited from the relationship, Mozambique was among the poorest countries in southern Africa. In June 1962 the Front for the Liberation of Mozambique (FRELIMO) formed, committed to end colonialism and establish an independent state. In 1964 FRELIMO began its operations in Mozambique; the attacks intensified, and by 1974 FRELIMO controlled the northern third of Mozambique, Portugal controlled the southern third, and the two disputed the center (Isaacman 1985, 134; Gunn 1988, 140–45). The Portuguese, their African supporters, and Rhodesian intelligence officers responded to FRELIMO's actions by organizing guerrilla forces to counter FRELIMO (Gunn 1988, 146–47).

The Portuguese Officers Coup of April 1974 resulted in Mozambican independence. The Front for the Liberation of Mozambique signed an agreement with the new Portuguese government on 7 September 1974, establishing a transition process that culminated in full independence on 25 June 1975. The newly independent Mozambican regime, under FRELIMO control, initially tried to implement a socialist model. Almost immediately FRELIMO instituted a number of socialist reforms, and in its Third Party Congress in 1977 declared itself a Marxist-Leninist vanguard party committed to "scientific socialism." Also in 1977, FRELIMO signed a Treaty of Friendship and Cooperation with the Soviet Union and began to receive Soviet economic and military aid and Soviet bloc advisers and technicians (M. Ottaway 1988, 213–16).[2] The late 1970s produced many reports of human rights abuses in Mozambique, including detentions, the use of reeducation camps, and other forms of brutality. These reports led the U.S. Congress to impose a ban on all aid to the country except food (Copson 1988a, 6).

Mozambique's domestic and international problems began almost immediately after it won independence. South Africa ceased using Mozambique's rail net and hiring Mozambican workers. In combination with the lost revenue suffered when Mozambique joined in enforcing international sanctions against the white minority regime in Rhodesia, this caused substantial economic problems (Isaacman 1985, 137, 139; Hanlon 1986, 134; P. Johnson and Martin 1986, 2). The combination of drought in the north and floods in the south ruined much of the agricultural output, and FRELIMO's socialist economic experiment turned into a disaster that left Mozambique's economy in shambles by 1980 (Isaacman 1985, 139; Gunn 1988, 146, 151).

Perhaps most damaging, however, the anti-FRELIMO guerrilla group,

RENAMO, began attacks in 1976.[3] First organized in 1974 by the white minority government of Rhodesia to combat Mozambique's support for the national liberation movements in Rhodesia, RENAMO was sponsored by South Africa after the dissolution of Rhodesia (U.S. Congress, House, Committee on Foreign Affairs, Subcommittee on Africa 1983c, 3–28). South African military and intelligence organizations equipped and trained RENAMO and supplied transport, communications, intelligence, and direct assistance (Crocker 1992, 243). Operating within Mozambique and out of sanctuaries in South Africa, RENAMO was able to conduct wide-ranging attacks and deny the regime control over its territory. From its inception, however, RENAMO was accused of indiscriminate and gruesome violence (see, e.g., Stacy 1987; U.S. Department of State 1987a; Gersony 1988; Minter 1989). Moreover, RENAMO seemed to have no identifiable political or social program and drew primarily on Shona-speaking peoples, a narrow slice of the Mozambican population (Morgan 1990, 605–7). Some U.S. officials pointed to these shortcomings as reasons to avoid contact with the movement (e.g., Crocker 1992, 242; Shultz 1993, 1111).

Faced with these challenges, FRELIMO responded by fundamentally changing its course. First, the government began to reverse its early commitment to socialism. It sold off many of its businesses, reduced the size of its state-run farms, and began emphasizing peasant agriculture. Internationally, Mozambique reached out to the West, establishing economic relationships with the United Kingdom, the Netherlands, Italy, France, Canada, Portugal, and Greece. Also, Mozambique helped to facilitate a peaceful transition to independence in Rhodesia. President Samora Machel of Mozambique convinced Robert Mugabe of the Zimbabwe African National Union (ZANU) to agree to British prime minister Margaret Thatcher's plan (see, e.g., Isaacman and Isaacman 1983, 182, 186–87; Legum 1988, 126–54). When Mugabe refused to sign the negotiated settlement, President Machel telephoned him in London and warned Mugabe that if he did not sign the agreement, he could return to Mozambique, ZANU's sanctuary, only to write his memoirs in retirement (Treverton and Levy 1989, 10). Hence, by 1980 FRELIMO had initiated its reorientation and had improved its ties to the West.

The United States had almost no dealings with or interest in Mozambique before its independence. Developments in Mozambique were filtered through broader concerns in the region and in the world, which generally translated into a desire for stability and containment of the influence and presence of the Soviet bloc.[4] In addition, southern Africa has some geostrategic significance, with its mineral wealth and its location commanding the sea routes between the Indian and Atlantic Oceans. Although U.S. relations with FRELIMO were strained in the 1970s, they were not hostile. Soon after Mozambican independence the United States established diplomatic relations, and when Mozambique began its reorientation, the U.S. Agency for International Development proposed a small aid plan (Copson 1988a, 4). However, in January 1981, just before President Reagan took office, FRELIMO responded to South African and rebel attacks and expelled American diplomats. It also invoked its 1977 treaty with the Soviet Union, sending U.S.-Mozambican relations to their nadir. The U.S. approach from that point on, led by the State Department, was based on attempts to stabilize relations between Mozambique and South Africa and to encourage Mozambique to reorient toward the West.

U.S. Policy and the Reagan Doctrine

The Bureau of African Affairs of the U.S. Department of State was the driving force behind U.S. policy toward Mozambique during the Reagan administration. American policy cannot be comprehended apart from this bureau's regional strategy, which focused on Namibian independence, peaceful change in South Africa, and the resolution of the Angolan civil war. As discussed more fully in Chapter 5, Assistant Secretary of State Chester Crocker convinced President Reagan and his secretaries of state—first Alexander Haig and then George Shultz—of the wisdom of this regional approach to southern Africa, in which the goals of regional stability and Cuban withdrawal remained primary. This approach, and Mozambique's role in it, are described in a still-classified national security decision directive from mid-1981 (NSDD 212 and NSDD 272 from 1986 and 1987, respectively, also touch briefly on Mozambique's role in the regional scheme). Though pressured by liberals and moderates on South Africa (to apply sanctions), and by conservatives on Angola and Mozambique (to assist the rebels), Crocker adhered to his regional strategy for eight years (B. Martin 1989, 24). Consequently, the Reagan Doctrine did not enter the official debate until 1984.

Phase I: Constructive Engagement: Mozambique, 1981–1985

Although the beginning of the Reagan administration coincided with a new low point in U.S.-Mozambican relations, Crocker hoped to improve that situation and eliminate the hostility between Mozambique and South Africa as a part of his "constructive engagement" strategy, by which he sought to hammer out settlements among the states of southern Africa. Crocker hoped that Mozambique would lend its support to the Angola-Namibia–South Africa negotiations (as Mozambique had supported the Zimbabwe-Rhodesia talks in 1979–80). Therefore, under the leadership of the State Department, the United States attempted to "wean" Mozambique away from the Soviet Union (Crocker 1980, 1989). This policy developed slowly. At first, Mozambique was punished for its expulsion of the American diplomats, who had been accused of espionage; on State Department advice the administration left the ambassador position vacant, blocked some equipment purchases and loans, and suspended a $5 million food aid program authorized for that year (*New York Times*, 14 March, 22 March 1981).

The decision drew fire from some members of Congress, who accused the administration of politicizing the food aid program. Acting Assistant Secretary of State for African Affairs Lannon Walker was forced to explain the decision to the House Foreign Affairs Subcommittee on African Affairs on 31 March 1981: "Because the circumstances that prevailed, the actions that were taken against our diplomats and the circumstances in which those actions were taken, we felt were anti-American and unhelpful [*sic*]. We felt it required the suspension and review of our assistance programs" (U.S. Congress, House, Committee on Foreign Affairs, Subcommittee on Africa 1981a, 243). Representative Gerry Studds (D-Mass.) spoke for the critics: "I for one cannot begin to comprehend how our stature is aided by such a decision, how anybody's perception of this, including our own perception of ourselves, could be enhanced by an action as petty as that. Maybe it is unfair to ask you, but do you think it portends a trend in the future, to which we have been alerted by other statements by the new administration, of a use of food as a political weapon in American policy?" (ibid., 243–44). Walker declined to speculate on that possibility.

From this cold beginning, U.S. relations with Mozambique gradually warmed up. Crocker conducted several trips through southern Africa and met with President Samora Machel and Foreign Minister Joaquim Chissano of Mozambique to garner their assistance with the negotiations on Namibia (Legum 1988, 214). In return, President Machel appealed to the United States to pressure South Africa to stop assisting the RENAMO guerrillas inside Mozambique. In 1982 Mozambique again approached the United States seeking improved relations and mediation with South Africa (B. Martin 1989, 27). By early 1983 a noticeable thaw had occurred. Crocker referred to the improvement before the House Foreign Affairs Subcommittee on Africa on 15 February 1983:

> This Administration took office just as US relations with Mozambique reached a low water mark. . . . But the utter incapacity of Marxist economics to cope with the problems of a developing country, and the conspicuous inability of the Soviet Union to assist Mozambique with security and political problems stemming from its isolation, led to indications that the Mozambican government wanted to reestablish communication with the United States. We responded by making clear that we, too, were interested in a positive relationship based on respect for each other's interests and were willing to engage in building bridges between us based on mutual respect. Within the past three months we have had two sets of discussions between senior American and Mozambican officials aimed at engaging the Mozambican Government in a constructive effort to improve regional stability and restore communication. We believe that a solid basis now exists for a meaningful improvement in relations between us. (U.S. Congress, House, Committee on Foreign Affairs, Subcommittee on Africa 1983a, 12–13)

In a demonstration of Congress's support for Crocker's approach to Mozambique, Representative Howard Wolpe (D-Mich.) described "genuine enthusiasm at . . . the state of growing relationships with Mozambique" and concluded that "it is a very important initiative on the part of the administration, and I applaud you for undertaking that effort" (ibid., 49). Eight million dollars in food aid was released in the first quarter of 1983 as an immediate reward for those talks (Crocker 1992, 237).

Mozambique speeded up its internal reforms and accelerated its turn toward the West (Isaacman 1985, 146–47; M. Ottaway 1988, 214). By October 1983 Crocker was persuaded that Machel had indeed turned away from the Soviet Union, and he rewarded Mozambique's actions by persuading the administration to appoint Peter Jon de Vos, a career diplomat, as the new ambassador to Mozambique (Cowell 1983; U.S. Department of State 1987a). As a further step, Crocker pressured the South African government to meet with Mozambique to negotiate an end to both countries' support for insurgencies. Following a series of meetings (on 20 December 1983, 16 January 1984, 20 February 1984, and 3 March 1984), Mozambique and South Africa signed the Nkomati Accord on 16 March 1984. This nonaggression pact, promising "good neighborliness" and an end to bases for rebels fighting in either country, was a sign that Crocker's approach to southern Africa was working. Crocker exulted over this agreement, stating, "The illusion that armed struggle will solve South Africa's problems has been dealt a body blow. It could even be an irreversible body blow" (quoted in Hanlon 1986, 39).[5]

The 1984 accord was a genuine turning point in Mozambique's relations with the West. Mozambique joined the International Monetary Fund and the World Bank and passed a new foreign investment law (Isaacman 1985, 149). Moreover, the United Kingdom began a military aid and training program, and Portugal and Italy also began to provide military aid. Mozambique eventually joined the Lomé Conference, the European Community's program for assisting developing countries. Finally, the United States pressured South Africa to sponsor FRELIMO-RENAMO talks in October 1984, which unfortunately failed to produce an accord (P. Johnson and Martin 1986, 32). Evidently, RENAMO's South African and Portuguese sponsors scuttled the talks: on 3 October 1984, South Africa hosted negotiations in Pretoria. In the midst of the talks RENAMO representative Evo Fernandes received a telephone call from Lisbon and walked out. Two weeks later RENAMO announced that it would not sign any agreement (U.S. Congress, Senate, Committee on Foreign Relations, Subcommittee on Africa 1987, 23).

U.S.-Mozambican relations also improved dramatically. In June 1984, at the instigation of Crocker and Secretary of State Shultz, the United States lifted a seven-year ban on aid and began guaranteeing investments by U.S. businesses (*New York Times,* 13 June 1984; Gunn 1985, 7). American economic assistance increased steadily thereafter (see Table 3). In 1985, the Reagan administration announced plans for a "limited military assistance relationship," justified by what the State Department characterized as "a major improvement in our bilateral relations with Mozambique" based on the expansion of Mozambique's

Table 3. U.S. Foreign Assistance to Mozambique (millions of dollars)

Type of aid	FY 1984	FY 1985	FY 1986	FY 1987	FY 1988
Development	1.0	—	—	—	15.0
Food	9.4	50.0	40.0	62.0	50.0
Economic support funds	7.0	13.0	9.6	10.0	—
Total	17.4	63.0	49.6	72.0	65.0

Source: Based on figures from Copson 1988b, p. 3.

ties with Europe, increased levels of Western aid and investment, positive and constructive relationships with U.S. officials, and its willingness to enter into negotiations and abide by agreements with South Africa. The proposed $1 million in aid consisted of nonlethal equipment (Ayres 1985). However, Congress, led by Representatives Mark Siljander (R-Mich.) and Dan Burton (R-Ind.) and Senator Malcolm Wallop (R-Wyo.), rejected military aid until all Soviet bloc personnel left Mozambique and insisted that any economic aid must go to the private sector. Amendments offered by Representative Siljander deleted the military aid and cut or restricted nonfood developmental aid because of the "Marxist nature of the government" (Felton 1985d, 1363; Clough 1986, 59; Martin 1989, 27).

In spite of criticism from conservative members of Congress and from some administration officials, in September 1985 President Machel was received warmly by President Reagan at the White House (U.S. Department of State 1987a, 1). According to Crocker (1992, 248), Machel greeted President Reagan warmly: "My dear friend Ronald! I've so long waited for this moment." As a result of their conversation, Machel convinced Reagan that his government sincerely desired friendly relations with the United States. The fact that Machel "regaled [the president] with anti-Soviet jokes and derogatory anecdotes about communism" did not hurt his standing (Shultz 1993, 1117). According to Shultz (1993, 1116), although Reagan had expressed some doubts about receiving Machel when the conservative criticism heated up, at the end of the meeting he praised Machel for his "step toward peace" and his economic and political reforms, and before Machel left the two presidents were calling each other by their first names. Reagan also told Shultz that Machel had convinced him of Mozambique's friendliness.

Hence, in late 1984 the U.S.-Mozambican relationship had progressed substantially. Crocker viewed the Mozambicans as "a voice for moderation" (U.S. State Department 1987a, 2) and a partner in a regional quest for peace, and Mozambique reciprocated by attempting to influence Angola to negotiate with the United States in good faith (Crocker 1992, 238). A State Department report (1987a, 1–2) noted that "one of the most important and positive developments in southern Africa in the 1980s has been Mozambique's turn away from the Soviet Union and toward the West. . . . [Mozambique] strongly supports efforts for peace and stability in the region. . . . No other country in southern Africa has worked more consistently with the US to further . . . peace and stability in southern Africa."

Phase II: The Conservative Challenge, 1985–1987

The first shots in the war to extend the Reagan Doctrine were fired in late 1984 and 1985 by private citizens and groups in the United States sympathetic to RENAMO, including Jack Wheeler (Freedom Research Foundation); Gordon Jones (Heritage Foundation); Thomas W. Shaaf, Jr. (Mozambique Research Center); Robert MacKenzie, a former Rhodesian intelligence officer (Freedom Inc.); and John K. Singlaub (World Anti-Communist League). Wheeler started his campaign through his accounts of visits with anticommunist insurgencies (see, e.g., Wheeler 1985b, 1985c). He also testified at a Senate Appropriations Committee hearing on U.S. policy toward anticommunist insurgencies (U.S. Congress, Senate, Committee on Appropriations 1985). Schaaf was a paid agent (lobbyist) for RENAMO, and the World Anti-Communist League claimed that it had begun to assist RENAMO in 1985 (Copson 1988, 7). Other major supporters included wealthy conservative businessman James Blanchard, who contributed $3,000 per month to RENAMO during 1985–88 (Pear and Brooke 1988);[6] former national security adviser William Clark; and former Reagan campaign aides John Sears and Stuart Spencer (Crocker 1992, 284; Shultz 1993, 1115–16). Moreover, RENAMO chartered a U.S. office, the Mozambique Information Office, located at the Heritage Foundation and headed by Professor Luis Seripaio, a professor at Howard University (A. Lewis 1987; Schmemann 1987a). These groups and individuals pressured Congress and the Reagan administration to support RENAMO and accused the State Department of treason.

The Bureau of African Affairs was convinced that the objections that these people and others raised in 1985 resulted from three related developments. The first was the change in U.S. relations with Mozambique, especially the provision of aid and President Machel's visit with President Reagan in the White House. Crocker said as much before the Senate Foreign Relations Subcommittee on Africa: "It is especially ironic that Mozambique got so little attention in Washington when it appeared to be firmly committed to Socialism, close relations with Moscow, and antagonism toward the United States. Only when Mozambique manifestly changed its course and began to reach out to us and to our Western allies did Mozambique and US policy toward that country become an issue in our own foreign policy debate" (Crocker 1987, 20). Moreover, the change in the relationship between South Africa and Mozambique, and its effect on South African–RENAMO ties, also influenced conservatives. As long as South Africa was actively involved in destabilizing Mozambique and providing aid to RENAMO, conservatives seemed satisfied. After Nkomati and the dramatic improvement in U.S.-Mozambican relations, RENAMO appeared to be without an official sponsor. Finally, hard-liners' success in repealing the Clark amendment banning aid to UNITA in July 1985 may have inspired them to extend the Reagan Doctrine to RENAMO. As Peter Rodman (1994, 270), an official who served in the State Department and on the NSC staff, noted, successes on Afghanistan and Angola were a kind of "rising tide" lifting all anticommunist rebel boats.

Constantine Menges (1988b, 231, 237–38), an NSC staff officer from 1983 to 1986, raised the issue of U.S. aid to RENAMO at a luncheon with conservative senators in July 1985. In August, at the request of the staff of Senators Steve Symms (R-Ida.) and Malcolm Wallop, Menges wrote a five-page draft for a "pro-Western strategy" of "full support for the pro-Western armed resistance, RENAMO" and gave it to Margaret Calhoun, a member of Symms's staff. Menges also pressed CIA director William Casey on the issue, claiming that the State Department and the national security adviser were not interested in supporting the "president's policy" toward Mozambique (ibid., 239).

These and other conservatives were angered by Machel's September 1985 visit to the White House. Senators Jesse Helms (R-N.C.) and Wallop and Representative Burton, who each had sponsored legislation to aid RENAMO only to see it die in committee, blamed the State Department for this particular perfidy. Senator Helms maintained that Machel's visit was orchestrated by the State Department in contradiction to President Reagan's policy objectives. He argued that the State

Department was trying to consolidate a communist government, just as it did, in his opinion, in Cuba in 1959 (U.S. Congress, Senate, Committee on Foreign Relations, Subcommittee on African Affairs 1987, 25–26). Wallop complained that "in Mozambique where they have a democratic opposition, we are siding with the communists" (Brooke 1985). Burton asserted flatly that "Mr. Machel is a communist dictator who is putting people in dungeons, who is violating all kinds of human rights, and who is deeply in bed with the Soviet Union," and blamed the State Department for ignoring these issues (*Congressional Quarterly Weekly Report*, 21 September 1985, 1987). Burton, with Menges's help, drafted a letter to President Reagan on 22 October 1985 advocating support for RENAMO against Mozambique, which they characterized as a Soviet client state with twenty thousand Soviet bloc troops and $1 billion of Soviet arms.

Although the president did not respond, a similar letter to Secretary of State Shultz elicited a short reply; Shultz stated that the current policy *was* pro-Western and effective (Menges 1988b, 238). Crocker attempted to blunt the hard-liner offensive by responding directly to the attacks of Congressman Burton in March 1987, refuting the charge that Mozambique was Marxist by describing its liberalization and moves toward greater freedom and orientation toward the West. He also challenged the depiction of RENAMO as a democratic resistance by characterizing the rebel group as a vicious gang of bandits (N. Lewis 1987a).

Members of the Defense Department also tried to force a policy review because of the Machel visit. In a memorandum for Caspar Weinberger outlining information and talking points for his visit with President Reagan and Machel, Undersecretary of Defense Fred Iklé and the Office of the Assistant Secretary of Defense for International Security Affairs (ISA) described Machel as "a self-avowed Marxist who has relied almost exclusively on the Soviets for arms." The authors urged Weinberger to "*stress that meaningful negotiations with RENAMO is* . . . the only possible and lasting solution to Mozambique's internal problems" (emphasis in original), and to "encourage FRELIMO to negotiate power sharing with RENAMO." This was, of course, contrary to official policy. An especially interesting aspect of this memorandum is the content of several handwritten amendments to the typed text. In the section describing objectives for the Machel visit, Fred Iklé crossed out the word "Administration" and replaced it with "State's," making the portion read "State's objectives for the Machel visit are . . . ," signifying clearly

204 Deciding to Intervene

that Iklé disagreed with the policy. Even more interesting are the hand-written comments at the end of the memorandum, in which Iklé and ISA agree that U.S. policy toward Mozambique should be reviewed because "the President [is] getting sold a bill of goods with [Machel]."[7]

In 1985 William Casey and the CIA worked in the background to generate support for RENAMO. At Casey's insistence, the CIA, relying primarily on South African sources, briefed administration and congressional officials on RENAMO's success while ignoring its atrocities (Crocker 1992, 284). Briefers reportedly utilized a map of Mozambique that showed RENAMO in control of nearly all the country. Casey and the CIA, with the support and active involvement of National Security Adviser John Poindexter, maintained a close relationship with elements of South Africa's security and intelligence officials through back channels from CIA headquarters. As on the Angola question (see Chapter 5), Casey used these channels to pursue his own policy agenda toward Mozambique and the region (Shultz 1993, 1113, 1116, 1119). Shultz and Crocker were incensed. The information Casey was supplying was false, and they viewed this as an attempt to undermine presidentially approved policy (Shultz 1993, 1116, 1113).

In 1986 a constellation of actors from Congress, the foreign policy bureaucracy, and the public renewed the effort to reformulate American policy toward Mozambique. Led by Senators Jesse Helms and Robert Dole (R-Kans.), hard-liners in the Senate blocked the appointment of Melissa Wells as ambassador to Mozambique in an attempt to pressure the administration to assist RENAMO. These senators had the support of William Casey, Patrick Buchanan (White House director of communications), Philip Ringdahl (NSC staff officer for African affairs), some members of the Defense Department, and the private network identified above (A. Lewis 1987; N. Lewis 1987b). In fact, contrary to official administration policy, Ringdahl met with RENAMO representatives in Congressman Dan Burton's office, and Buchanan met with RENAMO officials without the knowledge of State or the NSC (N. Lewis 1987b). Moreover, this network relied on the Mozambique Information Office, an agent of RENAMO, for assistance and information (A. Lewis 1987).

Ambassador designee Wells was a particularly unfortunate target of this network and a pawn in the larger game. Senator Helms, for instance, submitted 247 questions for her to answer, including "Is democracy the true goal in Mozambique? Or is it too much to expect of blacks committed to scientific socialism?" Helms also asked Wells if she had "[studied] socialism in [her] youth in Eastern Europe?" As Anthony Lewis (1987) of the *New York Times* pointed out, Melissa Wells had emigrated with her family from Estonia when she was three years old.

Robert Dole and twenty-eight other Senators joined Helms in blocking Wells's nomination. Dole, the Senate minority leader, opposed the administration's policy and the appointment of Wells as ambassador for three reasons: (1) he believed that relations with RENAMO would improve food distribution in Mozambique by prompting RENAMO to support the American supply efforts (*New York Times,* 24 May 1987); (2) he claimed that talks with RENAMO would hasten a cease-fire in which the good offices of the United States could facilitate negotiations; and (3) he believed that Wells opposed what he characterized as "an active peace search" (i.e., contacts with RENAMO) and wanted to continue a "policy of aiding a communist government" (Dole 1987).

A stalemate ensued when neither the State Department nor the hard-liners would budge, and President Reagan would not intervene to settle the dispute within his administration. A momentary respite for Crocker, Shultz, and the State Department occurred when William Casey, a major administration advocate of the RENAMO, resigned due to a brain tumor. Moreover, an NSC staff shakeup as a result of the Iran-contra debacle removed other hard-liners and eliminated other elements of support from the senators' effort. In particular, Philip Ringdahl was removed as NSC staff officer for African affairs and replaced with Herman Cohen, a career State Department official (N. Lewis 1987a; Crocker 1992, 343), Constantine Menges was forced out, and Frank Carlucci replaced John Poindexter as national security adviser. However, the Senate "RENAMO lobby" continued to block the Wells nomination, and the shift within the administration was tempered by the appointment of Edward J. Fuelner, former president of the Heritage Foundation, as a political consultant to the White House in March 1987. Fuelner, who had worked with RENAMO's representatives in their Heritage Foundation office, promoted RENAMO from his position inside the White House (P. Baker 1989, 57).

The issue came to a head in May and June 1987. First, Senator Helms promised to lift his objections to the Wells nomination if the Reagan administration met with RENAMO. In June, Greg Fergin, of the Mozambique desk in the Bureau for African Affairs, met with Luis Seripaio, the spokesman for RENAMO, at Seripaio's Heritage Foundation offices, ostensibly to discuss the kidnapping of Kendra Bryan, an American woman, by RENAMO in May (N. Lewis 1987d). This caused concern that the State Department was giving in to Helms.

Then, also in June, while Shultz and Crocker assured Mozambique of U.S. support (N. Lewis 1987c), Crocker squared off with Helms in a hearing before the Senate Foreign Relations Subcommittee on African Affairs. Helms challenged what he pointedly referred to as "State Department policy," portraying FRELIMO as a Soviet-sponsored, Marxist-oriented, totalitarian nightmare. He derided Crocker and the State Department and filled the record with letters, newspaper clips, and articles that depicted RENAMO members as democratic freedom fighters struggling against a Marxist oppressor (U.S. Congress, Senate, Committee on Foreign Relations, Subcommittee on Africa 1987, especially 8–9, 15–18, 20, 24–29, 38–41, 76–82, 103–23, 151–88). Helms even inserted outlandish testimony into the record by an adviser to the Mozambique Information Office, José A. Francisco, who accused Crocker of making American foreign policy to suit his own personal interests: "[Chester Crocker's] knowledge of Mozambique seems . . . influenced by his brief visits to the only functioning hotel in Maputo. . . . He has never contacted RENAMO. Yet Crocker advocates increased foreign involvement in Mozambique which can only be meant to increase foreign profits at the cost of Mozambican blood. What is behind Crocker's behavior I do not exactly know. But his Zimbabwean wife and family political connections do not give me optimism about his ability to conduct policy from an impartial position" (ibid., 79).

Crocker responded by dispelling what he referred to as the "myths" about Mozambique. First, he dismissed the charge that Mozambique was a Soviet client, pointing out that the Soviet aid and arms provisions had been declining since 1983, and that Western sources of aid exceeded Soviet bloc sources. He also noted that Mozambique never granted the Soviets access to a military base (in spite of their requests) or hosted Soviet or Cuban combat troops, and that Mozambique no longer voted with the Soviet Union in the UN (U.S. Congress, Senate, Committee on Foreign Relations, Subcommittee on Africa 1987, 4). Second, Crocker disputed the charge that Mozambique was using Western aid to bail out its socialist program. Mozambique, Crocker asserted, had actually jettisoned "its failed experiment in socialism and taken an economic U-turn. Its policies, as recognized by the international financial institutions, that is the World Bank and the IMF, represent one of the most far-reaching programs of economic restructuring undertaken by any African country" (U.S. Congress, Senate, Committee on Foreign Relations, Subcommittee on Africa 1987, 5). Finally, Crocker rejected the idea that RENAMO was a democratic alternative. As he discussed the actions of this group, which he later referred to as "an African Khmer Rouge" (Crocker 1992, 293) and a "low-tech killing machine" (Crocker 1989, 152), he reiterated that RENAMO had been created by Rhodesia and was sponsored by South Africa, and was not supported in Mozambique because of its brutality and lack of a program other than destruction. Because of this, he suggested, "the reality is that our NATO and Asian allies and friends continue to expand and deepen their support for the government of Mozambique. No Western democracy supports RENAMO. No country in the world has relations or official ties with it" (U.S. Congress, Senate, Committee on Foreign Relations, Subcommittee on Africa 1987, 6–7). He concluded, "In sum, Mr. Chairman, we believe our policy in Mozambique has been a success. . . . They are good for the United States, they are good for the region, and they are good for the people of Mozambique" (ibid., 8).

This clash did not resolve the stalemate, which continued through August 1987 despite a meeting between Secretary Shultz and Senators Helms and Dole on 15 July 1987. Shultz emphatically defended the official administration position that the United States would "not recognize or negotiate with RENAMO" (*New York Times,* 15 July 1987). National Security Adviser Frank Carlucci's similar conclusion also failed to break the deadlock (Crocker 1992, 250), and President Reagan did not make a public effort to resolve the dispute.

Ultimately, four developments intervened to settle the conflict. First, public opinion in the form of newspaper articles, editorials, and opinion pieces began to lambaste the "RENAMO lobby" for opposing what one *New York Times* editorial (13 July 1987) characterized as a "pragmatic and successful" policy. Second, according to Crocker (1992, 248), British prime minister Margaret Thatcher, a staunch conservative and "an ardent Machel fan," let it be known that she supported Crocker's policy. Thatcher's endorsement was critical for President Reagan and conservatives in Congress, and Secretary Shultz (1993, 1116) used it to encourage Reagan to resist the pressure from the right. Third, President Reagan's commitment to Crocker's approach was bolstered by his daughter, Maureen Reagan, who supported Crocker's initiative. She provided the president with "glowing reports" of Machel,

Chissano, and FRELIMO's reforms (Crocker 1992, 248), and her reports reinforced her father's support for Shultz and Crocker. Finally, reports of new RENAMO massacres undermined the claims of the right wing, although Helms called the reports a "clear setup" and other hard-liners maintained that FRELIMO members had dressed up as RENAMO guerrillas to commit the atrocities (Maren 1987; Wheeler 1990, 186).

Consequently, Senator Dole announced that he would drop his opposition to the Wells nomination, and the effort dissipated. Wells was confirmed on 9 September 1987 by a vote of 64 to 24, and, more important, the hard-liners lost their campaign to force a policy change (N. Lewis 1987e). Several weeks later, in a gesture of support for the State Department policy toward Mozambique, President Reagan welcomed Mozambique's new president, Joaquim Chissano, at the White House (New York Times, 2 October 1987). At that meeting, President Chissano asked President Reagan for increased aid and arms, and President Reagan promised U.S. assistance (New York Times, 7 October 1987).

The State Department–led approach continued, and Mozambique proved helpful in the 1988 negotiations that eventually led to the Angola-Namibia Accords in December 1988. Crocker noted in a State Department cable even before the clash between hard-liners and pragmatists that "the positive developments in US-Mozambican relations continue to have beneficial effects on our efforts with the MPLA leadership in Luanda."[8] Moreover, the stand was validated when, in April 1988, Robert Gersony (1988) submitted a report on violence in Mozambique to the State Department that described a pattern of abuses almost indescribable in its brutality. This report was reinforced one year later when William Minter (1989) reported similar conclusions to the Ford Foundation and the Swedish International Development Agency. According to Roy A. Stacy, a deputy assistant secretary for African Affairs, Gersony's report placed the responsibility for one of the "most brutal holocausts against ordinary human beings since World War II" squarely on RENAMO (Brooke 1988a). The press was stunned and critical of Senators Helms and Dole for their advocacy for such a group; Crocker, Shultz, and President Reagan were praised for their good sense in rejecting them (e.g., Brooke 1988b; New York Times, 23 April 1988). The State Department publicly announced that the report vindicated "our reluctance to enter into any sort of relationship" with RENAMO (Pear 1988). Finally, as neighboring states contributed forces to assist Mozambique and the British and Italian military assistance and training programs began to take effect, South Africa reopened talks with Mozambique in the fall of 1988 and agreed to discontinue its support for RENAMO (Gunn 1988, 172; Marcum 1989, 170).

Phase III: Defeat for the Reagan Doctrine, 1987–1992

The Bush administration continued the Reagan administration's policy toward Mozambique. After the Angola-Namibia Accords were signed in December 1988, the United States and South Africa pressed for peace talks between the FRELIMO government and RENAMO. With the United States as a facilitator, the Italian government and the Catholic church took up the role of mediators in direct RENAMO-FRELIMO negotiations, which began formally in Italy on 8 July 1990. In these talks, the mediators, with the assistance of Herman Cohen, Crocker's replacement in the Bush administration, brought about a cease-fire in December 1990. As the cease-fire went into effect, the United States participated in a ten-nation verification commission which monitored each side's actions. During intense negotiations over the next two years, the two sides agreed on a formal agenda (May 1991), a basic principles document (October 1991), and specific provisions for elections, military issues, and other safeguards (November 1991–August 1992). In August 1992, President Joaquim Chissano and RENAMO leader Afonso Dhlakama met in Rome and agreed to sign an accord by October. Finally, on 4 October 1992, Chissano and Dhlakama signed a peace accord ending the civil war (H. Cohen 1992).

A UN peacekeeping force was dispatched to Mozambique, and preparations were made for elections in October 1994. A 1992 Mozambican poll suggested FRELIMO would win legislative elections with 59.3 percent of the vote, and that RENAMO trailed even the fledgling opposition parties that had formed after Chissano's 1990 decision to allow them. The poll also showed that the majority in Mozambique considered RENAMO kind of a "dirty word" (Perlez 1992b). In October 1994, Mozambicans flocked to the polls and gave FRELIMO the presidency and the majority in the national assembly.[9]

Conclusions: The Reagan Doctrine and Mozambique

The Reagan Doctrine was not applied to Mozambique, in spite of concerted efforts by hard-liners in Congress, the administration, and the public. Instead, pragmatists led by the Bureau of African Affairs (Chester Crocker in particular), with support from many in Congress and some in the White House (including, in the end, President Reagan), managed to maintain control of policy toward Mozambique. The most determined effort to secure Reagan Doctrine aid for RENAMO came from the Senate through the obstructionist tactics of twenty-nine members of that body, aided by private individuals and groups and some administration officials in the NSC staff and the CIA. This group, led by William Casey, Jesse Helms, and Robert Dole, relied primarily on legislative tools, including hearings, filibusters, and the like, to block Melissa Wells's nomination for a full year in order to force President Reagan to abandon the policy preferred by Shultz, Crocker, and the majority of Congress. Prior to that showdown, this dissident network, or RENAMO lobby, worked through back channels to influence U.S. policy. In particular, Casey used the CIA and its ties to South African military and intelligence officials to work against the State Department–led policy. Neither approach succeeded.

In the end, only twenty-four senators voted against the Wells nomination. Secretary Shultz and President Reagan remained committed to Assistant Secretary Crocker's approach to the region and saw substantial benefits to the developing ties to Mozambique. In particular, the "weaning" strategy, as it was derisively labeled by conservatives, worked; Mozambique moved steadily away from its Marxist commitments after 1983, and the United States benefited from Mozambique's assistance in the Angola-Namibia negotiations. Finally, RENAMO's bloodthirsty reputation, backed by overwhelming evidence, persuaded the majority of policy makers in the administration and in Congress that Crocker's approach to Mozambique was the proper one.

Hence, the rejection of the Reagan Doctrine in Mozambique was driven by three fundamental issues. First, Mozambique was a part of a broad regional strategy coordinated by Crocker, who depended on Mozambique for assistance in negotiating with the MPLA in Angola and relied on improved South African–Mozambican relations to convince South Africa that peace could be achieved without resort to arms. This strategy was endorsed by Secretary Shultz, President Reagan, many members of Congress, and influential outsiders such as Margaret Thatcher and Reagan's daughter, Maureen. Second, the government of Mozambique embarked on a path of reform after 1982 that established its independence from the Soviet bloc. It made consistent efforts to court the West in both the economic and security spheres, and its policies after 1982 were consistently oriented toward market reforms and liberalization. Interestingly, in 1989 FRELIMO proposed a new constitution, which was completed in 1990. It established Mozambique as the most democratic country in southern Africa, guaranteeing a wide variety of rights and freedoms similar to the U.S. Bill of Rights (Knight 1991, 218–19; Bowen 1992, 256; Alden and Simpson 1993, 117). All this, coupled with the critical fact that Mozambique was never a base for Soviet or Cuban troops, undermined the characterization of Mozambique as a Soviet client and a totalitarian regime, weakening the basic argument of Reagan Doctrine proponents. Finally, RENAMO itself prevented the application of the Reagan Doctrine. Although insurgency is by nature violent, and all freedom fighters are guilty of abuses of one form or another, the origins of RENAMO and its substantial ties to South Africa, along with reports of its atrocities, persuaded the majority of policy makers in the United States that this group neither deserved the label "freedom fighters" nor warranted U.S. support. Only a small minority of hard-liners inside and outside the government advocated aid, and while they were vocal in 1986 and 1987, they failed to break the State Department–led consensus.

While it may be dangerous to vest too much importance in the case of Mozambique, it is ironic that, in the absence of any application of the Reagan Doctrine, the United States still achieved two goals. First, as noted above, a process of international realignment occurred. Mozambique's government, offered the benefits of good relations with the United States rather than the punishment of U.S. support for the insurgency it faced, opted to reorient its relations toward the West. While this does not demonstrate that the force of international developments and economic realities would have caused similar developments in Angola, Cambodia, and Nicaragua without the Reagan Doctrine, it is possible. The Reagan Doctrine obviously had no role in diminishing the Soviet influence in Mozambique; economic necessity appears to have been much more significant.

Second, and quite unlike the situation in its neighbor Angola, national reconciliation and democratization proceeded successfully in

Mozambique. It is likely that U.S. support for peaceful reconciliation, rather than siding with the rebels, played a role in the transition that occurred after 1989. Obviously, Reagan Doctrine aid was no factor in the peace settlements. In the end, under U.S. pressure, South Africa ceased its support for RENAMO in 1988, and the United States and the Soviet Union joined to monitor a cease-fire agreement in 1990. When, after four more years, elections were finally held under UN supervision, FRELIMO's presidential candidate, Joaquim Chissano, garnered 53 percent of the vote to the RENAMO candidate's 34 percent. A temporary scare occurred when Afonso Dhlakama, the RENAMO leader, announced a boycott on the eve of the elections, but pressure from former supporters and regional leaders in Zimbabwe and South Africa persuaded him to drop his opposition and participate. Without military force to fall back on, Dhlakama agreed to become the leader of the opposition instead of returning to war. More significantly, RENAMO's success (34 percent of the presidential vote and 38 percent of the parliamentary vote) indicated that the efforts spent since 1990 reorganizing it into a political party to compete in democratic elections had produced some positive results. From a "dirty word" in 1992 to a "minority party" in 1995 was a long road, but apparently a peaceful (and successful) one. In fact, it is likely that RENAMO representatives will be invited into a "national unity government" with FRELIMO, a step the Clinton administration is encouraging (Isaacs 1995).

Hence, the case of Mozambique is instructive for what it does not involve: once the cease-fire was signed, the interim process was peaceful, and even with FRELIMO the victor in the 1994 elections, it still seems unlikely that war will resume. To the extent that the United States has long-term interests in stability in southern Africa, Mozambique, where the Reagan Doctrine was not applied, offers the best prospects. In the end, lending support to those for whom carrots take precedence over sticks, the rejection of the Reagan Doctrine led to a successful result, both in Mozambique and in the broader region.

8

Conclusions: The Nature and Lessons

of the Reagan Doctrine

The Reagan Doctrine, conceived early in the 1980s, was applied or considered for application to five countries. The case studies examined in the preceding chapters leave us with two intriguing questions. The first concerns the overall character of this strategy and its impact in the waning period of the cold war: What did the Reagan Doctrine do? The second concerns the role and influence of different American policy makers in the formulation and implementation of the initiative: Who is responsible for devising this strategy?

Assessing the Reagan Doctrine

In his memoir of his time as secretary of state, George Shultz reflected on the Reagan Doctrine and its impact on U.S.-Soviet relations. During the two terms served by Ronald Reagan, "the Soviet attitude toward its relationship to world events had altered profoundly. The Brezhnev Doctrine was dead, with the execution due in some considerable part to its opposite number, the Reagan Doctrine" (Shultz 1993, 1129). Shultz's conclusion, which was echoed by other administration officials, members of Congress, and supporters, raises the complicated issue of the impact of the overall strategy. As the concluding section of each case study suggests, the impact of this initiative varied in each case. It remains to evaluate the broad characteristics and overall impact of the Reagan Doctrine as applied to Afghanistan, Cambodia, Angola, Nicaragua, and Mozambique.

The Characteristics of the Reagan Doctrine

In the most fundamental sense this book verifies that the Reagan Doctrine was devised early in the first term of Ronald Reagan as a calculated strategy to be applied in several instances, the claims of some observers notwithstanding. As Chapter 2 describes, and as the case studies demonstrate, a strategy was conceived and implemented, however unevenly. National Security Decision Directive 75 (January 1983) states clearly the strategic rationale of the Reagan Doctrine, and also indicates that it developed before the public declarations that triggered its identification. It is also evident that the original authors of this strategy, mainly hard-liners in the White House and the National Security Council staff, were driven by a compelling logic centered on the need to challenge Soviet gains from previous years and the belief that those gains were traceable to shortcomings in the containment strategy and détente.

Nevertheless, a doctrine conceived and a doctrine implemented are two different issues. As foreign policy insider Anthony Lake (1989, 58–59) noted, most U.S. foreign policy emerges from compromise. The Reagan Doctrine was no exception: as the initiative was considered and applied, four versions of it emerged, each of which had proponents in different parts of the policy-making community. The authors and primary advocates of the Reagan Doctrine imagined a "universal" version that would be applied consistently and uniformly in situations in which a pro-Soviet regime faced opposition. In this version, the strategy was to be policy; that is, Reagan Doctrine aid was to be the principal means with which to address the existence of the regime, Soviet bloc influence, and Soviet power in a particular region. Other policy makers defined a "two-track" version that joined the force of the Reagan Doctrine to diplomacy in order to resolve regional issues. To these people, the Reagan Doctrine was not an end but a means to address more limited U.S. goals within the region in question. A "truncated" version of the doctrine included the rationale of the two-track approach but limited the scope to situations in which foreign troops were present. This group saw a use for the Reagan Doctrine in situations where such "invaders" existed, and rejected the application of the strategy as inappropriate, unnecessary, and self-defeating where they did not. Finally, a "Soviet aggressor" version of the doctrine was supported by policy makers who believed the Reagan Doctrine was

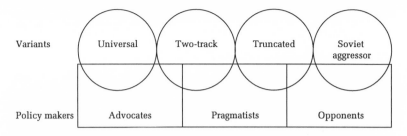

Figure 2. Variants of Reagan Doctrine and Their Supporters

appropriate only in situations in which the Soviet Union had actually invaded, installed a puppet government, and conducted military operations in support of that regime.

These four versions of the Reagan Doctrine had support from three different factions within the foreign policy community (see Figure 2). Most "advocates" in the administration, Congress, and the public held the universal view, and most "opponents" in Congress and the public held the Soviet aggressor view. "Pragmatists" in the administration, Congress, and the public adopted a more restrictive view than advocates and a more expansive view than opponents. Even pragmatists, however, were divided between the two-track and truncated versions of the doctrine.

In practice, the existence of these factions and versions had significant consequences. The logic of the universal approach led its adherents to advocate Reagan Doctrine aid in all five of the cases considered in this study, and to oppose diplomatic settlements in each. The logic of the Soviet aggressor view led its supporters to oppose Reagan Doctrine assistance in all cases but Afghanistan, although some also equated the Vietnamese invasion of Cambodia with the Soviet invasion of Afghanistan. The pragmatic faction insisted on three features: (1) active diplomacy, for which Reagan Doctrine aid was to be a complement; (2) careful consideration of the relationship between the regime and the Soviet bloc, especially as it related to foreign troops; and (3) careful evaluation of the nature of the rebel groups, particularly the extent to which they were indigenous. All pragmatists rejected the application of the Reagan Doctrine to Mozambique, and most, especially in Congress, rejected its application to Nicaragua, except during 1985–86.

Ultimately, the Reagan Doctrine emerged from the complex struggle between the three factions over these four versions. Neither the universal nor the Soviet aggressor version prevailed. In the end, a combination of the truncated and two-track versions was applied to Afghanistan, Cambodia, and Angola. The absence of foreign troops or a diplomatic track led to the rejection of the Reagan Doctrine for Mozambique and Nicaragua (although, as Chapter 6 shows, this rejection was not consistent).

This suggests that the authors of the strategy were unsuccessful in implementing it according to their conception. Instead, a wider group of policy makers altered the original strategy and embedded it into a more limited, case-by-case approach to be utilized in conjunction with other instruments of foreign policy, including diplomacy and inducements. The coherent "grand design" suggested by NSDD 75 was filtered through a complex institutional setting, resulting in a more cautious compromise. Lake (1989, 59) suggested that this situation is far from rare: he identified contending interests as the central cause of "an important central truth about . . . foreign policy: with very rare exceptions, foreign policy decisions represent compromises," whether forced or voluntary.

The explanation behind the compromise that resulted in this modification of the Reagan Doctrine rests in large part on varying assessments of threat and beliefs about the utility and appropriateness of certain foreign policy tools. The case studies examined in the preceding chapters indicate that differing perceptions of threat account for much of the disagreement among U.S. policy makers: variation in policy maker response to the five cases tracks closely with varying assessments of the threat involved. Policy makers' consensus on Afghanistan rested on their agreement that the presence and operations of Soviet troops constituted a threat to U.S. interests in the region and the world. Diminished but still significant agreement existed on Cambodia and Angola, largely because of the threat posed by the presence and operation of Vietnamese and Cuban troops, respectively, in those countries. No such consensus existed on Nicaragua, in part because many U.S. policy makers, particularly in Congress, remained unconvinced that the Sandinista regime posed a threat to U.S. interests, especially in the absence of Soviet bloc combat troops. In the Mozambique case, there was a consensus that no threat existed.

Along with threat assessment was disagreement over the appropriate tools with which to protect U.S. interests. Distinctions among the three factions of U.S. policy makers rested in part in their attitudes toward various instruments of foreign policy, the most significant of which was the relationship between military and diplomatic approaches: hard-liners eschewed diplomatic tools, liberal policy makers rejected military tools, and the pragmatic middle tried to wed the two.

The Reagan Doctrine's Strengths and Weaknesses

Differences between the doctrine as conceived and the doctrine as applied complicate the evaluation of the strengths and weaknesses of the Reagan Doctrine. As conceived, the strategy had several strengths. As a response to the Brezhnev Doctrine and Soviet expansionism in the 1970s, the Reagan Doctrine clearly and unequivocally challenged Moscow's practices in various parts of the world. This assertiveness can be defended as a necessary response to the failure of the Soviet Union to act with restraint, as was expected during détente. Moreover, there is a kind of "just desserts" logic as well, in that the Soviets' support for "national liberation movements" came full circle and caught them in a web similar to those engendered by their own previous efforts.

The Reagan Doctrine also accommodated the realities of post-Vietnam foreign policy. As the editor of *Foreign Policy*, Charles William Maynes (1990, 267), concluded, the strategy met the requirements of both realism and restraint. In essence, the doctrine did not propose U.S. military intervention in the Third World, which was probably impossible in terms of public and congressional opinion. Moreover, the doctrine proposed to challenge the Soviet Union along its periphery, not in Eastern Europe, where the forerunner of the Reagan Doctrine (the Dulles Doctrine?) met its demise. The combination of these two factors meant that U.S.-Soviet confrontation was impossible and that direct Soviet military intervention or escalation was unlikely (except, ironically, in Afghanistan, the scene of the Reagan Doctrine's greatest— or only—success).

As applied, the Reagan Doctrine had two additional strengths. First, and probably most significant, because of the insistence of pragmatists throughout the government, the Reagan Doctrine was wedded to other instruments of policy and embedded in other initiatives vis-à-vis the Soviet Union. This allowed "carrots" to be combined with "sticks," and pressure to be applied as required by the situation at hand. To those who supported the two-track and truncated policy variants, this was crucial. As Undersecretary of State Michael Armacost remembered, this calibration helped to produce "a balance of forces that . . . convinced the parties involved that a military solution [was not] possible. . . . [The Reagan Doctrine helped] preserve that balance, making a political solution more likely" (Talbott 1989, 33). Second, the Reagan Doctrine differentiated between regimes put in place or supported by the presence of foreign troops and those that emerged and existed largely on their own. The policy implemented by the United States proved more focused and less sweeping than its rhetoric (and authors) claimed.

However, a number of weaknesses also existed in the Reagan Doctrine. One fundamental problem with the overall strategy stemmed from the Manichaean view of the world on which it was based. Consistent with the worldview of the hard-liners who were the primary authors and supporters of the initiative, this simplistic "dualism" caused three predominantly negative consequences. First, the situations in which the Reagan Doctrine was to be applied tended to be oversimplified as East-West issues. While Afghanistan was clearly such an issue, the other cases were not. Cambodia, for instance, concerned the Khmer Rouge dilemma and Khmer Rouge–Vietnamese hostility, making the foundation of the Reagan Doctrine's application potentially troubling to the extent that Vietnam's actions were viewed as a seamless part of Soviet expansionism. Angola poses another puzzle, given the impact of South African aggression on the region. At least part of the Cuban and Soviet involvement was a function of South African interventionism, and "good" and "evil" in this case are difficult to determine, especially in light of post-1988 events. Finally, the issues involved in Nicaragua clearly exceeded the East-West dimension. To the extent that the problem was forced into this prism, Nicaragua was inaccurately examined and interpreted, with harmful effects on U.S. policy.

The Reagan Doctrine's Manichaean simplification also resulted in the demonization of the target regimes. According to the Kirkpatrick-Gerson thesis (see Chapter 2), each of these regimes was illegitimate and a Soviet client. In truth, however, considerable variation existed among the regimes, especially in their relationship to the Soviet Union. Afghanistan, Cambodia, Angola, Nicaragua, and Mozambique, in that order, had diminishing levels of ties to and dependence on the USSR. In fact, as detailed elsewhere (e.g., J. Scott 1993), only Afghanistan and

Cambodia really deserved the "client" label. Moreover, in the case of Cambodia, the puppet nature of the regime changed over time to a much more Cambodian orientation. To the extent that several regimes were not clearly, if at all, tied to the Soviet Union, application of the Reagan Doctrine, predicated as it was on the presumption of such ties, probably exacerbated the situation and encouraged greater reliance on the Soviet bloc. In those situations, the Reagan Doctrine was, in a sense, self-defeating, at least in the short term. For example, most of the evidence suggests that the Soviet and Cuban commitment to Nicaragua increased substantially in 1984, *after* the application of the Reagan Doctrine. Before that time, Soviet economic and military aid was limited and the Sandinista regime was repeatedly encouraged to maintain friendly ties to the West. The extent to which each regime was committed to Soviet-style Marxism and was illegitimate varied considerably as well.

Another consequence of this Manichaean simplification was the glorification of the rebel groups. Proponents of the doctrine consistently exaggerated the virtues of the rebels. Whether it was the mujahidin's supporters extolling the virtues of these rebels and their abiding faith in God, UNITA supporters characterizing Jonas Savimbi as the greatest democrat in Africa, or contra supporters describing the Nicaraguan rebels as morally equal to the founders of the United States, such oversimplifications tarnished U.S. policy and obscured the fact that in some cases the differences between the rebels and the regimes were more imagined than real. Nowhere is this clearer than in the case of Savimbi and UNITA. A careful analysis of UNITA's organization, purposes, policies, and practices finds little difference between UNITA and the MPLA regime in Angola. The false dichotomy—"democratic freedom fighters" versus "totalitarian puppets of Moscow"—obfuscated efforts to design a nuanced policy. In each case, this oversimplification resulted in policy problems, especially—but not exclusively—after 1988.

A second overall weakness of the Reagan Doctrine stemmed directly from its logic. The doctrine was difficult to combine with other measures of foreign policy, especially diplomacy. The logic of the Reagan Doctrine—as demonstrated especially in the latter stages of the Afghanistan case, throughout the Nicaragua case, and in much of the Angola and Mozambique cases—made the pursuit and acceptance of negotiated settlements very difficult, especially for the faction embracing the universal version of the doctrine. Moreover, the underlying logic tended to be escalatory, ratcheting up the role of violence and arms in the problem area. The logic also was somewhat self-defeating, as noted above, in that it may have encouraged greater reliance on and involvement by the Soviet Union (and Cuba or Vietnam) rather than less. In fact, as Ted Hopf (1994, 110–14) noted, at least initially the application of the Reagan Doctrine to Afghanistan, Angola, and Nicaragua triggered dramatic increases in Soviet aid and operations in those countries. In fairness, however, it should be noted that this may have been an intended consequence for the short term, in order to achieve a long-term gain. That is, by forcing greater Soviet involvement in the short term, the Reagan Doctrine's application probably increased the costs associated with the ventures, and in the end may have actually contributed to the decline of Soviet influence, commitment, and power.

The third overall weakness embodied in the Reagan Doctrine was the difficulty it presented in determining victory. The underlying purposes of the Reagan Doctrine made it almost impossible to prevent the extension of the doctrine to civil conflict, even after the foreign troops had been withdrawn. In two cases (Afghanistan and Angola) continued U.S. support probably fueled the continued violence and civil war.

The inevitable costs and trade-offs prompted by the application of the policy were a fourth weakness. To apply the Reagan Doctrine to meet the high-priority threat identified by its underlying logic, policy makers were forced to ignore or discount other costs. Turning a blind eye to Pakistani nuclear proliferation, providing tacit support for the Khmer Rouge, ignoring the drug trade in Afghanistan, (mis)allocating scarce foreign aid resources, and creating the perception of U.S. alignment with South Africa were all undesirable concomitants of the policy. To these should be added a final note: while a strength of the Reagan Doctrine was its limited cost to the United States in terms of lives and resources, the fact that the strategy depended on fostering insurgencies proved costly to the civilians in the target countries. Deaths, injuries, hardships, and retaliations all took their toll on the societies of Afghanistan, Angola, Nicaragua, and Cambodia.

The Impact of the Reagan Doctrine

An overall evaluation of the Reagan Doctrine's impact yields mixed conclusions, as the assessments accompanying each case study suggest. In sum, however, the Reagan Doctrine made three concrete contributions to the achievement of broad U.S. foreign policy goals. First, the rhetoric of the doctrine proved to be an important component of broad U.S. foreign policy. In foreign policy, declarations are often as significant as actions, and the declaration of the Reagan Doctrine indicated the potential, if not the likelihood, of increasing costs to the Soviet Union, which Moscow recognized. As Raymond Garthoff (1994) indicated in his detailed examination of U.S.-Soviet relations in this final phase of the cold war, not only did administration officials press the issue of regional conflicts in nearly every meeting with Soviet officials, but pressure was also raised publicly (and rhetorically) by President Reagan in several notable forums, including the U.S. Congress, the UN General Assembly, and the British Parliament. Moreover, as Garthoff recognized, Soviet officials viewed the declarations as a direct challenge to their "achievements" of the 1970s. In combination with more concrete pressure stemming from military and economic competition and confrontation, this rhetorical pressure played a significant role.

Second, the application of the Reagan Doctrine to Afghanistan was a vital cog in broader U.S. efforts to moderate Soviet policy and, indeed, the Soviet Union. The costs imposed on the Soviet Union associated with this application were real and heavy in terms of reputation, prestige, resources, and lives. In relation to other, particularly economic, costs, the burden imposed by the doctrine was less but still significant. Moreover, as National Security Decision Directive 75 declared, and as Peter Schweizer (1994) described, Afghanistan especially was viewed by administration officials as a critical element of a broad strategic offensive against Moscow that included economic, propaganda, military, and other pressures. Additionally, the application of the Reagan Doctrine to Afghanistan precipitated breakthroughs in other regions, including Cambodia and Angola, and almost certainly contributed to the reformation of Soviet foreign policy undertaken by General Secretary Mikhail Gorbachev.[1] Hence, for this one application alone, proponents of the Reagan Doctrine may claim success. On the other hand, this specific application actually began under the Carter administration, without the enunciation of a "doctrine." Moreover, if this case alone was critical, then the Reagan Doctrine had served its purpose by 1988 and need not have been continued after that time, which is particularly ironic given the attempts by its advocates to extend the doctrine in Mozambique, Nicaragua, and Angola in 1987 and after.

Finally, this analysis of the application of the Reagan Doctrine to Afghanistan, Cambodia, and Angola prior to 1989 suggests that the Reagan Doctrine contributed to the withdrawal of foreign troops by strengthening diplomatic efforts in those countries. This suggests, as Bruce Jentleson's (1991) look at the strategy of coercive diplomacy concluded, that the Reagan Doctrine as a component of U.S. strategy was successful in "restraining more than re-making governments." The doctrine helped in attaining the goal of restraining the behavior of the Soviet Union and its allies through a combination of force and diplomacy, but failed in the more expansive goal of replacing the existing regimes. As the Bush administration's assistant secretary of state for East Asian affairs, Richard Solomon, concluded, "it is relatively easy to withdraw foreign occupation forces. The really tough job is to deal with the internal political process" (U.S. Congress, House, Committee on Foreign Affairs, Subcommittee on Asian and Pacific Affairs 1990c, 11). In this respect, pragmatists proved more accurate and dependable in their arguments and assessments than hard-liners or liberals. The only variant of the Reagan Doctrine that achieved success was the combined two-track–truncated version designed to achieve the withdrawal of foreign troops.

Three qualifications or caveats arise. First, the continued application of the Reagan Doctrine after 1988 was ill-advised and counterproductive, especially in light of the Soviet Union's decision to respond to continued U.S. military pressure by continuing its own military support (as it did in Angola). In fact, as Garthoff (1994), Hopf (1994), and Mark Katz (1991) have argued, the continued application of the Reagan Doctrine prompted the Soviet Union to continue its own aid to the regimes, making internal reconciliation more difficult. Second, the Reagan Doctrine as applied hardly resembled the Reagan Doctrine as conceived by its hard-line authors in the White House and the National Security Council staff. Third, the timing of Reagan Doctrine aid lends support to those who wonder whether it preceded or followed Soviet reform efforts. The implication touches on the impact of the doctrine; if, as seems the case in Angola, for example, the Reagan Doctrine aid followed the initiation of Soviet reforms, it can hardly be said to have caused them. Hence, it is difficult to say whether it was the Reagan Doctrine or the Gorbachev Doctrine (Gorbachev's reform policies) driving these events. In the end, only the Afghan case clearly predated Soviet reassessments and had positive results.

The Reagan Doctrine and Post–Cold War American Foreign Policy

The demise of the Reagan Doctrine followed the demise of the cold war. Given the strategic logic behind the doctrine, this is not especially surprising. Whether an observer credits the strategy with having some role in the end of the cold war or not, the Reagan Doctrine itself is irrelevant in the post–cold war period. Nevertheless, this cold war initiative provides some substantive lessons for post–cold war American foreign policy. The most significant of these concern the rationales underlying future doctrines and the relevance of doctrines per se in the world to come.

The Reagan Doctrine was founded on the wedding of strategic and moral considerations. The initiative proposed action to counter perceived Soviet expansion *and* to "go on the offensive with a forward strategy for freedom" (Reagan 1983c, 1383). The doctrine therefore rested on the supposition that what was necessary had to be coupled with a defense of what was right. This foundation, which permeates most presidential doctrines, can be expected to continue in the post–cold war period. But what is necessary (i.e., strategic justification) is less clear in an environment in which the United States has "fewer permanent enemies and fewer permanent allies" (Deese 1994, xi). Hence, it is likely that the defense of foreign policy initiatives will involve an even tighter link between moral justification and more narrowly circumscribed "national interests," if not a greater emphasis on the moral justification. Hence, the absence of a clear threat to the United States provides greater freedom for positive, rather than negative, policy (i.e., promoting rather than resisting).

Interestingly, this dual foundation is particularly evident in the clearest broad policy statement yet to emerge from the Clinton administration. According to National Security Adviser Anthony Lake, the combination of U.S. interests and ideals requires a new foreign policy strategy: "Throughout the Cold War, we contained a global threat to market democracies; now we should seek to enlarge their reach, particularly in places of special significance to us. *The successor to a policy of containment must be a strategy of enlargement—enlargement of the world's free community of market democracies* (Lake 1993, 41; emphasis added). According to Lake, such a strategy would make the United States more secure and would make the world more humane and peaceful.

The ties between this statement and the Reagan Doctrine rest on the link between the notion of a forward strategy for freedom and the strategy of enlargement. This foundation also rests on deeper cultural values that can be traced through the history of U.S. relations with other countries. Long-standing public beliefs in the innocence, benevolence, and exceptionalism of the United States, and the historical pattern that can best be described as "mission," suggest that post–cold war initiatives will play on these appeals. In this sense, policy doctrines in the post–cold war era will resemble the Reagan Doctrine and other cold war presidential doctrines in that they will almost certainly rest on what Cecil Crabb (1982) described as the broad "doctrines" of American foreign policy: exceptionalism, unilateralism, and mission.

Still, the Reagan Doctrine, and in fact all presidential doctrines, suggest that appeal to mission and morality is not an adequate basis for a successful doctrinal statement. All the cold war presidential doctrines—Truman's, Eisenhower's, Nixon's, Carter's, and Reagan's—shared a common element that seems likely to be missing from post–cold war policy. Each emphasized danger and fear more than benevolence and morality. Whether it was Truman seeking to frighten the American people with visions of an international communist threat, or members of the Reagan administration warning of a noose tightening around the United States, the central theme was a clear and significant threat to the "American way of life" that required action. Again, it is difficult to see such a threat in the post–cold war period, at least in the near term. Basing a doctrine on the desire for a more humane and peaceful world does not carry the same weight with an American public that has always been reluctant to commit resources to foreign policy goals that do not involve tangible interests or clear dangers to U.S. security. Put another way, doctrines require both moral and strategic justifications; while the moral end is significant, it cannot compel action without the strategic element any more than the strategic argument can succeed without the moral component.

In fact, other aspects of the Reagan Doctrine suggest additional limits to the impact of such policy statements. Far from triggering a doctrinaire application of its principles, in fact, the strategy succeeded primarily as an agenda-setting device; policy proceeded on a case-by-case basis due to the complexity of the international setting and the U.S. policy-making environment. If this was the case for a doctrine in the cold war, with its relatively simple imperatives, it should be even more pronounced in the post–cold war era. Without a clear threat to U.S. security, and given the absence of consensus among U.S. policy makers and the public on the interests, role, and appropriate resource commitment in the post–cold war environment, it is difficult to imagine a presidential doctrine that can combine a definition of interests, threat, purpose, and action in such a way as to command the broad support necessary to see it implemented. Hence, in the absence of consensus and a clear threat with which to mobilize opinion and action, a case-by-case approach, with its potential inconsistencies and policy reversals, seems likely to become the norm. This suggests that future foreign policy will exhibit a more general, "results-oriented pragmatism" rather than a set of guiding doctrines (see Warburg 1989, 310).

At the same time, the Reagan Doctrine teaches that a case-by-case approach is not necessarily harmful. One of the lessons for post–cold war foreign policy taught by the Reagan Doctrine is the need to assess carefully the specific circumstances of a particular situation. The doctrine was successful when the context was considered; its failures generally stemmed from insufficient attention to complexity, subtle distinctions, or changes in context. Thus, if post–cold war presidential doctrines were limited to the expression of general purposes and the establishment of "terms of reference" for more specific policy debates, the effect might be advantageous rather than problematic.

The Reagan Doctrine also sheds some light on the place of the Third World in U.S. foreign policy. It is clear from the logic of the initiative that the primary concern with the targets of the strategy stemmed from connections to issues and events outside the Third World itself. That is, the significance of the Third World to the Reagan Doctrine was essentially as an arena in which to confront the Soviet Union. While the doctrine's rationale specified the need to confront Moscow and the desire to promote democracy and freedom in the Third World, the commitment of resources was clearly tied directly to the first purpose, not the second. Moreover, the actions by the United States during the Bush administration suggest that as the perception of threat from the Soviet Union declined, the willingness of policy makers throughout the system to continue expending time, energy, and resources on the cases also declined. Hence, while the Reagan Doctrine called for a "crusade for freedom" in the Third World, and while the Clinton administration, consistent with this appeal, has argued for a strategy of enlargement, U.S. policy in the late 1980s and early 1990s has shown a distinct lack of zeal to expend the resources necessary for either. In the post–cold war world the lesson is this: without a compelling strategic interest (generally stemming from outside the particular region in question) or powerful economic concern, U.S. policy makers will not make many Third World issues a major priority. For all the attention provided during the Reagan administration, the activity of the United States in such places as Angola, Afghanistan, and Nicaragua after 1989 was decidedly limited. In the absence of a crisis (economic or strategic), the post–cold war Third World will be similarly treated.

Making the Reagan Doctrine: The Policy Makers

The manner in which the Reagan Doctrine was formulated and applied reveals a number of important characteristics about U.S. foreign policy making. The origins of the strategy, its diverse versions, and its uneven application all point to the complexity of the process and the variation in the roles and influence of the policy makers. The case studies teach three lessons about American foreign policy making: (1) policy is shaped by four circles of policy makers; (2) the role and influence of each of these circles shifts, and policy-making leadership may come from the White House, Congress, the foreign policy bureaucracy, or all three; and (3) like-minded individuals from different circles form complex rival alliances to combat other policy makers and shape policy according to their preferences. The complexity and broad involvement of many actors in the making of Reagan Doctrine foreign policy carry implications for post–cold war U.S. foreign policy as well.

The Four Circles of Policy Makers

As the case studies make abundantly clear, the development and application of the Reagan Doctrine cannot be traced to any single actor or institution in the U.S. foreign policy community. Rather, the involvement of many actors from four different circles caused the strategy to evolve as it did. Each circle was involved, and each influenced policy in important ways. In truth, the Reagan Doctrine cannot be comprehended without looking to each of these groups. Therefore, the first lesson of the Reagan Doctrine for U.S. foreign policy making is that the policy emerged from the interaction of four circles of policy makers.

President Reagan and his advisers. The Reagan Doctrine was initially formulated by the White House, which then took steps to implement it in several situations. Members of this circle, then, were the authors of the Reagan Doctrine, and as such were responsible for outlining the broad strategic goals of the initiative, establishing the framework for discussion, and setting the agenda for policy making. The initial choice on policy toward Nicaragua during 1981 emerged most clearly from the leadership of this group. Moreover, this group was deeply involved in subsequent policy making regarding Nicaragua, in combination with Congress. Furthermore, the White House could, and did, dominate the agenda when it wished. In the Nicaragua case, for example, the White House forced Congress to return to the issue again and again. In the case of Afghanistan, this high-level group made two key decisions in 1985 and 1986, although the decisions occurred in the context of bureaucratic and congressional pressure. While this circle of actors was often involved in the policy-making process, however, it did not always lead. It cannot be said to have occupied the center of American foreign policy making in that regard.

Perhaps the most striking characteristic of this group concerns the episodic involvement of President Reagan. It is clear from the case studies that, with the exception of the Nicaragua case and a few instances in the others, President Reagan was largely absent from executive-branch decision making. Stemming from his detached style of governing, his lack of interest, and other idiosyncratic characteristics, as well as more general constraints on his time and priorities, this uneven involvement had several consequences. First, high-level advisers to the president had to compete for attention and support, and they engaged in diverse efforts to manipulate the president and one another. Unfortunately, President Reagan often refrained from resolving disagreements and conflicts among this advisers, prompting sometimes bitter rivalry (e.g., Shultz versus Casey) and often contradictory policy efforts.[2] In effect, rather than serving as a set of advisers to the president, administration high-level officials were often semiautonomous actors pursuing what they considered to be official policy.

The president's lack of attention had at least three other consequences. In addition to fostering disputes among his advisers, it also prompted related bureaucratic disputes and "wheel spinning," or stalemates. President Reagan had the authority to decide policy disputes, but in several critical instances (e.g., regarding Afghanistan, Angola, Mozambique, and Cambodia) he refused to do so. For example, President Reagan refused to resolve the disagreement over whether or not to give Stinger missiles to the Afghan rebels. Only when the State Department sided with those in favor of supplying the missiles was the logjam broken. When presented with a consensus, Reagan agreed and "decided" to send the missiles. Hence, this lack of presidential assertiveness produced two different kinds of results: policy was sometimes frozen in the status quo until the dispute was resolved by other means; and the disputants pursued contradictory policies, attempting to undermine other approaches, until one side emerged victorious in the bureaucratic struggle or external events (in Congress or outside the United States) intervened to resolve the conflict. The president's inattention and lack of assertiveness made it possible for advisers and bureaucrats to shape policy more by the specific actions they took than through official interagency or high-level policy reviews. Finally, presidential inattention provided numerous opportunities for Congress, either as an institution or through the actions of individual members, to take up leadership roles. Ironically, when the president brought his attention to bear, the first two consequences were largely mitigated.

The foreign policy bureaucracy. The bureaucracy was involved in every Reagan Doctrine case in several ways: it generated most of the options and analyses that prompted policy reviews and decisions; the various agencies and departments carried out policy; and this circle often led in making policy, especially in the early phases of policy making on Mozambique, Cambodia, and Angola, and in the later stages on Mozambique and Angola.

Several characteristics stand out from the case studies. This group (indeed, the executive branch in general) dominated the early stages and cycles of policy making in all the cases. In addition, as foreign policy insiders have long noted (e.g., Lake 1989, 31), the work of members of the bureaucracy on specific, day-to-day issues shaped broad policy, often as much as official reviews or presidential decision directives. Hence, in implementing decisions and responding to daily developments, bureaucrats made policy and established precedents. More troubling, however, this circle's activities were dominated by conflict, disagreement, bargaining, compromise, and sometimes stalemates. In many instances, the adage that the only final decision is the one with which a bureaucrat agrees seemed to pertain, as the "losing" officials often seemed to treat such verdicts as obstacles rather than as the end to debate. Especially in the Angola, Mozambique, and Nicaragua cases, different parts of the foreign policy bureaucracy reacted to a decision by increasing their attempts to change the policy.

Some of the disagreements reflected the divisive power of organizational purposes and missions. On the overall policy, for example, the CIA and the Department of Defense tended to adhere to the "Reagan Doctrine as policy" viewpoint, emphasizing assistance to anticommunist rebels to coerce changes in the targeted country and in the Soviet Union. The State Department, on the other hand, emphasized the initiative as a component of a larger strategy that included diplomacy, and its officials advocated negotiated settlements in the targeted countries and in the larger regions.

The debilitating effects of bureaucratic conflict took a frequent toll on U.S. policy. Divisions, disagreements, and conflicts were common within and between State and Defense, State and CIA, CIA and Defense, and State and the NSC staff. In some cases, bureaucratic conflict produced a compromise that did not satisfy any organization fully, and may thus be said to have been suboptimal (e.g., aid to the Cambodian resistance). In others, feuding between two or more organizations produced confusing and contradictory actions that undermined the effectiveness of American policy. This occurred to some extent over Nicaragua, where disagreements between the NSC staff and the CIA, on the one hand, and the State Department, on the other, produced the contradictory result of an administration at once opposed to negotiations and proposing negotiations, and attempting to accommodate Congress while taking action to confront, polarize, and deceive that institution.

Even more egregious bureaucratic conflict occurred over Angola and Mozambique, where hard-liners in the Defense Department and the CIA worked actively to undermine and defeat the presidentially approved and congressionally supported policy by using their control over certain channels of implementation and information to shape policy. In the case of Afghanistan, the State Department utilized its control over the diplomatic option to shape U.S. policy in 1986–88. When the details of the State Department's approach became public, institutional and interbranch conflict broke out as other elements of the foreign policy–making community rejected State's actions. Thus, parallel or simultaneous policy making occurred in which different parts of the bureaucracy pursued different policies, or each agency responsible for a particular "track" of U.S. policy tended to emphasize that track as the primary channel and attempted to minimize, or even scuttle, the other track(s).

Divisions between career specialists and political appointees were evident in several cases, including Nicaragua, where careerists in State and Defense were inclined to be more accommodating toward the Sandinistas and less in favor of the contras, while political appointees were much more supportive of both the contras and of a maximalist solution to the problem (e.g., overthrowing the Sandinista government). Even more significant, the appointees on the NSC staff were uniformly more hard-line than the careerists at State and Defense.[3] The most obvious split of this sort occurred over the Reagan Doctrine and Afghanistan. Careerists in the CIA and the Defense Department were extremely cautious toward the prospect of supporting the Afghan rebels for fear of direct confrontation with the Soviet Union and the potential that sophisticated American weapons would fall into the hands of terrorists or the Soviet Union, while appointees in the same agencies were strong advocates of the program.

Congress. A key feature revealed in the preceding chapters is the extent to which members of Congress were major factors in the formulation and application of the Reagan Doctrine. In truth, the institution and individual members had access to potentially potent avenues of influence. When institutional consensus existed, Congress could make or shape policy through substantive legislation (e.g., Afghanistan and Cambodia). When serious cleavages occurred, as in the case of Nicaragua, members of Congress could freeze policy, because any faction could block action but no single group could take action. Also, the different factions could ally themselves with those in the executive branch and the public with whom they agreed and force the others to adopt their version of policy.

The first route of congressional influence lay in the nature of the policy process, which presented regular opportunities for congressional action. The nature of the policy-making process for the Reagan Doctrine ensured a role for Congress by providing stages suited to its particular powers and by progressing in cycles that allowed Congress to take part in policy formulation in successive iterations of the process, even if it ceded initial policy making in each case to the executive branch.

Certain direct powers also gave Congress a role and influence.

Members of Congress enacted their preferences into law, and just as often threatened legislation to force policy into line with their preferences. On multiple occasions in each of the Reagan Doctrine cases, members used the institution's legislative powers to either set policy or force the administration to compromise. Additionally, Congress shaped policy by granting or withholding funds. The control of the treasury gave members a formidable tool, and the regularity of the annual budget cycle presented them with recurring opportunities to wield it. Members used this power to expand dramatically U.S. aid to the Afghan rebels; to constrain, attempt to channel, and eventually set policy in the Nicaragua case; to force a rethinking and expansion of the Reagan Doctrine to portions of the rebel groups operating in Cambodia; and to restrain U.S. efforts in Mozambique by eliminating funds from programs they did not support.

Members of Congress also used the institution's oversight responsibilities to monitor and evaluate existing policy. One of the most striking patterns in the case studies is Congress's reliance on this avenue to gain access to policy making, which occurred regularly and in every case. Moreover, U.S. senators have the constitutional authority to advise and consent in the treaty process and in the appointment of administration officials. Using this power, senators affected the Reagan Doctrine. For example, members of the Senate blocked the nomination of Melissa Wells as ambassador to Mozambique to force a fundamental change in U.S. policy. The Senate's threats to block the Intermediate Nuclear Forces (INF) Treaty if the president did not accede to its desires on Afghanistan are another example of this instrument of influence.

In addition, Congress used other informal avenues to affect policy in each case.[4] Members merely threatened to exercise their congressional powers, issued warnings and requests directly to the executive branch (often in the form of letters), and passed nonbinding resolutions to convince the president to incorporate their preferences into the policy. While the outcomes varied from case to case, in general these methods were quite effective at influencing policy. In the case of Afghanistan, the Tsongas resolution, the Senate staff study, and the Senate resolution on the 1988 diplomatic settlement all forced changes in the administration's approach. On Cambodia, a good example can be seen in the 1988 congressional resolution on the UN statement and corresponding U.S. policy, since it clearly influenced the administration's actions. For Nicaragua, the early Boland amendments and the persistent efforts by some members to promote negotiations between the United States and the Nicaraguan government constitute such signals. Finally, in both the Angola and Mozambique cases, steady pressure by aid supporters in the form of legislative proposals, hearings, letters, and other measures all had a major role in shaping U.S. policy and the administration's actions.

A few other avenues were also utilized. Members of Congress attempted to affect policy by framing opinion through debate, hearings, public appeals, and other events, often vying with similar administration efforts, as the s/LPD episode in the Nicaragua case suggests (see Chapter 6). When disagreements among executive branch officials occurred, as they did in each case, members were able to seize on them and join with one faction or another to try to achieve a specific set of policy goals. Such alliances provided opportunities for coalitions that cut across the branches to influence the policy debate and shape policy in line with their preferences. Members of Congress also used procedural legislation to structure administration processes. For instance, members agreed to provide nonlethal assistance to the contras in 1985 but stipulated that it would have to be disbursed through a new State Department agency in order to minimize the influence of the CIA and Defense Department and maximize the openness and accountability of the process (i.e., make certain Congress could supervise the aid). In the same measure, Congress required that the aid be provided in three individual installments, each accompanied by a report detailing the precise expenditures.

Finally, the Afghanistan and Cambodia cases suggest that members of Congress used their positions on specialized subcommittees to create policy; the efforts of Representative Charles Wilson detailed in the Afghanistan case study are a fair example. Wilson used his position and influence on the defense appropriations subcommittee of the House Appropriations Committee to reshape the application of the Reagan doctrine toward Afghanistan; his alliance with Defense and CIA officials succeeded in obtaining a virtual tripling of the assistance, and a qualitative expansion as well. His efforts were then presented to the Congress and the president for approval.

The public. This broadest circle, which includes public opinion, the media, diverse interest groups (e.g., trade, ethnic, ideological, corporate, transnational and foreign groups, government, business, or otherwise), and research institutions played a role, if secondary, in the formulation and application of the Reagan Doctrine. The involvement of the public was supportive rather than primary, but it was significant. It can be seen most clearly in the Afghanistan, Angola, and Mozambique cases, in which nongovernmental actors were important sources of pressure and support on which policy makers could draw. In particular, the Angola and Mozambique case studies show that various networks of groups formed a significant part of the attempts to reformulate U.S. policy. It is also the case that, at least regarding Nicaragua, broad public opinion acted as a constraint on U.S. policy, perhaps preventing more direct U.S. action (Sobel 1993).

Shifting Constellations of Policy Makers

The fact that the formulation and application of the Reagan Doctrine occurred through the activities of President Reagan and his advisers, the foreign policy bureaucracy, Congress, and the public leads to a second broad lesson. In the process of making the Reagan Doctrine, these four broad circles of actors had varied and fluctuating relationships, and each governmental circle exercised policy leadership at some point.

As the case studies clearly indicate, the president and the White House did not determine foreign policy. This suggests that, at least with regard to the Reagan Doctrine, policy making is better represented by the shifting constellations image (see Figure 1b on p. 10) than the presidential preeminence image, because the roles and influence of these four circles shifted throughout the cases. Only the shifting constellations image accommodates leadership by the president, as expected by the conventional representation, *and* leadership by other circles. Therefore, the shifting constellations image is both more accurate and of greater utility and applicability; it allows for the leadership of different policy makers and does not presume that the president is always at the center of policy making. It suggests that studies of U.S. foreign policy include each of the four groups, be aware that complex interrelationships can occur, and examine the full process by which they formulate, implement, and evaluate policy. Following these cues increases the likelihood that case studies will capture the complexity of U.S. foreign policy making and its impact on the ensuing policy.

The effect of the cyclical policy-making process through which the Reagan Doctrine was formulated and applied contributes to this second lesson. The initiative began in the White House or the foreign policy bureaucracies, but in every case it then progressed to include the interbranch actor set—or, in the case of Afghanistan, Cambodia, and Nicaragua, to policy leadership by Congress. The shifting constellations suggest that the president is preeminent in policy making only initially. Other actors soon become engaged and may wrest leadership away from the White House or the foreign policy bureaucracy.

The case studies indicate that the shift in initiative is a consequence of two factors. First, the pattern stems from the stages and cyclical nature of the process. Policy, once decided, must be implemented and reviewed. The foreign policy bureaucracy and Congress are involved in both steps, and each may make subsequent attempts to reformulate or refine the original policy. Moreover, control over resources (e.g., the treasury) or responsibility for implementation allow both Congress and the foreign policy bureaucracy to shape policy after the formal decisions are made, a consequence repeatedly exhibited in each Reagan Doctrine case. Second, the pattern is, it seems, partly related to the nature of the tool with which policy is implemented. Robert Pastor (1992, 112) perceptively suggested that the "vehicle that carries a particular policy" heavily influences the group involved in setting and carrying out the policy. Policy tools requiring appropriations "hardwire" Congress into the policy-making process and may prompt shifts from executive branch leadership to interbranch or congressional leadership. Additionally, the tools trigger the involvement of particular elements of the foreign policy bureaucracy, which then have an opportunity to shape policy by the specific actions they take when implementing the chosen course.

The changing role and influence of the four circles of policy makers across and within the Reagan Doctrine cases display five general configurations or constellations formed by the shifting relationships among the four main circles of actors, each representing leadership by a different circle or circles.

Constellation I: White House leadership. The president and his top advisers exerted policy leadership in a manner consistent with the orthodox model. However, sole leadership occurred less often than the presidential preeminence image (see Chapter 1) would indicate. In fact, the White House led primarily in the initial formulation of the overall doctrine (i.e., in creating the initial framework and providing the "plan" to which others reacted), in the doctrine's initial application to Nicaragua and Afghanistan, and in its 1985–86 expansion in Afghanistan. Three general comments on the policy making stemming from this group's leadership seem warranted. First, in the cases of Afghanistan (1985–86) and Nicaragua (1981), this high-level group assessed developments, considered information, and devised a response. These cases illustrate that White House leadership is *capable* of producing coherent and rational decision making. Second, however, the Nicaragua case clearly shows signs of the small-group effect known as group-think (e.g., Janis 1982): an ideologically homogeneous circle of high-level officials considered a narrow range of alternatives and eliminated dissenters (i.e., officials advocating negotiation and accommodation) from the ranks of policy makers. This illustrates the problems to which White House Leadership is *susceptible.* Third, these cases emphatically underscore the importance of presidential attention and involvement. As Jerel Rosati (1981) and Peter Schraeder (1994) concluded, given interest, attentiveness, involvement, and activity, the White House may bend the foreign policy bureaucracy to its policy preferences (e.g., at some moments in the Afghanistan, Nicaragua, and Angola cases). However, as President Reagan's general disinterest in several of the cases and his utter unwillingness to settle disagreements among his own advisers and agencies in others (e.g., Afghanistan, Angola, and Mozambique) suggest, such characteristics are far from given and appear to depend on the president's management style and personality.

Constellation II: Foreign policy bureaucracy leadership. When the foreign policy bureaucracy exercised policy leadership, the White House and Congress tended to be ratifiers of bureaucratic options rather than initiators of policy. The Reagan Doctrine cases suggest that this constellation may be the default option when the White House and Congress are not assertive. Leadership from this constellation develops because of the control by the foreign policy bureaucracy over the day-to-day conduct of foreign affairs; specific actions set precedents and combine to create policy by their cumulative effect and momentum. In the absence of White House or congressional attention, this control over implementation and information provides the basis for policy leadership, as was the case in the early phases of policy toward Mozambique, Cambodia, and Angola, and in the later phases of Mozambique and Angola. The most significant pattern of behavior of this constellation stems from its "multivoice" character, which tends to generate disagreement and conflict between advisers, agencies, and departments. The consequence might be compromise that does not satisfy any organization fully, stalemate, confusing and contradictory actions, or parallel policies.

Constellation III: Interbranch leadership. Interbranch leadership, in which all three governmental circles shared responsibility and non-governmental actors played supporting roles, prevailed at some stage or cycle in all the cases. Interbranch policy making showed at least four characteristics (Jentleson 1990). First, there was cooperation, in which the circles worked together to make policy. Through the combination of legislation, hearings, and executive actions, policy emerged that was supported and furthered by each circle (e.g., Afghanistan). Second, constructive compromise developed in which members of the circles found enough common ground or were able to devise solutions that garnered enough support for policy to proceed, although these sometimes satisfied no group completely and sometimes contained inherent contradictions (e.g., Cambodia). Third, institutional competition developed involving legislative-executive or interagency contention (e.g., later Afghanistan, Angola, and Mozambique). Two subpatterns emerged in this development: either the circles pursued parallel policy making, seeking to act independently of one another to make policy fit the preferences of the dominant view (or majority, in the case of Congress), or members of each circle forged alliances with like-minded members of the other circles to compete over policy (e.g., Mozambique and Angola). It is important to note that parallel policy making may involve two bureaucratic agencies competing as well as competition between the White House and Congress. Finally, policy confrontation and stalemate occurred, in which each circle, endowed with some "negative power," blocked the preferences of the others (Nicaragua, and Mozambique in 1987).

Constellation IV: Subgovernment leadership. Subgovernment, closed policy systems based on alliances between members of subcommittees and bureaucratic agencies, nominally led by the legislative component, also exerted some influence and leadership. This occurred principally in the second phase of policy toward Afghanistan, when Representative Charles Wilson used his position on an appropriations subcommittee to double aid to the rebels, but it can also be seen in Representative Steven Solarz's efforts to forge U.S. policy toward Cambodia. Policy was made through bargaining and logrolling by actors with reinforcing objectives and interests without the involvement of the upper levels of the executive branch or Congress (see, e.g., Ripley and Franklin 1991). However, multiple policy systems usually exist, and there may be clashes over their "turf," as the appropriations and intelligence committees clashed over aid to the Afghan rebels. When this occurs, the involvement of higher levels of the executive and legislative branches is usually required to settle the dispute. As Ripley and Franklin (1991) noted and the Reagan Doctrine cases indicate, subgovernment leadership is most common on issues involving defense policy and appropriations.

Constellation V: Congressional leadership. Congress controlled policy making through its legislative procedures in phases of the Cambodia and Nicaragua cases. Although the executive branch was called on for information and opinions during hearings, policy was formulated and the initial legitimation occurred in Congress. The president was asked to endorse the legislation (by signing it), and the foreign policy bureaucracy was asked to implement the policy, but the policy emerged from bargaining and compromise among members of Congress. Because of both the bargaining and the desire by some members to allow flexibility, the legislation had loopholes or ambiguities, which allowed the executive branch to interpret it with flexibility (e.g., the Solarz initiative, Boland I and II). Congressional leadership occurred only when consensus existed within the institution. In such cases, Congress acted as a unified institution and made policy. (When such consensus does not exist, the rival factions of Congress will often form alliances with elements of the executive branch to influence policy.) The case studies indicate that, given consensus, congressional leadership is likely under two circumstances: (1) agreement on the need for a policy exists, but the president or executive branch has not acted; and (2) the administration adopts a policy that a substantial part of Congress rejects.

Latent hierarchy. The shifting constellations formed by the White House, the foreign policy bureaucracy, Congress, and the public during the formulation and application of the Reagan Doctrine indicate that the president is not always at the center of policy making. As the case studies show, a president may be largely absent from policy making, appearing only to ratify a decision made by other actors (usually a consensus or compromise) or to break a deadlock. Thus, a condition exists within the executive branch that might be labeled "latent hierarchy."

This concept is based on a recognition of the substantial powers conferred on a president which enable that individual to choose advisers, establish structure, make and enforce decisions, and settle disagreements. However, latent hierarchy predicates such leadership by the president on the interest, attentiveness, involvement, and activity of that individual. Therefore, presidential leadership is a variable, not a given (Rockman 1994, 67).

Within the executive branch, the implication of latent hierarchy is that both presidential advisers and members of the foreign policy bureaucracy enjoy greater autonomy than is often assumed. Since personalities and management styles vary, and since priorities must be set and the president's interest cannot be focused on all foreign policy issues at once, numerous instances are likely to exist in which the president is no more than a spectator. Thus, latent hierarchy stems from constraints flowing from idiosyncratic factors and the more general constraints of time, complex agendas, and issue importance. A president can assert leadership over the bureaucracy, cut through or minimize the effects of bureaucratic disagreement, and mitigate differences of opinion among high-level advisers, but only with attention and participation. In the absence of presidential attention and direction, the advisers may act semiautonomously and the foreign policy bureaucracy will exert leadership and suffer from its internal divisions and organizational complexity. Hence, the relationship between the White House and the foreign policy bureaucracy (and Congress, for that matter) is subject to variation based on the president's style, time, and interests.

In the Reagan Doctrine cases, four consequences of latent hierarchy can be identified. When President Reagan focused on a case, the White House was influential, although not necessarily dominant. Given the interest and activity of the president (e.g., in Nicaragua and Afghanistan), the White House succeeded in reducing the impact of bureaucratic and advisory disputes, and it dominated the agenda with respect to Congress, setting the terms of the debate. This consequence represents the "hierarchy" aspect of latent hierarchy and basically corresponds to the orthodox image, which places the president at the center of policy making. Of course, as the Nicaragua case indicates, presidential attention does not ensure high-quality policy making or results.

The other three consequences spring from the "latent" component of the concept. In the Reagan Doctrine cases, more often than not President Reagan was uninvolved and uninterested. His lack of involvement affected his circle of high-level advisers, the foreign policy bureaucracy, and relations between the legislative and executive branches. His top advisers acted not as his agents but as independent policy makers. William Casey, Alexander Haig, George Shultz, Caspar Weinberger, William Clark, Robert McFarlane, and John Poindexter all pursued their own agendas and attempted to manipulate the president and each other to achieve their goals. The president's lack of vigor also made it possible for bureaucratic disputes to affect policy (e.g., in the Angola, Afghanistan, and Mozambique cases). In particular, his unwillingness to assert himself allowed different agencies to pursue parallel policies, which were often mutually contradictory; to attempt to undermine existing policy in favor of their own preferences; and to block action entirely, either by their own control over implementation or by forging alliances with members from other circles (e.g., Congress and nongovernmental actors). Finally, President Reagan's lack of involvement and the corresponding actions by his advisers and the foreign policy bureaucracy provided Congress with a motive to be more assertive. In the Afghanistan, Angola, Cambodia, and Mozambique cases, the president's disinterest and inaction prompted individual members and the institution as a whole to act. In some cases, individual members used their positions on committees and subcommittees to seize the agenda; in others, the action stemmed from the institutional involvement of Congress. Significantly, though, congressional involvement was not limited to cases in which the president failed to lead, as the Nicaragua case clearly indicates.

Congressional influence. In addition, the shifting constellations image also indicates that Congress matters more in foreign policy than conventional approaches suggest. The role of Congress in the application of the Reagan Doctrine indicates that various avenues of influence, formal (e.g., legislation and appropriation) and informal (e.g., procedural, anticipated reactions, and rival alliances), present the institution and its individual members with ample opportunity to shape foreign policy. As the case studies suggest, the combination of formal and informal paths of influence create formidable possibilities if members of Congress choose to exercise them. Congress was a full partner in the policy-making process in all the Reagan Doctrine cases. Moreover, even when members failed to pass a single substantive measure, their activities affected foreign policy. In addition, Congress did not simply react to the president; in certain instances, members took the lead in formulating policy options (e.g., Cambodia and Nicaragua). Hence, the Reagan Doctrine lends support to those who have argued for increased attention to the role of Congress in foreign policy (e.g., Mann 1990; Lindsay 1993, 1994c; Ripley and Lindsay 1993) and raises questions for those who have dismissed such involvement as a myth (e.g., Hinckley 1994). Indeed, the array of formal and informal avenues of influence indicates that no evaluation of congressional foreign policy making that examines only legislation can possibly assess the influence of the institution, and no examination of foreign policy that ignores members of Congress can hope to comprehend policy making (or policy).

The cyclical nature of this complex process stands out as a key to congressional influence. Although the executive branch had the initial advantage in policy making, Congress played a crucial role in each case. This suggests that although members may be reluctant to take an initial leadership role, they will react to a sluggish, disinterested, or defiant White House. Representative Norman Dicks (D-Wash.) put it nicely: "Congress abhors a vacuum" (Stockton 1993, 241). Furthermore, while many analysts argue that members of Congress do not care about foreign policy ("Afghanistan is not in my district"), the case studies show that member involvement was broad, indicating some interest, and that interested individuals in Congress used their access to avenues of influence to force broader institutional attention. This last point seems a key one. For example, although few members (of Congress or the executive branch) were interested in Cambodia, Representative Solarz used policy-making tools that forced the entire institution to act (vote). Furthermore, key individuals were also able to use indirect methods to affect the executive branch and their own colleagues. In short, a few members of Congress can prompt institutional action. Hence, whether all the members care about Afghanistan is irrelevant; whether Congress acts is what matters.

Interbranch leadership thus best characterizes the overall formulation and application of the Reagan Doctrine. With regard to Afghanistan, each policy-making group seized the initiative at various times: the White House was important at one moment, the foreign policy bureaucracy at another, and Congress at a third. The final stage saw a complex interaction among the executive and legislative branches. In the case of Cambodia, policy-making leadership shifted from the executive branch to Congress and then to joint leadership. Those two cases thus provide examples of interbranch cooperation. The application of the Reagan Doctrine to Angola in 1985 was a result of multiple branch processes that simultaneously included bureaucratic policy making, presidential policy making, congressional policy making, rival alliances, and parallel policy making. Policy for Nicaragua took shape through a process that began with presidential dominance but quickly moved to interbranch conflict and then to congressional leadership for the final year and a half of the Reagan administration.

Rival Alliances of Policy Makers

The third broad lesson to be gained from the formulation and application of the Reagan Doctrine concerns the formation and influence of rival alliances that cut across the branches. Just as the United States does not speak with a single voice on foreign policy but instead depends on the interaction of four circles of policy makers, many different individuals constitute the White House, the foreign policy bureaucracy, Congress, and the public. No circle of actors can be viewed as a monolith with only one perspective and one policy preference. Instead, the different individuals who make up each group will have different policy views. Disagreements, disputes, and divisions will occur within each circle as well as between them.

Like-minded individuals from different circles can unite to force their preferences into policy. A presidential adviser may find sympathetic members of Congress and careerists from the foreign policy bureaucracy who agree on a particular perspective. They have access to different instruments and avenues, which allows them to complement and supplement each other in their effort to shape or reshape policy. Clashes between rival alliances may produce stalemates, in which each can cancel the other's preference but none can enact its own. Compromise and bargaining may also occur, as may the simultaneous pursuit of different approaches or strands of policy (e.g., one alliance pursuing a diplomatic option and another implementing paramilitary action). In these situations, policy, if it emerges at all, is the result of a complex interaction involving presidential advisers, bureaucrats, members of Congress, and the public.

The formation of and potential clashes between such alliances constitute a basic feature of U.S. foreign policy making, especially when disagreement over objectives or instruments exists. In fact, this sub rosa involvement of many people with access to many levers of influence is a central arena of foreign policy making. The factions may contend with one another to establish policy; once policy is determined, they may alternatively conspire to undermine the existing policy or unite to preserve the status quo. Moreover, these alliances shift, both in their composition and in their status. New policies and changes in existing ones prompt changing membership and renewed actions by reconstituted alliances: dissident alliances become status quo alliances which attempt to protect their gains, while status quo alliances become dissident alliances and try to reverse or mitigate the changes. The arena for action and debate also shifts constantly. It may rest in the bowels of the foreign policy bureaucracy or be elevated to the White House; it may take place in back rooms and offices, in committees and subcommittees, or on the floor of Congress.

Such alliances formed in all the cases in which the Reagan Doctrine was applied or considered. In the debate over policy toward Nicaragua, for instance, an alliance between members of the White House, parts of the foreign policy bureaucracy (especially the NSC staff and the CIA), and members of Congress colluded to sustain the application of the Reagan Doctrine and prevent alternatives to or abandonment of that option. In the case of Afghanistan, a hard-liner alliance with members from each circle consistently tried to expand U.S. support for the rebels and, after 1985, to limit the scope of the diplomatic effort. A more pragmatic alliance, while agreeing on expanded U.S. aid to the rebels, sought meaningful negotiations in addition. The two alliances clashed in 1987 and 1988 when a settlement began to take shape. The ensuing U.S. policy, which supported both diplomacy *and* continuing U.S. assistance, resulted from a very uneasy compromise between the two alliances.

Rival alliances were most pronounced and had the greatest impact in the Mozambique and Angola cases. In the Mozambique case, hard-liners in the White House (e.g., Casey and Poindexter), foreign policy bureaucracy (e.g., CIA, NSC staff), Congress (e.g., Helms, Burton, and Roth), and the public (e.g., the Heritage Foundation) who did not subscribe to the regional strategy approved in 1981 united and tried to reverse U.S. policy and begin sending aid to the rebels. The presence of members from each of the circles provided the alliance with access to public pressure, executive branch instruments (e.g., information and control of day-to-day conduct), and legislative tools (e.g., hearings and budget debates). These channels allowed a number of actions that ranged in scope from simple information sharing, to attempts at mobilization and pressure tactics in support of a particular option, to semiautonomous actions to implement the preferred version of policy (e.g., clandestine contacts with rebels and foreign leaders).

These channels were utilized to attack existing policy, block its implementation, and force its refinement or reversal. Specifically, Casey and elements from the CIA, NSC staff, and Defense Department used intelligence back channels to aid and encourage South African support for the rebels and attempted to bring information from those channels to bear on administration reviews. Their allies in Congress also had access to this information, which they used to attack administration representatives and persuade colleagues. In addition, the nomination of Melissa Wells as ambassador to Mozambique created an opportunity for the Senate portion of the alliance to obstruct official policy and press for a reevaluation by blocking the appointment and holding additional hearings. These private and public actors carefully orchestrated their attempts to frame opinion—presidential, congressional, and public. Ultimately these mutually reinforcing efforts failed to reverse existing policy. Instead, a less organized but more broadly based alliance of pragmatists and liberals from each of the four circles sustained the conciliatory approach to Mozambique. This alliance persuaded President Reagan and the broader membership of Congress to reject the hard-liners' arguments and maintain the status quo (e.g., Reagan affirmed the State Department–led approach by meeting with Mozambican president Chissano in September 1987, and the Senate voted to confirm Wells).

The Angola case provides an even more extensive example of rival alliances contending with one another to shape policy (see Chapter 5). Disagreement over U.S. objectives in Angola and southern Africa was evident in 1981 when the administration officially adopted the constructive engagement approach and attempted to begin assisting the Angolan rebels, an effort that failed in the face of congressional opposition. Once the general course emerged, predicated on U.S. mediation of the Angola-Namibia–South Africa disputes, disagreement among policy makers caused three different alliances to form. First, hard-liners from the White House (e.g., Casey, Clark, and Poindexter), the foreign policy bureaucracy (e.g., certain officials from CIA, Defense, and NSC staff), Congress (e.g., Kemp, Burton, Dornan, Symms, Wallop, and

Helms), and the public (e.g., the Cuban-American National Foundation and the Heritage Foundation) formed one dissident alliance that worked doggedly to begin U.S. aid to rebels in Angola and work more cooperatively with South Africa. Another dissident alliance, made up of more liberal members of Congress and the public, pressed for more forceful action to combat apartheid and South African regional aggression while advocating better, more cooperative relations with both the Angolan and Mozambican governments. A status quo alliance of pragmatists from all four circles sought to preserve the regional diplomatic approach and balance U.S. support for the rebels, opposition to Cuban troops, and moderation of the Angolan regime, and avoid an outright alliance with South Africa.

The jockeying among these three alliances caused U.S. policy to develop as it did. The alliances gave each component greater access and influence in the policy-making debate. Members of Congress received inside information and some voice in internal administration debates, administration officials had their preferences represented in congressional debates and written into legislation, and supportive members of the public received access to information and support for their activities while helping the other members of their alliance to shape the terms of the debate. All three alliances utilized the tools at their disposal to structure the debate, seize the initiative, take action, and protect their preferences. In particular, the hard-liner alliance conducted a carefully timed and coordinated effort that harnessed various legislative and executive branch actions in an organized campaign. The efforts were especially acute during the 1985 debate on whether to begin aid to the UNITA rebels; the arena began in Congress with the fight to repeal the Clark amendment and then expanded to include both branches as administration deliberations followed. The clash prompted a lengthy and acrimonious debate in all arenas, and the resulting policy uneasily combined some sanctions against South Africa, some assistance for the rebels, and U.S. diplomatic efforts to negotiate a regional settlement.

These two examples and the evidence from the other cases suggest that the opportunity to form such alliances improves the ability of members of each circle to shape policy to their liking. Each component—adviser, bureaucrat, member of Congress, and private citizen or group—contributes to and benefits from the alliance. A White House adviser advocating a particular viewpoint gains avenues through which to marshall support for a particular position. If that position is consistent with the established policy, the alliances serve as backstops which help to sustain the approach and ensure faithful implementation. Conversely, if the adviser's position has been rejected or has not been given a hearing, alliances can generate pressure to review existing policy, manipulate the process, and reopen a policy debate, giving the adviser an (additional) opportunity to advocate the desired option. Moreover, alliances provide dissenting advisers with post hoc opportunities to try to block the implementation of an undesired decision. Hence, such alliances provide means by which advisers manipulate the process, each other, and the president in order to turn their policy preferences into official policy, prevent undesired options from being implemented, and undermine existing policy with the purpose of prompting a revision.

Similar advantages present themselves to foreign policy bureaucrats. While providing the source of information and the avenues by which to affect implementation, bureaucrats benefit from alliances in several ways. Perhaps most fundamentally, such alliances provide authorization for bureaucratic actions, a route through which to shape the policy debate, and an avenue for dissent from official policy. An alliance with a sympathetic presidential adviser and members of Congress provides "patrons" who may champion the perspective of a bureaucrat who dissents from existing policy, bring the official into deliberations or reviews, and use the information that the bureaucrat provides. At a minimum, the member of the foreign policy bureaucracy who dissents from existing policy gains another channel through which to push a preferred option. At most, control by different alliances over certain channels of implementation and information in the foreign policy bureaucracy prompts parallel or simultaneous policy making in which different parts of the bureaucracy pursue different policies, or each agency responsible for a particular track of U.S. policy emphasizes that track as the primary channel and attempts to minimize, or even scuttle, the other track(s).

Similarly, members of Congress stand to gain, perhaps more than any other circle. First, members of these alliances gain access to executive branch information and debates. Moreover, members are given a voice in the internal administrative debates through their executive branch allies; congressional support also strengthens the positions of adviser and bureaucrat in administration deliberations. These alliances also constitute additional channels through which members of Congress can send signals, advocate options, and apply pressure or provide support. Access to executive branch allies provides special opportunities for some members to attend otherwise restricted meetings, receive personal reports and briefings, and participate in executive branch deliberations. Such access also helps members of Congress to time their actions carefully to maximize their impact, and members can shape statements, letters, and legislative proposals in light of the inside information they receive from advisers and bureaucrats. Hence, in addition to improving knowledge and information, alliances provide support for actions taken in pursuit of policy preferences.

Together the alliances represent formidable forces that magnify the potential for bargaining, compromise, conflict and stalemate in the formulation and application of policy. Strong alliances with well-orchestrated campaigns can steamroll opponents and undermine rivals with the purpose of sustaining or reversing existing policy. Finally, with members in each circle, alliances can conduct parallel policy making, with each existing network developing and implementing a separate strand of policy. The Angola case provides a good example of this phenomenon: the pragmatist alliance, centered on the State Department, developed a diplomatic approach, while the hard-liner alliance, centered on the CIA, developed a covert, paramilitary stance. At times the two alliances operated as if they were independent of one another, and their supporters barely tolerated the existence of the other track.

In sum, cross-branch alliances provide advantages to their members in at least five ways: (1) they expand access to and sharing of information across the circles; (2) they help their constituents set the agenda, bring issues to the forefront, and force consideration of certain options; (3) they enhance the ability of each individual component to structure the terms of the debate and apply pressure or persuasion, whether in policy deliberations, legislative efforts, or the framing of public opinion; (4) well-developed alliances with members in each circle acquire opportunities to act, allowing coordination and orchestration of efforts and sometimes providing openings to conduct their own policies; and (5) alliances enhance the ability of their members to sustain preferred initiatives or to obstruct undesired policies by expanding the range of access points and policy instruments at their disposal. Combined, these effects increase the influence of the components and amplify their impact of policy. They also ensure that policy emerges from interbranch interaction.

Post–Cold War Foreign Policy Making

Although it is certain that the Reagan Doctrine itself has little specific relevance for the post–cold war world, given its focus on fighting communism and confronting the now-defunct Soviet Union, the same cannot be said for the processes by which U.S. foreign policy makers formulated and implemented this initiative. On the contrary, a final set of lessons from the Reagan Doctrine apply directly to future American foreign policy making. The underlying theme is that foreign policy making is a messy, complicated affair involving many different actors, and that probably will not change. The presidential preeminence that generally characterized the cold war era is unlikely to return, for several reasons.

First, the level of threat has diminished significantly. The formulation and application of the Reagan Doctrine occurred through the complex interaction of many individuals and groups, even in the presence of a very real threat from the Soviet Union. Disputes over interests, instruments, and roles occurred among U.S. policy makers in spite of the presence of this dominant adversary. In the cases analyzed in this book, variation in the perception of threat produced varying levels and types of agreement, disagreement, and policy activism. Where threat was perceived, consensus developed (e.g., Afghanistan); where threat was disputed, conflict and disagreement developed (e.g., Nicaragua). This suggests that the post–cold war world, with no Soviet Union and no clear replacement threat, can be expected not only to sustain the complex policy-making process exhibited in the Reagan Doctrine cases, but even to increase it.

Second, increasing interdependence and transnational ties make a return to presidential preeminence unlikely. Foreign policy making has become more like domestic policy making: subject to conflict, bargaining, and persuasion among competing groups within and outside the government. David Deese has noted that "the foreign policy environment is no longer the arena of contending national interests," which has caused the growth of domestic interests, the fragmentation of responsibility, and the competition for influence among actors from all four circles (Deese 1994, xl). One cause of this is the increasingly important link between domestic interests and international events, which has given rise to the expansion of "intermestic" issues. This growing permeability between foreign and domestic issues reduces the role of the president as the preeminent foreign policy maker, triggers greater fragmentation of responsibility and control, and increases the competition for influence (Rockman 1994, 73).

The third reason flows from these factors: the end of the cold war and heightened interdependence have created a situation in which consensus over the proper role, important interests, and necessary actions of the United States in the world is noticeably lacking. As many analysts have argued (e.g., Mann 1990, 2-3, 10), presidential preeminence depends as much on substantive agreement on the purposes and instruments of U.S. foreign policy as it does on institutional powers and levers of influence. In the post–cold war period—indeed, in a growing trend since the shattering of the cold war consensus in the late 1960s and early 1970s—such basic agreement has become more elusive than ever. Policy makers and the public are increasingly divided over foreign policy goals and instruments; they do not agree on even such basic issues such as the appropriate role of the United States in the world (Holsti and Rosenau 1984; Holsti 1994). Hence, even more debate over foreign policy can be expected, and increased fragmentation—or what another observer called the "democratization of foreign policy-making" (Moreno 1990, 12)—should continue for the foreseeable future.

Finally, institutional changes, when combined with international developments, suggest that the complexity of foreign policy making is irreversible. As Thomas E. Mann (1990, 28) argued, this is a consequence of "a broader transformation of the process of foreign policy-making. . . . The institutional legacy of Vietnam, Watergate, and the Iran-Contra Affair, the political incentives for foreign policy activism, and the culture of Capitol Hill" ensure continued "messiness." This firmly establishes fragmentation of responsibility and competition for influence as "the new politics of American foreign policy" in the post–cold war period (e.g., Deese 1994).

The dynamics of the post–cold war world therefore ensure continued policy-making activity by each of the four circles. Tradition, the president's role as chief executive, the sprawling foreign policy bureaucracy, and the combination of other formal and informal roles guarantee presidential involvement, if not dominance. Members of Congress have a formidable set of tools and, if anything, greater motives than ever before to engage in foreign policy activity. The erosion of consensus over foreign policy goals and appropriate instruments signals the likelihood of congressional activism on substantive grounds, while expanding interdependence and growing "intermestic" policy issues reduce the gap between foreign and domestic policy, thus increasing the political incentives for activism. Furthermore, the post–cold war period will see greater bureaucratic fragmentation as well. The changing agenda, in which economic concerns challenge traditional security issues for saliency, suggests two results: an expanding definition of the "foreign policy" bureaucracy, which will increasingly include economic and other, more traditionally domestic, agencies; and an increasingly broad spectrum of interests and perspectives, combined with new bureaucratic missions to be defended. These changes in the foreign policy bureaucracy point to a decline in presidential control; more access for members of Congress, perhaps to form alliances such as those that characterized so much of the Reagan Doctrine; and more numerous points of contact for nongovernmental groups and individuals to press for policy that reflects their concerns. Finally, the erosion of consensus and the expanding category of intermestic issues probably herald heightened involvement by nongovernmental actors. Even if the public exhibits little general interest in foreign policy, specific groups and individuals have more incentive to engage in the kind of pressure politics more typically characteristic of domestic policy.

Summary: The Implications of the Reagan Doctrine's Lessons

The lessons taught by the Reagan Doctrine indicate that a varied and complex policy-making environment is likely to persist into the foreseeable future. The cases suggest that the president and the executive branch enjoy several advantages, most notably those of initiative and control over implementation, but that other actors also have influence and play an important role, even to the extent of exercising policy leadership. When considered in the light of the broad historical context of American foreign policy making—pre–cold war, cold war, and post–cold war—the patterns of policy making exhibited in the Reagan Doctrine cases represent the norm rather than the exception. In fact, the cold war was the unique situation; American foreign policy typically emerges from the complex interaction of shifting constellations.

Hence, the post–cold war period presages a return to pre–World War II patterns.

The Reagan Doctrine also suggests that the constellations of policy makers shift according to a number of factors. These include previously described elements such as the particular stage or cycle in the process, the level of substantive agreement, the instruments required to implement the policy, and the interest, style, and personality of the president and members of Congress. They also include the type of policy involved. As noted in Chapter 1, one of the advantages of studying the Reagan Doctrine rests in its nature: it included structural, strategic, and crisis policy in different stages and cases. As others have noted, differences in these types trigger different roles for different actors (e.g., Ripley and Franklin 1991; Ripley and Lindsay 1993; Lindsay 1994c). The shifts in the constellations responsible for the Reagan Doctrine reinforce this argument. When the issue involved crisis characteristics (e.g., Afghanistan in 1979 and 1985), the White House dominated policy making. When the issue involved structural characteristics such as appropriations (e.g., specific stages in Afghanistan, Cambodia, and Nicaragua), Congress played an important role, even exercising policy leadership. When long-term, noncrisis strategic issues were addressed, the White House and the foreign policy bureaucracy had advantages, stemming from initiative and control of day-to-day conduct, which allowed them to dominate the initial stages and cycles of policy making and set the agenda. In later stages and cycles, Congress played a more important and assertive role (e.g., the overall initiative).

The consequences for policy that emerges from such a complicated process are mixed. Complexity slows down the process and makes it more difficult to produce policy. It also ensures politicization and the need for bargaining, persuasion, and compromise. Moreover, complexity makes stalemate possible and allows for conflict and contradictory actions. At the same time, the democratization of foreign policy making acts as a brake on ill-conceived policy and broadens the debate to include more interests and a wider perspective. It also may make innovation more likely, given the greater opportunity, and even imperative, for policy entrepreneurship by non–executive branch policy makers. Finally, policy that does emerge from this environment is likely to be more sustainable and more legitimate (Lindsay 1994c, 179–82).

Hence, complexity of the policy-making process is not necessarily debilitating. Indeed, the Reagan Doctrine was successful because of the wider debate and the broad involvement of policy makers. In fact, it was precisely the broad involvement of actors outside the White House that transformed the Reagan Doctrine into a more subtle, nuanced strategy that combined force with diplomacy, a transformation that was essential for its limited success. Moreover, the individual successes of the strategy, especially in Afghanistan, Cambodia, and Angola, also occurred as a consequence of the input by all four circles. Policy was improved in each case by the broad involvement, even if it suffered in the short term from the conflict triggered by diverging perspectives (e.g., Angola). Where the Reagan Doctrine was not applied (Mozambique), or where it was curtailed and eventually suspended because of stalemate (Nicaragua), broad U.S. objectives were still achieved, indicating that here, too, U.S. foreign policy was improved by the actions of Congress and other actors who resisted the application of the doctrine for practical, moral, and strategic reasons. Thus, the messiness and conflict of the process, while frustrating and potentially destructive, are not necessarily harmful to policy.

Conclusion

In 1980, when Ronald Reagan won the presidential election, many observers saw a world that had turned against the United States. Just eight short years later, the world looked quite different, and all but the most obtuse recognized the dramatic changes that had taken place. This "great transition," as one author labeled it (Garthoff 1994), occurred because of a complex mix of political, economic, diplomatic, and military factors involving many countries and many places. This examination of one much-celebrated component of the U.S. attempt to manufacture that shift suggests two fundamental complexities that make cause-and-effect statements difficult.

First, on the substance of the policy, a significant lesson of this analysis points to the complexity of the events that brought about the end of the cold war. The Reagan Doctrine was envisioned as a component of a broad strategy of pressure designed to "win the cold war." As this analysis suggests, however, attribution is difficult. The strategy, as applied, had mixed results; it was the primary contributor to victory in only one case. The ultimate irony is that at the precise moment when agreement was reached on the need for the Reagan Doctrine within much of the foreign policy community, the justification for the strategy in the world evaporated. In the end, the Reagan Doctrine was a relatively small part of forty years of U.S. foreign policy. It was, however, present at the demise, and that accounts for much of its celebrity.

Second, the formulation and application of the Reagan Doctrine was the result of procedural complexity. This intriguing strategy was developed through the efforts of many policy makers and members of the public. It was conceived by a group of ideologues in the White House, who then watched as others in the foreign policy bureaucracy and Congress altered the initiative and truncated its application. Ironically, these changes were responsible for the major successes of the initiative. This suggests that future studies should pay more attention to policy makers outside the White House, since the Reagan Doctrine is as easily attributed to them as to the president. The constellations identified in this chapter and in Chapter 1, which shifted regularly throughout the process of formulating and applying the Reagan Doctrine, produced a relatively coherent strategy, even if it was more limited than its authors intended. In the final analysis, then, such shifting constellations might be looked for in other foreign policy issues, outside this time period and apart from the administrations of Presidents Reagan and Bush.

The involvement and interaction of each of the four circles casts doubt on the ownership of the strategy—that is, the extent to which the approach was truly "Reagan's" doctrine. While the strategy was Reagan's in the sense that the president's strategic "vision" was its foundation and because he selected key upper-level officials who shared his outlook and more directly authored the initiative, the foreign policy bureaucracy and Congress played equally critical roles. For instance, William Casey was important in devising the strategy, but others in the State Department and Congress were the authors of the dual-track version, the dominant variant of the strategy. Moreover, although some key decisions were clearly President Reagan's (e.g., to expand the Afghanistan operation in 1985 and 1986 and to provide covert aid to the Angolan rebels in 1985), even these were taken only after other actors pushed, prodded, and even manipulated the process. For example, in the Afghanistan case, William Casey and members of Congress had been pushing for expanded aid since 1981. Bureaucratic disagreement prevented such action until 1986 because Reagan would not settle the dispute between various parts of the bureaucracy and other advocates and opponents over the wisdom of expanded U.S. assistance. Only in 1985, when Congress, Shultz, Casey, and Weinberger finally agreed, did the president "decide" to accelerate the program. Thus, while the strategy bears President Reagan's name in deference to his overall vision and his "seat at the helm" during the 1980s, it is clear that it might well have received a different label. To the extent that the doctrine contributed to the "great transition," it did so as a consequence of the efforts of actors from each of the four circles; credit, if it is due, must be shared.

Notes

1 Introduction

1 The questions used to examine each case in this "structured, focused comparison" are grouped into four clusters: (1) background (antecedents of U.S. involvement; groups and countries involved); (2) actors (policy makers, interests, and
resources); (3) policy making (who was involved and what patterns occurred
in agenda setting, formulation, legitimation, implementation, and evaluation);
and (4) results (application of the Reagan Doctrine, impact, success, failure,
effect of process on policy).

2 For example, Copson and Cronin (1987), Pastor (1987), R. Johnson (1988), and
Elliott Abrams and Alan Keyes (Lagon 1991, 385–86) all suggested that the
strategy was developed only to justify aid to the contras, while Rodman (1994,
259) maintained that no strategy, consideration, national security study directive, or national security decision directive embodying the initiative existed
prior to 1985.

3 This is my adaptation of Jones 1984 and Ripley and Franklin 1991.

2 The Reagan Doctrine

1 Ted Carpenter (1986, note 1) suggested that the intellectual roots of the Reagan
Doctrine may be found in the writings of Laurence W. Beilenson (e.g., 1972,
1984), who advocated the use of insurgencies against vulnerable Soviet clients.
Not coincidentally, Beilenson was one of Ronald Reagan's friends.

2 On the worldview and ideology of the Reagan administration, see Kegley and
Wittkopf 1982.

3 This quote is from a 31 July 1986 Soviet document, "On Measures to Strengthen
Our Counteractions to the American Policy of Neoglobalism," cited in Garthoff
1994, 696–97.

4 Casey had been working on this for some time, as seen in his early policy recom-

mendations and his speeches before the Society of the Four Arts (23 February 1982); the Denver Chief Executive Officers (30 July 1982); Westminster College, Missouri (29 October 1983); the Mid-America Club (4 April 1984); Fordham University (25 February 1986); the American-Israel Public Affairs Committee (6 April 1986); the OSS/Donovan Symposium (19 September 1986); and Ashland College (27 October 1986). These speeches are contained in a collection edited by Herbert Meyer (1989).

5   According to Gutman (1988, 268–69), Casey's speech resulted from a meeting between Casey and private adventurer Jack Wheeler. Wheeler toured Nicaragua, Angola, Afghanistan, Cambodia, Ethiopia, and Mozambique for six months and returned to give an illustrated lecture to twenty-five White House aides in which he advocated U.S. support for movements in each country. He then had a ninety-minute meeting with Casey in November 1984 and left him with a memo on the potential policy initiative. Given Casey's ongoing efforts at such a program (see note 4, above), Gutman (and Wheeler) probably exaggerated the importance of this event.

6   Other noteworthy references include a 1985 radio address in which President Reagan (1985c, 1303) noted that "the deep desire to be free moves people everywhere to resist oppression, from Afghanistan to Cambodia, Angola, Ethiopia, and Nicaragua. . . . This is why our support for struggling resistance forces shall not cease." In another 1985 address Reagan (1985d, 1523–24) praised the development of "a new, bipartisan foreign policy consensus . . . which unites Democrats and Republican alike in support of a strong national defense and help for freedom fighters around the globe."

7   Rodman (1994, 259), for example, erroneously asserted that no such policy was discussed prior to 1985. His error may be due in part to the fact that such discussions took place in the NSPG, and not in the National Security Council, and because Casey cut the NSC staff off from the CIA (see, e.g., Schweizer 1994, xix, 19).

8   One report stated that the CIA *may* have given Ethiopian exiles and dissidents hundreds of thousands of dollars over several years because they said they could start a democratic resistance that the Reagan administration could support as freedom fighters. The reporters further indicated that as of 1986, the only freedom fighters in Ethiopia were separatists and Marxists. The reporters stated that no American official they talked to could see any chance for a successful democratic resistance through covert operations, and suggested that certain hard-liners "jettison their quixotic campaign to arm a non-existent democratic resistance movement in Ethiopia" (Tinker and Wise 1986). Bob Woodward (1987) also spread this story. Richelson (1989, 344) noted that a request was made by a dissident group but rejected in 1982. Donald Crummey of the University of Illinois Center for African Studies indicated in a personal letter to me (19 July 1993) that although he suspected some involvement by the United States, particularly with respect to the TPLF's radio operations, no evidence of financial or material transfers exists. In addition, I questioned nu-

merous academics and former policy makers, and every one stated flatly that there was no Reagan Doctrine aid to rebel groups in Ethiopia. Paul Henze and Marina Ottaway, widely regarded as two of the most knowledgeable Ethiopia analysts, agree. Henze wrote to me that no assistance was provided (personal letter, 4 November 1992), and Ottaway wrote in 1986 that no aid was offered. Moreover, published accounts by several people with "inside" information concur (see Korn 1986; D. Ottaway 1989; Lefebvre 1992; Schraeder 1994).

3   Afghanistan

1 The study was declassified in 1979 and included in *The Declassified Documents Collection, 1979,* item 33a.

2 On the PDPA, see Dupree 1979a, 1979b, 1980a, 1980b; Arnold 1983, 1985; Hammond 1984; Bradsher 1985; Bonner 1987; Anwar 1988; and Hyman 1992.

3 On the resistance in Afghanistan, see Hammond 1984; Bradsher 1985; Karp 1986; Roy 1986; Bonner 1987; Arnold 1990; Khalilzad 1991; and Hyman 1992.

4 The sanctions are discussed in U.S. Congress, House, Committee on Foreign Affairs, Subcommittee on Europe and the Middle East 1981; Hammond 1984, 122–24; Bradsher 1985, 194–99; and Garthoff 1985, 951–62. Between the invasion and 4 January 1980, the Department of State and the NSC staff prepared a list of forty possible sanctions from which to choose; this list included nearly every aspect of the U.S.-Soviet relationship to which sanctions might be applied. Eventually nearly all the sanctions on this list were enacted, even though the list was intended to be a "menu."

5 This statement appears in the memoir of General Mohammed Yousaf of Pakistan (*The Bear Trap*), published in Pakistan and Europe in June 1992 and cited in Cogan 1993, 80.

6 This proved to be a very real fear. Press reports in 1993 indicated that the United States had initiated a $55 million program to purchase three hundred Stinger missiles left over from the war. Iran had already acquired some, and a few were used in rebel attacks in Tajikstan (Weiner 1993; Garthoff 1994, 713).

7 The following account of Wilson's efforts is from Felton 1984b; Bradsher 1985, 278; *Washington Post,* 13 January 1985; Prados 1986, 364–65; Woodward 1987, 357–59; and Richelson 1989, 341.

8 For example, in 1981 President Reagan spoke of the "courageous people of Afghanistan" (*Weekly Compilation of Presidential Documents,* 4 January 1982, 1). In 1982 the president declared that "the freedom-fighters of Afghanistan are defending principles of independence and freedom that form the basis of global security and stability" (*Weekly Compilation of Presidential Documents,* 15 March 1982, 281–82). In the same vein, in 1983 the president stated that "the resistance of the Afghan freedom-fighters is an example to all the world of the invincibility of the ideals we in this country hold most dear" (*Weekly Compilation of Presidential Documents,* 28 March 1983, 436). Finally, in 1987, President Reagan attributed the rebels' success to their religious faith: "With an abiding

faith in God and a passionate love of freedom, they have shown the world what price free people are willing to pay to remain free" (U.S. Department of State 1988c, 80–81).

9 In 1982, President Reagan stated that "despite blanket bombing and chemical and biological weapons, the brave Afghan freedom-fighters have prevented the . . . Soviet occupation force from extending its control over a large portion of the country" (*Weekly Compilation of Presidential Documents,* 15 March 1982, 281– 82). In 1985 President Reagan referred to the Soviets' use of "barbaric methods of waging war in their effort to crush this war of national liberation," including "indiscriminate air and artillery bombardments . . . savage reprisals . . . and the calculated destruction of crops and irrigation systems" (U.S. Department of State 1986c, 22). In remarks in 1987 he denounced the Soviet attempt "to ruthlessly and systematically destroy the ability of the Afghan people to resist" (Department of State 1988c, 80–81).

On the fourth anniversary of the Soviet invasion, President Reagan encouraged Americans and others "who live in lands of freedom, along with those who dream of doing so, [to] take inspiration from the spirit and courage of the Afghan patriots. Let us resolve that their quest for freedom will prevail and that Afghanistan will become, once again, an independent member of the family of nations" (U.S. Department of State 1984c, 38). Finally, the president warned in 1985 that the Soviet Union was "waiting for world attention to slip, for our outrage to wane. Then, they believe, the support which the free world has been providing to the freedom-fighters will dwindle. . . . My friends, we cannot, we must not allow that to happen" (*Weekly Compilation of Presidential Documents,* 6 January 1986, 1).

10 These resolutions can be found in the annual editions of United Nations General Assembly, *Resolutions and Decisions Adopted by the General Assembly* (November 1980–88).

11 Both Dobbs (1992b) and Coll (1992b) discussed these plans. Coll gained access to the information through U.S. intelligence sources. Dobbs was able to use Politburo documents released by Boris Yeltsin in 1992. The U.S. Department of State (1985d, 1986b) reported all the Soviet actions but not the intelligence information.

12 Several sources identify CIA and Defense Department opposition to the idea, including Harrison 1988, 201; Persico 1990, 429–30; Cannon 1991, 371; Cogan 1993, 78, 81; Rodman 1994; and Schweizer 1994.

13 Those who argued that the aid exceeded $600 million in 1987 include Harrison (1988, 203), Rupert (1989, note 1), Cannon (1991, 371), and various press accounts (e.g., *Washington Post,* 3 December 1986; Felton 1988h, 995). Representative Bill McCollum (1989) wrote that U.S. aid from 1980 to 1989 totaled approximately $2.8 billion; arithmetic using the numbers that are not in dispute indicates more than $600 million in aid in 1987. Cogan (1993, 76) set the amount at $470 million.

14 The remainder of this paragraph is drawn from an article by Michael Dobbs

(1992b), who obtained copies of the Politburo documents and excerpted from them extensively.

15   On this "endgame" in Afghanistan, see the works by Schultz (1993, ch. 49), Rodman (1994, ch. 13), and especially Khan (1991), whose position as a Pakistani diplomat gave him an inside perspective.

16   This characterization was provided by Edward Luttwak of the Georgetown Center for Strategic and International Studies (U.S. Congress, House, Committee on Foreign Affairs, Subcommittee on Asian and Pacific Affairs 1986, 16).

17   This point is still ambiguous. Rodman (1994, 331–34) noted that Shultz briefed Reagan and got his approval, and also stated that the NSC staff agreed with the measure primarily because its members were convinced it would be ignored by the Soviet Union, which they thought would never negotiate its way out of Afghanistan. Robert A. Peck told Congress in 1986 that Shultz had approved, and press reports in 1988 concurred. Shultz's memoir is unclear. He acknowledged that "our negotiators in Geneva had taken the position" (1993, 1087) but did not indicate whether he had approved of their actions beforehand. He further indicated that "as the possibility of Soviet withdrawal became increasingly real, and as the Soviets made clear their intentions to continue supplying arms and other support to their allies in Kabul, this position seemed to me incomplete and unwise, to say the least. We had to have the same rights as the Soviets. If they could supply their puppet regime, we must be able to supply the Afghan freedom fighter. The Soviets, of course, tried to lock us in to an unbalanced outcome" (ibid., 1087). This seems to imply that Shultz approved the initiative but reassessed the situation and changed his mind later, perhaps as a result of the criticism.

18   In early January, Soviet foreign minister Eduard Shevardnadze informed a press agency that the United States had agreed to end covert aid as a part of a larger agreement (B. Keller 1988; Shultz 1993, 1087). Secretary Shultz responded the following day by insisting on reciprocity, claiming that such was the U.S. position all along. Shultz maintained that he had informed Shevardnadze that the United States "would stop the flow of arms if the Soviets did the same; if the Soviets continued military supplies to the Najibullah regime, we would do likewise for the mujaheddin. We would not abandon our friends to superior firepower" (Shultz 1993, 1087). Shultz also acknowledged that the Soviet Union regarded this as a shift in the U.S. position (ibid., 1087).

19   See U.S. Congress, House, Committee on Foreign Affairs, Subcommittee on Asian and Pacific Affairs 1989b, 51–69, for the text of the accords. See also U.S. Department of State 1988b for a discussion of the final round of negotiations and the implementation of the accords in 1988. According to Menges (1990, 76), he and several other "Republican foreign policy experts" met with President Reagan on 12 April 1988 and urged him "not to sign the accords until they provided for the immediate installation of an independent, non-communist government in place of the Kabul regime," but Reagan acceded to the State Department's advice.

20 On the Bush administration's application of the Reagan Doctrine to Afghani-
    stan, see B. R. Rubin 1989a, 1989b, 1989c; Rupert 1989; Cogan 1990, 1993;
    Doherty 1990b, 1990c, 1990d, 1990e; U.S. Congress, House, Committee on For-
    eign Affairs, Subcommittee on Asian and Pacific Affairs 1990a, 1990b, 1993;
    U.S. Congress, Senate, Committee on Foreign Relations 1990; Khalilzad 1991;
    Coll 1992b; and Rodman 1994.
21 The Bush administration's national security directive that resulted from this
    review, which is entitled "U.S. Aid to Afghan Guerrilla Groups," remains clas-
    sified.
22 An analysis of the AIG may be found in a report by Zalmay Khalilzad (1991), a
    State Department official in the Reagan administration.
23 The United States made several attempts to improve the AIG, including sus-
    pending payments to the exile parties, supplying the local commanders di-
    rectly, and enlisting the assistance of Zahir Shah (former king of Afghanistan).
    See B. R. Rubin 1989a, 1989b, and 1989c for an account of the initial fail-
    ures of these efforts. The rebels' brutality also reduced the support among U.S.
    policy makers after the Soviet withdrawal. The rebels were guilty of atrocities
    against the PDPA, its supporters, and Soviet troops, but they themselves had
    suffered greatly from the terrible violence and atrocities of the PDPA and Soviet
    policies, and their actions may be considered an unfortunate consequence of
    the fourteen-year guerrilla war. However, the rebels also massacred civilians
    and surrendering or defecting Afghan military personnel and indiscriminately
    shelled cities such as Jalalabad (B. R. Rubin 1989c, 157–58; Rupert 1989, 769–70;
    U.S. Congress, House, Committee on Foreign Affairs, Subcommittee on Asian
    and Pacific Affairs 1990b, 141, 157–58; U.S. Congress, Senate, Foreign Relations
    Committee 1990, 3–4; Khalilzad 1991, vii–viii). Also, Hekmatyar's forces con-
    ducted a campaign of assassination against rival leaders (B. R. Rubin 1989c,
    159–60; Rupert 1989, 770; Khalilzad 1991, 18).

4   Cambodia

1   Good treatments of Cambodia include Kiernan and Boua 1981; Chanda 1986;
    Chandler 1991, 1992a, 1992b; and Vickery 1984, on which this summary de-
    pends.
2   On the Khmer Rouge holocaust, see Ponchaud 1978; Vickery 1984; Jackson 1989;
    and Chandler 1991, ch. 7).
3   On the KPRP regime, see Vickery 1984, 1986; Chanda 1986; Brown 1989; Carney
    1990; and Chandler 1992a.
4   On American interests in Cambodia and Southeast Asia, see Leifer 1983, 1986;
    Brown 1989; Harding and Lincoln 1989; Jordan et al. 1989, ch. 17; and Scala-
    pino 1990.
5   On the KPNLF, see van der Kroef 1990; Corfield 1991; Sutter 1991a; and Chandler
    1992a, ch. 13. On FUNCINPEC and Sihanouk, see also Chandler 1991, 1992b. On

the Khmer Rouge, see Asia Watch 1989, 1990; Jackson 1989; Evans and Rowley 1990; and Heder 1991.

6   Several sources argue that American aid to the resistance factions, including the Khmer Rouge, began in 1979. According to Elizabeth Becker (1986, 440), National Security Adviser Zbigniew Brzezinski persuaded Thailand and China to rebuild the Khmer Rouge and supply the NCR factions. She stated that Brzezinski told her he "encouraged the Chinese to support Pol Pot" and "the Thai to help the [Khmer Rouge]. . . . [The United States] could never support [Pol Pot] but China could." Brzezinski did not mention this in his memoir, and Becker did not indicate that Brzezinski mentioned anything other than encouragement. Michael Haas (1991a, 1991b) also maintained that the United States was active in the 1979–80 decisions to rebuild the Khmer Rouge. He argued that the United States worked with China and Thailand to support the Khmer Rouge against the Vietnamese as early as 1979, and, citing Clymer 1990, that the United States began supplying arms to the NCR factions in 1979 (see, e.g., Haas 1991a, 49, 83). However, in addition to a number of factual errors (e.g., he stated that the United States provided $500 million annually in excess non-lethal Defense Department supplies under the McCollum program; the amount was actually $500,000), Haas also misrepresented a number of key points made by other analysts. He cited Hood and Ablin (1987, lv) regarding U.S. pressure on ASEAN in 1979 to rebuild the Khmer Rouge, but Hood and Ablin made no such statement on that page, describing only *ASEAN and Chinese pressure in 1982*. In a later work, they identified 1982 as the starting point of U.S. aid (Ablin and Hood 1990, 418). Moreover, although Haas (1991a, 84) claimed that increased U.S. aid to Thailand (beginning in 1980) was "available for resale to the Cambodian resistance," he failed to identify any American role in this and acknowledged that Thailand has denied the allegation. Also, Haas did not explain why, if aid and involvement began in 1979, ASEAN officials needed to lobby the U.S. government from 1982 to 1985 to encourage support for the resistance (see the analysis in the text). Finally, Haas, Eva Mysliwiec (1988, 83), and Michael Vickery (1989a, 35) referred to a letter from Jonathan Winer, counsel to Senator John Kerry (D-Mass.), to Larry Chartiennes (Vietnam Veterans of America), dated 22 October 1986, that apparently said the United States had provided about $85 million to the Khmer Rouge from 1980 to 1985, including $54 million in 1980 and $18 million in 1981. The U.S. State Department explicitly denies this, and Winer himself stated that this money was the amount of U.S. *humanitarian aid delivered by the UN* to Khmer Rouge–controlled refugee camps. While the United States acquiesced in China's (and Thailand's) rebuilding of the Khmer Rouge (Chanda 1989a, 40; Solarz 1990, 102–3) and encouraged the initial development of the NCR, the evidence indicates that the United States did not take an active part in these deeds and did not begin to fund the resistance until 1982.

7   The program, "From the Killing Fields," aired on 26 April 1990. Transcripts are available from Journal Graphics in New York. See also Babcock and Woodward

1985; Sutter 1985, 4; Chanda 1986, 392, 402; McAuliff and McDonnell 1989, 89; and Richburg 1991, 115–16.

8   On the conference, see U.S. Department of State 1981e; Mahbubani 1984; and Chanda 1986, 383–92. An excellent source of material on ASEAN's strategy, initiatives, and statements from 1979 to 1985 is Royal Thai Government 1985, in which are collected documents on ASEAN and Indochinese proposals, ASEAN documents and statements, CGDK documents, UN documents, and Vietnamese-Cambodian documents. For a concise overview of the diplomatic efforts, see Acharya et al. 1991, introduction.

9   These resolutions may be found in the annual editions of United Nations General Assembly, *Resolutions and Decisions Adopted by the General Assembly* (1979–89).

10   On this, see Babbadge 1989; Zagoria 1989, 1991b; Alagappa 1990; Becker 1991; and Blacker 1993, 130–39.

11   On the Bush administration's policy toward Cambodia, see Brown 1989, 1991; McAuliff and McDonnell 1989; Solarz 1990; Stern 1990; U.S. Congress, House, Committee on Foreign Affairs, Subcommittee on Asian and Pacific Affairs 1990c, 1991a, 1991b, 1992a, 1992b; U.S. Congress, Senate, Committee on Foreign Relations, Subcommittee on East Asian and Pacific Affairs 1990a, 1990b; Becker 1991; Haas 1991a, 1991b; Richburg 1991; Thayer 1991; and Rodman 1994.

12   A useful source of information on the Paris Conference is Acharya et al. 1991, in which the complete set of documents is compiled and edited. McAuliff and McDonnell (1989) argued that the United States was to blame for Sihanouk's reversal.

5   Angola

1   On U.S. interests in southern Africa and Angola, see Kitchen 1983; Bender et al. 1985; Clough 1986; Coker 1986; Oye et al. 1987, ch. 12; Jordan et al. 1989, ch. 19; B. Martin 1989; and Newsom 1990. For a discussion of this lack of attention, see Lefebvre 1991; and Schraeder 1994.

2   Kissinger's conclusion is cited in Robert H. Johnson's statement before the House Foreign Affairs Subcommittee on Africa on 31 October 1985 (U.S. Congress, House, Committee on Foreign Affairs, Subcommittee on Africa 1986b, 17).

3   On the MPLA prior to Angolan independence, see Marcum 1978. On MPLA-Soviet ties, see Kempton 1989, ch. 2. On the MPLA in power, see M. Ottaway 1986; and M. Ottaway and Ottaway 1986.

4   On UNITA, see Marcum 1978; Dohning 1984; Bridgland 1986; and Radu 1990b.

5   I use the rather awkward present tense here since UNITA remains a rebel movement and it is by no means certain that the 1994 cease-fire will hold.

6   See Crocker's briefing memorandum to George Schultz, "Your Meeting with the President on the Southern Africa Negotiations, Thursday, September 23 at 11:00 a.m.," Briefing memorandum from Chester A. Crocker to the Secretary, 22 September 1982 (declassified 6 August 1991), p. 2.

7   Ibid.

8   Ibid.

9   Ibid.

10 On these negotiations, see also the State Department cable, "Update on Southern Africa Negotiations," 12 January 1984 (declassified 26 April 1991).

11 The negotiations leading to the Lusaka Accord are described in Crocker 1992, ch. 7; the State Department cable identified in note 9 above; and "South Africans and Angolans Reach Agreement," State Department cable from 14 February 1984 (declassified on 26 May 1991). The United States pressured South Africa to make the deal, as illustrated by the decision to refrain from blocking a UN Security Council Resolution condemning South Africa's occupation of southern Angola and calling for a withdrawal; previous resolutions had been vetoed (*New York Times,* 13 December 1983).

12 See "Update on Southern Africa Negotiations" (cited in note 9, above), p. 3.

13 Hanlon (1986, 161) noted that the agreement was initially honored but stalled when South Africa refused to withdraw from the last area of Angola in July 1984. Ben Martin (1989, 36) maintained that only U.S. pressure convinced South Africa to finish the withdrawal in April 1985, nearly a year after the specified date. Crocker (1992, 196–99) blamed both regimes for not following through on their requirements.

14 While significant for U.S. policy toward Angola, the sanctions campaign is not directly relevant to the application of the Reagan Doctrine and is thus not discussed in detail here; see Hanlon and Omond 1987; P. Baker 1989; and Crocker 1992, esp. chs. 11, 13 for good treatments of the issue.

15 "Meeting with UNITA Leader, Jonas Savimbi, February 6, 1986, 6:30 p.m.–7:00 p.m.," Briefing memorandum from Chester A. Crocker to the Secretary, 5 February 1986 (declassified 15 July 1992), p. 3.

16 Ubiquitous criticism of U.S. policy toward southern Africa and elsewhere may be found in nearly every speech or publication by the aforementioned conservative individuals and groups. Representative examples are Alexiev 1986; Hart 1986; Menges 1988a, 1988b, 1988c, 1990; and the letter that Howard Phillips, chairman of the Conservative Caucus, wrote to Secretary of State Shultz in 1983 criticizing the State Department's "abandonment of Jonas Savimbi" (quoted in Crocker 1992, 284).

17 The MLPA undertook a similar effort with Washington firms, first Gray and Company and then Hill and Knowlton.

18 See "Freedom Fighters International," Memorandum for Robert C. McFarlane from Walter Raymond, Jr., and Oliver L. North, 21 May 1985 (declassified 9 July 1987).

19 Ibid.

20 This directive affirmed NSDD 212's objective while strengthening the pressures on the MPLA.

21 See the memorandum cited in note 15, above.

22 Savimbi, who had made this point many times, repeated it to a reporter in Sep-

tember 1987, stating that "there is no prospect of a military victory for UNITA. Our objective is to deny the enemy a victory" (Battersby 1987). It should also be noted that the CIA and State Department both agreed that UNITA could not win militarily; only the Defense Intelligence Agency concluded that a UNITA victory was possible (D. Ottaway and Tyler 1987).

23   On these operations, see "The 1987–1988 Combat in Southern Angola: Lessons Learned," an 11 May 1988 Defense Intelligence Agency briefing script.

24   See "Update on Southern Africa Negotiations," 13 March 1984 (declassified 21 April 1991), p. 4.

25   A good description of the Bush administration's policy toward Angola is Weitz 1992. See also Gunn 1990; Katz 1991; Crocker 1992, 483–94; Tvedten 1992, 44–52; Marcum 1993; and Rodman 1994, 391–99.

26   On post-1992 election developments in Angola, see Holmes 1993a, 1993b; Meldrum 1993a, 1993b; Shiner 1994; and Keller 1995.

6   Nicaragua

1   For general treatments of American interests in Latin and Central America, see Lafeber 1983; Blasier 1985; Molineau 1986; Best 1987; and Pastor 1992. On Nicaragua, see Millet 1977; Diederich 1981; and Pastor 1987.

2   On the rule of the Somoza family, see Booth 1985, 51–95; Walker 1991a; and, especially, Millet 1977.

3   On the FSLN, see Nolan 1984; Booth 1985; Walker 1985, 1991a, 1991b; Spalding 1987; and Gilbert 1988.

4   According to SIPRI's annual *World Armament and Disarmament,* the Soviet Union provided $255 million in arms from 1979 to 1984, and $2.4 billion from 1985 to 1989. The bulk ($1.5 billion) was provided during 1984–86.

5   On the contras, see Dickey 1985; Ronfeldt and Jenkins 1989; and Pardo 1990.

6   See Owen's 17 October memorandum, "Overall Perspective," acquired by the National Security Archive for its document collection, *The Iran Contra Affair: The Making of a Scandal, 1983–1988* [hereafter, NSA 1990].

7   See Gates's 14 December 1984 memorandum, "Nicaragua," pp. 1, 5 (in NSA 1990).

8   See "Covert Action Proposal for Central America," a 27 February 1981 memorandum (in NSA 1990).

9   Missing from the review of options was a U.S. Army War College classified report prepared for Lieutenant General Wallace Nutting, commander of U.S. forces in Latin America, in October 1981 entitled "The Role of the US Military—Caribbean Basin." The War College stated flatly that a paramilitary option would not work in Nicaragua because the FSLN was widely supported; no effective or organized internal opposition existed; and the rebels, former Somocistas, could not gather enough support from Nicaraguans to achieve a successful counterrevolution. Should the United States decide to pursue a confrontational role, the policy would strengthen the anti-American bias in the FSLN

and the Nicaraguan populace, reinforce the interventionist image of the United States in the region, unite FSLN decision makers, diminish the legitimacy of the emerging internal opposition groups and parties, force alignment with the Soviet Union and Cuba, legitimize the export of revolution as defense against counterrevolution, and provide justification for a clampdown on the internal opposition before it matured into an effective force. The War College report concluded that aid should be provided only to help the internal opposition create a viable political movement (Gutman 1988, 81–82).

10   Gates's characterization of the division on policy toward Nicaragua is contained in a 14 December 1984 memorandum for Director of Central Intelligence William Casey entitled "Nicaragua" (in NSA 1990).

11   Ibid.

12   See "Ronald Reagan, Presidential Finding on Covert Operations in Nicaragua, December 1, 1981" (in NSA 1990).

13   In March, the administration presented intelligence photographs depicting military expansion (construction sites) and repression (burned villages). Bobby Ray Inman, deputy director of the CIA, pointed out thirty-six new military facilities and many destroyed Indian villages that the administration attributed to Sandinista repression (Taubman 1982a).

14   According to Roy Gutman (1988, 115–18), William Casey was a key source for this article. Gutman maintained that Casey discussed the covert war with the magazine staff prior to the printing of the issue, and that *Newsweek* made it a cover story on the basis of Casey's confirmation of key facts. Casey, who agreed to be quoted as "one senior official involved in the decisions," stated that the rebels might topple the Nicaraguan government.

15   According to Cynthia Arnson (1989, 120), CIA attorneys told Michael Barnes that since the United States did not seek the overthrow of Nicaragua, it did not matter what course the contras pursued. However, a U.S. ambassador to the region, Frank McNeil (1988, 152–53) maintained that the CIA instructed the contras to seek the overthrow of the regime.

16   See the memorandum from William Clark entitled "Public Diplomacy (Central America), July 1 1983" (in NSA 1990).

17   This paper, entitled "US Policy in Central America and Cuba through Fiscal Year 1984, Summary Paper," was printed in the *New York Times,* 7 April 1983.

18   See "Minutes, National Security Planning Group Meeting on Central America, June 25 1984," p. 7 (in NSA 1990).

19   "Ronald Reagan, Presidential Finding on Covert Operations in Nicaragua, September 19, 1983," p. 1 (in NSA 1990).

20   See "Public Diplomacy Action Plan: Support for the White House Educational Campaign," a memorandum from Daniel Jacobowitz dated 12 March 1985; and "White Propaganda Operation," memorandum from Johnathan Miller to Patrick Buchanan dated March 13, 1985 (both in NSA 1990). Parry and Kornbluh 1988 describes additional (possibly illegal) efforts.

21   See W. Cohen and Mitchell 1988; Draper 1991, arguably the most thorough; and

the reports of the Tower Commission (*Report of the President's Special Review Board* 1987), the congressional investigating committees (ICFR 1987a), and Independent Counsel Lawrence Walsh (1993).

22 A 1 May 1985 memorandum from Oliver North to Robert McFarlane entitled "FDN Military Operations" (in NSA 1990) stated that between July 1984 and May 1985 $24.5 million was obtained, of which $17 million went for arms. This memorandum described another $8.5 million in pledges and included a careful accounting of expenditures. Also, Independent Counsel Walsh (1993, 376–78) showed that the nonlethal aid delivered by the Nicaraguan Humanitarian Assistance Office was inextricably intermingled with the secret supply operation providing lethal aid.

23 "Minutes, National Security Planning Group Meeting on Central America, June 25 1984" (in NSA 1990). Baker later stated that the United States could not "do indirectly what we can't do directly" and claimed to be worried about what "the crazies" would do in order to circumvent the congressional restrictions (Cannon 1991, 382).

24 Memorandum from William Casey to Robert McFarlane, "Supplemental Assistance to Nicaragua Program, March 27, 1984"; and CIA cable, "South African Assistance to Nicaraguan Project, April 4, 1984." Israel's support and the involvement of Honduras and Guatemala are described in a 1989 court document entitled "US Government Stipulation on Quid Pro Quo with Other Governments as Part of Contra Operations," thirteen pages of "stipulated facts" for the trial of Oliver North (all in NSA 1990). See Robert C. McFarlane, "Memorandum for the President, Approach to the Hondurans Regarding the Nicaraguan Resistance, February 19, 1985"; "Recommended Telephone Call to His Excellency Roberto Suazo Cordova, President of the Republic of Honduras, with Reagan's Notes, April 25, 1985"; and Oliver North, "Memorandum for Robert McFarlane with Attachments, Guatemalan Aid to the Nicaraguan Resistance, March 5, 1985" (all in NSA 1990).

25 For a description of the meeting, see Steven Berry, "Memo to the Files: August 6, 1986, 8:35 a.m. White House Situation Room Discussion with Mr. Ollie North Regarding House Resolution 485, September 3, 1986" (in NSA 1990).

26 Ibid., p. 2.

27 On policy and events from 1987 to 1993, see L. Robinson 1991; Vickers and Spence 1992; Pastor 1992; W. Robinson 1992; Arnson 1993, chs. 8–9; and Rodman 1994, ch. 15. William Robinson argued that the Bush administration gave up aid to the contras in favor of direct use of the CIA to corrupt the 1990 elections in favor of the opposition.

28 For more on this pattern, see Sanchez 1988; Larkin 1989; and J. Scott 1993, 294–303.

7 Mozambique

1 The case examined in this chapter differs from the others in that Mozambique did not receive any Reagan Doctrine aid. Although the option reached the agenda and formulation stages, it did not proceed any further. Consequently, this chapter examines only the efforts made to consider the Reagan Doctrine for Mozambique, the process by which it was rejected, and the rationale behind the decision to pursue another policy alternative.

2 For fuller discussions of socialism in Mozambique, see Hanlon 1984; and M. Ottaway and Ottaway 1986, especially ch. 4.

3 On RENAMO, see Legum 1983; Isaacman 1985; Gersony 1988; Gunn 1988; Minter 1989; Morgan 1990; and Crocker 1992.

4 For treatments of U.S. interests in southern Africa, see Crocker 1980a; Bender et al. 1985; Coker 1986; Oye et al. 1987, ch. 12; Jordan et al. 1989, ch. 12; and Newsom 1990.

5 On Nkomati, see Hanlon 1984, 1986; Gunn 1986; and Legum 1988, 289–300.

6 In a letter to Senator Jesse Helms (R-N.C.) Blanchard wrote, "I have talked with the RENAMO leadership personally and I am extremely impressed and convinced that they are not only a successful indigenous anti-Communist political and military organization, but they are explicitly pro-West and pro-United States. . . . They even have a fairly articulate free market oriented economic program planned. As I have told many others, when you see the director of information for . . . RENAMO reading a book on the American revolution and pro–free market literature such as Milton Friedman's *Free to Choose,* you know something has got to be wrong with our State Department." Senator Helms described Mr. Blanchard as "a distinguished economist . . . a brilliant mind . . . and a dedicated American." The letter and Helms's comments are in U.S. Congress, Senate, Committee on Foreign Relations, Subcommittee on Africa 1987, 18.

7 Memorandum (Secret) for the Secretary of Defense through the Under-Secretary of Defense for Policy, "Your Call on President and Field Marshall Samora Machel of Mozambique—Information Memorandum," 19 September 1985 (declassified 20 December 1991).

8 State Department cable, "Update on Southern African Negotiations," 21 January 1984 (declassified 26 April 1991), p. 5.

9 For reporting on the situation in Mozambique after the peace accord, see Ayisi 1992; S. McCormick 1993; Meldrum 1993a, 1993c; Wurst 1994; and Isaacs 1995.

8 Conclusions

1 On these two broader consequences, see Garthoff 1994; and Schweizer 1994.

2 See, for example, Shultz's (1993, ch. 51) reflection on Reagan's style.

3 In addition to this analysis, see Menges 1988b, 1990; Shultz 1993; and Rodman 1994.

4 On these "avenues" of influence, see Lindsay 1993, 1994a, 1994b.

References

Ablin, David A., and Marlowe Hood, eds. 1990. *The Cambodian Agony*. Armonk, N.Y.: M. E. Sharpe.

Abrams, Elliott. 1982. Human rights situation in Nicaragua: statement before the Western Hemisphere Affairs Subcommittee of the Senate Foreign Relations Committee, 25 February 1982. *Department of State Bulletin*, April, 69–71.

———. 1984. Persecution and restrictions of religion in Nicaragua: address before the United Jewish Appeal, 28 June 1984. *Department of State Bulletin*, September, 49–51.

———. 1986. Permanent dictatorship in Nicaragua? Statement before the Subcommittee on Western Hemisphere Affairs of the House Foreign Affairs Committee, 5 March 1986. *Department of State Bulletin*, April, 83.

Acharya, Amitav, Pierre Lizée, and Sorpong Peou. 1991. *Cambodia—The 1989 Paris Peace Conference: Background Analysis and Documents*. Millwood, N.Y.: Kraus International Publications.

Alagappa, Muthiah. 1990. Soviet policy in Southeast Asia: toward constructive engagement. *Pacific Affairs* 63:351–65.

Alden, Chris, and Mark Simpson. 1993. Mozambique: a delicate peace. *Journal of Modern African Studies* 31.1:109–30.

Alexiev, Alexander. 1983. *The New Soviet Strategy in the Third World*. Santa Monica: Rand Corporation.

———. 1985. Soviet strategy and the Mujahidin. *Orbis* 29.1:31–40.

———. 1986. *U.S. Policy in Angola: A Case of Nonconstructive Engagement*. Santa Monica: Rand Corporation.

———. 1989. *Marxism and Resistance in the Third World: Cause and Effect*. Santa Monica: Rand Corporation.

Allison, Graham T. 1971. *The Essence of Decision*. Boston: Little, Brown.

America's secret war: Nicaragua. 1982. *Newsweek*, 8 November.

Americas Watch. 1985a. *Violations of the Laws of War by Both Sides in Nicaragua 1981–1985*. New York: Americas Watch. March.

————. 1985b. *Human Rights in Nicaragua: Reagan, Rhetoric, and Reality.* New York: Americas Watch. July.

————. 1986. *Human Rights in Nicaragua, 1985–1986.* New York: Americas Watch. March.

————. 1988. *Human Rights in Nicaragua, August 1987–August 1988.* New York: Americas Watch. August.

Amnesty International. 1982. *People's Republic of Angola.* London: Amnesty International.

————. 1986a. *Nicaragua: The Human Rights Record.* London: Amnesty International.

————. 1986b. *Report 1986.* London: Amnesty International.

————. 1986c. *Afghanistan: Torture of Political Prisoners.* London: Amnesty International.

————. 1987. *Kampuchea: Political Imprisonment and Torture.* London: Amnesty International.

Anwar, Raja. 1988. *The Tragedy of Afghanistan.* New York: Verso.

Armacost, Michael. 1969. *The Politics of Weapons Innovation.* New York: Columbia University Press.

————. 1987. U.S. policy toward the Third World. *Department of State Bulletin,* January, 56–59.

————. 1988a. Regional issues and U.S.-Soviet relations: address before the General Federation of Women's Clubs in Grand Rapids, Michigan, on 22 June 1988. *Department of State Bulletin,* September, 18–23.

————. 1988b. Status report on Afghanistan: statement before the Senate Foreign Relations Committee, 23 June 1988. *Department of State Bulletin,* September, 55–59.

————. 1988c. Military power and diplomacy: the Reagan legacy. *Department of State Bulletin,* November, 40–44.

Arnold, Anthony. 1983. *Afghanistan's Two-Party Communism: Parcham and Khalq.* Stanford: Hoover Institution Press.

————. 1985. The stony path to Afghan socialism: problems of Sovietization in an alpine Muslim society. *Orbis* 29.1:40–57.

————. 1990. Afghanistan. In *The New Insurgencies: Anticommunist Guerrillas around the World,* ed. Michael Radu, 233–58. New Brunswick, N.J.: Transaction Books.

Arnson, Cynthia J. 1989. *Crossroads: Congress, the Reagan Administration, and Central America.* New York: Pantheon Books.

————. 1993. *Crossroads: Congress, the President, and Central America, 1976–1993.* University Park: Pennsylvania State University Press.

Asia Watch. 1989. *Khmer Rouge Abuses along the Thai-Cambodian Border.* Washington: Asia Watch.

————. 1990. *Violations of the Rules of War by the Khmer Rouge.* Washington: Asia Watch.

Austen, James, Jonathon Fox, and Walter Kruger. 1985. The role of the revolutionary state in the Nicaraguan food system. *World Development* 13.1:15–40.

Ayisi, Ruth Ansah. 1992. And now the peace. *Africa Report*, November–December, 31–33.

Ayres, Drummond, Jr. 1985. U.S. plans to aid Mozambique army. *New York Times*, 17 January.

Babbadge, Ross, ed. 1989. *The Soviets in the Pacific in the 1990s*. Canberra: Brassey's (Australia) Press.

Babcock, Charles, and Bob Woodward. 1985. CIA covertly aiding pro-West Cambodians. *Washington Post*, 8 July.

Bach, William. 1986. A chance in Cambodia. *Foreign Policy* 62:75–95.

Baker, James A. 1989. Secretary's statement, July 30, 1989. *Department of State Bulletin*, September, 25.

Baker, Pauline H. 1985. Erring on southern Africa. *New York Times*, 23 July.

———. 1989. *The United States and South Africa: The Reagan Years.* New York: Ford Foundation and Foreign Policy Association.

Battersby, John. 1987. Angola and U.S. to keep talking. *New York Times*, 14 September.

Becker, Elizabeth. 1986. *After the War Was Over: The Voices of Cambodia's Revolution and Its People.* New York: Simon and Schuster.

———. 1987. Stalemate in Cambodia. *Current History*, April, 86:156–59, 186.

———. 1991. Neither tiger nor horse: Soviet-American cooperation in the Cambodian War. In *Soviet-American Conflict Resolution in the Third World*, ed. Mark N. Katz, 139–68. Washington: United States Institute of Peace Press.

Beilenson, Laurence W. 1972. *Power through Subversion.* Washington: Public Affairs Press.

———. 1984. Aid to freedom fighters. In *Defending a Free Society*, ed. Robert W. Poole, 295–316. Lexington, Mass.: D. C. Heath.

Bender, Gerald. 1981. Angola: left, right, and wrong. *Foreign Policy* 43:53–69.

———. 1985. American policy toward Angola: a history of linkage. In *African Crisis Areas and U.S. Foreign Policy*, ed. Gerald J. Bender et al., 110–28. Berkeley: University of California Press.

———. 1987. The eagle and the bear in Angola. *Annals of the American Academy of Political Science* 489:123–32.

———. 1988. Washington's quest for enemies in Angola. In *Regional Conflict and U.S. Policy: Angola and Mozambique*, ed. Richard J. Bloomfield, 186–206. Algonac, Mich.: Reference Publishers.

Bender, Gerald J., James S. Coleman, and Richard L. Sklar, eds. 1985. *African Crisis Areas and U.S. Foreign Policy.* Berkeley: University of California Press.

Bernstein, Alvin H. 1987. Insurgents against Moscow: the Reagan Doctrine can put Soviet imperialism on the defensive. *Policy Review* 41:26–29.

Bernstein, Carl. 1980. Arms for Afghanistan. *New Republic*, 18 July, 8–10.

Best, Edward. 1987. *U.S. Policy and Regional Security in Central America.* New York: St. Martin's Press.

Beyond Containment. The future of U.S.-Soviet relations: a symposium. 1985. *Policy Review* 31:16–41.

Blachman, Morris J., William LeoGrande, and Kenneth E. Sharpe. 1986. *Confronting Revolution: Security through Diplomacy in Central America.* New York: Pantheon Books.

Blacker, Coit D. 1993. *Hostage to Revolution: Gorbachev and Soviet Security Policy, 1985–1991.* New York: Council on Foreign Relations.

Blakely, Steve. 1986. House hands Reagan victory on covert aid to Angolans. *Congressional Quarterly Weekly Report,* 20 September, 2202–3.

Blasier, Cole. 1984. *The Giant's Rival: The USSR and Latin America.* Pittsburgh: University of Pittsburgh Press.

———. 1985. *The Hovering Giant: U.S. Response to Revolutionary Change in Latin America, 1910–1985.* Pittsburgh: University of Pittsburgh Press.

Bloomfield, Richard J., ed. 1988. *Regional Conflict and U.S. Policy: Angola and Mozambique.* Algonac, Mich.: Reference Publishers.

Bode, William R. 1986. The Reagan Doctrine. *Strategic Review* 14:21–28.

Bonner, Arthur. 1986. Afghan rebels' victory garden: opium. *New York Times,* 18 June.

———. 1987. *Among the Afghans.* Durham: Duke University Press.

Booth, John A. 1985. *The End and the Beginning: The Nicaraguan Revolution.* 2d ed. Boulder, Colo.: Westview Press.

Bowen, Merle L. 1992. Beyond reform: adjustment and political power in contemporary Mozambique. *Journal of Modern African Studies* 30.2:255–79.

Bradsher, Henry. 1985. *Afghanistan and the Soviet Union.* Durham: Duke University Press.

Brenner, Philip, and William M. LeoGrande. 1991. Congress and Nicaragua: the limits of alternative policy-making. In *Divided Democracy: Cooperation and Conflict between the President and Congress,* ed. James Thurber, 219–53. Washington: Congressional Quarterly Press.

Bridgland, Fred. 1986. *Jonas Savimbi: A Key to Africa.* New York: Paragon House.

Brooke, James. 1985. Mozambican displays pin-stripe diplomacy. *New York Times,* 13 October.

———. 1987a. CIA said to send weapons via Zaire to Angola rebels. *New York Times,* 1 February.

———. 1987b. U.S. arms airlift to Angola rebels said to go on. *New York Times,* 27 July.

———. 1988a. Visiting State Department official condemns Mozambique's rebels. *New York Times,* 27 April.

———. 1988b. Rebels leave Mozambique a bloodied and fallow land. *New York Times,* 11 May.

Brown, Frederick Z. 1989. *Second Chance: The United States and Indochina in the 1990s.* New York: Council on Foreign Relations.

———. 1991. Normalization of relations with Vietnam. In *The Challenge of Indo-*

china: An Examination of the U.S. Role, ed. Dick Clark, 29–32. Queenstown, Md.: Aspen Institute.

Brzezinski, Zbigniew. 1983. *Power and Principle: Memoirs of the National Security Advisor.* New York: Farrar, Straus and Giroux.

Buchanan, Patrick J. 1984. Selling Savimbi down the river. *Washington Times,* 29 February.

———. 1986. The contras need our help. *Washington Post,* 5 March.

Burnham, James. 1950. *The Coming Defeat of Communism.* New York: J. Day Press.

———. 1953. *Containment or Liberation: An Inquiry into the Aims of U.S. Foreign Policy.* New York: J. Day Press.

Burns, John F. 1985. Sihanouk urges US to help set up coalition. *New York Times,* 11 June.

———. 1995a. New Afghan force takes hold, turning to peace. *New York Times,* 16 February.

———. 1995b. With Kabul largely in ruins, Afghans get respite from war. *New York Times,* 20 February.

Butler, Stuart M., Michael Sanera, and W. Bruce Weinrod. 1984. *Mandate for Leadership II.* Washington: Heritage Foundation.

Campbell, Colin. 1982a. 3 Cambodian groups forming coalition. *New York Times,* 21 June.

———. 1982b. 3 Cambodians sign accord on exile regime. *New York Times,* 23 June.

———. 1983a. Cambodia is armed camp of soldiers and guerrillas. *New York Times,* 4 April.

———. 1983b. Cambodian rebel accuses Vietnam of massacring civilians. *New York Times,* 10 April.

———. 1985. Cambodia issue again flares in US. *New York Times,* 29 April.

Campbell, Kurt M. 1986. *Soviet Policy toward Southern Africa.* New York: St. Martin's Press.

———. 1988. *Southern Africa in Soviet Foreign Policy.* Adelphi Papers 227. London: International Institute of Strategic Studies.

Campbell, Kurt M., and S. Neil MacFarlane. 1989. *Gorbachev's Third World Dilemmas.* London: Routledge.

Cannon, Lou. 1991. *President Reagan: The Role of a Lifetime.* New York: Simon and Schuster.

Carney, Timothy. 1989. The unexpected victory. In *Cambodia, 1975–1978: Rendezvous with Death,* ed. Karl D. Jackson, 13–35. Princeton: Princeton University Press.

———. 1990. The Heng Samrin armed forces and the military balance in Cambodia. In *The Cambodian Agony,* ed. David A. Ablin and Marlowe Hood, 180–209. Armonk, N.Y.: M. E. Sharpe.

Carpenter, Ted Galen. 1986. *U.S. Aid to Anti-communist Rebels: The Reagan Doctrine and Its Pitfalls.* Cato Institute Policy Analysis 74. Washington: Cato Institute.

Carter, Jimmy. 1982. *Keeping Faith.* New York: Bantam Books.

Chanda, Nayan. 1984. CIA no, U.S. aid, yes. *Far Eastern Economic Review*, 16 August, 16–18.

———. 1986. *Brother Enemy: The War after the War. A History of Indochina since the Fall of Saigon*. New York: Collier Books.

———. 1989a. Civil war in Cambodia? *Foreign Policy* 76:26–43.

———. 1989b. Lethal diplomacy. *Far Eastern Economic Review*, 22 June 1989, 22–23.

———. 1990. For reasons of state. *Far Eastern Economic Review*, 2 August, 10–11.

Chandler, David P. 1991. *The Tragedy of Cambodian History: Politics, War and Revolution since 1945*. New Haven: Yale University Press.

———. 1992a. *A History of Cambodia*. 2d ed. Boulder, Colo.: Westview Press.

———. 1992b. *Brother Number One: A Political Biography of Pol Pot*. Boulder, Colo.: Westview Press.

Christian, Shirley. 1985. Shultz, at Cambodia border: a gut understanding. *New York Times*, 10 July.

———. 1986. *Nicaragua: Revolution in the Family*. New York: Vintage Books.

———. 1992. As quake wreaks havoc, Chamorro appeals to U.S. *New York Times*, 3 September.

Clark, Dick, ed. 1991. *The Challenge of Indochina: An Examination of the U.S. Role*. Queenstown, Md.: Aspen Institute.

Clinton, William J. 1993. U.S. recognition of Angolan government. *US Department of State Dispatch* 4.21 (24 May).

Clough, Michael, ed. 1986. *Reassessing the Soviet Challenge in Africa*. Berkeley: University of California, Institute of International Studies.

Clymer, Kenton J. 1990. American assistance to the Cambodian resistance forces. *Indochina Issues* 90:1–7.

Codevilla, Angelo. 1988. The Reagan Doctrine: as yet a declaratory policy. In *Bureaucratic Politics and National Security*, ed. David C. Kozak and James M. Keagle, 243–57. Boulder, Colo.: Lynne Reinner.

Cody, Edward. 1984. Shadow of Somoza haunts rebels' image. *Washington Post*, 17 December.

———. 1985. Nicaraguan rebel keeps command as shifts buffet his forces. *Washington Post*, 28 February.

Cogan, Charles G. 1990. Shawl of lead: from holy war to civil war in Afghanistan. *Conflict* 10.3:189–204.

———. 1993. Partners in time: the CIA and Afghanistan since 1979. *World Policy Journal* 10.2:73–82.

Cohen, Herman J. 1991. Cease-fire and political settlement in Angola. *US Department of State Dispatch* 2.18 (6 May).

———. 1992. Mozambique and Angola: prospects for peace and democracy. *US Department of State Dispatch* 3.41 (12 October).

Cohen, Shari. 1985. Hill probes into contra funds stalled over lack of evidence. *Congressional Quarterly Weekly Report*, 16 November, 2388.

Cohen, William S., and George J. Mitchell. 1988. *Men of Zeal: A Candid Inside Story of the Iran-Contra Hearings*. New York: Viking Press.

Cohn, Betsy, and Patricia Hynds. 1987. The manipulation of the religion issue. In *Reagan versus the Sandinistas: The Undeclared War on Nicaragua*, ed. Thomas Walker, 97–122. Boulder, Colo.: Westview Press.

Coker, Christopher. 1986. *The United States and Southern Africa, 1968–1985: Constructive Engagement and Its Critics.* Durham: Duke University Press.

Colbert, Evelyn. 1984. Southeast Asia: standing pat. *Foreign Policy* 54:139–55.

Coll, Steve. 1992a. Afghan leader gives up power. *Washington Post,* 17 April.

———. 1992b. Anatomy of a victory: CIA's covert Afghan war. *Washington Post,* 19 July.

———. 1992c. In CIA's covert Afghan war, where to draw the line was key. *Washington Post,* 20 July.

Copson, Raymond W. 1986. *Angola: Conflict Assessment and U.S. Policy Options.* Washington: U.S. Library of Congress, Congressional Research Service.

———. 1987a. Angola: U.S. options. *Congressional Research Service Review,* March, 19–20.

———. 1987b. Contra aid and the Reagan Doctrine: an overview. *Congressional Research Service Review,* March, 1–5.

———. 1988a. The Reagan Doctrine: U.S. assistance to anti-Marxist guerrillas. *Congressional Research Service Issue Brief,* 11 March.

———. 1988b. Mozambique: U.S. foreign assistance facts. *Congressional Research Service Issue Brief,* 8 July.

Copson, Raymond W., and Richard P. Cronin. 1987. The Reagan Doctrine and its prospects. *Survival* 29.1:40–55.

Copson, Raymond W., and Robert B. Shepard. 1988. Angola: issues for the United States. *Congressional Research Service Issue Brief,* no date given.

Corfield, Justin. 1991. *A History of the Cambodian Non-communist Resistance, 1975–1983.* Centre of Southeast Asian Studies, Working Paper 72. Clayton, Australia: Monash University.

Cowell, Alan. 1982a. Tanzanian military advisors will be sent to Mozambique. *New York Times,* 23 February.

———. 1982b. Leftist Mozambique sidles up to West. *New York Times,* 13 November.

———. 1983. Mozambique finds its freedom is full of thistles. *New York Times,* 3 June.

———. 1984. South Africa and Mozambique in security accord. *New York Times,* 3 March.

———. 1985a. 4 rebel units sign anti-Soviet pact. *New York Times,* 6 June.

———. 1985b. S. Africa acknowledges for first time it supports anti-Marxist rebels in Angola. *New York Times,* 21 September.

———. 1986. Mozambican chief dies in air crash in South Africa. *New York Times,* 21 October.

———. 1992a. Mozambique leader and rebel chief talk peace. *New York Times,* 6 August.

———. 1992b. Mozambique leader and rebels sign pact. *New York Times,* 5 October.

Crabb, Cecil V. 1982. *The Doctrines of American Foreign Policy: Their Meaning, Role, and Future.* Baton Rouge: Louisiana State University Press.

Crocker, Chester. 1980a. African policy in the 1980s. *Washington Quarterly* 3.3:72–86.

———. 1980b. South Africa: strategy for change. *Foreign Affairs* 59.2:323–51.

———. 1981a. U.S. policy on Namibia: statement before the Subcommittee on Africa of the House Foreign Affairs Committee, 17 June 1981. *Department of State Bulletin*, August, 55–56.

———. 1981b. Regional strategy for southern Africa: address before the American Legion in Honolulu, 29 August 1981. *Department of State Bulletin*, September, 24–27.

———. 1982a. Communist influence in southern Africa. *Department of State Bulletin*, June, 46–47.

———. 1982b. U.S. response to the challenge of regional security in Africa: address before the Baltimore Council on Foreign Relations, 28 October 1982. *Department of State Bulletin*, December, 22–25.

———. 1985. An update of constructive engagement in South Africa: statement before the Subcommittee on African Affairs of the Senate Foreign Relations Committee, 26 September 1984. *Department of State Bulletin*, January, 5–9.

———. 1986. U.S. and Soviet interests in the Horn of Africa: address before the World Affairs Council, 13 November 1985. *Department of State Bulletin*, January, 29–32.

———. 1987. U.S. policy toward Mozambique. *Department of State Bulletin*, September, 19–22.

———. 1988. Review of events in Ethiopia. *Department of State Bulletin*, August, 62–65.

———. 1989. Southern Africa: eight years later. *Foreign Affairs* 68.2:144–64.

———. 1992. *High Noon in Southern Africa: Making Peace in a Rough Neighborhood.* New York: W. W. Norton.

Crocker, Chester, Mario Greszes, and Robert Henderson. 1981. Southern Africa: a U.S. policy for the 80s. *Africa Report,* January–February, 7–14.

Cronin, Richard P. 1985. *The United States, Pakistan, and the Soviet Threat to Southern Asia: Options for Congress.* Washington: U.S. Library of Congress, Congressional Research Service.

———. 1987. Afghanistan: issues for U.S. policy. *Congressional Research Service Review*, March, 15–18.

———. 1988. Central American peace prospects: overview. *Congressional Research Service Review*, April, 1–4.

Cronin, Thomas E., and Sanford D. Greenberg. 1969. *The Presidential Advisory System.* New York: Harper and Row.

Crossette, Barbara. 1982. Nicaragua accepts U.S. plan for talks on reconciliation. *New York Times*, 15 April.

———. 1985a. Vietnamese attack Cambodia camp. *New York Times*, 8 January.

———. 1985b. Cambodia rebel unit orders pullout from its main camp. *New York Times*, 9 January.

———. 1985c. US official rules out arms for Cambodia rebels. *New York Times*, 19 January.

———. 1985d. Cambodia rebels are pushed into Thailand, and cornered. *New York Times*, 24 February.

———. 1985e. Cambodian rebels driven from base. *New York Times*, 12 March.

———. 1985f. Cambodia rebel to visit US. *New York Times*, 31 March.

———. 1992. Life for Afghans after Najibullah: warring clans and deprivation. *New York Times*, 14 October.

Darnton, John. 1994. Forgotten by world, Afghans plunge into misery. *New York Times*, 11 August.

Davidow, Jeffrey. 1992. An update on US-Angola Policy. *US Department of State Dispatch* 3.49 (7 December).

Davis, Nathaniel. 1978. The Angola decision of 1975: a personal memoir. *Foreign Affairs* 57.1:109–24.

Deese, David, ed. 1994. *The New Politics of American Foreign Policy*. New York: St. Martin's Press.

Demuth, Christopher, Owen Harries, Irving Kristol, Joshua Muravchik, Stephen Rosenfeld, and Stephen Solarz. 1987. *The Reagan Doctrine and Beyond*. AEI Forum 67. Washington: American Enterprise Institute for Public Policy Research.

De Onis, Juan. 1981a. U.S. halts Nicaragua aid over help for guerrillas. *New York Times*, 23 January.

———. 1981b. Wheat sale to Nicaragua delayed. *New York Times*, 11 February.

———. 1981c. House panel favors keeping curbs on aid to Angolan rebels. *New York Times*, 28 April.

Destler, I. M., Leslie Gelb, and Anthony Lake. 1984. *Our Own Worst Enemy: The Unmaking of American Foreign Policy*. New York: Simon and Schuster.

Dickey, Christopher. 1982. Nicaraguan moderates assail U.S. for alleged destabilization plan. *Washington Post*, 18 March.

———. 1983a. Well-armed units show strongholds. *Washington Post*, 3 April.

———. 1983b. Rebel odyssey: foes of Sandinistas seek to purge Somoza stigma. *Washington Post*, 4 April.

———. 1985. *With the Contras: A Reporter in the Wilds of Nicaragua*. New York: Simon and Schuster.

Diederich, Bernard. 1981. *Somoza and the Legacy of U.S. Involvement in Central America*. New York: E. P. Dutton.

Diskin, Martin. 1987. The manipulation of indigenous struggles. In *Reagan versus the Sandinistas: The Undeclared War on Nicaragua*, ed. Thomas Walker, 80–96. Boulder, Colo.: Westview Press.

Dobbs, Michael. 1992a. Secret memos trace Kremlin's march to war. *Washington Post*, 15 November.

———. 1992b. Dramatic Politburo meeting led to end of war. *Washington Post,* 16 November.

Doherty, Carroll J. 1990a. Bush team rethinking aid as hill wariness grows. *Congressional Quarterly Weekly Report,* 14 July, 2232–33.

———. 1990b. Wars of proxy losing favor as cold war tensions end. *Congressional Quarterly Weekly Report,* 25 August, 2721–25.

———. 1990c. Intelligence authorization bill facing House floor fights. *Congressional Quarterly Weekly Report,* 13 October, 3438–39.

———. 1990d. House votes to put conditions on aid to Angolan rebels. *Congressional Quarterly Weekly Report,* 20 October, 3532–34.

———. 1990e. New openness marks debate on intelligence bill. *Congressional Quarterly Weekly Report,* 27 October, 3625–26.

Dohning, W. 1984. *UNITA.* Kwacha, Angola: UNITA Press.

Dole, Robert. 1987. Why the food initiative for Mozambique? *New York Times,* 2 June.

Donaldson, Robert H., ed. 1984. *The Soviet Union in the Third World.* 2d ed. Boulder, Colo.: Westview Press.

Doyle, Michael. 1986. Liberalism and world politics. *American Political Science Review* 80.4:1151–63.

Draper, Theodore. 1991. *A Very Thin Line: The Iran-Contra Affairs.* New York: Hill and Wang.

Drischler, Alvin Paul. 1986. The activist Congress and foreign policy. *SAIS Review* 6.2:193–204.

Duncan, W. Raymond, ed. 1980. *Soviet Policy in the Third World.* New York: Pergamon Press.

———. 1984. Soviet interests in Latin America. *Journal of Inter-American Studies and World Affairs* 26:163–98.

———. 1985. *The Soviet Union and Cuba: Interests and Influence.* New York: Praeger.

Duncan, W. Raymond, and Carolyn McGiffert Ekedahl. 1990. *Moscow and the Third World under Gorbachev.* Boulder, Colo.: Westview Press.

Dupree, Louis. 1977. Afghanistan 1977: does trade plus aid guarantee development? *American University Field Staff Reports, Asia* 21.

———. 1979a. Red flag over Hindu Kush. Part I: Leftist movements in Afghanistan. *American University Field Staff Reports, Asia* 44.

———. 1979b. Red flag over Hindu Kush. Part II: The accidental coup, or Taraki in Blunderland. *American University Field Staff Reports, Asia* 45.

———. 1979c. Afghanistan under the Khalq. *Problems of Communism* 28:34–50.

———. 1980a. Red flag over Hindu Kush. Part III: Rhetoric and reforms, or promises! promises! *American University Field Staff Reports, Asia* 23.

———. 1980b. Red flag over Hindu Kush. Part V: Repression, or security through terror purges, I–IV. *American University Field Staff Reports, Asia* 28.

———. 1980c. *Afghanistan.* Princeton: Princeton University Press.

Eliot, Theodore L., Jr. 1979. Afghanistan after the 1978 revolution. *Strategic Review* 7.2:57–62.

Enders, Thomas. 1982a. Strategic situation in Central America: statement before the Subcommittee of Western Hemisphere Affairs of the Senate Foreign Relations Committee, 14 December 1981. *Department of State Bulletin*, February, 80–81.

———. 1982b. Democracy and security in the Caribbean Basin: statement before the Senate Foreign Relations Subcommittee on Western Hemisphere Affairs, 1 February 1982. *Department of State Bulletin*, March, 61–62.

———. 1983. Nicaragua: threat to peace in Central America: statement before the House Foreign Affairs Committee on 14 April 1983. *Department of State Bulletin*, June, 76–80.

Engelberg, Steven. 1985. Reagan approval reported on plan to weaken Libya. *New York Times*, 4 November.

———. 1986a. Pentagon deputy ousted over a disclosure of secret information. *New York Times*, 30 April.

———. 1986b. House backs covert aid to rebels in Angola. *New York Times*, 18 September.

———. 1987. Iranians captured Stinger missile from Afghan guerrillas. *New York Times*, 17 October.

Epstein, Barbara. 1989. The Reagan Doctrine and right-wing democracy. *Socialist Review* 19.1:9–38.

Ermacora, Felix. 1985a. Report on the situation of human rights in Afghanistan—prepared by the special rapporteur, Mr. Felix Ermacora, in accordance with Commission on Human Rights Resolution 1985/88. UN Document E/CN.4/1985/21, 21 February.

———. 1985b. Report on the situation of human rights in Afghanistan—prepared by the special rapporteur, Mr. Felix Ermacora, in accordance with Commission on Human Rights Resolution 1985/88. UN Document A/40/843, 5 November.

———. 1986. Report on the situation of human rights in Afghanistan—prepared by the special rapporteur, Mr. Felix Ermacora, in accordance with Commission on Human Rights Resolution 1985/88. UN Document E/CN.4/1986/24, 17 February.

———. 1987a. Report on the situation of human rights in Afghanistan—prepared by the special rapporteur, Mr. Felix Ermacora, in accordance with Commission on Human Rights Resolution 1985/88. UN Document A/41/778.9, 9 January.

———. 1987b. Report on the situation of human rights in Afghanistan—prepared by the special rapporteur, Mr. Felix Ermacora, in accordance with Commission on Human Rights Resolution 1985/88. UN Document E/CN.4/1987/22, 19 January.

Etcheson, Craig. 1985. *The Rise and Demise of Democratic Kampuchea.* Boulder, Colo.: Westview Press.

Evans, Grant, and Kelvin Rowley. 1990. *Red Brotherhood at War.* Rev. ed. London: Verso.

Farer, Tom. 1985. Contadora: the hidden agenda. *Foreign Policy* 59:59–72.

Feinberg, Richard. 1986. *The Intemperate Zone: Third World Challenge to U.S. Foreign Policy.* New York: W. W. Norton.

Felton, John. 1982a. Members seeking leverage on foreign policy decisions resort to letter campaign. *Congressional Quarterly Weekly Report,* 30 October, 2763–65.

———. 1982b. State pledges El Salvador murder report. *Congressional Quarterly Weekly Report,* 18 December, 3056–57.

———. 1983a. Nicaragua reports raise concern in Congress. *Congressional Quarterly Weekly Report,* 9 April, 703–4.

———. 1983b. Democrats falter on Nicaragua covert aid ban. *Congressional Quarterly Weekly Report,* 21 May, 1008–9.

———. 1983c. House panel votes to cut off aid to Nicaragua insurgents. *Congressional Quarterly Weekly Report,* 11 June, 1174–76.

———. 1983d. Secret House session focuses on covert aid to Nicaragua. *Congressional Quarterly Weekly Report,* 23 July, 1492–93.

———. 1983e. House quashes covert Nicaragua aid. *Congressional Quarterly Weekly Report,* 30 July, 1535–37.

———. 1983f. House: no covert aid to Nicaragua rebels. *Congressional Quarterly Weekly Report,* 22 October, 2163.

———. 1984a. Hill presses Reagan on Central America policy. *Congressional Quarterly Weekly Report,* 14 April, 831–35.

———. 1984b. Budget item opens a window on Afghan war. *Congressional Quarterly Weekly Report,* 4 August, 1903–6.

———. 1984c. CIA role in Nicaragua manual getting scrutiny on Capitol Hill. *Congressional Quarterly Weekly Report,* 3 November, 2874–75.

———. 1984d. House panel echoes CIA on probe of manual. *Congressional Quarterly Weekly Report,* 8 December, 3074.

———. 1985a. Intelligence panels: fresh faces, familiar issues. *Congressional Quarterly Weekly Report,* 19 January, 117–19.

———. 1985b. Ethiopian war impedes food aid, panel is told. *Congressional Quarterly Weekly Report,* 19 January, 121.

———. 1985c. House panel opens the door to aiding Cambodian rebels. *Congressional Quarterly Weekly Report,* 23 March, 543–46.

———. 1985d. House votes amendment-laden foreign aid bill. *Congressional Quarterly Weekly Report,* 13 July, 1359–63.

———. 1985e. From insurgencies to culture to human rights. *Congressional Quarterly Weekly Report,* 9 November, 2284–86.

———. 1985f. Some strings on Nicaragua eased by intelligence measure. *Congressional Quarterly Weekly Report,* 23 November, 2451–52.

———. 1985g. Congress is considering aid to Angolan rebels. *Congressional Quarterly Weekly Report,* 30 November, 2505–6.

———. 1986a. Reagan, hill gear up for new round on "contras." *Congressional Quarterly Weekly Report,* 25 January, 158–59.

———. 1986b. Congress cool to covert Angolan arms bid. *Congressional Quarterly Weekly Report,* 1 February, 185.

———. 1986c. Savimbi: selling Washington on Angola's war. *Congressional Quarterly Weekly Report,* 8 February, 264–65.

————. 1986d. Reagan gets conflicting advice on contra aid. *Congressional Quarterly Weekly Report,* 15 February, 306.

————. 1986e. Reagan wants $100 million in new contra aid. *Congressional Quarterly Weekly Report,* 22 February, 456–57.

————. 1986f. Reagan asks hill to approve arms, other aid for "contras." *Congressional Quarterly Weekly Report,* 1 March, 489–90.

————. 1986g. Reagan loses ground on contra aid program. *Congressional Quarterly Weekly Report,* 8 March, 535–37.

————. 1986h. Cloudy policy goals, cloudy outlook on hill. *Congressional Quarterly Weekly Report,* 15 March, 601–5.

————. 1986i. After House defeat, Reagan to push contra aid. *Congressional Quarterly Weekly Report,* 22 March, 648–53.

————. 1986j. Senate narrowly backs Nicaragua contra aid. *Congressional Quarterly Weekly Report,* 29 March, 695–98.

————. 1986k. House Republicans go for broke on contra aid. *Congressional Quarterly Weekly Report,* 19 April, 835–37.

————. 1986l. Compromise on contra aid proves elusive in the House. *Congressional Quarterly Weekly Report,* 21 June, 1388.

————. 1986m. For Reagan, a key House win on contra aid. *Congressional Quarterly Weekly Report,* 28 June, 1443–47.

————. 1986n. Senate foes of contra money weigh filibuster, other tactics. *Congressional Quarterly Weekly Report,* 19 July, 1608.

————. 1986o. Rebuffing Democrats' attack, Senate approves contra aid. *Congressional Quarterly Weekly Report,* 16 August, 1876–81.

————. 1986p. Reagan facing hill challenge to US role in Angolan war. *Congressional Quarterly Weekly Report,* 6 September, 2065–67.

————. 1986q. New questions about US role in Nicaragua. *Congressional Quarterly Weekly Report,* 11 October, 2575.

————. 1986r. US reopening the pipeline for military aid to contras. *Congressional Quarterly Weekly Report,* 1 November, 2787.

————. 1987a. Leadership reform or more "soap opera"? *Congressional Quarterly Weekly Report,* 21 February, 315.

————. 1987b. Legal loopholes: Reagan promises Congress he'll tighten covert rules. *Congressional Quarterly Weekly Report,* 8 August, 1780–82.

————. 1987c. Reagan, critics face off over Nicaragua plan. *Congressional Quarterly Weekly Report,* 16 October, 2444–45.

————. 1987d. Nicaragua peace process moves to Capitol Hill. *Congressional Quarterly Weekly Report,* 14 November, 2789–91.

————. 1987e. Shultz, Wright: a truce on contra diplomacy. *Congressional Quarterly Weekly Report,* 21 November, 2867–68.

————. 1987f. Republicans fold their hands on contra aid—for present. *Congressional Quarterly Weekly Report,* 5 December, 2978.

————. 1987g. Wrangling over contra aid sets stage for battle in 1988. *Congressional Quarterly Weekly Report,* 19 December, 3120–21.

————. 1987h. Hill, Reagan compromise on aid to contras. *Congressional Quarterly Weekly Report*, 26 December, 3195–99.

————. 1988a. Reagan seeks compromise to win contra aid. *Congressional Quarterly Weekly Report*, 23 January, 143–45.

————. 1988b. Contra vote may not be a clear test after all. *Congressional Quarterly Weekly Report*, 30 January, 198–201.

————. 1988c. Reagan, GOP remain aloof from new contra-aid plan. *Congressional Quarterly Weekly Report*, 13 February, 292.

————. 1988d. House defeat clouds outlook for contra aid. *Congressional Quarterly Weekly Report*, 5 March, 555–58.

————. 1988e. Cease-fire pact changes political equations. *Congressional Quarterly Weekly Report*, 26 March, 804–8.

————. 1988f. US-Soviet impasse remains over pullout from Afghanistan. *Congressional Quarterly Weekly Report*, 26 March, 814.

————. 1988g. Solemn Congress approves contra-aid package. *Congressional Quarterly Weekly Report*, 2 April, 839–41.

————. 1988h. Afghan deal won't end war, policy questions. *Congressional Quarterly Weekly Report*, 16 April, 993–96.

————. 1988i. House panel backs covert action notice bill. *Congressional Quarterly Weekly Report*, 14 May, 1295–96.

————. 1988j. Reagan, Democrats renew contra-aid disputes. *Congressional Quarterly Weekly Report*, 21 May, 1395–96.

————. 1988k. House defeats GOP attempt to resume contra arms aid. *Congressional Quarterly Weekly Report*, 28 May, 1464.

————. 1988l. . . . and a new bid for contra funds. *Congressional Quarterly Weekly Report*, 4 June, 1517.

————. 1988m. Angolan gets sympathy, little fresh support. *Congressional Quarterly Weekly Report*, 2 July, 1831–32.

————. 1988n. Lines forming for another contra-aid battle. *Congressional Quarterly Weekly Report*, 23 July, 2036–37.

————. 1988o. Contra aid entangled in US, regional politics. *Congressional Quarterly Weekly Report*, 30 July, 2084–85.

————. 1988p. Contra aid: Democratic muscle, partisan fallout. *Congressional Quarterly Weekly Report*, 13 August, 2285–87.

————. 1988q. Contra talks may revive as aid package nears. *Congressional Quarterly Weekly Report*, 17 September, 2573–74.

————. 1988r. Wright at center of Nicaragua policy storm. *Congressional Quarterly Weekly Report*, 24 September, 2631–33.

————. 1988s. Reagan Doctrine: how far will Bush take aid to "freedom fighters"? *Congressional Quarterly Weekly Report*, 17 December, 3504–6.

————. 1989. Bush, hill agree to provide contras with new aid. *Congressional Quarterly Weekly Report*, 25 March, 655–57, 669–70.

Felton, John, and Nadine Cohodas. 1985. Reagan agrees to compromise on contra aid. *Congressional Quarterly Weekly Report*, 20 April, 707–14.

Felton, John, and Steven Pressman. 1987a. When it all unraveled: some insiders' views. *Congressional Quarterly Weekly Report*, 1 August, 1706–10.

———. 1987b. Senate panel votes to tighten procedures on covert action. *Congressional Quarterly Weekly Report*, 19 December, 3126.

Finkel, Vicki R. 1992. Brothers in arms. *Africa Report*, March–April, 60–64.

———. 1993. Savimbi's sour grapes. *Africa Report*, January–February, 25–28.

Fisher, Louis. 1985. *Constitutional Conflicts between Congress and the President*. Washington: CQ Press.

Foreign Policy Bulletin. 1993. A quartet of foreign policy speeches. 4.3 (November–December): 36–53.

Freeman, Charles. 1989. The Angola-Namibia Accords. *Foreign Affairs* 68.3:126–41.

French, Howard W. 1993a. Nicaraguans say the army had a hand in attack. *New York Times*, 26 July.

———. 1993b. In Nicaragua, no peace, and nostalgia for Somoza. *New York Times*, 27 July.

Fromkin, David. 1980. The great game in Asia. *Foreign Affairs* 58.2:936–51.

Fuerbringer, Jonathon. 1985a. House approves a measure to aid Cambodia rebels. *New York Times*, 10 July.

———. 1985b. House acts to allow Angola rebel aid. *New York Times*, 11 July.

Fukuyama, Francis. 1985. The new Marxist-Leninist states and internal conflict in the Third World. In *Third World Marxist-Leninist Regimes: Strengths, Vulnerabilities, and U.S. Policy*, ed. Uri Ra'anan et al., 18–44. Washington: Pergamon-Brassey.

Gaddis, John Lewis. 1982. *Strategies of Containment*. New York: Oxford University Press.

Gargan, Edward. 1993a. 6 days of battle kill 700 in Kabul. *New York Times*, 18 May.

———. 1993b. In a corner of Afghanistan, mines are cleared and a bold emir emerges. *New York Times*, 27 July.

Garrett, Banning N., and Bonnie S. Glaser. 1987. From Nixon to Reagan: China's changing role in American strategy. In *Eagle Resurgent: The Reagan Era in American Foreign Policy*, ed. Kenneth A. Oye et al., 255–95. Boston: Little, Brown.

Garthoff, Raymond. 1985. *Détente and Confrontation: American-Soviet Relations from Nixon to Reagan*. Washington: Brookings Institution.

———. 1994. *The Great Transition: American-Soviet Relations and the End of the Cold War*. Washington: Brookings Institution.

Gastil, Raymond, ed. 1981. *Freedom in the World: Political Rights and Civil Liberties, 1981*. Westport, Conn.: Greenwood Press, with Freedom House.

———. 1985. *Freedom in the World: Political Rights and Civil Liberties, 1984*. Westport, Conn.: Greenwood Press, with Freedom House.

Gelb, Leslie. 1981. U.S. seeks Angolan compromise as price for accord on Namibia. *New York Times*, 1 June.

———. 1982. U.S. said to plan covert action in Latin area. *New York Times*, 14 March.

———. 1983a. Change is hinted in Angola stand. *New York Times*, 3 February.

———. 1983b. U.S. said to increase arms aid to Afghan rebels. *New York Times*, 4 May.

———. 1984. Officials say US plans to double supply of arms to Afghan rebels. *New York Times*, 28 November.

———. 1986a. The doctrine/undoctrine of covert/overt aid. *New York Times*, 21 January.

———. 1986b. '85 Reagan ruling on Afghans cited. *New York Times*, 19 June.

George, Alexander. 1979. Case studies and theory development: the method of structured focused comparison. In *Diplomacy: New Approaches in History, Theory, and Policy*, ed. Paul Gordon Lauren, 107–20. New York: Free Press.

———. 1980. *Presidential Decision-making and Foreign Policy*. Boulder, Colo.: Westview Press.

———. 1982. Case studies and theory development: paper presented to the Second Annual Symposium on Information Processing in Organizations, Carnegie Mellon University, Pittsburgh, 15–16 October 1982.

George, Alexander, Philip J. Farley, and Alexander Dallin, eds. 1988. *U.S.-Soviet Security Cooperation: Achievements, Failure, Lessons*. New York: Oxford University Press.

George, Alexander, David K. Hall, and William E. Simons. 1971. *The Limits of Coercive Diplomacy*. Boston: Little, Brown.

George, Alexander, and T. J. McKeown. 1985. Case studies and theories of organizational decision-making. In *Advances in Information Processing in Organizations*, vol. 2, ed. Robert Coulam and Richard Smith, 21–58. Greenwich, Conn.: JAI Press.

George, Alexander, and Richard Smoke. 1974. *Deterrence in American Foreign Policy*. New York: Columbia University Press.

Gersony, Robert. 1988. *Summary of Mozambican Refugee Accounts of Principally Conflict-related Experience in Mozambique: Report Submitted to Ambassador Jonathan Moore and Dr. Chester A. Crocker*. Washington: U.S. Department of State, Bureau of Public Affairs.

Gigot, Paul A. 1981. Bitter struggle: Afghans are determined, but so are the Soviets, and they appear ready to stay a long while. *Wall Street Journal*, 28 April.

Gilbert, Dennis. 1988. *Sandinistas*. Cambridge, Mass.: Basil Blackwell.

Goodfellow, William, and James Morrell. 1991. From Contadora to Esquipulas to Sapoa and Beyond. In *Revolution and Counter-revolution in Nicaragua*, ed. Thomas Walker, 369–93. Boulder, Colo.: Westview Press.

Gordon, Bernard. 1986. The third Indochina conflict. *Foreign Affairs* 65.1:66–85.

Goshko, John M. 1992a. Baker seeks answer from UNITA leader. *Washington Post*, 30 March.

———. 1992b. End of last cold war conflict. *Washington Post*, 17 April.

Gunn, Gillian. 1985. Post-Nkomati Mozambique. *CSIS Africa Notes* 38 (8 January).

———. 1986. Mozambique after Machel. *CSIS Africa Notes* 67 (29 December).

———. 1988. Learning from adversity: the Mozambique experience. In *Regional*

Conflict and U.S. Policy: Angola and Mozambique, ed. Richard J. Bloomfield, 134–85. Algonac, Mich.: Reference Publishers.

———. 1990. Unfulfilled expectations in Angola. *Current History,* May, 213–16, 234.

Gupta, Bhabani Sen. 1986. *Afghanistan: Politics, Economics, and Society.* London: Frances Pinter.

Gutman, Roy. 1984. Nicaragua: America's diplomatic charade. *Foreign Policy* 56:3–23.

———. 1988. *Banana Diplomacy: The Making of American Policy in Nicaragua 1981–1987.* New York: Simon and Schuster.

Gwertzman, Bernard. 1981a. Aide terms Haig "wounded lion" over Bush's role. *New York Times,* 28 March.

———. 1981b. Sihanouk is ready for Pol Pot talks. *New York Times,* 27 February.

———. 1981c. Haig cites "hit list" for Soviet control of Central America. *New York Times,* 19 March.

———. 1981d. U.S. plans a mission to southern Africa. *New York Times,* 29 March.

———. 1981e. U.S. decides to back resistance groups active in Cambodia. *New York Times,* 3 May.

———. 1982a. Haig says captive proves Nicaragua has Salvadoran role. *New York Times,* 7 March.

———. 1982b. Nicaragua given new U.S. proposal to mend relations. *New York Times,* 10 April.

———. 1984. U.S. moves to end Namibia deadlock. *New York Times,* 25 January.

———. 1985a. U.S. may help 2 rebel groups of Cambodians. *New York Times,* 10 April.

———. 1985b. Angola, angry over rebel aid issue, ends talks. *New York Times,* 14 July.

———. 1985c. U.S. policy on Angola moves closer to rebel aid. *New York Times,* 2 November.

———. 1985d. Shultz backs aid to foes of Soviet Union. *New York Times,* 11 December.

———. 1986a. Reagan to offer Angolan rebels more backing. *New York Times,* 26 January.

———. 1986b. President decides to send weapons to Angola rebels. *New York Times,* 19 February.

———. 1986c. Reagan bars ties to Afghan rebels. *New York Times,* 17 June.

———. 1986d. Stingers aiding Afghans' fight, U.S. aides say. *New York Times,* 13 December.

Haas, Michael. 1991a. *Genocide by Proxy: Cambodia Pawn on a Superpower Chessboard.* New York: Praeger.

———. 1991b. *Cambodia, Pol Pot, and the United States: The Faustian Pact.* New York: Praeger.

Haig, Alexander. 1981a. News conference at Manila, 20 June 1981. *Department of State Bulletin,* August, 44.

———. 1981b. A strategic approach to American foreign policy. *Department of State Bulletin*, September, 12.

———. 1984. *Caveat.* New York: Macmillan.

Halliday, Fred. 1989. *From Kabul to Managua: Soviet-American Relations in the 1980s.* New York: Pantheon Books.

Halloran, Richard. 1984. Pentagon in dispute over aid abroad. *New York Times*, 9 November.

———. 1986. U.S. may establish Afghan rebels ties. *New York Times*, 18 June.

Hammond, Thomas T. 1984. *Red Flag over Afghanistan: The Communist Coup, the Soviet Invasion, and the Consequences.* Boulder, Colo.: Westview Press.

Halon, Joseph. 1984. *Mozambique: The Revolution under Fire.* London: ZED Books.

———. 1986. *Beggar Your Neighbors: Apartheid Power in Southern Africa.* Bloomington: Indiana University Press.

Hanlon, Joseph, and Roger Omond. 1987. *The Sanctions Handbook.* New York: Viking Penguin.

Harding, Harry, and Edward J. Lincoln. 1989. The East Asian laboratory. In *Restructuring American Foreign Policy*, ed. John D. Steinbruner, 185–220. Washington: Brookings Institution.

Harrison, Selig S. 1983. A breakthrough in Afghanistan. *Foreign Policy* 51:3–26.

———. 1986. Cut a regional deal. *Foreign Policy* 62:126–47.

———. 1988. Afghanistan: Soviet intervention, Afghan resistance, and the American role. In *Low-Intensity Warfare: Counterinsurgency, Proinsurgency, and Antiterrorism in the 1980s*, ed. Michael T. Klare and Peter Kornbluh, 183–206. New York: Pantheon Books.

Hart, Benjamin. 1986. Rhetoric vs. reality: how the State Department betrays the Reagan vision. *Heritage Foundation Backgrounder* 484 (31 January).

Hayes, Michael. 1995. Trading places: Khmer Rouge weakened by defections. *Far Eastern Economic Review*, 19 January, 21–22.

Heder, Stephen. 1991. *Pol Pot and Khieu Samphan.* Centre of Southeast Asian Studies, Working Paper 70. Clayton, Australia: Monash University.

Heller, Mark. 1980. The Soviet invasion of Afghanistan. *Washington Quarterly* 3.3: 36–59.

Helsinki Watch Committee. 1986. *Afghan Children: The Other War.* New York: Helsinki Watch Committee.

Henkin, Louis. 1972. *Foreign Affairs and the Constitution.* New York: W. W. Norton.

Henkin, Louis, Stanley Hoffman, Jeane J. Kirkpatrick, Allan Gerson, William D. Rogers, and David J. Scheffer. 1989. *Might v. Right: International Law and the Use of Force.* New York: Council on Foreign Relations Press.

Henze, Paul B. 1983. Getting a grip on the Horn. In *The Pattern of Soviet Conduct in the Third World*, ed. Walter Z. Laqueur, 150–86. New York: Praeger.

———. 1985. *Rebels and Separatists in Ethiopia: Regional Resistance to a Marxist Regime.* Santa Monica: Rand Corporation.

———. 1986. Eritrea: the endless war. *Washington Quarterly* 9.2:23–36.

———. 1989. *The Ethiopian Revolution: Mythology and History.* Santa Monica: Rand Corporation.

———. 1990a. *The United States and the Horn of Africa: History and Current Challenge.* Santa Monica: Rand Corporation.

———. 1990b. Eritrea. In *The New Insurgencies: Anticommunist Guerrillas in the Third World,* ed. Michael Radu, 95–126. New Brunswick, N.J.: Transaction Books.

———. 1991a. *Ethiopia in 1990: The Revolution Unraveling.* Santa Monica: Rand Corporation.

———. 1991b. *Ethiopia in 1991: Peace through Struggle.* Santa Monica: Rand Corporation.

———. 1991c. *The Horn of Africa: From War to Peace.* New York: St. Martin's Press.

———. 1992. *The Defeat of the Derg and the Establishment of New Government in Ethiopia and Eritrea.* Santa Monica: Rand Corporation.

Hijazi, Ihsan A. 1986. U.S. Yemeni offer reported. *New York Times,* 25 April.

Hinckley, Barbara. 1994. *Less Than Meets the Eye: Foreign Policy Making and the Myth of the Assertive Congress.* Chicago: University of Chicago Press.

Hoge, Warren. 1982a. Its border raided, Nicaragua trains civilians. *New York Times,* 4 January.

———. 1982b. Salvador war also puts squeeze on Managua. *New York Times,* 10 January.

Holdridge, John H. 1982. Southeast Asia and U.S. Policy. *Department of State Bulletin,* August, 58–59.

Holmes, Steven A. 1993a. Ending long enmity, U.S. plans ties with Angola's government. *New York Times,* 19 May.

———. 1993b. U.S. lifts ban on sale of nonlethal military equipment to Angola. *New York Times,* 1 July.

Holsti, Ole R. 1994. Public opinion and foreign policy: attitude structures of opinion leaders after the cold war." In *The Domestic Sources of American Foreign Policy,* ed. Eugene R. Wittkopf, 36–56. 2d ed. New York: St. Martin's Press.

Holsti, Ole R., and James N. Rosenau. 1984. *American Leadership in World Affairs: Vietnam and the Breakdown of Consensus.* London: Allen and Unwin.

Hood, Marlowe, and David A. Ablin. 1987. The path to Cambodia's present. In *The Cambodian Agony,* ed. David A. Ablin and Marlowe Hood, xv–lxi. Armonk, N.Y.: M. E. Sharpe.

Hopf, Ted. 1994. *Peripheral Visions: Deterrence Theory and American Foreign Policy in the Third World, 1965–1990.* Ann Arbor: University of Michigan Press.

Hough, Jerry. 1986. *The Struggle for the Third World: Soviet Debates and U.S. Options.* Washington: Brookings Institution.

House, Karen Elliott. 1980. Reagan's world: Republican policies stress arms buildup, a firm line to Soviet. *Wall Street Journal,* June 3.

Hyde, Henry J., and Charles Wilson. 1990. More, not less aid to Afghan rebels. *New York Times,* 29 August.

Hyman, Anthony. 1992. *Afghanistan under Soviet Domination, 1964–1991.* 3d ed. London: Macmillan.

Iklé, Fred C. 1983. U.S. policy for Central America—can we succeed? News release, 12 September 1983. Washington: Office of the Assistant Secretary of Defense for Public Affairs.

International Institute of Strategic Studies. 1985–. *Strategic Survey, 1984–85.* London: Brassey's.

Isaacman, Allen. 1985. Mozambique: tugging at the chains of dependency. In *African Crisis Areas and U.S. Foreign Policy,* ed. Gerald J. Bender et al., 129–57. Berkeley: University of California Press.

Isaacman, Allen, and Barbara Isaacman. 1983. *Mozambique: From Colonialism to Revolution.* Harare: Zimbabwe Publishing House.

Isaacs, Dan. 1995. Fulfilling a dream. *Africa Report,* January–February, 13–21.

Iyer, Pico. 1984. Caravans on moonless nights: how the CIA supports and supplies the anti-Soviet guerrillas. *Time,* 11 June, 38–40.

Jackson, Karl D. 1989. *Cambodia, 1975–1978: Rendezvous with Death.* Princeton: Princeton University Press.

Janis, Irving. 1982. *Groupthink: Psychological Studies of Policy Decisions and Fiascos.* Boston: Houghton Mifflin.

Jentleson, Bruce W. 1990. American diplomacy: around the world and along Pennsylvania Avenue. In *A Question of Balance: The President, the Congress and Foreign Policy,* ed. Thomas E. Mann, 146–200. Washington: Brookings Institution.

———. 1991. The Reagan administration and coercive diplomacy: restraining more than remaking governments. *Political Science Quarterly* 106.1:57–82.

Johnson, Robert H. 1985. Exaggerating America's stakes in Third World conflicts. *International Security* 10.3:32–68.

———. 1988. Misguided morality: ethics and the Reagan Doctrine. *Political Science Quarterly* 103.3:509–29.

Johnson, Phyliss, and Dave Martin. 1986. *Destructive Engagement: Southern Africa at War.* Harare: Zimbabwe Publishing House.

Jones, Charles O. 1984. *An Introduction to the Study of Public Policy.* 3d ed. Monterey, Calif.: Brooks/Cole.

Jordan, Amos A., William J. Taylor, Jr., and Lawrence J. Korb. 1989. *American National Security: Policy and Process.* 3d ed. Baltimore: Johns Hopkins University Press.

Kamm, Henry. 1981a. Reagan facing limited decisions on South East Asia. *New York Times,* 26 February.

———. 1981b. Cambodians trying to forge united front against Hanoi. *New York Times,* 3 September.

———. 1981c. Three Cambodian ex-leaders sign pact on anti-Hanoi front. *New York Times,* 5 September.

———. 1981d. Pol Pot group unyielding at Cambodian talks. *New York Times,* 13 September.

Kaplan, Robert D. 1990. *Soldiers of God: With the Mujahidin in Afghanistan.* Boston: Houghton Mifflin.

Karp, Craig M. 1986. The war in Afghanistan. *Foreign Affairs* 64.5:1026–47.

Katz, Mark N. 1986. Anti-Soviet insurgencies: growing trend or passing phase? *Orbis* 30.2:365–91.

———. 1991. Beyond the Reagan Doctrine: reassessing U.S. policy toward regional conflicts. *Washington Quarterly* 14.1:169–79.

Kaufman, Michael. 1981. Afghans said to get better guns after trip to Egypt. *New York Times,* 22 January, 22.

Kegley, Charles W., Jr., and Eugene R. Wittkopf. 1982. The Reagan administration's world view. *Orbis* 26.1:223–44.

Keller, Bill. 1984. Conservative group urges aid to anti-communist guerrillas. *New York Times,* 20 November.

———. 1988. Charting the road out. *New York Times,* 10 January.

———. 1993. Mozambique's outlook brightens and truce holds and drought ends. *New York Times,* 22 February.

———. 1995. Will Angolan rebels give peace a chance? *New York Times,* 14 February.

Kelly, John H. 1991. Current situation in Afghanistan. *US Department of State Dispatch* 2.26 (1 July).

Kempton, Daniel. 1989. *Soviet Strategy toward Southern Africa: The National Liberation Movement Connection.* New York: Praeger.

Khalilzad, Zalmay. 1991. *Prospects for the Afghan Interim Government.* Santa Monica: Rand Corporation.

Khan, Riaz M. 1991. *Untying the Afghan Knot: Negotiating Soviet Withdrawal.* Durham: Duke University Press.

Kiernan, Ben. 1981a. Resisting the French 1946–54: The Khmer Issarak. In *Peasants and Politics in Kampuchea, 1942–1981,* ed. Ben Kiernan and Chanthou Boua, 127–33. London: ZED Press.

———. 1981b. The Samlaut Rebellion, 1967–68. In *Peasants and Politics in Kampuchea, 1942–1981,* ed. Ben Kiernan and Chanthou Boua, 166–205. London: ZED Press.

———. 1981c. The 1970 uprisings against Lon Nol. In *Peasants and Politics in Kampuchea, 1942–1981,* ed. Ben Kiernan and Chanthou Boua, 206–23. London: ZED Press.

———. 1981d. Pol Pot and the Kampuchean communist movement. In *Peasants and Politics in Kampuchea, 1942–1981,* ed. Ben Kiernan and Chanthou Boua, 227–317. London: ZED Press.

———. 1981e. Kampuchea stumbles to its feet. In *Peasants and Politics in Kampuchea, 1942–1981,* ed. Ben Kiernan and Chanthou Boua, 363–85. London: ZED Press.

———. 1985. *How Pol Pot Came to Power.* London: Verso.

———. 1991. China, Cambodia and the UN plan. In *The Challenge of Indochina: An Examination of the U.S. Role,* ed. Dick Clark, 13–16. Queenstown, Md.: Aspen Institute.

Kiernan, Ben, and Chanthou Boua, eds. 1981. *Peasants and Politics in Kampuchea, 1942-1981*. London: ZED Press.

Kirby, Harmon E. 1985. U.S. policy on Afghanistan. In *Afghan Alternatives: Issues, Options and Policies*, ed. Ralph H. Magnus, 143–51. New Brunswick, N.J.: Transaction Books.

Kirkpatrick, Jeane. 1982. Afghan situation and implications for peace: statement to the United Nations General Assembly, 18 November 1981. *Department of State Bulletin*, January, 57–59.

———. 1983. Call for Soviet withdrawal from Afghanistan: statement to the United Nations General Assembly, 24 November 1982. *Department of State Bulletin*, January, 78–81.

———. 1985a. *The Reagan Doctrine and U.S. Foreign Policy*. Washington: Heritage Foundation.

———. 1985b. Supporting the contras—in Angola. *Washington Post*, 27 October.

———. 1985c. Afghanistan: five years of tragedy. *Department of State Bulletin*, January, 45–48.

Kirkpatrick, Jeane J., and Alan Gerson. 1989. The Reagan Doctrine, human rights, and international law. In *Right v. Might: International Law and the Use of Force*, ed. Louis Henkin et al., 19–36. New York: Council on Foreign Relations Press.

Kitchen, Helen. 1983. *U.S. Interests in Africa*. CSIS Washington Paper 98. New York: Praeger.

Klass, Rosanne. 1988. Afghanistan: the accords. *Foreign Affairs* 67.3:922–43.

———, ed. 1990. *Afghanistan: The Great Game Revisited*. Rev. ed. New York: Freedom House.

Klinghoffer, Arthur Jay. 1980. *The Angolan War: A Study in Soviet Policy in the Third World*. Boulder, Colo.: Westview Press.

Knight, Virginia Curtin. 1991. Mozambique's search for stability. *Current History*, May, 217–20.

Koh, Harold Hongju. 1990. *The National Security Constitution*. New Haven: Yale University Press.

Korbonski, Andrezj, and Francis Fukuyama. 1987. *The Soviet Union and the Third World: The Last Three Decades*. Ithaca, N.Y.: Cornell University Press.

Korn, David A. 1986. *Ethiopia, the United States, and the Soviet Union*. Carbondale: Southern Illinois University Press.

Kornbluh, Peter. 1987. The covert war. In *Reagan versus the Sandinistas: The Undeclared War on Nicaragua*, ed. Thomas Walker, 21–38. Boulder, Colo.: Westview Press.

———. 1988. "Nicaragua: U.S. proinsurgency warfare against the Sandinistas." In *Low Intensity Warfare*, ed. Michael T. Klare and Peter Kornbluh, 136–57. New York: Pantheon Books.

———. 1991. The U.S. role in the counter-revolution. In *Revolution and Counterrevolution in Nicaragua*, ed. Thomas Walker, 323–66. Boulder, Colo.: Westview Press.

————. 1992. Nicaragua. In *Intervention into the 1990s: U.S. Foreign Policy in the Third World,* ed. Peter J. Schraeder, 285–301. Boulder, Colo.: Lynne Rienner.

Kornbluh, Peter, and Malcolm Byrne, eds. 1993. *The Iran-Contra Scandal: The Declassified History.* New York: New Press.

Korolyov, Yuri. 1987. The USSR and Latin America: toward a greater understanding. *International Affairs* 12:73–81.

Kozak, David C., and James M. Keagle, eds. 1988. *Bureaucratic Politics and National Security: Theory and Practice.* Boulder, Colo.: Lynne Reinner Publishers.

Krakowski, Elie. 1990. Afghanistan: the geopolitical implications of Soviet control. In *Afghanistan: The Great Game Revisited,* rev. ed., ed. Rosanne Klass, 161–85. New York: Freedom House.

Krauthammer, Charles. 1985. The Reagan Doctrine. *Time,* 1 April, 54–56.

————. 1986a. The poverty of realism. *New Republic,* 17 February, 14–18.

————. 1986b. Interventionism: an exchange. *New Republic,* 28 April, 20–21.

————. 1986c. Morality and the Reagan Doctrine. *New Republic,* 8 September, 17–24.

————. 1987. The day Harry Truman remade the world. *Washington Post,* 12 March.

Laber, Jeri, and Barnett R. Rubin. 1984. *Tears, Blood and Cries: Human Rights in Afghanistan since the Invasion, 1979-1984.* New York: Helsinki Watch Committee.

————. 1988. *"A Nation Is Dying": Afghanistan under the Soviets, 1979-1987.* Evanston, Ill.: Northwestern University Press.

Lafeber, Walter. 1983. *Inevitable Revolutions: The United States in Central America.* New York: W. W. Norton.

Lagon, Mark P. 1991. "Crusade for freedom": international and ideological sources of the Reagan Doctrine. Ph.D. dissertation, Georgetown University, Washington, D.C.

————. 1992. The international system and the Reagan Doctrine: can realism explain aid to "freedom fighters"? *British Journal of Political Science* 22.1:39–70.

————. 1994. *The Reagan Doctrine: Sources of American Conduct in the Cold War's Last Chapter.* Westport, Conn.: Praeger.

Lake, Anthony. 1989. *Somoza Falling. The Nicaraguan Dilemma: A Portrait of Washington at Work.* Boston: Houghton Mifflin.

————. 1993. National Security adviser Anthony Lake's speech at The Johns Hopkins University, September 21, 1993. *Foreign Policy Bulletin,* November/December, 39–45.

Lambertson, David F. 1989. Update on Cambodia: statement before the Subcommittee on Asian and Pacific Affairs of the House Foreign Affairs Committee, 1 March 1989. *Department of State Bulletin,* May, 37–40.

Lardner, George, Jr. 1990. Afghan, Cambodia covert aid cut. *Washington Post,* 24 October.

Larkin, Bruce, ed. 1989. *Vital Interests: The Soviet Issue in U.S. Central American Policy.* Boulder, Colo.: Lynne Rienner Press, 1989.

Lawyers Committee for Human Rights. 1985. *Kampuchea: After the Worst.* New York: Lawyers Committee for Human Rights.

Layne, Christopher. 1988. Requiem for the Reagan Doctrine. *SAIS Review* 8.1:1–18.

Ledeen, Michael. 1988. *Perilous Statecraft: An Insider's Account of the Iran-Contra Affair.* New York: Charles Scribner's Sons.

Lefevbre, Jeffrey A. 1991. *Arms for the Horn: U.S. Security Policy in Ethiopia and Somalia 1953-1991.* Pittsburgh: University of Pittsburgh Press.

———. 1992. The geopolitics of the Horn of Africa. *Middle East Policy* 1.3:1-16.

Legum, Colin. 1983. The counter-revolutionaries in Southern Africa: the challenge of the Mozambique National Resistance. *Third World Reports,* March, 1-22.

———. 1987. USSR policy in sub-Saharan Africa. In *The Soviet Union and the Third World: The Last Three Decades,* ed. Andrezj Korbonski and Francis Fukuyama, 228-46. Ithaca, N.Y.: Cornell University Press.

———. 1988. *The Battlefronts of Southern Africa.* New York: Africana Publishing House.

Leifer, Michael. 1983. The security of sea-lanes in South-East Asia. *Survival* 25.1:16-24.

———, ed. 1986. *The Balance of Power in East Asia.* New York: St. Martin's Press.

Leiken, Robert S. 1982. *Soviet Strategy in Latin America.* New York: Praeger.

———. 1984. Fantasies and fact: the Soviet Union and Nicaragua. *Current History* 83:314-15, 344-45.

Leiken, Robert S., and Barry Rubin, eds. 1987. *Central American Crisis Reader.* New York: Summit Books.

Lelyveld, Joseph. 1982a. Linkage in Africa. *New York Times,* 15 July.

———. 1982b. Angola rebels yield 2 Soviet captives. *New York Times,* 16 November.

———. 1983. Report of truce plan. *New York Times,* 3 February.

Lemarchand, Rene, ed. 1978. *American Policy in Southern Africa: The States and the Stances.* Washington: University Press of America.

LeMoyne, James. 1985. Some contra leaders are their own worst enemies. *New York Times,* 24 March.

LeoGrande, William. 1985. Through the looking glass: the report of the National Bipartisan Commission on Central America. *World Policy Journal* 1.2:251-84.

———. 1986. Rollback or containment: the U.S., Nicaragua, and the search for peace in Central America. *International Security* 11.2:89-120.

LeoGrande, William, and Philip Brenner. 1993. The House divided: ideological polarization over aid to the Nicaragua "contras." *Legislative Studies Quarterly* 17.1:105-36.

Lewis, Anthony. 1981. After mistakes, Angola turns toward realism. *New York Times,* 8 February.

———. 1982. Hypocrisy wins again. *New York Times,* 4 January.

———. 1983a. Living with neighbors. *New York Times,* 20 January.

———. 1983b. Mozambique seeks Western investment. *New York Times,* 5 February.

———. 1985. Marching for Pretoria. *New York Times,* 31 October.

———. 1986. Arranging to lose. *New York Times,* 2 January.

———. 1987. How to isolate America. *New York Times,* 19 May.

Lewis, Neil. 1987a. Bid to have U.S. back Mozambique rebels halted. *New York Times,* 16 March.

———. 1987b. Dole dissents on Mozambique policy. *New York Times,* 20 May.

———. 1987c. Schultz assures Mozambique aide U.S. won't withdraw its support. *New York Times,* 23 May.

———. 1987d. U.S. meets Mozambique rebel figure. *New York Times,* 13 July.

———. 1987e. Senate confirms Mozambique envoy. *New York Times,* 10 September.

———. 1988. US insists Soviets stop sending arms to Afghan regime. *New York Times,* 5 March.

Lewis, Paul. 1988. Pro-guerrilla senator urges president to reject Afghan pact. *New York Times,* 7 April.

———. 1992. UN sends peacekeeping force to supervise Mozambique truce. *New York Times,* 17 December.

Lindsay, James M. 1986. Congress and defense policy: 1961–1986. *Armed Forces and Society* 13:371–401.

———. 1991. *Congress and Nuclear Weapons.* Baltimore: Johns Hopkins University Press.

———. 1993. Congress and foreign policy: why the hill matters. *Political Science Quarterly* 107.4:607–28.

———. 1994a. Congress and foreign policy: avenues of influence. In *The Domestic Sources of American Foreign Policy: Insights and Evidence,* 2d ed., ed. Eugene R. Wittkopf, 191–207. New York: St. Martin's Press.

———. 1994b. Congress, foreign policy, and the new institutionalism. *International Studies Quarterly* 38.2:281–304.

———. 1994c. *Congress and the Politics of US Foreign Policy.* Baltimore: Johns Hopkins University Press.

Lindsay, James M., and Randall B. Ripley. 1992. Foreign and defense policy in Congress: a research agenda for the 1990s. *Legislative Studies Quarterly* 17:417–49.

Lindsey, Robert. 1982. Forces of Nicaragua regime train in California. *New York Times,* 18 January.

Linfield, Michael. 1991. Human rights. In *Revolution and Counter-revolution in Nicaragua,* ed. Thomas Walker, 275–94. Boulder, Colo.: Westview Press.

Lowenthal, Abraham. 1987. *Partners in Conflict: The U.S. and Latin America.* Baltimore: Johns Hopkins University Press.

Macchiarola, Frank J., and Robert B. Oxnam, eds. 1991. *The China Challenge: American Policies in East Asia.* Proceedings of the Academy of Political Science 38, no. 2. New York: Academy of Political Science.

Magnus, Ralph, ed. 1985. *Afghan Alternatives: Issues, Options, and Policies.* New Brunswick, N.J.: Transaction Books.

Magnuson, Ed. 1987. Yet another Saudi connection. *Time,* 29 June.

Mahbubani, Kishore. 1984. The Kampuchean problem: a Southeast Asian perspective. *Foreign Affairs* 62.2:407–25.

Makinda, Samuel. 1992. *Security in the Horn of Africa.* Adelphi Paper 269. London: International Institute of Strategic Studies.

Mann, Thomas E. 1990. *A Question of Balance: The President, the Congress and Foreign Policy.* Washington: Brookings Institution.

Marcum, John. 1969. *The Angolan Revolution*. Vol. 1: *The Anatomy of an Explosion, 1950-1962*. Cambridge: MIT Press.

———. 1978. *The Angolan Revolution*. Vol. 2: *Exile Politics and Guerrilla Warfare (1962-1976)*. Cambridge: MIT Press.

———. 1986. Bipolar dependency: the People's Republic of Angola. In *Reassessing the Soviet Challenge in Africa*, ed. Michael Clough, 12–30. Berkeley: University of California, Institute of International Studies.

———. 1989. Africa: a continent adrift. *Foreign Affairs* 68.1:159–79.

———. 1993. Angola: war again. *Current History*, May, 218–23.

Maren, Michael. 1987. US callousness and Mozambique massacres. *New York Times*, 22 August.

Martin, Ben L. 1989. American policy towards southern Africa in the 1980s. *Journal of Modern African Studies* 27.1:23–46.

Martin, David, and Phyliss Johnson. 1981. *The Struggle for Zimbabwe*. Harare: Zimbabwe Publishing House.

Maynes, Charles William. 1990. The rise and fall of the Reagan Doctrine. In *Gorbachev's New Thinking and Third World Conflicts*, ed. Jiri Valenta and Frank Cibulka, 265–75. New Brunswick, N.J.: Transaction Books.

McAuliff, John, and Mary Byrne McDonnell. 1989. The Cambodian stalemate. *World Policy Journal* 7.1:71–106.

McCollum, Bill. The CIA has bungled it. *Washington Post*, 10 September, C1.

McColm, R. Bruce, ed. 1991. *Freedom in the World: Political Rights and Civil Liberties, 1990*. Lanham, Md.: University Press of America, with Freedom House.

McCormick, James. 1992. *American Foreign Policy and Process*. 2d ed. Itasca, Ill.: F. E. Peacock.

McCormick, Shawn H. 1993. Mozambique's cautious steps toward lasting peace. *Current History*, May, 224–28.

McFaul, Michael. 1989. Rethinking the Reagan Doctrine in Angola. *International Security* 14.3:99–135.

McNeil, Frank. 1988. *War and Peace in Central America*. New York: Charles Scribner's Sons.

Melanson, Richard A. 1991. *Reconstructing Consensus: American Foreign Policy since the Vietnam War*. New York: St. Martin's Press.

Meldrum, Andrew. 1992. Hungry to vote. *Africa Report*, November–December, 26–30.

———. 1993a. Lessons from Angola. *Africa Report*, January–February, 22–24.

———. 1993b. Two steps back. *Africa Report*, March–April, 44–46.

———. 1993c. Peace at last. *Africa Report*, March–April, 47–50.

Menges, Constantine. 1968. *Democratic Revolutionary Insurgency as an Alternative Strategy*. Santa Monica: Rand Corporation.

———. 1988a. Has anyone seen the Reagan Doctrine? State's Angola sellout. *National Review*, 28 October, 26–29.

———. 1988b. *Inside the National Security Council*. New York: Simon and Schuster.

———. 1988c. The diplomacy of defeat. *Policy Review* 45:10–14.

———. 1990. *The Twilight Struggle: The Soviet Union v. the United States Today.* Washington: AEI Press.

Meyer, Herbert. 1989. *Scouting the Future: The Public Speeches of William J. Casey.* Washington: Regnery Gateway.

Michel, James H. 1984. U.S. relations with Honduras and Nicaragua: statement before the Subcommittee on Military Installations and Facilities of the House Armed Services Committee, 28 March 1984. *Department of State Bulletin*, June, 81–85.

Middendorf, J. William, III. 1984. Review of Nicaragua's commitments to the OAS. *Department of State Bulletin*, September, 69–71.

Miller, Judith. 1981a. Reagan searching for more "flexibility" to set foreign policy. *New York Times*, 20 March.

———. 1981b. House panel acts to maintain ban on military aid to Angolan rebels. *New York Times*, 13 May.

Miller, Nicola. 1989. *Soviet Relations with Latin America 1959–1987.* Cambridge: Cambridge University Press.

Millet, Richard. 1977. *Guardians of the Dynasty: A History of the U.S.-Created Guardia Nacional and the Somoza Family.* Maryknoll, N.Y.: Maryknoll Press.

Minter, William. 1989. The Mozambican National Resistance (RENAMO) as described by ex-participants. *Development Dialogue* 1:89–132.

Mittelman, James. 1983. Be fair to Mozambique. *New York Times,* 27 July.

Molineau, Harold. 1986. *U.S. Policy toward Latin America: From Regionalism to Globalism.* Boulder, Colo.: Westview Press.

Moreno, Dario. 1990. *U.S. Policy in Central America: The Endless Debate.* Miami: Florida International University Press.

Morgan, Glenda. 1990. Violence in Mozambique: toward an understanding of RENAMO. *Journal of Modern African Studies* 28.4:603–19.

Moser, Charles, ed. 1985. *Combat on Communist Territory.* Lake Bluff, Ill.: Regnery Gateway.

Motley, Langhorne. 1984a. Is peace possible in Central America: address before the Foreign Policy Association, 19 January 1984. *Department of State Bulletin*, March, 67–69.

———. 1984b. U.S. Central American policy at a crossroads. *Department of State Bulletin*, August, 77–84.

———. 1985. The new opportunity for peace in Nicaragua: statement before the Subcommittee on Western Hemisphere Affairs of the House Foreign Affairs Committee, 17 April 1985. *Department of State Bulletin*, June, 80–83.

Muravchik, Joshua. 1986. The Nicaragua debate. *Foreign Affairs* 65.2:366–82.

Mysliwiec, Eva. 1988. *Punishing the Poor: The International Isolation of Kampuchea.* Oxford: OXFAM.

Nash, Philip. 1987. Dangling carrots before Marxists: U.S.-Mozambican relations since 1981. *Fletcher Forum* 11:331–45.

Nation, R. Craig, and Mark V. Kauppi, eds. 1984. *The Soviet Impact in Africa.* Lexington, Mass.: Lexington Books.

National Security Archive. 1990. *The Iran-Contra Affair: The Making of a Scandal, 1983–1988* (microfiche). Alexandria, Va.: Chadwyck-Healey.

National Security Decision Directive 17 [NSDD 17]. 1982. National security decision directive on Cuba and Central America. 4 January (declassified 19 December 1991).

National Security Decision Directive 37 [NSDD 37]. 1982. National security decision directive on Cuba and Central America. 28 May (declassified 19 December 1991).

National Security Decision Directive 57 [NSDD 57]. 1982. United States policy toward the Horn of Africa. 17 September (declassified 31 October 1990).

National Security Decision Directive 59 [NSDD 59]. 1982. Cuba and Central America. 5 October (declassified 19 December 1991).

National Security Decision Directive 75 [NSDD 75]. 1983. U.S. relations with the USSR. 17 January (declassified 16 July 1994).

National Security Decision Directive 100 [NSDD 100]. 1983. Enhanced US military activity and assistance for the Central American region. 28 July (declassified 19 December 1991).

National Security Decision Directive 124 [NSDD 124]. 1984. Central America: promoting democracy, economic improvement, and peace. 7 February (declassified 19 December 1991).

National Security Decision Directive 158 [NSDD 158]. 1985. United States policy in Southeast Asia (the Kampuchea problem). 9 January.

National Security Decision Directive 212 [NSDD 212]. 1986. United States policy toward Angola. 10 February (declassified 17 May 1991).

National Security Decision Directive 264 [NSDD 264]. 1987. Central America. 27 February (unclassified).

National Security Decision Directive 272 [NSDD 272]. 1987. United States objectives in southern Africa. 7 May (declassified 17 May 1991).

National Security Decision Directive 274 [NSDD 274]. 1987. United States policy toward Angola. 7 May (declassified 20 December 1991).

National Security Decision Directive 319 [NSDD 319]. 1988. United States policy toward Indochina. 14 November (declassified 21 October 1993).

A New Inter-American Policy for the Eighties: Report of the Committee of Santa Fe. 1980. Washington: Council for Inter-American Security.

Newsom, David D. 1990. After the cold war: U.S. interest in sub-Saharan Africa. In *U.S. Foreign Policy after the Cold War,* ed. Brad Roberts, 143–58. Cambridge: MIT Press. (First published in *The Washington Quarterly* 13.1.)

Noble, Kenneth B. 1992a. Violence is building in Angola as election nears. *New York Times,* 24 September.

———. 1992b. Millions cast votes in Angola's first election since end of 16 year civil war. *New York Times,* 30 September.

———. 1992c. Fair or fixed Angola vote? Stability hangs in balance. *New York Times,* 1 October.

———. 1992d. Ruling party takes lead in Angola. *New York Times,* 2 October.

———. 1992e. Angola opposition charges election fraud as ruling party leads. *New York Times*, 6 October.

———. 1992f. Angola's leader seems the victor, but rebel threat prompts recount. *New York Times*, 7 October.

———. 1992g. Savimbi party indicates it might accept Angola vote results. *New York Times*, 8 October.

———. 1992h. Renewed fighting in Angola follows a car-bomb blast. *New York Times*, 12 October.

———. 1992i. Angolan parties begin indirect talks on elections. *New York Times*, 15 October.

———. 1992j. Runoff vote expected in Angola as leader apparently falls short. *New York Times*, 16 October.

———. 1993. Angolan rebels rebound within reach of victory. *New York Times*, 13 April.

Nolan, David. 1984. *The Ideology of the Sandinistas and the Nicaraguan Revolution*. Coral Gables, Fla.: University of Miami Press.

Noorzoy, M. Siddieq. 1990. Soviet economic interests and policies in Afghanistan. In *Afghanistan: The Great Game Revisited*, rev. ed., ed. Rosanne Klass, 71–95. New York: Freedom House.

Oksenberg, Michael. 1982. A decade of Sino-American relations. *Foreign Affairs* 61:1.

Okun, Robert S. 1988. UN calls on Soviet Union to withdraw from Afghanistan: statement to the United Nations General Assembly on 10 November 1987. *Department of State Bulletin*, January, 54–56.

Ottaway, David. 1986. Massacre charges taint "freedom fighters." *Washington Post*, 29 July.

———. 1989. What are the constraints on the U.S. role in Third World protracted warfare? In *Guerrilla Warfare and Counterinsurgency: U.S.-Soviet Policy in the Third World*, ed. Richard H. Schultz et al., 47–58. Lexington, Mass.: D. C. Heath.

Ottaway, David, and Patrick Tyler. 1986. DIA alone in optimism for Savimbi. *Washington Post*, 7 February.

Ottaway, Marina. 1982. *Soviet and American Influence in the Horn of Africa*. New York: Praeger.

———. 1986. African Marxist regimes and U.S. policy: ideology and interest. *SAIS Review* 6.2:137–50.

———. 1988. Mozambique: from symbolic socialism to symbolic reform. *Journal of Modern African Studies* 26.2:211–26.

Ottaway, Marina, and David Ottaway. 1986. *Afrocommunism*. 2d ed. New York: Africana.

Oye, Kenneth A. 1987. Constrained confidence and the evolution of Reagan foreign policy. In *Eagle Resurgent: The Reagan Era in American Foreign Policy*, ed. Kenneth A. Oye et al., 3–40. Boston: Little, Brown.

Oye, Kenneth, Robert J. Lieber, and Donald Rothchild. 1987. *Eagle Resurgent: The Reagan Era in American Foreign Policy*. Boston: Little, Brown.

Pardo, Maurer. 1990. *The Contras, 1980–1989: A Special Kind of Politics.* Washington: Center for Strategic and International Studies.

Parry, Robert, and Peter Kornbluh. 1988. Iran-contra's untold story. *Foreign Policy* 68:3–36.

Pastor, Robert A. 1987. *Condemned to Repetition: The U.S. and Nicaragua.* Princeton: Princeton University Press.

———. 1992. *Whirlpool: U.S. Foreign Policy toward Latin America and the Caribbean.* Princeton: Princeton University Press.

Pazzanita, Anthony G. 1991. The conflict resolution process in Angola. *Journal of Modern African Studies* 29.1:83–114.

Pear, Robert. 1988. Mozambicans fled rebels, United States says. *New York Times,* 21 April.

Pear, Robert, and James Brooke. 1988. Rightists in U.S. aid Mozambique rebels. *New York Times,* 22 May.

Perlez, Jane. 1991. A hard line Marxist who mellowed. *New York Times,* 30 May.

———. 1992a. A Mozambique formally at peace is bled by hunger and brutality. *New York Times,* 13 October.

———. 1992b. Rebel group in Mozambique is trying its hand at politics. *New York Times,* 15 October.

———. 1992c. Mozambique gets U.N. observer unit. *New York Times,* 16 October.

Persico, Joseph E. 1990. *Casey: From the OSS to the CIA.* New York: Viking Penguin.

Petterson, Donald. 1986. Ethiopia abandoned? An American perspective. *International Affairs* 62.4:627–45.

Ponchaud, F. 1978. *Cambodia: Year Zero.* New York: Holt, Rhinehart and Winston.

Porter, Bruce D. 1983. The Soviet Union in Asia: a strategic survey. *Radio Free Europe-Radio Liberty, Radio Liberty Research* 148/82 (1 April 1983).

Porter, Gareth. 1981. Vietnamese policy and the Indochina crisis. In *The Third Indochina Conflict,* ed. David W. P. Elliott, 69–137. Boulder, Colo.: Westview Press.

———. 1988. Cambodia: Sihanouk's initiative. *Foreign Affairs* 66.2:809–26.

Potter, Anne L. 1987. *The Battle over Nicaragua.* Washington: U.S. Library of Congress, Congressional Research Service.

Poullada, Leon B. 1990. The road to crisis 1919–1980—American failures, Afghan errors and Soviet successes. In *Afghanistan: The Great Game Revisited,* rev. ed., Rosanne Klass, 37–69. New York: Freedom House.

Powell, Colin L. 1988. American foreign policy: opportunities and challenges. *Department of State Bulletin,* October, 51–53.

Prados, John. 1986. *Presidents' Secret Wars: CIA and Pentagon Covert Operations from World War II through Iranscam.* New York: Quill Press.

Prasso, Sheri. 1994. Cambodia: a heritage of violence. *World Policy Journal* 11.3:71–77.

Pressman, Steven. 1985. Massive lobbying campaign waged over aid for "contras." *Congressional Quarterly Weekly Report,* 20 April, 715–16.

———. 1987a. Senate panel votes to cut off all US funds for the contras. *Congressional Quarterly Weekly Report,* 21 February, 314.

————. 1987b. House Democrats moving to halt contra aid. *Congressional Quarterly Weekly Report,* 7 March, 421.

————. 1987c. House, in a symbolic action, votes contra aid moratorium. *Congressional Quarterly Weekly Report,* 14 March, 460–63.

————. 1987d. Moratorium on contra funds runs aground in the Senate. *Congressional Quarterly Weekly Report,* 28 March, 563.

————. 1987e. House members try to tighten strings on covert operations. *Congressional Quarterly Weekly Report,* 18 April, 720–22.

————. 1987f. CIA aide points to a hands-on role by Casey. *Congressional Quarterly Weekly Report,* 22 August, 1944–45.

————. 1987g. New contra aid: political pitfall for Reagan? *Congressional Quarterly Weekly Report,* 12 September, 2178–79.

————. 1987h. Fresh Iran-contra evidence fuels questions about Bush. *Congressional Quarterly Weekly Report,* 12 September, 2180–81.

————. 1987i. Wright steers middle course on contra aid. *Congressional Quarterly Weekly Report,* 19 September, 2255.

————. 1987j. Arias sounds call for peace, end to contra aid. *Congressional Quarterly Weekly Report,* 26 September, 2297–98.

Quinn, Kenneth M. 1989a. The pattern and scope of violence. In *Cambodia, 1975–1978: Rendezvous with Death,* ed. Karl D. Jackson, 179–208. Princeton: Princeton University Press.

————. 1989b. Explaining the terror. In *Cambodia, 1975–1978: Rendezvous with Death,* ed. Karl D. Jackson, 215–40. Princeton: Princeton University Press.

Quinn-Judge, Paul. 1984. Asia allies want open U.S. aid for Kampuchea guerrillas. *Christian Science Monitor,* 12 October.

Radu, Michael. 1990a. *The New Insurgencies: Anticommunist Guerrillas around the World.* New Brunswick, N.J.: Transaction Books.

————. 1990b. Angola. In *The New Insurgencies: Anticommunist Guerrillas around the World,* ed. Michael Radu, 127–60. New Brunswick, N.J.: Transaction Books.

Ramet, Pedro, and Fernando Lopez-Alves. 1984. Moscow and the revolutionary left in Latin America. *Orbis* 34:342–63.

Ranelagh, John. 1987. *The Agency: The Rise and Decline of the CIA.* New York: Simon and Schuster.

Raphel, Robin. 1994. US policy toward Afghanistan, Bangladesh, Nepal, and Sri Lanka. *US Department of State Dispatch* 5.35 (29 August).

Rashid, Abdul. 1990. The Afghan resistance: its background, its nature, and the problems of unity. In *Afghanistan: The Great Game Revisited,* rev. ed., ed. Rosanne Klass, 203–27. New York: Freedom House.

Rashid, Ahmed. 1995. Sword of Islam: new force challenges Afghan warlords. *Far Eastern Economic Review,* 5 January.

Reagan, Ronald. 1981a. Interview with the president. *Weekly Compilation of Presidential Documents* 17.10:231–33.

————. 1981b. University of Notre Dame commencement address. *Weekly Compilation of Presidential Documents* 17.21:531–34.

————. 1983a. State of the Union Address. *Weekly Compilation of Presidential Documents* 19.4:105–15.

————. 1983b. Remarks at the annual convention of the National Association of Evangelicals. *Weekly Compilation of Presidential Documents* 19.10:364–70.

————. 1983c. Remarks at the 10th Anniversary Dinner, Heritage Foundation. *Weekly Compilation of Presidential Documents* 19.40:1380–84.

————. 1983d. Challenge to U.S. security interests in Central America: remarks to the National Association of Manufacturers, 10 March 1983. *Department of State Bulletin*, May, 6–9.

————. 1983e. Central America: defending our vital interests: address before a joint session of Congress, 27 April 1983. *Department of State Bulletin*, June, 1–5.

————. 1983f. Saving freedom in Central America: address before the International Longshoremen's Association, 18 July 1983. *Department of State Bulletin*, August, 1–4.

————. 1984a. Radio address to the nation, 2 April 1984. *Weekly Compilation of Presidential Documents* 20.13:427–28.

————. 1984b. Address to the nation, 9 May 1984. *Weekly Compilation of Presidential Documents* 20.19:676–82.

————. 1984c. Remarks to a White House outreach working group, 18 July 1984. *Weekly Compilation of Presidential Documents* 20.29:1038–39.

————. 1985a. State of the Union Address. *Weekly Compilation of Presidential Documents* 21.6:140–46.

————. 1985b. A foundation for enduring peace: message to the United Nations General Assembly. *Department of State Bulletin*, November, 1–7.

————. 1985c. Establishment of Nicaraguan Humanitarian Assistance Office, 30 August 1985. *Weekly Compilation of Presidential Documents* 21.35:1015–16.

————. 1985d. Radio address to the nation. *Weekly Compilation of Presidential Documents* 21.44:1303–4.

————. 1985e. Radio address to the nation. *Weekly Compilation of Presidential Documents* 21.52:1523–24.

————. 1986a. Freedom, regional security, and global peace: message of the president to Congress. *Weekly Compilation of Presidential Documents* 22.11:356–64.

————. 1986b. State of the Union Address. *Weekly Compilation of Presidential Documents* 22.6:135–40.

————. 1987a. Los Angeles, California. Remarks at a Luncheon (26 August 1987). *Weekly Compilation of Presidential Documents* 23.34:964–69.

————. 1987b. Central America at a critical juncture: address to the OAS, 7 October 1987. *Department of State Bulletin*, December, 1–4.

————. 1988. Peace and democracy for Nicaragua: address to the nation, 2 February 1988. *Department of State Bulletin*, April, 32–34.

————. 1989. *Speaking My Mind: Selected Speeches.* New York: Simon and Schuster.

Report of the National Bipartisan Commission on Central America. 1984. Washington: National Bipartisan Commission on Central America.

Report of the President's Special Review Board. 1987. Washington, February 17 (Tower Commission Report). Washington: USGPO.

Richburg, Keith. 1991. Back to Vietnam. *Foreign Affairs* 70.4:111–31.

Richelson, Jeffrey T. 1989. *The U.S. Intelligence Community.* 2d ed. Cambridge, Mass.: Ballinger.

Riding, Alan. 1981a. Nicaragua seeking accord in Salvador. *New York Times,* 12 February.

———. 1981b. Fearful Nicaraguans building 200,000-strong militia. *New York Times,* 18 February.

———. 1981c. Nicaragua, attacked on rights, defends its record. *New York Times,* 5 March.

———. 1981d. Nicaragua at the crossroads: U.S. is forcing a choice. *New York Times,* 9 March.

———. 1981e. Rightist exiles plan invasion of Nicaragua. *New York Times,* 2 April.

———. 1982a. Nicaragua places forces on alert. *New York Times,* 17 March.

———. 1982b. Mexican officials obtain U.S. plan for region. *New York Times,* 16 August.

———. 1982c. Nicaraguan rebels build up strength. *New York Times,* 7 November.

———. 1982d. Nicaragua says Argentines will quit region. *New York Times,* 19 December.

Ripley, Randall B., and Grace A. Franklin. 1991. *Congress, the Bureaucracy, and Public Policy.* 5th ed. Chicago: Dorsey Press.

Ripley, Randall B., and James M. Lindsay, eds. 1993. *Congress Resurgent: Foreign and Defense Policy on Capitol Hill.* Ann Arbor: University of Michigan Press.

Roberts, Steven V. 1981. Senate votes to end ban on aid to Angolan rebels. *New York Times,* 1 October.

———. 1985. House approves foreign aid bill opposing Marxists around the world. *New York Times,* 12 July.

———. 1986. House panel said to ask Reagan to rethink aid for Angola rebels. *New York Times,* 8 February.

Robinson, Linda. 1991. *Intervention or Neglect: The United States and Central America beyond the 1980s.* New York: Council on Foreign Relations Press.

Robinson, William I. 1992. *A Faustian Bargain: U.S. Intervention in the Nicaraguan Elections and American Foreign Policy in the post–Cold War Era.* Boulder, Colo.: Westview Press.

Rockman, Bert A. 1994. Presidents, opinion, and institutional leadership. In *The New Politics of American Foreign Policy,* ed. David A. Deese, 59–75. New York: St. Martin's Press.

Rodman, Peter W. 1994. *More Precious Than Peace: The Cold War and the Struggle for the Third World.* New York: Scribner's.

Ronfeldt, David, and Brian Jenkins, eds. 1989. *The Nicaraguan Resistance and U.S. Policy: Report on a May 1987 Conference.* Santa Monica: Rand Corporation.

Rosati, Jerel A. 1981. Developing a systematic decision-making framework: bureaucratic politics in perspective. *World Politics* 3:233–52.

———. 1993. *The Politics of United States Foreign Policy.* Fort Worth, Tex.: Harcourt, Brace, Jovanovich.

Rothchild, Donald, and Caroline Hartzell. 1994. The case of Angola: four power intervention and disengagement. In *Foreign Military Intervention: The Dynamics of Protracted Conflict,* ed. Ariel E. Levite, Bruce W. Jentleson, and Larry Berman, 163–208. New York: Columbia University Press.

Rothchild, Donald, and John Ravenhill. 1987. Subordinating African issues to global logic: Reagan confronts political complexity. In *Eagle Resurgent: The Reagan Era in American Foreign Policy,* ed. Kenneth Oye et al., 393–430. Boston: Little, Brown.

Rourke, John T. 1983. *Congress and Presidency in U.S. Foreign Policymaking: A Study of Interaction and Influence, 1945–1982.* Boulder, Colo.: Westview Press.

Rourke, John T., Ralph G. Carter, and Mark A. Boyer. 1994. *Making American Foreign Policy.* Guilford, Conn.: Dushkin.

Roy, Olivier. 1986. *Islam and Resistance in Afghanistan.* Cambridge: Cambridge University Press.

Royal Thai Government, Ministry of Foreign Affairs, Department of Political Affairs. 1985. *Documents on the Kampuchean Problem, 1979–1985.* Bangkok, Thailand: Ministry of Foreign Affairs.

Rubin, Barnett R. 1985. *To Die in Afghanistan.* New York: Helsinki Watch Committee.

———. 1989a. Afghanistan: the next round. *Orbis.* 33.1:57–72.

———. 1989b. Afghanistan: "back to fuedalism." *Current History,* December, 421–24, 444–46.

———. 1989c. The fragmentation of Afghanistan. *Foreign Affairs* 68.5:150–68.

———. 1990. Human rights in Afghanistan. In *Afghanistan: The Great Game Revisited,* rev. ed., ed. Rosanne Klass, 335–58. New York: Freedom House.

Rubin, Barry. 1985. *Secrets of State: The State Department and the Struggle over U.S. Foreign Policy.* New York: Oxford University Press.

Rubinstein, Alvin Z. 1982. *Soviet Policy toward Turkey, Iran, and Afghanistan: The Dynamics of Influence.* New York: Praeger.

———. 1986. Afghanistan at war. *Current History,* March, 117–20, 128–31.

———. 1987. Speculations on a national tragedy. *Orbis* 30.4:589–608.

———. 1989a. *Moscow's Third World Strategy.* Princeton: Princeton University Press.

———. 1989b. *Soviet Foreign Policy since World War II.* 3d ed. Glenview, Ill.: Scott, Foresman.

Rule, Sheila. 1987. Mozambican rebels step up raids in Zimbabwe. *New York Times,* 7 October.

———. 1988. The guerrilla fight in Mozambique also takes toll on Zimbabwe. *New York Times,* 21 February.

Rupert, James. 1989. Afghanistan's slide toward civil war. *World Policy Journal* 6.4:759–86.

Safire, William. 1988. Derailing day one. *New York Times,* 24 March.

Sanchez, Robert E. 1988. Soviet bloc and Cuban assistance to Nicaragua. *Congressional Research Service Review,* April, 12–14.

Savimbi, Jonas. 1986. The war against Soviet colonialism. *Policy Review* 35:18–24.

Scalapino, Robert A. 1990. Asia and the United States: the challenges ahead. *Foreign Affairs* 69.1:89–115.

Schmemann, Serge. 1987a. Mozambican seeks U.S. investment. *New York Times,* 28 January.

———. 1987b. Mozambique rethinking its dreams. *New York Times,* 19 February.

Schoultz, Lars. 1987. *National Security and United States Policy toward Latin America.* Princeton: Princeton University Press.

Schraeder, Peter, ed. 1989. *Intervention in the 1980s: U.S. Foreign Policy in the Third World.* Boulder, Colo.: Lynne Rienner.

———. 1991. Speaking with many voices: continuity and change in U.S. Africa policies. *Journal of Modern African Studies* 29.3:373–412.

———, ed. 1992a. *Intervention into the 1990s: U.S. Foreign Policy in the Third World.* Boulder, Colo.: Lynne Rienner.

———. 1992b. Paramilitary intervention. In *Intervention into the 1990s: U.S. Foreign Policy in the Third World,* ed. Peter Schraeder, 131–51. Boulder, Colo.: Lynne Rienner.

———. 1994. *United States Foreign Policy toward Africa: Incrementalism, Crisis, and Change.* Cambridge: Cambridge University Press.

Schultz, Richard H., Jr., Robert L. Pfaltzgraff, Jr., Uri Ra'anan, William J. Olson, and Igor Lukes, eds. 1989. *Guerrilla Warfare and Counterinsurgency: U.S.-Soviet Policy in the Third World.* Lexington, Mass.: D. C. Heath.

Schweizer, Peter. 1994. *Victory: The Reagan Administration's Secret Strategy That Hastened the Collapse of the Soviet Union.* New York: Atlantic Monthly Press.

Sciolino, Elaine. 1987. Possible theft of U.S. Afghan aid being investigated by GAO. *New York Times,* 24 March.

Scott, James M. 1993. American foreign policy-making and the Reagan Doctrine. Ph.D. dissertation, Northern Illinois University, De Kalb.

Scott, Peter Dale, and Jonathan Marshall. 1991. *Cocaine Politics: Drugs, Armies, and the CIA in Central America.* Berkeley: University of California Press.

Serafino, Nina M. 1987a. Contra aid: debate in Congress. *Congressional Research Service Review,* March, 6–9.

———. 1987b. *Contra Aid 1981–1987: Summary and Chronology of Major Congressional Action on Key Legislation concerning U.S. Aid to the Anti-Sandinista Guerrillas.* Washington: U.S. Library of Congress, Congressional Research Service.

———. 1988. The U.S. response: the problem of Nicaragua. *Congressional Research Service Review,* April, 9–11.

Shafer, Michael. 1982. Mineral myths. *Foreign Policy* 47:171.

Shawcross, William. 1979. *Sideshow: Kissinger, Nixon, and the Destruction of Cambodia.* New York: Simon and Schuster.

———. 1984. *The Quality of Mercy: Cambodia, Holocaust, and Modern Conscience.* New York: Simon and Schuster.

Shenon, Philip. 1992a. Sihanouk says he'd pursue peace even if Khmer Rouge rebels balk. *New York Times,* 3 September.

———. 1992b. Cambodians say Khmer Rouge fail to adhere to U.N. peace plan. *New York Times,* 4 November.

———. 1993a. Sihanouk forms government, regaining power after 23 years. *New York Times,* 4 June.

———. 1993b. Rival parties in Cambodia agree to form a coalition government. *New York Times,* 17 June.

———. 1993c. Sihanouk reunited with son; secession bid over. *New York Times,* 18 June.

———. 1993d. Sihanouk backs Khmer Rouge talks. *New York Times,* 27 July.

———. 1993e. Khmer Rouge violent acts said to signal their goals. *New York Times,* 4 August.

———. 1995a. US considers providing arms to Cambodia to fight guerrillas. *New York Times,* 30 January.

———. 1995b. Rebels still torment Cambodia 20 years after their rampage. *New York Times,* 6 February.

Shiner, Cindy. 1994. The world's worst war. *Africa Report,* January–February, 13–20.

Shipler, David K. 1988a. Shultz urges end of Soviet arms aid in Afghan pullout. *New York Times,* 8 January.

———. 1988b. Reagan didn't know of Afghan deal. *New York Times,* 11 February.

———. 1988c. US official meets Afghan alliance. *New York Times,* 25 February.

Shroder, John F., Jr., and Abdul Tawab Assifi. 1990. Afghan resources and Soviet exploitation. In *Afghanistan: The Great Game Revisited,* ed. Rosanne Klass, 97–134. Rev. ed. New York: Freedom House. 97–134.

Shultz, George. 1983a. Struggle for democracy in Central America: address before the World Affairs Council. *Department of State Bulletin,* May, 10–13.

———. 1983b. Statement before Senate Foreign Relations Committee. *Department of State Bulletin,* July, 65–72.

———. 1984. Letter to the Congress, 18 October 1983. *Department of State Bulletin,* January, 85.

———. 1985a. America and the struggle for freedom: address to the Commonwealth Club of San Francisco, 22 February 1985. *Current Policy* 659. Washington: Department of State, Bureau of Public Affairs.

———. 1985b. Shaping American foreign policy: new realities and new ways of thinking. *Foreign Affairs* 64:3.

———. 1986. Nicaragua: will democracy prevail? statement before the Senate Foreign Relations Committee, 27 February 1986. *Department of State Bulletin,* April, 32–39.

———. 1987. Power in the service of peace in Central America: statement before the House Foreign Affairs Committee, 13 October 1987. *Department of State Bulletin,* December, 8–11.

———. 1993. *Turmoil and Triumph: My Years as Secretary of State.* New York: Charles Scribner's Sons.

Simon, Sheldon W. 1981. The Soviet Union and Southeast Asia: interests, goals, and constraints. *Orbis* 25.2:53–88.

———. 1990. U.S. security policy and ASEAN. *Current History,* March, 98–100, 130–32.

Simpson, Chris. 1993. Worsening situation. *West Africa,* 18 April, 594–95.

Sliwinski, Marek. 1989. Afghanistan: the decimation of a people. *Orbis* 33.1:39–56.

Smist, Frank J. 1990. *Congress Oversees the United States Intelligence Community, 1947–1989.* Knoxville: University of Tennessee Press.

Smith, Jean Edward. 1989. *The Constitution and American Foreign Policy.* New York: West.

Smith, Wayne S. 1986. A trap in Angola. *Foreign Policy* 62:61–74.

———. 1987. Lies about Nicaragua. *Foreign Policy* 67:87–103.

Sobel, Richard, ed. 1993. *Public Opinion in U.S. Foreign Policy: The Controversy over Contra Aid.* Lanham, Md.: Rowman and Littlefield.

Solarz, Stephen. 1985. Why the US is helping Cambodia. *New York Times,* 30 July.

———. 1986. When to intervene. *Foreign Policy* 63:20–39.

———. 1989. Pol Pot could return. *Washington Post,* 19 April.

———. 1990. Cambodia and the international community. *Foreign Affairs* 68.2:99–115.

Solomon, Richard H. 1991a. Cambodia and Vietnam: time for peace and normalization. *US Department of State Dispatch* 2.16 (22 April).

———. 1991b. Prospects for peace in Cambodia. *US Department of State Dispatch* 2.42 (21 October).

Sorzano, José. 1985. Contadora: a process for Central American peace: statement at a plenary session of the UN General Assembly, 25 October 1984. *Department of State Bulletin,* January, 59–62.

Spalding, Rose. 1987. *The Political Economy of Revolutionary Nicaragua.* Boston: Allen and Unwin.

Spanier, John, and Joseph Nogee. 1981. *Congress, the Presidency, and American Foreign Policy.* New York: Pergamon Press.

Spanier, John, and Eric Uslaner. 1989. *American Foreign Policy-Making and the Democratic Dilemmas.* Pacific Grove, Calif.: Brooks/Cole.

Stacy, Roy. 1987. Food situation in Mozambique and Angola. *Department of State Bulletin,* December, 38–40.

Stern, Lewis M. 1990. Cambodia: diplomacy falters. *Current History,* March, 109–12, 135–38.

Stockton, Paul N. 1993. Congress and defense policy-making for the post–cold war era. In *Congress Resurgent: Foreign and Defense Policy on Capitol Hill,* ed. Randall B. Ripley, and James M. Lindsay, 235–59. Ann Arbor: University of Michigan Press.

Stockwell, John. 1978. *In Search of Enemies: A CIA Story.* New York: W. W. Norton.

Sullivan, Mark P. 1987. *Nicaragua: An Overview of U.S. Policy.* Washington: U.S. Library of Congress, Congressional Research Service.

Sutter, Robert G. 1985. *The Fighting in Cambodia: Issues for U.S. Policy.* Washington: U.S. Library of Congress, Congressional Research Service.

———. 1987. Cambodia: U.S. assistance to the non-communist resistance. *Congressional Research Service Review,* March, 21–22.

———. 1991a. *The Cambodian Crisis and U.S. Policy Dilemmas.* Boulder, Colo.: Westview Press.

———. 1991b. A settlement in Cambodia: U.S. interests, options, and policy debate. In *The Challenge of Indochina: An Examination of the U.S. Role,* ed. Dick Clark, 9–12. Queenstown, Md.: Aspen Institute.

Symms, Steve. 1985. Good riddance to the Clark amendment. *New York Times,* 10 August.

Talbott, Strobe. 1989. Credit where credit is due. *Time,* 23 January, 33.

Taubman, Philip. 1982a. U.S. offers photos of bases to prove Nicaragua threat. *New York Times,* 10 March.

———. 1982b. Nicaraguan youth is returned by U.S. *New York Times,* 14 March.

———. 1982c. U.S. reportedly sending millions to foster moderates in Nicaragua. *New York Times,* 11 March.

———. 1982d. CIA is making a special target of Latin region. *New York Times,* 4 December.

———. 1982e. Background noise on direct covert CIA plot. *New York Times,* 19 December.

———. 1988. Gorbachev and Afghan leader say way seems clear to start Soviet pullout by May 15. *New York Times,* 8 April.

Taylor, Paul. 1993. In Angola, learning the hard way. *Washington Post,* weekly edition, 5–11 April.

Taylor, Stuart. 1981. Latins training in U.S. raises questions of criminal and international law. *New York Times,* 24 December.

Thayer, Nate. 1991. Cambodia: misperceptions and peace. *Washington Quarterly* 14.2:179–91.

Thomas, Jo. 1981a. Nicaraguans train in Florida as guerrillas. *New York Times,* 17 March.

———. 1981b. Latin exiles focus on Nicaragua as they train urgently in Florida. *New York Times,* 23 December.

Thurber, James A. 1991. *Divided Democracy: Cooperation and Conflict between the President and Congress.* Washington: Congressional Quarterly Press.

Tinker, Jerry, and John Wise. 1986. A misguided policy on Ethiopia. *New York Times,* 16 August.

Tolchin, Martin. 1981. House-Senate conferees approve foreign aid bill. *New York Times,* 15 December.

Tomsen, Peter. 1994. Cambodia: recent developments. *US Department of State Dispatch* 5.21 (23 May).

Toth, Robert. 1983. Reagan seeks to sway Soviet internal policies. *Washington Post,* 21 March.

Towell, Pat. 1987a. House passes intelligence bill; extends covert contra aid ban. *Congressional Quarterly Weekly Report,* 13 June, 1252.

———. 1987b. The issue ahead: will peace plans head off fight over new contra aid? *Congressional Quarterly Weekly Report,* 8 August, 1783–84.

———. 1988. Senate urges continuation of Afghan rebel aid. *Congressional Quarterly Weekly Report,* 5 March, 561.

Towell, Pat, and Sheldon P. Yett. 1990. House passes spending bill after shifting priorities. *Congressional Quarterly Weekly Report,* 30 June, 2077–78.

Trainor, Bernard. 1987. Afghan air war: US missile scores on Russians. *New York Times,* 7 July.

Treverton, Gregory F. 1987. *Covert Action: The Limits of Intervention in the Postwar World.* New York: Basic Books.

Treverton, Gregory F., and Marc Levy. 1989. *Rhodesia Becomes Zimbabwe.* Pittsburgh: Pew Program in Case Teaching and Writing in International Affairs.

Tucker, Robert C. 1985. *Intervention and the Reagan Doctrine.* New York: Council on Religion and International Affairs.

———. 1989. Reagan's foreign policy. *Foreign Affairs* 68.1:1–27.

Tvedten, Inge. 1992. U.S. policy towards Angola since 1975. *Journal of Modern African Studies* 30.1:31–52.

Tyler, Patrick E., and Bob Woodward. 1982. U.S. approves covert plan on Nicaragua. *Washington Post,* 10 March.

United States Congress. Arms Control and Foreign Policy Caucus. 1985. *Who Are the Contras?* 98th Congress, 2d session.

United States Congress. House. Committee on Appropriations. 1983. *Foreign Assistance and Related Programs Appropriations for 1984.* Part 4: *Hearings before the Committee on Appropriations.* 98th Congress, 1st session, 9 March, 19, 27, and 28 April, 24 May 1983.

———. 1985. *Foreign Assistance and Related Programs Appropriations for 1986: Hearings before the Committee on Appropriations.* 99th Congress, 1st session, 27 March, 16, 17 May, 19 June 1985.

United States Congress. House. Committee on Foreign Affairs. 1981. *Soviet Policy and United States Response in the Third World.* Report prepared by the Congressional Research Service. 97th Congress, 1st session.

———. 1982a. *Africa: Observations on the Impact of American Foreign Policy and Development Programs in Six African Countries.* Report of a congressional study mission to Zimbabwe, South Africa, Kenya, Somalia, Angola, and Nigeria, 4–22 August 1981. 97th Congress, 2d session.

———. 1982b. *The Soviet Occupation of Afghanistan and Certain Human Rights Matters: Hearing and Markup on H. Con. Res. 100.* 97th Congress, 2d session, 16 March 1982.

———. 1983. *Congress and Foreign Policy, 1982.* Washington, D.C.: U.S. Government Printing Office.

————. 1984. *Congress and Foreign Policy, 1983.* Washington, D.C.: U.S. Government Printing Office.

————. 1985a. *Congress and Foreign Policy, 1984.* Washington, D.C.: U.S. Government Printing Office.

————. 1985b. *The Soviet Union in the Third World, 1980–1985: An Imperial Burden or Political Asset?* Report prepared by the Congressional Research Service. 99th Congress, 1st Session, 23 September 1985. Committee print.

————. 1986. *Report to Accompany H. J. Res. 540.* H. Rept. 99–483, pts. 1–4. 99th Congress, 1st session.

————. Subcommittee on Africa. 1981a. *Foreign Assistance Legislation for Fiscal Year 1982.* Part 8: *Hearing before the Committee on Foreign Affairs.* 97th Congress, 1st session, 19, 24, 26, and 31 March, 1, 2, and 27 April 1981.

————. Subcommittee on Africa. 1981b. *The Possibility of a Resource War in Southern Africa: Hearing before the Committee on Foreign Affairs.* 97th Congress, 1st session, 8 July 1981.

————. Subcommittee on Africa. 1983a. *Namibia and Regional Destabilization in Southern Africa: Hearings before the Committee on Foreign Affairs.* 98th Congress, 1st session, 15 February 1983.

————. Subcommittee on Africa. 1983b. *United States Policy toward Southern Africa, Focus on Namibia, Angola, and South Africa: Hearings and Markup on H. Res. 214 and H. Con. Res. 183.* 97th Congress, 1st session, 16 September 1981.

————. Subcommittee on Africa. 1983c. *Regional Destabilization in Southern Africa: Hearings before the Committee on Foreign Affairs.* 97th Congress, 2d session, 8 December 1982.

————. Subcommittee on Africa. 1985. *Namibia: Internal Repression and United States Diplomacy: Hearing before the Committee on Foreign Affairs.* 99th Congress, 1st session, 21 February 1985.

————. Subcommittee on Africa. 1986a. *Namibia: The Exploitation of Natural Resources and U.S. Policy: Hearing before the Committee on Foreign Affairs.* 99th Congress, 1st session, 29 October 1985.

————. Subcommittee on Africa. 1986b. *Angola: Intervention or Negotiation: Hearings before the Committee on Foreign Affairs.* 99th Congress, 1st session, 31 October, 12 November 1985.

————. Subcommittee on Africa. 1986c. *Legislation to Require That Any United States Government Support for Military or Paramilitary Operations in Angola Be Openly Acknowledged and Publicly Debated: Hearing and Markup before the Committee on Foreign Affairs.* 99th Congress, 1st session, 22, 23 April 1986.

————. Subcommittee on Africa. 1988a. *U.S. Response to Relief Efforts in Sudan, Ethiopia, Angola, and Mozambique: Hearing before the Committee on Foreign Affairs.* 100th Congress, 2d session, 10 March 1988.

————. Subcommittee on Africa. 1988b. *Possible Violation or Circumvention of the Clark Amendment. Hearing before the Committee on Foreign Affairs.* 100th Congress, 1st session, 1 July 1987.

————. Subcommittee on Africa. 1989. *New Reports of Human Rights Violations in the Angolan Civil War: Hearing before the Committee on Foreign Affairs.* 101st Congress, 1st session, 12 April 1989.

———. Subcommittee on Africa. 1990. *A Review of United States Policy toward Political Negotiations in Angola: Hearing before the Committee on Foreign Affairs.* 101st Congress, 1st session, 27 September 1989.

———. Subcommittee on Asian and Pacific Affairs. 1981a. *Foreign Assistance Legislation for Fiscal Year 1982.* Part 5: *Hearings and Markup before the Committee on Foreign Affairs,* 23–26, 30, and 31 March, 6 April 1981.

———. Subcommittee on Asian and Pacific Affairs. 1981b. *U.S. Policy toward Indochina since Vietnam's Occupation of Kampuchea: Hearings before the Committee on Foreign Affairs.* 97th Congress, 1st session, 15, 21, and 22 October 1981.

———. Subcommittee on Asian and Pacific Affairs. 1982. *Kampuchea and American Foreign Policy Interests: Hearing before the Committee on Foreign Affairs.* 97th Congress, 1st session, 23 July 1981.

———. Subcommittee on Asian and Pacific Affairs (with the Subcommittee on Human Rights and International Organizations). 1983a. *The Democratic Kampuchea Seat at the United Nations and American Interests: Hearing before the Committee on Foreign Affairs.* 97th Congress, 2d session, 15 September 1982.

———. Subcommittee on Asian and Pacific Affairs. 1983b. *Cambodia after 5 Years of Vietnamese Occupation: Hearing and Markup before the Committee on Foreign Affairs.* 98th Congress, 1st session, 15 September, 6, 18 October 1983.

———. Subcommittee on Asian and Pacific Affairs. 1985a. *Foreign Assistance Legislation for Fiscal Years 1986–87.* Part 5: *Hearings and Markup before the Committee on Foreign Relations.* 99th Congress, 1st session, 20, 27, and 28 February, and 5, 6, 12, and 20 March 1985.

———. Subcommittee on Asian and Pacific Affairs. 1985b. *Cambodian Refugees in Southeast Asia: Hearing before the Committee on Foreign Affairs.* 99th Congress, 1st session, 31 July 1985.

———. Subcommittee on Asian and Pacific Affairs. 1986. *The Situation in Afghanistan: Hearing before the Committee on Foreign Affairs.* 99th Congress, 2d session, 1 May 1986.

———. Subcommittee on Asian and Pacific Affairs. 1988. *Foreign Assistance Legislation for Fiscal Years 1988–89.* Part 5: *Hearings and Markup before the Committee on Foreign Affairs.* 100th Congress, 1st session, 25 February, 3, 4, 5, 11, 12, 17, and 18 March 1987.

———. Subcommittee on Asian and Pacific Affairs. 1989a. *Developments in Afghanistan, February 1988: Hearings before the Committee on Foreign Affairs.* 100th Congress, 1st session, 17, 25 February 1988.

———. Subcommittee on Asian and Pacific Affairs. 1989b. *The Geneva Accords on Afghanistan: Hearing before the Committee on Foreign Affairs.* 100th Congress, 2d session, 19 May 1988.

———. Subcommittee on Asian and Pacific Affairs. 1989c. *Hope for Cambodia: Preventing the Return of the Khmer Rouge and Aiding the Refugees: Hearing and*

Markup before the Committee on Foreign Affairs. 100th Congress, 2d session, 30 June, 28 July 1988.

———. Subcommittee on Asian and Pacific Affairs. 1990a. *Developments in Afghanistan and Their Implications for U.S. Policy: Hearings before the Committee on Foreign Affairs.* 101st Congress, 1st session, 21 February, 14 June 1989.

———. Subcommittee on Asian and Pacific Affairs. 1990b. *United States Policy toward Afghanistan: Hearing before the Committee on Foreign Affairs.* 101st Congress, 2d session, 7 March 1990.

———. Subcommittee on Asian and Pacific Affairs. 1990c. *The Paris Peace Conference on Cambodia: Implications for U.S. Policy: Hearing before the Committee on Foreign Affairs.* 100th Congress, 1st session, 14 September 1989.

———. Subcommittee on Asian and Pacific Affairs. 1991a. *United States Policy toward Cambodia: Prospects for a Negotiated Settlement: Hearing before the Committee on Foreign Affairs.* 101st Congress, 2d session, 12 September 1990.

———. Subcommittee on Asian and Pacific Affairs. 1991b. *Recent Developments in Cambodia: Hearing before the Committee on Foreign Affairs.* 101st Congress, 2d session, 10 December 1990.

———. Subcommittee on Asian and Pacific Affairs. 1992a. *The Cambodia Peace Agreement: Hearing before the Committee on Foreign Affairs.* 102d Congress, 1st session, 17 October 1991.

———. Subcommittee on Asian and Pacific Affairs (with the Subcommittee on Human Rights and International Organizations). 1992b. *Implementation of the Cambodian Peace Accord: Joint Hearing before the Committee on Foreign Affairs.* 102d Congress, 2d session, 27 February 1992.

———. Subcommittee on Asian and Pacific Affairs. 1993. *Recent Developments in U.S. Policy toward Afghanistan: Hearing before the Committee on Foreign Affairs.* 102d Congress, 1st session, 20 June 1991.

———. Subcommittee on Europe and the Middle East. 1981. *An Assessment of the Afghanistan Sanctions: Implications for Trade and Diplomacy in the 1980s.* Report prepared by the Congressional Research Service. 97th Congress, 1st session.

———. Subcommittee on Human Rights and International Organizations (with the Commission on Security and Cooperation in Europe). 1981. *Soviet Violation of Helsinki Final Act: Invasion of Afghanistan: Hearing before the Committee on Foreign Affairs.* 97th Congress, 1st session, 22 July 1981.

———. Subcommittee on Western Hemisphere Affairs. 1986. *Nicaraguan Incursion into Honduras: Hearing before the Committee on Foreign Affairs.* 99th Congress, 2d session, 8 April 1986.

United States Congress. House. Permanent Select Committee on Intelligence. 1986. *Angola: Should the United States Support UNITA? Hearing before the Permanent Select Committee on Intelligence.* 99th Congress, 1st session, 13 March 1986.

United States Congress. House. Select Committee on Hunger. Committee on Foreign Affairs. Subcommittee on Africa. 1988. *U.S. Response to Relief Efforts in Sudan, Ethiopia, Angola, and Mozambique: Joint Hearing before the Select Committee on Hunger and the Committee on Foreign Affairs.* 100th Congress, 2d session, 10 March 1988.

United States Congress. House. Select Committee to Investigate Covert Arms Transactions with Iran, and Senate Select Committee on Secret Military Assistance to Iran and the Nicaraguan Opposition [ICFR]. 1987a. *Report of the Congressional Committees Investigating the Iran-Contra Affair with Supplemental, Minority, and Additional Views.* 100th Congress, 1st session (H. Rept. 100–433; S. Rept. 100–216).

———. 1987b. *Testimony at Joint Hearings before the House Select Committee to Investigate Covert Arms Transactions with Iran and Senate Select Committee on Secret Military Assistance to Iran and the Nicaraguan Opposition.* 100th Congress, 1st session (vols. 100-1–100-12).

United States Congress. Senate. Committee on Appropriations. 1985. *U.S. Policy toward Anti-communist Insurgencies: Hearing before the Committee on Appropriations.* 99th Congress, 1st session, 8 May 1985.

United States Congress. Senate. Committee on Foreign Relations. 1984. *Hidden War: The Struggle for Afghanistan.* Staff report prepared by John B. Ritch III. 98th Congress, 2d session. Committee print 181.

———. 1986a. *Angola: Options for American Foreign Policy: Hearing before the Committee on Foreign Relations.* 99th Congress, 2d session, 18 February 1986.

———. 1986b. *U.S. Policy toward Nicaragua: Aid to Nicaraguan Resistance Proposal: Hearings before the Committee on Foreign Relations.* 99th Congress, 2d session, 27 February, 4 March 1986.

———. 1987a. *United States Policy Options with Respect to Nicaragua and Aid to the Contras: Hearings before the Committee on Foreign Relations.* 100th Congress, 1st session, 28 January, 5 February 1987.

———. 1990. *Stalemate in Afghanistan, Democracy in Pakistan.* Report prepared by Senator Claiborne Pell. 101st Congress, 1st session. Committee print 65.

———. 1992. *Nicaragua Today.* Republican staff report prepared by Deborah DeMoss. 102d Congress, 2d session. Committee print 102.

———. Subcommittee on Africa. 1987. *Mozambique and United States Policy: Hearing before the Committee on Foreign Relations.* 100th Congress, 1st session, 24 June 1987.

———. Subcommittee on East Asia and Pacific Affairs. 1981. *U.S. Policy in Southeast Asia: Hearings before the Committee on Foreign Relations.* 97th Congress, 1st session, 15, 21, and 22 July 1981.

———. Subcommittee on East Asia and Pacific Affairs. 1990a. *U.S. Policy toward Indochina: Hearing before the Committee on Foreign Relations.* 100th Congress, 1st session, 2 October 1989.

———. Subcommittee on East Asia and Pacific Affairs. 1990b. *Prospects for Peace in Cambodia: Hearing before the Committee on Foreign Relations.* 101st Congress, 2d session, 28 February 1990.

———. Subcommittee on Near Eastern and South Asian Affairs. 1980. *U.S. Secu-*

rity Interests and Policies in Southwest Asia: Hearings before the Committee on Foreign Relations. 96th Congress, 2d session, 18 March 1980.

———. Subcommittee on Western Hemisphere Affairs. 1982. *Human Rights in Nicaragua: Hearings before the Committee on Foreign Relations.* 97th Congress, 2d session, 25 February, 1 March 1982.

United States Congress. Senate. Committee on the Judiciary. Subcommittee on Security and Terrorism. 1982. *The Role of the Soviet Union, Cuba, and East Germany in Fomenting Terrorism in Southern Africa: Hearings before the Committee on the Judiciary,* vols. 1 and 2. 97th Congress, 2d session, 22, 24, 25, 29, and 31 March 1982.

United States Department of Defense. 1981 (annual). *Soviet Military Power.* Washington: U.S. Department of Defense.

———. Defense Intelligence Agency. 1982. *Weekly Intelligence Survey.* 16 July. Washington: U.S. Department of Defense.

United States Department of State. 1981a. *Communist Interference in El Salvador.* Special Report 80. Washington: U.S. State Department, Bureau of Public Affairs.

———. 1981b. U.S. suspends economic aid to Nicaragua. *Department of State Bulletin,* May, 71.

———. 1981c. Question and answer following Secretary of State Alexander Haig's address before the American Society of Newspaper Editors. *Department of State Bulletin,* June, 8–10.

———. 1981d. Afghanistan: a year of occupation. *Department of State Bulletin,* March, 18–22.

———. 1981e. International Conference on Kampuchea. *Department of State Bulletin,* August, 86–88.

———. 1982a. Cuba's renewed support for violence in Latin America. *Department of State Bulletin,* February, 68–75.

———. 1982b. Angola: department statements. *Department of State Bulletin,* March, 34.

———. 1982c. Cuban and Nicaraguan support for the Salvadoran insurgency. *Department of State Bulletin,* May, 72–75.

———. 1982d. The United States and Afghanistan. *Department of State Bulletin,* March, 1–25.

———. 1982e. *Chemical Warfare in Southeast Asia and Afghanistan.* Special Report 98. Washington: U.S. Department of State, Bureau of Public Affairs.

———. 1982f. *Chemical Warfare in Southeast Asia and Afghanistan: An Update.* Special Report 104. Washington: U.S. Department of State, Bureau of Public Affairs.

———. 1983a. *Soviet and East European Aid to the Third World, 1981.* Washington: U.S. Department of State, Bureau of Public Affairs.

———. 1983b. Afghanistan: 3 years of occupation. *Department of State Bulletin,* February, 53–62.

———. 1983c. *Afghanistan: 4 Years of Soviet Occupation.* Special Report 112. Washington: U.S. Department of State, Bureau of Public Affairs.

———. 1984a. U.S. policy in Central America: White House statement, 10 April 1984. *Department of State Bulletin*, June, 85.

———. 1984b. *Afghanistan: 5 Years of Soviet Occupation.* Special Report 120. Washington: U.S. Department of State, Bureau of Public Affairs.

———. 1984c. Anniversary of the Soviet invasion of Afghanistan: text of the president's statement, Dec. 12, 1983. *Department of State Bulletin*, February, 37–38.

———. 1984d. Afghanistan Day, 1984: text of the secretary's statement, Mar. 21, 1984. *Department of State Bulletin*, May, 82.

———. 1985a. Central American initiative proposed. *Department of State Bulletin*, July, 74–76.

———. 1985b. *Revolution beyond Our Borders: Sandinista Intervention in Central America.* Washington: U.S. Department of State, Bureau of Public Affairs.

———. 1985c. Economic sanctions against Nicaragua. *Department of State Bulletin*, July, 74–77.

———. 1985d. *Afghanistan: 6 Years of Soviet Occupation.* Special Report 135. Washington: U.S. Department of State, Bureau of Public Affairs.

———. 1986a. *Documents on the Nicaraguan Resistance: Leaders, Military Personnel, and Program.* Special Report 142. Washington: U.S. Department of State, Bureau of Public Affairs.

———. 1986b. *Afghanistan: 7 Years of Soviet Occupation.* Special Report 155. Washington: U.S. Department of State, Bureau of Public Affairs.

———. 1986c. Soviet occupation of Afghanistan: text of the President's statement, Dec. 27, 1985. *Department of State Bulletin*, February, 22.

———. 1987a. Mozambique: charting a new course. *Current Policy* 980 (June), 1–3. Washington: U.S. Department of State, Bureau of Public Affairs.

———. 1987b. U.S. policy toward Mozambique. *Current Policy* 983 (September), 1–3. Washington: U.S. Department of State, Bureau of Public Affairs.

———. 1987c. *Afghanistan: 8 Years of Soviet Occupation.* Special Report 173. Washington: U.S. Department of State, Bureau of Public Affairs.

———. 1988a. *Nicaraguan Biographies: A Resource Book.* Washington: U.S. Department of State, Bureau of Public Affairs.

———. 1988b. *Afghanistan: Soviet Occupation and Withdrawal.* Special Report 179. Washington: U.S. Department of State, Bureau of Public Affairs.

———. 1988c. Afghanistan: text of the president's statement, Dec. 27, 1987. *Department of State Bulletin*, March, 80–81.

———. 1989a. Soviets withdraw from Afghanistan. *Department of State Bulletin*, April, 48.

———. 1989b. *Mozambique. Background Notes.* May. Washington: U.S. Department of State, Bureau of Public Affairs.

———. 1989c. U.S. support for democracy and peace in Central America. *Department of State Bulletin*, June, 55–59.

———. 1989d. Cambodian independence. *Department of State Bulletin*, January, 17.

———. 1989e. Efforts toward a Cambodian settlement. *Department of State Bulletin*, February, 65–68.

————. 1991. A comprehensive political settlement in Cambodia. *US Department of State Dispatch* 2.42 (21 October).

Urban, Mark. 1988. *War in Afghanistan*. New York: St. Martin's Press.

Valenta, Jiri, and Frank Cibulka, eds. 1990. *Gorbachev's New Thinking and Third World Conflicts*. New Brunswick, N.J.: Transaction Books.

Valkenier, Elizabeth Kridl. 1983. *The Soviet Union and the Third World: An Economic Bind*. New York: Praeger.

Vance, Cyrus. 1983. *Hard Choices: Critical Years in America's Foreign Policy*. New York: Simon and Schuster.

Van der Kroef, Justus. 1990. Cambodia. In *The New Insurgencies: Anticommunist Guerrillas around the World*, ed. Michael Radu, 197–231. New Brunswick, N.J.: Transaction Books.

Vickers, George R., and Jack Spence. 1992. Two years after the fall: Nicaragua's balancing act. *World Policy Journal* 9.3:533–62.

Vickery, Michael. 1984. *Cambodia, 1975–1982*. Boston: South End Press.

————. 1986. *Kampuchea: Politics, Economics, and Society*. Boulder, Colo.: Lynne Rienner.

————. 1989a. Cambodia: history, tragedy, and uncertain future. *Bulletin of Concerned Asian Scholars* (Twentieth Anniversary Issue on Indochina and the War) 21.2–4:35–58.

————. 1989b. Cambodia and the Khmer Rouge. *Far Eastern Economic Review*, 30 November, 4–5.

Walker, Thomas, ed. 1982. *Nicaragua in Revolution*. New York: Praeger.

————. 1985. *Nicaragua: The First Five Years*. New York: Praeger.

————. 1987. *Reagan versus the Sandinistas: The Undeclared War on Nicaragua*. Boulder, Colo.: Westview Press.

————. 1991a. *Nicaragua: The Land of Sandino*. 3d ed. Boulder, Colo.: Westview Press.

————, ed. 1991b. *Revolution and Counter-revolution in Nicaragua*. Boulder, Colo.: Westview Press.

Walsh, Lawrence E. 1993. *Final Report of the Independent Counsel for Iran/Contra Matters*. Washington: United States Court of Appeals for the District of Columbia.

Walters, Vernon. 1986. UN Calls for Soviet withdrawal: statement to the United Nations General Assembly on 12 November 1985. *Department of State Bulletin*, February, 20–22.

Warburg, Gerald Felix. 1989. *Conflict and Consensus: The Struggle between Congress and the President over Foreign Policymaking*. New York: Harper and Row.

Watson, Alexander F. 1993. US policy toward Nicaragua. *US Department of State Dispatch* 4.43 (25 October).

Weiner, Tim. 1993. U.S. will try to buy antiaircraft missiles back from Afghans. *New York Times*, 24 July.

Weitz, Richard. 1992. The Reagan Doctrine defeated Moscow in Angola. *Orbis* 36.1:57–68.

Wheeler, Jack. 1984a. Fighting the Soviet imperialists: UNITA in Angola. *Reason* 15 (April): 22–30.

———. 1984b. Fighting the Soviet Imperialists: the Mujaheddin in Afghanistan. *Reason* 16 (September): 22–30.

———. 1985a. Fighting the Soviet imperialists: the Khmer in Cambodia. *Reason* 16 (February): 24–33.

———. 1985b. Fighting the Soviet imperialists: the new liberation movements. *Reason*, 17 (June–July): 36–44.

———. 1985c. From Rovuma to Maputo: Mozambique's guerrilla war. *Reason* 17 (December): 31–38.

———. 1990. Mozambique. In *The New Insurgencies: Anticommunist Guerrillas in the Third World*, ed. Michael Radu, 161–96. New Brunswick, N.J.: Transaction Books.

Whitaker, Jennifer S., ed. 1978. *Africa and the United States: Vital Interests*. New York: New York University Press.

———. 1983. South Africa extends military offensive. *New York Times*, 21 January.

Whitehead, John C. 1986. Afghanistan's struggle for freedom: address before the World Affairs Council of Washington, D.C., 13 December 1985. *Department of State Bulletin*, February, 1–3.

Whittle, Richard. 1981a. Reagan wants looser ties on military aid. *Congressional Quarterly Weekly Report*, 21 March, 523.

———. 1981b. Repeal of Clark amendment faces fight. *Congressional Quarterly Weekly Report*, 4 April, 589.

———. 1981c. Reagan foreign policy requests challenged. *Congressional Quarterly Weekly Report*, 18 April, 685–88.

Wolfers, Michael, and Jane Bergerol. 1983. *Angola in the Frontline*. London: ZED Press.

Wolfowitz, Paul D. 1984. Cambodia, the search for peace. *Department of State Bulletin*, November, 51–54.

Woodward, Bob. 1987. *Veil: The Secret Wars of the CIA, 1981–1987*. New York: Pocket Books.

Wootten, James P. 1987. Contra prospects: the military situation in Nicaragua and Honduras. *Congressional Research Service Review*, March, 10–12.

Wren, Christopher S. 1982. Cambodians press anti-Vietnam pact. *New York Times*, 22 February.

Wudunn, Sheryl. 1992. 10-nation meeting on Cambodia fails. *New York Times*, 9 November.

Wurst, Jim. 1994. Mozambique: peace and more. *World Policy Journal* 11.3:78–82.

Zagoria, Donald S. 1983. *Soviet Policy in East Asia*. New Haven: Yale University Press.

———. 1989. Soviet policy in East Asia: a new beginning? *Foreign Affairs* 68.1:120–38.

———. 1991a. The great powers and Indochina. In *The Challenge of Indochina: An*

Examination of the U.S. Role, ed. Dick Clark, 33–38. Queenstown, Md.: Aspen Institute.

———. 1991b. Soviet policy in East Asia: the quest for constructive engagement. In *Soviet-American Relations after the Cold War,* ed. Robert Jervis and Seweryn Bialer, 164–82. Durham: Duke University Press.

Zakaria, Fareed. 1990. The Reagan strategy of containment. *Political Science Quarterly* 105.3:373–95.

Zartman, William. 1989. *Ripe for Resolution: Conflict and Intervention in Africa.* Rev. ed. New York: Oxford University Press.

Zelikow, Philip. 1994. Foreign policy engineering: from theory to practice and back again. *International Security* 18.4:143–71.

Index

Central Intelligence Agency (*cont'd*)
158, 159, 161, 164, 168–169, 170, 173;
role in foreign policy bureaucracy, 7,
229–230; role in mining Nicaraguan
harbors, 168–169, 192; U.S. Congress
and, 94, 126. *See also* Casey, William;
Clarridge, Duane; Gates, Robert;
McMahon, John
Chamorro, Edgar, 169
Chamorro, Pedro Joaquin, 153
Chamorro, Violeta Barrios de. *See*
Barrios de Chamorro, Violeta
Channell, Carl R.: role in Iran-Contra
affair, 179–180
China, 84, 103; ASEAN negotiations with
92; and Ethiopian Marxist groups, 36;
and Khmer Rouge, 83, 85, 100, 104,
110; and mujahidin, 46, 63; and NCR,
90; and UNITA and FNLA, 113
Chissano, Joaquim, 198, 208, 212
Citizens for America, 126, 128
Clark, William, 18, 121, 239; opposition
to diplomacy, 125, 162, 166; as Reagan
Doctrine advocate, 20, 25, 201
Clark amendment (of 1976), 113; congressional support for, 119–120, 202;
Reagan administration and hard-
liners opposition to, 117, 128; Reagan
Doctrine prohibited by, 115–116, 118–
121, 127–130, 130–131; repeal of, 112,
126, 127–131, 139
Clarridge, Duane, 159, 160, 169; role in
Iran-contra, 158
Clinton administration policy: in Af-
ghanistan, 77; in Angola, 145–146,
151; in Cambodia, 111; enlargement,
225; in Mozambique, 212; in post-
cold war, 223–226
Coalition Government of Democratic
Kampuchea (CGDK), 92, 99; U.S. aid
to, 88–89, 111
Cohen, Herman, 142, 145, 205, 209
Cold War, 77
Coleman, Ron, 181
Committee for a Free Afghanistan, 51
Committee of Sante Fe, 17

Conservative Caucus, 126
Conservatives, 17, 26, 27 (Table, 1),
28; and Angola, 127; and Mozambique, 202–207; network of, 127–130,
201; and Nicaragua, 173; and Reagan
Doctrine, 15; and South Africa, 124,
125–126
Constructive engagement, 116–118, 142;
in Angola, 131–132; in Mozambique,
196–201; opposition to, 132–133
Contadora, 166–167
Containment, 2, 4, 14–15, 17, 19, 214;
U.S. interests in Cambodia and, 84;
vs. rollback, 160
Contras, 121, 164; banning of U.S. aid
to, 164–170; cease-fire agreement with
FSLN, 185–186; CIA relations with, 158,
161, 168–170, 192; dependence on
U.S. support, 155–156; foreign policy
bureaucracy and, 229–230; Reagan
administration support for, 161–162,
165–167, 168–169, 176–181; Reagan
Doctrine and, 33, 219; U.S. aid to,
154, 158–162, 163, 170–173, 175–176,
184, 185, 232; violence of, 192. *See
also* Iran-contra affair; Nicaragua;
Sandinistas
Cordovez, Diego, 56–57, 68
Costa Rica, 153, 164. *See also* Arias,
Oscar
Cranston, Alan, 26
Crocker, Chester: and Angola, 116, 118,
121–123, 128–129, 135, 138, 141–142;
Brazzaville Accords and, 139, 146;
constructive engagement and, 116,
146, 196–201; and Ethiopia, 38; and
Mozambique, 196–199, 200–201,
205–207; opposition to Clark amendment, 119, 129; as Reagan Doctrine
pragmatist, 25; support for two-track
approach to diplomacy, 131–132
Cruz, Arturo, 171
Cuba: and Angola, 113–116, 127, 135,
140–143, 216; and Brazzaville Accords, 139; and Ethiopia, 36; and
Nicaragua, 154, 160, 162, 172; role in

Angola-Namibian linkage proposal, 113, 114, 115, 117, 148; support for Marxist groups in Ethiopia, 36; troops in Angola, 216, 218, 220; U.S. policy toward, 15, 19

Cuban-American National Foundation, 126, 127, 130

Deaver, Michael, 160; as Reagan Doctrine pragmatist, 25

DeConcini, Dennis, 133, 140; as Reagan Doctrine pragmatist, 25

Defense Intelligence Agency (DIA), 94, 140

Department of Defense, U.S. 243, 244; and Afghanistan, 40, 45, 47, 48, 52, 59, 61; and Angola, 121, 126, 132, 138, 140; and Cambodia, 94, 96; and Ethiopia, 37, 38; and Mozambique, 203–204; and Nicaragua, 162, 170, 173, 176; and UNITA, 132, 138; role in foreign policy bureaucracy, 229–230, 243, 244

Department of State, U.S.: and Afghanistan, 40, 56–57, 60–61, 64–71; and Angola, 112, 121–123, 128, 131–132, 136; and Cambodia, 84, 94, 96, 97; and Clark amendment, 131; criticism of, 133; diplomacy and, 56, 63, 64, 144; and Ethiopia, 37, 38; and Mozambique, 199–202, 205–208; and Nicaragua, 155, 157, 159, 162, 165–166, 171, 174; opposition to aiding rebels, 37, 38, 52, 88, 136; and PDPA, 69; role in Reagan Doctrine, 7, 94, 229; and Solarz initiative, 95, 96–97. See also constructive engagement; diplomacy; and individual State Department officials

Destablization, 28, 30. See also Frontline states; South Africa

Detente, 16, 19, 214, 217

Dickey, Christopher, 164

Diplomacy, 28; in Afghanistan, 54–57, 64–71, 222; in Angola, 135, 222; in Cambodia, 86, 91–93, 105–106, 107,

222; hard-liners opposition to, 29, 166; in Mozambique, 196–202; in Nicaragua, 159–160, 166–167, 171–172, 183–184; pragmatists support for, 217–218; rejection of, 215, 217; two-track approach to, 82, 95, 162, 174, 135–138, 190, 192, 222. See also constructive engagement

Doctrines, 224–225

Dodd, Christopher, 26, 133

Dole, Robert, 204, 205, 207, 208

Dornan, Robert, 126, 130, 133

Dos Santos, Jose Eduardo, 122, 144, 145

Dubs, Adolph, 44

Dulles, John Foster, 15

Dulles Doctrine, 15, 79, 217

Dunbar, Charles, 65, 68

Durenburger, David: as Reagan Doctrine pragmatist, 25

Eagleburger, Lawrence: and constructive engagement, 116

Eastern Europe, 20, 144

Egypt, 36, 37; and Afghanistan, 38, 49, 78

Eisenhower, Dwight D., 15

Eisenhower administration, 15

Eisenhower Doctrine, 1, 224

El Salvador, 164, 165; FSLN support for rebels in, 155, 162

Enders, Thomas, 18; and diplomacy, 159, 160, 162, 166; as Reagan Doctrine pragmatist, 25

Enlargement strategy, 223, 225

Eritrean People's Liberation Front (EPLF), 36

Esquipulas Accord, 183, 184

Ethiopia, 2, 3, 16, 21, 23, 31; as noncase of Reagan Doctrine, 36–39

Europe, 37; in NSDD 57, 37

Evans, Gareth, 106

Fahd, King (Saudi Arabia): and Iran-contra, 178

Falwell, Jerry, 126

Fascell, Dante, 133, 139, 140

—relations with Soviet Union, 219, 220
—Sandinistas in, 154
—Sapoa cease-fire agreement, 185–186
—U.S. occupation of, 153
—U.S. policy toward, 126, 172–173, 226
Nicaraguan contras. *See* contras
Nicaraguan Democratic Force (FDN),
   155. *See also* contras
Nicaraguan Humanitarian Assistance
   Office, 173, 174
Nicaraguan National Guard, 153–155
Nixon administration: and Cambodia,
   84
Nixon Doctrine, 224
Nkomati Accord, 199, 202
Non-Communist Resistance (NCR), 8;
   ASEAN aid to, 89–90; diplomacy and,
   91; Khmer Rouge and, 107; Solarz
   initiative and, 93–104; U.S. aid to,
   84–85, 87, 97–98, 104–108. *See also*
   Coalition Government of Democratic
   Kampuchea
Non-proliferation Treaty, 80
North, Oliver, 126, 129, 160; role in
   gaining support for contras, 161–
   162, 170; role in Iran-contra affair,
   177, 179–181; role in U.S. mining of
   Nicaraguan harbors, 169
North Vietnam, 16, 21, 105, 220; and
   Cambodia, 82–84, 98–104, 216; and
   Khmer Rouge, 218; and NSDD 319, 103;
   U.S. bombing of, 83

OAS. *See* Organization of American
   States
Office for Public Diplomacy for Latin
   America and the Caribbean (S/LPD),
   165–166, 171, 232
O'Neill, Tip, 175, 176
Operation Askari, 122
Organization of American States (OAS),
   154, 184
Ortega, Daniel, 173, 175, 186
Ovimbundos: and UNITA, 114, 151
Owen, Robert, 155–156

Pakistan, 60, 63, 77, 78; and Afghani-
   stan, 41, 42, 56, 61–62, 67; and devel-
   opment of nuclear weapons, 80; and
   Geneva accords, 70–71; and NSDD 75,
   51; role in Reagan Doctrine, 46, 47,
   48–49, 221
Pakistani Inter-Services Intelligence
   Agency (ISI): role in Reagan Doctrine
   application in Afghanistan, 48–49
Panama Canal, 152
Paris Peace Conference, 105–106
Pashtuns, 42
Peck, Robert A., 65, 68–69
Pell, Claiborne, 69, 105, 133; support for
   negative symmetry, 75
Pentagon. *See* Department of Defense
Pentagon Special Forces, 59
People's Democratic Party of Afghani-
   stan (PDPA): criticism of, 74, 77, 81;
   Geneva Accords and, 70–71; resis-
   tance against, 41–42; Soviet Union
   and, 41, 72–73; United States and, 64,
   67
People's Republic of China. *See* China
People's Republic of Kampuchea (PRK),
   99, 105; as Vietnamese client, 83, 91
Pepper, Claude, 139; opposition to
   Clark amendment, 130; and Reagan
   Doctrine, 133
Percy, Charles, 50
Perez de Cuellar, Javier, 56
Persian Gulf, 1, 43, 144
Persian Gulf War: and Reagan Doctrine,
   76–77
Pezzullo, Lawrence, 157, 159
Philippines, 82
Phnom Penh, 83
Pillsbury, Michael, 61, 63
Pipes, Richard, 20
Poindexter, John, 126, 239; and Iran-
   contra affair, 178, 179, 181
Policy makers: four circles of, 226–233;
   and Reagan Doctrine, 24–30, 214–216;
   shifting constellations of, 233–237
Policy making, 10; broad involvement
   in, 250–251; cold war, 249–250; con-

James M. Scott is Assistant Professor of Political Science at Illinois
State University.

Library of Congress Cataloging-in-Publication Data
Scott, James M., 1964–
Deciding to Intervene: the Reagan doctrine and American foreign policy
/ James M. Scott
Includes bibliographical references and index.
ISBN 0-8223-1780-x (alk. paper)—ISBN 0-8223-1789-3 (pbk.: alk.paper)
1. United States—Foreign relations—1981–1989. 2. United States—
Foreign relations—Soviet Union. 3. Soviet Union—Foreign relations—
United States. 4. United States—Foreign relations—Developing
countries. 5. Developing countries—Foreign relations—United States.
E876.S36 1996   327.73—dc20   95-53041 CIP